NAPA VALLEY

Land of Golden Vines

SECOND EDITION

by Kathleen Thompson Hill
&
Gerald N. Hill

Guilford, Connecticut

The prices and rates listed in this book were confirmed at press time. We recommend, however, that you call establishments before traveling to obtain current information.

Cover painting entitled *Napa Valley in the Spring* by Judy Theo Lehner, M. F. A. Studio address: 134 Church Street, Sonoma, CA 95476; (707) 996–5111. Medium: monotype.
Cover and text design by Lana Mullen
Maps by Mary Ballachino
Illustrations by Mauro Magellan
Photos by Kathleen and Gerald N. Hill
Historical illustrations by an anonymous newspaper illustrator, circa 1800s.

Library of Congress Cataloging-in-Publication Data
Hill, Kathleen, 1941-
    Napa Valley: land of golden vines / by Kathleen Thompson Hill & Gerald N. Hill.— 2nd ed.
        p. cm. — (Hill guides series)
    Includes index
    ISBN 0–7627–0652–X
    1. Napa Valley (Calif.)—Guidebooks. 2. Wine and wine making—California—Napa Valley—Guidebooks. I. Hill, Gerald N. II. Title

F868.N2 H55 2001
    917.94'190454—dc21

                                                                                    00–046656

Manufactured in the United States of America
Second Edition/Second Printing

CONTENTS

ACKNOWLEDGMENTS v

PREFACE vii

INTRODUCTION ix

How to Get Here x

Getting Around Once You're Here xiii

How to Be a Visitor and Not a Tourist in Napa Valley xiv

CHAPTER 1: *Los Carneros District* 1

CHAPTER 2: *In the City of Napa Itself* 25

CHAPTER 3: *Highway 29 (The St. Helena Highway)* 37

CHAPTER 4: *The Silverado Trail* 185

CHAPTER 5: *Where to Stay in the Napa Valley* 235

CHAPTER 6: *Beyond Wine Tasting* 249

CHAPTER 7: *History of the Napa Valley* 257

CHAPTER 8: *The Napa Valley List of Lists* 289

ABOUT THE AUTHORS 300

INDEX 301

ACKNOWLEDGMENTS

We particularly want to thank our old friends Senator John Dunlap and his wife, Janet, for their historical and personal insights into the Napa Valley and for spending so much time with us.

Our friend Jane Mosier of Napa, whom we met initially through politics, gave us incomparable assistance by faxing us piles and piles of facts she collected with her usual energetic and intellectual care. Dear friends Susan Weeks and Sue Holman helped us with the arduous duty of joining us to sample restaurants. Artist Judy Theo Lehner has, once again, created the perfect cover for our book. Our kids, Erin and Mack, gave their tolerant support, as usual.

And, of course, we thank the hundreds of winemakers, winery staff, chefs, restaurateurs, and shopkeepers for giving us their time, their stories, their soul, and their recipes. Thanks, too, to the people of Napa Valley for their encouragement and hospitality.

PREFACE

he Napa Valley continues to add new wineries and restaurants and somehow manages to become increasingly beautiful. The roadside community wildflower planting efforts make visitors smile almost at the instant they enter Napa County.

We will introduce you to small, rustic, family-run wineries, as well as some of the largest corporate-owned wineries in the world. In this guide, we will take you to chefs who are cooking world-class food for world-class prices. But we also visit ethnic and home cooks who share their best cultural traditions with the public at extremely reasonable prices.

Movie directors and cartoon developers, video-game and computer-program inventors, traditional vintners, and pilots and doctors all nurse their vineyards and wineries in their own way, each offering their personal taste and expression to the public. The contrasts are astounding and wonderful.

Napa Valley has more restaurants, more people, more money, more wineries, more applauded wines, more visiting movie stars, and more attention than Sonoma Valley, its nextdoor neighbor. Things are often done with much greater flair and at greater expense in Napa. The Napa wineries tend to have more expensive and dramatic designs; some wineries' art collections are brilliant and extensive, drawing more viewers than the local art galleries and museums.

A friendly rivalry exists between the Napa and Sonoma valleys. Sonoma resident and comedian Tommy Smothers's line, "Sonoma makes wine, Napa makes auto parts," adorns T-shirts and posters and fuels the fires to keep this good-natured competition going. Still, vintners have grafted and traded vine cuttings, winemakers, and phylloxera back and forth between Napa and Sonoma for decades. They are also joining together in the fight against the shiny-winged sharpshooter to prevent it from destroying vineyards, as it did in Temecula in the southern part of the state.

Each valley has its special charms. We encourage you to visit both Napa and Sonoma to maximize your pleasure!

—Kathleen Thompson Hill
—Gerald N. Hill

". . . where . . . the wine is bottled poetry . . ."

—Robert Louis Stevenson, *Silverado Squatters*

INTRODUCTION

*N*apa Valley stretches about 30 miles from its northwestern end to its southeastern end, sprawling between the Mayacamas Mountains on the west and the Vaca Range (sometimes called the Silverado Range of hills) on the east. It is widest (5 miles) in the south around the city of Napa and narrowest (1 mile) in the north near Calistoga. The Napa River is widest around the city of Napa—which it often floods in the winter—but the river is just a trickling stream where it begins in the north. Napa Valley ranges from windswept flats, to the Palisade Cliffs at the foot of Mount St. Helena, to the forests of the Mayacamas Mountains.*

Napa Valley's mildest climate is in the south, which benefits from breezes off the San Pablo Bay. The farther north you go, the rainier it gets, and the more extreme the temperatures. Microclimates are everywhere and contribute to some of the Valley's most unique wines.

The Napa Valley has two principal north–south roads: Highway 29 (locals prefer to call it the St. Helena Highway as it gets closer to St. Helena) and the Silverado Trail. A number of smaller roads connect the two.

In this guide, we first take you on a route up one side of the Napa Valley, on Highway 29. After meandering up Highway 29, you'll cross the Valley at Tubbs Lane, north of Calistoga, through Calistoga, then head back south on the gorgeous Silverado Trail.

On each route, we recommend that you crisscross the highway as few times as possible, for your safety and that of others. These busy roads can be quite dangerous. (Remember, other drivers have been sipping wine, too.)

On the way you will find restaurants judiciously interspersed with wineries. Napa Valley is one place where you will never go thirsty for wine or hungry for good food. Or is it hungry for wine and thirsty for food?

Napa Valley's towns are as attractive to visit as the wineries. Each has its own personality. We take you street by street, shop by shop, gallery by gallery through Napa, Yountville, Oakville, Rutherford, St. Helena, and Calistoga. We review every restaurant, from drive-up hamburger and taco stands to The French Laundry and the Culinary Institute of America, as we go along the route.

APPELLATIONS

Several microclimates and soil characteristics have been identified in the Napa Valley, and more attention is now paid to the unique terrain and terroir, a French term that reflects the effect that a particular vineyard site, the earth, and its sociology have on its wine.

Within the original Napa Valley Appellation, several subappellations have become recognized and named. These include the Stag's Leap District, Atlas Peak, Howell Mountain, Los Carneros, Mt. Veeder, Oakville, Rutherford, St. Helena, Spring Mountain, and Wild Horse Valley.

This guide also takes you mile by mile through the quasi-industrial auxiliary wine businesses south of the city of Napa—the part of the Valley you come to first if you travel from Oakland, Berkeley, the rest of the East Bay, or Sacramento. In addition, you will explore the fascinating Los Carneros District, in the southern part of the Valley between the two main roads. (Carneros extends from Napa Valley into Sonoma Valley.)

In this guide, we also offer the only concise and complete history of the Napa Valley. Read about the trials and travails of Robert Louis Stevenson, winemaking, wine lore, and wine fights.

And watch for elegant recipes throughout the book, provided by generous winemakers and chefs from throughout the Napa Valley. These luscious gems will allow you to bring some of your Valley experience into your own home.

HOW TO GET HERE

Napa Valley is only about an hour from San Francisco or forty-five minutes from Berkeley and Oakland. But there's a catch: You can't reach the Valley via public transportation. You must have a car or private airplane to get here. (The only bus from the Bay Area airports is the Evans Airporter, a private bus service. It makes eight trips from Oakland International Airport and eleven trips from San Francisco International Airport to the Napa Valley daily. Fares on all runs are $18.)

Getting Here by Car

From San Francisco: Take the Golden Gate Bridge north and continue on Highway 101 past San Rafael and through Marin County for about 30 miles. Turn east on Highway 37 toward Napa. Turn left (north) onto Highway 121 at Sears Point Raceway, heading toward Napa and Sonoma. Here you enter the prized and highly esteemed Carneros Wine District, which traverses the county line between Sonoma and Napa.

At the Schellville Fire Station, Highway 12 goes north into Sonoma, while 121 from here is also Highway 12 and goes east to Napa. So, to get to Napa, continue eastward (straight) toward Napa from the intersection of Highways 12 and 121. This segment of road is known locally as Fremont Drive. It takes you to or past the Cherry Tree plant and store, Babe's Drive-In (great hamburgers), eventually Clover-Stornetta Dairy (where Laura Chenel makes wonderful chèvre cheeses), and on to Napa.

After you pass (or even visit) Carneros wineries, turn north (left) onto Highway 121, which also becomes Highway 29. Highway 121 will turn eastward on Imola Avenue in Napa, and eventually becomes the Silverado Trail, running along the eastern side of the Napa Valley.

At this point, you have two Napa wine-touring choices: Follow Highway 29 northward along the western side of Napa Valley, or follow Highway 121 to the Silverado Trail and the eastern side of the Valley. We suggest that you explore both.

From Berkeley, Oakland, and the East Bay: From Berkeley and Oakland take Highway 80 east (it says east, but you are actually traveling north) through El Cerrito, Crockett, and across the Carquinez Bridge. Get in the left lanes of the bridge, because just after the toll gate you can turn leftish toward Napa and Highway 29, which will take you northward through Vallejo and American Canyon (no canyon in sight) to Napa.

Or you can follow Highway 80 to the Columbus Parkway exit and head toward Marine World Africa U.S.A. From Marine World continue westward on Highway 37 to Highway 29 in Vallejo's outskirts. Turn right (north) on Highway 29 and follow it into Napa.

Just past the intersection of Highways 29 and 12, you can stop at the Hakusan Sake Company, Seguin Moreau cooperage, and Napa Brewing Company before you even get to the city of Napa.

From Downtown Sonoma: From Sonoma Plaza in the middle of downtown Sonoma, go south on Broadway, then turn left (east) on Napa Road. Follow this road through two flashing red lights, and on through the hills to the stoplight and intersection of Highway 12. Turn left onto Highway 12/121 toward Napa and take the road through the hills. Off to the wineries you go!

Getting Here by Air

Napa Valley Airport, "Skyport to the Wine Country," is located conveniently south of the city of Napa and west of Highway 29 across from its intersection with Highway 12. (While no commercial jets land at the airport, Japan Airlines maintains an enormous flight-training school here.)

From Other Airports via Private Aircraft: Twenty-nine nmi NW of Oakland International (OAK) airport, 30 nmi SE of Sonoma County (STS) airport, 17 nmi NW of Concord (CCR) airport, and 18 nmi SW of Nut Tree (045) airport, Napa Airport is 4 NM south of the city of Napa, 1 NMi(-) east of the Napa River, and 1 NM west of Highways 12 and 29 intersection. The control tower is south side of runway 06/24, with rotating beacon east side of airport and a golf course 2 NM east.

Communication Frequencies: Napa Tower 118.7, Napa Ground Control 121.7, Napa Atis 124.05, Scaggs VOR (SGD) 112.1, Napa ILS Localizer 111.3, KVON (BDCST) 1440 KH 153, 4 NM to airport, Oakland Center 127.8, Oakland Radio 122.1T/112.1R.

Airport Information (APC): Field elevation 33 ft MSL; TPA: 1,033 ft MSL; Tower operates from 0700 to 2000 daily (may vary with season); VOR and localizer approaches available through Oakland Center (127.8); runway lights pilot activated. Key 118.7-3,5, or 7 times; San Francisco Sectional and L1-L2 Chart; Latitude 38-13; Longitude 122-17; Reil Runway 06; Papi Runway 18R.

Winds at Napa generally favor the use of either Runway 18 or 24. Landings and takeoffs are frequently conducted simultaneously from several runways, so pilots should be alert for other traffic.

At the airport, **Bridgeford Flying Service** (707–224–0887 or 707–644–1658) offers multitudinous goods and services, including Chevron fuel, flight instruction, ground school, pilot supplies, flying club, Cessna Pilot Center, maintenance, sales, and charter and scenic tours and rides. Office manager Adriann Harpst, a pilot herself, is most helpful and knowledgeable. Her office doubles as supply and gift shop, which includes pilot necessities, souvenirs, and an unusual collection of flying-related manuals and history books.

GETTING AROUND ONCE YOU'RE HERE

Once you arrive at the airport, you have to rent a car, which you can arrange at the airport or at your hotel, or take a taxi escorted tour.

Car Rental Agencies

AFFORDABLE AUTO RENTAL, 473 Soscol Avenue, Napa; (707) 257–1911
BUDGET RENT-A-CAR, 407 Soscol Avenue, Napa; (707) 224–7845
ENTERPRISE RENT-A-CAR, 230 Soscol Avenue, Napa; (707) 253–8000
HERTZ, 1895 Salvador Avenue, Napa; (707) 226–2037
RENT-A-WRECK, 555 Main Street, St. Helena; (800) 300–3213
SEARS RENT-A-CAR, 407 Soscol Avenue, Napa; (707) 224–7847
ZUMWALT FORD, 21 Main Street, St. Helena; (707) 963–2771

Taxi Companies

NAPA VALLEY CAB ("The Red Ones"), (707) 257–6444
TAXI CABERNET, (707) 942–2226, (707) 963–2620, or (888) 333–TAXI
(8294)

Public Transportation

NAPA VALLEY TRANSIT, (800) 696–6433 or (707) 255–7631, runs its route
between ten towns along Highway 29 from Vallejo in Solano County to
Calistoga at the northern end of Napa Valley, Monday–Saturday. Buses also stop
at Oakville Grocery, Beaulieu Winery, Freemark Abbey, and Bothe Napa State
Park.

THE V.I.N.E. (Valley Intracity Neighborhood Express), (707) 255–7631,
follows five routes within the city of Napa.

BEAR FLAG EXPRESS, (707) 944–4815, provides bus service within Yountville.

HOW TO BE A VISITOR AND NOT A TOURIST
IN NAPA VALLEY

Don't worry about looking like a tourist in Napa Valley. The Valley is
made for tourists! The wineries and restaurants thrive on your visit and are
well aware of that fact, so you will be treated well. Just dress comfortably and
bring your taste buds and money. There's no currency exchange—everyone's
must be green or plastic.

It does help to know a few of the local rules, however. Smoking is not
allowed in tasting rooms or restaurants, but it's occasionally okay outdoors. A
few wineries even sell cigars. In addition, be sure to make dinner and accommodations reservations—this is a popular region.

CHAPTER 1

LOS CARNEROS DISTRICT

os Carneros, a world-famous wine region, runs from the southern part of Sonoma Valley across the hills to the southern end of Napa Valley. Less formally known as Carneros, it also has its own appellation.

The Carneros region is cooler than most other parts of the Napa and Sonoma valleys due to the cool breezes and summer fog from the San Francisco Bay. These elements also provide for the slow maturation of the grapes—enhancing their flavor, color, and character—and are the ideal conditions for growing and producing Pinot Noir, Chardonnay, and Merlot.

In 1846 General Mariano Vallejo granted 18,000 acres of what is now known as Carneros to his brother-in-law, Jacob Leese. At that time, the land was called Rancho Huichica; a nearby, smaller grant of 2,500 acres known as Rincon de los Carneros gave its name to the region.

In the mid-1850s many farmers planted grapes on their parcels of land in Carneros. A stagecoach ran between the farms and Sonoma along what is now Highway 12/121, known locally as the Carneros Highway. In 1870 the first winery in the region opened (first known as Winter Winery and subsequently as Talcoa Vineyards).

In the late 1800s, the first wave of phylloxera, a devastating disease of grape plants spread by the phylloxera louse, struck. Then Prohibition in the 1920s temporarily eliminated wine production in the Carneros. After the repeal of Prohibition in 1933, a winery named Garetto began making wine again. Louis Martini and Beaulieu both planted in the Carneros from the 1940s to the 1960s. In the 1970s Carneros Creek, Saintsbury, and Acacia all achieved recognition as a new breed of winery.

How to Get to the Carneros District

To get here from San Francisco, take the Golden Gate Bridge and Highway 101 north, turn east on Highway 37, left at Sears Point Raceway to Highway 12/121, and follow toward Napa. The Domaine Carneros chateau, vineyards, and sign on the right mean soon you will take an extremely sharp hairpin right onto Duhig Road and the first winery on our tour. From Oakland/Berkeley, take I–80 east, take Highway 37, north on Highway 29, and left on Highway 12/121. In about 1 mile Domaine Carneros and Duhig Road will be on your left. Before stopping at Domaine Carneros, however, you should make an appointment to visit the di Rosa Preserve, which is right across the way. When you see wooden cutouts of animals against the hillside and a newish corrugated metal building, turn right (north) into the di Rosa driveway.

Wineries and Distillery of the Carneros Region

Wineries and grape growers in the area have created The Carneros Quality Alliance, an organization dedicated to improving and promoting the wines of Carneros with dignity and gusto. A small group, its members believe intensely in their mission and group individuality. In Napa Valley's part of the Carneros, you can visit Domaine Carneros, Acacia, Saintsbury, RMS (Rémy-Martin Sonoma) Distillery, Madonna Estate/Mont St. John, Carneros Creek, and Artesa.

Just west of the wineries, though, you come to the fascinating DI ROSA PRESERVE: ART & NATURE, on the north side of Highway 12/121, a highly unusual and personal collection of unconventional and experimental indoor and outdoor art. These pieces are dramatically presented throughout Rene di Rosa's fifty-three-acre property, which includes Winery Lake, the Gatehouse Gallery, and the Main Gallery.

Rene di Rosa collects San Francisco Bay Area artists' work and exhibits his 1,500-piece collection according to his own instincts, not according to curator's school standards. So you might find an unknown artist's work next to William Wiley's, an artist from San Jose next to Napa's Earl Thollander, or perhaps a lesser piece next to the drama of Joan Brown.

What many critics miss in describing Rene as a collector is the mission he feels to help artists. A former journalist who bought 460 Carneros acres when "experts" said you couldn't grow grapes here, di Rosa and his late wife, Veronica, took tremendous pleasure from helping artists by buying their work—a kind of sponsorship of the arts.

Veronica was the backbone of the restoration of the Napa Opera House. Tragically, she fell over a cliff in France while collecting flower seeds for her garden in Carneros. (Our mutual friend, the late Bob Ernest, who designed the di Rosa's chapel and some of the gardens, had told the di Rosas exactly where to find the seeds.) Veronica died as a result of the fall, just after Bob passed away.

Rene di Rosa sold most of his vineyards to Joseph E. Seagram & Sons in 1986 for a few million. He then created the Rene and Veronica di Rosa Foundation, part of whose mission is to support and inspire the work of Bay Area artists.

We guarantee that you will have an artistic experience at the di Rosa Preserve unlike any you will have in a museum—or anywhere else, for that matter. Di Rosa's collection will wake up your mind and your senses and stimulate your imagination as well as your funny bone.

 Fine points: Call for an appointment to take the two-hour tour. Everyone is welcome, and guides limit each group to twenty-five. Park in the lot below the corrugated-metal Gatehouse Gallery; the tours begin at the Gatehouse. Open your receptors and enjoy!

꙳⚘ *Di Rosa Preserve, 5200 Highways 12/121, Napa 94558; phone (707) 226–5991. Tours start at 9:25 A.M. and 12:55 P.M. Monday, Wednesday, and Thursday; 12:55 and 6:25 P.M. Tuesday; 9:25 and 10:25 A.M. Saturday. Admission is $10, but free to Napa County residents with photo ID. Visa and MasterCard. Wheelchair-accessible.*

The first winery you come to—and one of the grandest of Carneros—lies right across from di Rosa's property. The fabulous **DOMAINE CARNEROS** is owned by the Taittinger family of France.

In 1931 Pierre Taittinger acquired the venerable Champagne house Fourneaux, founded in 1734, and established Champagne Taittinger, which today is the last major French Champagne house still controlled by its founding family. Pierre Taittinger created a lighter Champagne wine, which now is the elegant wine that other producers emulate.

His son, Claude Taittinger, now president of Champagne Taittinger, selected this 138-acre parcel in Carneros in 1970 to build his American enterprise, a joint venture with Taittinger's distributor, Kobrand Corporation. Following his father's death in 1965, Claude Taittinger established the Prix Culinaire International Pierre Taittinger, now the ultimate recognition of a chef's skills.

Domaine Carneros was established in 1987. The building's design, inside and out, was inspired by the Taittinger family's French residence in Champagne, Chateau de la Marquetterie. Beautiful and slightly imposing, it is set on a knoll overlooking Carneros and the Napa Valley from the southwest.

DOMAINE CARNEROS' ENTRANCE DECK

As you enter the elegant winery, a grand portrait of Madame de Pompadour greets you. Turn right to the tasting room, with its vast views of the di Rosa Preserve and Artesa. Enjoy well-known designer Mary Steer's interior decoration, featuring blue upholstered maple chairs, glass and brass tables, maple walls, an exquisite collection of wine and food books, and a warm and welcoming tasting bar.

If the ambience here seems familiar to you, there's an excellent reason: Winemaker Eileen Crane contributed to the design of both Domaine Carneros and Gloria Ferrer Champagne Caves in the Sonoma Valley part of the Carneros. An exceptional person who taught nutrition science in Venezuela, Eileen has a master's degree in nutrition and graduated from both the University of California at Davis enology program and from the Culinary Institute of America. She left Gloria Ferrer for Domaine Carneros to help design, develop, and lead this facility.

Have a seat in the salon, and a server will explain the day's tastings and bring them to you with a complimentary hors d'oeuvre of chèvre and herb mousse with melba toast.

 Fine points: Mother's Day celebrations include music and treats with wine tasting. Winery tours hourly from 11:00 A.M. to 4:00 P.M. daily, April–October; same hours on Friday–Saturday, rest of the year; with tours at 11:00 A.M. and 1:00 and 3:00 P.M. Monday–

Thursday, winter. Featured wines: Sparkling wines made in the *méthode champenoise*, including Brut, Brut Vintage, La Rêve Blanc de Blancs, Brut Rose, and Famous Gate Pinot Noir. Tasting fees: $5.00–$10.00 a glass. Managing Director/Winemaker: Eileen Crane. Cases: 35,000 sparkling, 10,000 Pinot Noir. Acres: 138 here, 70 at Pompadour Vineyard.

❧ *Domaine Carneros, 1240 Duhig Road at Highway 12/121, Napa 94559; phone (707) 257–0101, fax (707) 257–3020, Web site www.domainecarneros.com. Open 10:30 A.M. to 6:00 P.M. daily. MasterCard, Visa, and American Express. Wheelchair-accessible from upper parking lot.*

As you come out of the Domaine Carneros driveway, turn right up Duhig Road. Follow it for about 2 miles, up the hill, down, and past a Mondavi vineyard on the right. Turn left on Las Amigas at Beaulieu's vineyard, and in 0.3 mile turn left into the driveway of ACACIA WINERY, the Carneros sister of the Chalone Wine Group.

Acacia Winery is a surprise, located in a pleasant, adobe-colored stucco building with leaf-green trim. It is surrounded by cow pasture and Beaulieu Vineyard across the road.

In 1986 Chalone Wine Group founder Dick Graf and Phil Woodward bought Acacia from Mike Richmond and partners, adding it to their Chalone Vineyard near Soledad, California; Edna Valley Vineyard near San Luis Obispo; Carmenet in Sonoma; Canoe Ridge Vineyard in eastern Washington; Sagelands (formerly Staton Hills) in Yakima, Washington; and Jade Mountain in Napa.

CHÈVRE AND HERB MOUSSE
from Eileen Crane, Director/Winemaker, Domaine Carneros

INGREDIENTS:

½ cup parsley leaves

½ tsp crushed garlic

1 bunch (about 1/4 cup) of tarragon leaves

1 cup chèvre (goat cheese)

1 ½ lbs cream cheese

PREPARATION:

Chop parsley leaves, crushed garlic, and tarragon leaves in a food processor, turning on and off in short pulses until finely minced but not liquefied. Remove to a small bowl. Blend the chèvre and cream cheese in the food processor until creamy and smooth. Add the herb/garlic mixture, and lightly combine the ingredients by turning on and off the processor in short pulses.

The mousse can be piped or spooned into a serving dish. Present with mini toasts, crackers, or bread. Makes 25 small ramekin-size servings. Serve with Domaine Carneros' Famous Gate Pinot Noir or sparkling wines.

The Acacians, as Acacia's loyal and jovial staff members call themselves, stress their sensitivity to terroir, the French concept that each vineyard has a character different from others. That character emanates from its geography, geology, climate, and biological and sociological influences, and it should not be disturbed. Acacians call themselves "a friendly if a bit eccentric bunch" who "have never had a black tie event . . . and intend to keep it that way." The staff here are taught that no matter what the request, the answer is yes. The Acacians clearly enjoy themselves, their work, and their wine, and they will do everything possible to be sure that you do, too. But please, be sure to call ahead for reservations.

Acacia gives killer tours, with barrel tastings and technical tours. In the "sky's the limit" attitude, the staff put on Famous Chef Dinners, bicycle tours, "picnics, breakfast with the winemaker, bowling for Pinot, bar crawling, horseshoes, old wines, young wines, old dogs, new tricks. You name it, we'll try it."

Fine points: Acacia has bottled its wines with private labels for Tra Vigne, Spago, the Mauna Kea Beach Hotel, Ruth's Chris Steak House, Burlingame Country Club, and the Claremont Country Club. Tasting fee: none, except $5.00 per person for groups of 10 or more. Featured wines: Chardonnay, Chardonnay Brandy, Pinot Noir, Rosé, Viognier, Mutts Mongrel Rouge, Old Vines blend, Amethyst Vinalia, Brut. Winemaker/General Manager: Michael Terrien. Cases: 60,000. Acres: 150.

✤ *Acacia Winery, 2750 Las Amigas Road, Napa 94559; phone (707) 226–9991, fax (707) 226–1685, Web site www.acaciawinery.com. Open "by*

ACACIA WINERY IN CARNEROS

appointment" from 10:00 A.M. to 4:30 P.M. Monday–Saturday, noon to 4:30 P.M. Sunday. MasterCard, Visa, and American Express. Wheelchair-accessible.

As you leave Acacia Winery, turn left on Las Amigas Road, and in about one mile turn right onto Buchli Station Road to **BOUCHAINE VINEYARDS,** a rapidly rising star of Los Carneros. Notice the late architect William Turnbull's winery design trademark of natural vertical wood on the winery's exterior, which in this case comes from recycled redwood wine tanks from the 1900s. Enjoy the colorful herb and perennial garden near the monogrammed gate.

Bouchaine is both the maiden name of owner Gerret Copeland's mother and, according to the staff, the French word for a person who puts corks in wine bottles. Residents of Delaware, Gerret is a Dupont, and Tatiana, his wife, is a native of Buenos Aires, Argentina, of Russian heritage.

In 1980 the Copelands purchased what was the Boon Fly ranch in the mid-1800s and completed the winery and tasting room renovations in 1997. It was once owned by the Garretto Brothers, who made sacramental wines and distilled Grappa and whiskey

---

GRANDMA'S PINEAPPLE UPSIDE DOWN CAKE
from
Bouchaine Vineyards

INGREDIENTS:

4 Tbs butter
½ cup brown sugar
1 can sliced pineapple
2 eggs
¼ tsp salt
1 cup sugar
1 tsp vanilla
¼ cup water
1 cup cake flour
1 tsp baking powder

PREPARATION

Melt 3 Tbs butter in 9-inch iron skillet. Remove from heat and sprinkle with brown sugar. Arrange pineapple slices in bottom of skillet.

Beat eggs until light and add (while beating) salt, sugar, and vanilla. Heat to boiling: water and 1 Tbs butter or shortening. Sift together cake flour and baking powder. Add wet ingredients to mixture, beating thoroughly. Pour over fruit in skillet.

Bake at 350° F for 25–30 minutes or until the cake pulls away from the edge of the pan. Turn out while warm and serve with whipped cream and Bouchaine Tsarina.

---

before and after Prohibition, delivering their stash on the back of a truck. Beringer bought the property from Boon, and later sold it to the Copelands. Bouchaine is the longest continually operated winery in Carneros.

Now lovely sculpture, a cozy fireplace, living room furniture, a deck, and views of Carneros' rolling hills create a casually elegant but homey ambience.

Fine points: No tasting fee except for large groups. Featured wines: Late Harvest Tsarina, Rosé of Pinot Noir, Pinot Noir, Chardonnay, Cabernet Franc. Owners: Gerret and Tatiana Copeland. Winemaker: David Stevens. Cases: 15,000. Acres: 105.

❧ *Bouchaine Vineyards, 1075 Buchli Station Road, Napa 94559; phone (707) 252–9065 or (800) 654–9463, fax (707) 252–0401, Web site www.bouchaine. com. Open from 10:30 a.m. to 4:00 p.m. daily by appointment. Visa, MasterCard, and American Express. Wheelchair-accessible.*

From Bouchaine turn left (north) onto Cuttings Wharf Road until you reach **RMS** (Rémy-Martin Sonoma) BRANDY DISTILLERY, which makes American luxury brandies. (You can also get here by turning south on Cuttings Wharf Road from the Carneros Highway [Highway 12/121] 1.3 miles west of Highway 29, or by coming eastward across Withers Road from Saintsbury on Los Carneros.)

RMS president and CEO Pierre-Michel Alsac, who is also president and CEO of the Grand Vin de Gironde division of Remy-Cointreau, in 1998 changed the name to RMS, meaning Rare, Mature, and Special.

As you approach RMS, be sure to notice the lush fields and ponds, pine trees, and French-looking gray stone buildings with red tile roofs. Hundreds of

RMS (RÉMY-MARTIN SONOMA) BRANDY DISTILLERY
WITH SWALLOWS CIRCLING

swallows nest under the buildings' eaves, dotting the parking lot and paths with surprisingly uniform little white splats.

You truly feel as if you are in France in this protective complex of stone buildings with lawns and patios in the center and housing the Visitor Center, Still House, Barrel House, and offices. Enjoy the Visitor Center's soft blue sofa and fireplace, Gail Chase-Bien's three-panel painting titled *Angels of Carneros,* angel wind chimes, brandy maple syrup, Vine Village oils and vinegars, and French Prairie marionberries in brandy, pears in brandy, and black cherries. Here you can also view a display of French brandy making and a traditional Alambic Charentais pot.

Alambic Still House and Barrel House tours are a real treat. They provide a rare chance to see the centuries-old *méthode charentaise* or traditional Cognac method of double wine distillation, culminating in the Aroma Room. Be sure to try samples of chocolate sauce with RMS Special Reserve Brandy, caramel sauce with RMS Pear de Pear, and any others offered.

 Fine points: RMS affords the affluent among us the chance to select personal brandy blends and to create signature barrels. These can cost from $5,000 on up and come from French Colombard, Chenin Blanc, Pinot Noir, Palomino, Folle Blanche, and Muscat grapes. Featured brandies: SR (Special Reserve), Carneros QE (Quality Extraordinaire), Pear de Pear from North Coast California Bartlett pears, Folle Blanche, Trilogy, and Heavenly Pair. Cellarmaster: Rick Estes. Cases: Undefined. Acres: 30.

❧ *RMS (Rémy-Martin Sonoma) Brandy Distillery , 1250 Cuttings Wharf Road, Napa 94559; phone (707) 253–9055, fax (707) 253–0116. Web site: www.rmsbrandy.com. Open from 10:00 A.M. to 5:00 P.M. daily in summer, 10:00 A.M. to 4:30 P.M. during standard time. MasterCard, Visa, and American Express. Wheelchair-accessible.*

On the south side of the Carneros Highway (12/121), don't miss Saintsbury, renowned producer of Carneros Pinot Noir and Chardonnay. To get there, turn right (south) from the highway onto Los Carneros Avenue. Turn left (east) onto Withers Lane, then turn south into Saintsbury's driveway.

Saintsbury has a Ned Forrest–designed, elegant rural barn with gray stucco walls and beamed ceilings. An English garden of native plants and blond pebbles provides a charming setting.

As you enter the Mexican tiled office and tasting area, you are struck with the quality of art everywhere, much of it from the San Francisco Museum of Modern Art Rental Center.

UC Davis enology classmates David Graves and Dick Ward discovered in 1977 that they liked "knocking back a decent glass of Morey-Saint-Denis." In 1981 they moved their wine friendship into a wine partnership. Original wine-maker Bill Knuttel joined them in 1983, and Byron Kosuge came in as "Bill's right hand man."

Dick and Dave both named their winery for "the old codger" George E. B. Saintsbury (1845–1933), a Scottish professor of literature at the University of Edinburgh and wine fan. In his *Notes on a Cellar Book*, first published in 1920, Saintsbury wrote: "Well! A cellar is an interesting place to fill, to contemplate when filled, and to empty in the proper way."

Dick and Dave believe, and hopefully they are correct, that Carneros is the Beaune of California. They were among the first wineries to produce 100 per-cent malolactic Chardonnay, which means that the wine goes through malo-lactic fermentation, in which the conversion of malic acid to lactic acid makes the wine softer and richer. While their first devotion is to their exceptional Pinot Noirs, their reality also includes the fact that, as Dick puts it, "You need to have something for the fish course."

Fine points: Featured wines: Carneros Chardonnay, Pinot Noir, Garnet, Marc Brandy, and Vin Gris of Pinot Noir. Winemaker: Byron Kosuge. Cases: 48,000. Acres: 55.

᠅ *Saintsbury, 1500 Los Carneros Avenue, Napa 94559; phone (707) 252–0592. Call for appointment. No credit cards. Wheelchair-accessible.*

On the north side of Highway 12/121 you will find three more wineries with vastly different and distinct personalities: Madonna Estate/Mont St. John, Carneros Creek, and Artesa.

To get there from Napa, Cuttings Wharf Road, or Los Carneros Avenue, turn right off Highway 12/121 onto Old Sonoma Road. (If you decide to forgo Saintsbury and go there from Domaine Carneros, get back onto the highway and immediately turn left onto Old Sonoma Road.)

MADONNA ESTATE/MONT ST. JOHN WINERY, with its arched windows, is at the northeast corner of Old Sonoma Road and Highway 12/121, so turn right into its driveway. The Bartolucci family founded the winery in 1922 in the shadow of Mt. St. John near Oakville. They were among the first to plant pre-mium grape varieties in the Napa Valley.

Andrea (Andy) Bartolucci came to the United States from Italy in 1913 expressly to make wine. He settled in St. Helena in 1919. In 1922 he pur-chased a twenty-four-acre vineyard and winery, where he made sacramental wines and sold grapes to home winemakers during Prohibition. He made his

MADONNA ESTATE/MONT ST. JOHN WINERY

PEACHY WALNUT SALAD
from Madonna Estate/
Mont St. John Winery

INGREDIENTS:

   large bowl of mixed greens
   2 ripe peaches, sliced
   ¼ cup blue cheese, crumbled
   ¼ cup toasted walnuts brushed with honey and broiled or baked until brown
   1 small red onion, sliced thinly
   ½ cup cherry tomatoes
   Toasted Walnut Grapeseed Oil
   Late Harvest Riesling Vinegar

PREPARATION:

   Drizzle Toasted Walnut Grapeseed Oil and Late Harvest Riesling Vinegar over ingredients and toss.

first table wine with his son Louis in 1933, selling the 5,000 gallons for 20 cents a gallon. Louis studied enology at UC Davis, began to modernize Madonna Winery, bought out his father, and began production of wines under the Mont St. John label. By 1947 Mont St. John Cellars was the twelfth-largest winery in California.

Louis's son, Andrea (Buck) Bartolucci, grew up in Louis's varietal-specific vineyards, studied viticulture and enology at Cal State University at Fresno, and came home in 1967 to work as assistant winemaker to his father. When Louis and his brothers sold the winery in 1970, Buck bought and planted 160 acres in the not yet "discovered" Carneros Region, which he still farms organically and dry—meaning nature runs things. Buck's Madonna Vineyards is one of the few vineyards in Napa County with the California Certified Organic Farmers Association designation and produces the fine pesticide- and herbicide-free wines of Madonna Estate/ Mont St. John. Buck believes that "herbicides and pesticides . . . are shortcuts that ultimately throw things in the vineyards out of balance, causing more problems down the road."

Buck's daughter, Brette, has joined the winery as director of public relations.

As you enter the tasting room with its wood-paneled walls and obviously linoleum floors, you instantly know that this is a casual, fun place with warm hospitality and humor. The staff's motto is "No question's too dumb; the only dumb question is the one unasked." Here you can purchase some of our favorites: Angelo's garlic-stuffed olives, garlic marinara sauce and salsa, mustard, Cuisine Perel pastas, grapeseed oils, Madonna Estate vinegars, such as orange, spicy peach, and black fig, olive oils, and Merlot blackberry grilling sauce.

TRUFFLE RISOTTO
from Madonna Estate/
Mont St. John Winery

INGREDIENTS:

 2 cups Arborio rice

 2 oz dry porcini mushrooms

 ½ stick butter (⅛ lb)

 4 Tbs truffle oil

 1 bunch scallions, chopped

 3 carrots, minced

 2 cups grated Parmesan cheese

PREPARATION:

Add hot water to the dry porcini mushrooms and let stand 30 minutes. In another pan, melt butter, add oil, scallions, and carrots. Cook for 10 minutes. Add the rice and cook for 5 minutes. Drain the porcini by slowly pouring the water over the rice. Simmer until the rice is tender but firm, about 25 minutes. When done, drizzle with a little extra truffle oil and sprinkle with Parmesan cheese.

Don't miss the white truffle oil. You'll also find "Life Is a Cabernet" mouse pads, espresso shortbread cookies, and wine-country posters and books.

 Fine points: Reserve ahead to spend some entertaining time with Buck or other wine guys on their vineyard and tasting tours, particularly on the second and fourth Saturdays of the month. These exceptionally personal and informative tours of organic farming and wine tasting cost $5.00 for tour and tastings. Tasting only: $2.00. Featured wines (all estate-bottled): Chardonnay, Pinot Grigio, Merlot, Johannisberg Riesling, Gewürztraminer, Muscat di Canelli, Pinot Noir, Cabernet Sauvignon. Owner: Andrea (Buck) Bartolucci. Winemakers: Buck Bartolucci and John Kreiger. Cases: 10,000. Acres: 160 certified organic.

❦ *Madonna Estate/Mont St. John Winery, 5400 Old Sonoma Road, Napa 94559; phone (707) 255–8864, fax (707) 257–2778, Web site www.madonna estate.com. Open from 10:00 A.M. to 5:00 P.M. daily. Call for a tour appointment. MasterCard, Visa, and American Express. Wheelchair-accessible.*

Carneros Creek Winery is next on our tour. As you leave Madonna Estate/Mont St. John, turn right up Old Sonoma Road. (If you skipped Madonna Estate/Mont St. John, just continue up the road.) Turn left (west) onto Dealy Lane 0.3 mile from Madonna Estate/Mont St. John, and travel west 1 mile. After you pass a private golf course, watch for the Irish and American flags near what looks like a yellow wood house, which it was before it became Carneros Creek. Turn left into Carneros Creek's parking lot at the flags.

An Irishman making wine? You bet! In fact, Carneros Creek Pinot Noir is the official wine of the Irish city of Cork, one of San Francisco's sister cities. Here's the story.

Owner Francis Mahoney's parents left County Cork in the 1920s for California. Their families, the O'Mahoneys and O'Riordans, still farm around Cork. In the 1960s Francis took off to work the family farms and travel the wine regions of France, Germany, and Italy. After carefully developing his affinity for Burgundian wines, Francis taught for a while, then decided to follow his true love: wine. He studied enology at UC Davis, worked at Connoisseur Wine Imports in San Francisco and as vineyard manager for Mayacamas Vineyards, and established his own winery in the Carneros district in 1972. His goal was to make wines that would stand up to French Burgundies. Eventually he cofounded the Carneros Quality Alliance.

In a brilliant move, Francis offered his land for a UC Davis field study to improve grape varietal quality. He selected the enology department's top student, Melissa Moravec, to lead the clonal research project. Francis learned along with the researchers, hired Melissa as enologist, then winemaker, and now sets

CARNEROS CREEK WINERY

a standard for Pinot Noir. Melissa has been the winemaker here for twenty years, and 2002 will be the winery's thirtieth anniversary. Four cats have taken over the tasting room's chairs with pride. Already fully utilizing its new production building, Carneros Creek will soon build a new hospitality center.

No surprise, but Carneros Creek's wines were served by President Clinton to then President Mary and Mr. Robinson of Ireland.

Fine points: The tasting fee of $2.50, or $5.00 for vineyard designates, goes toward your purchase of wine. Featured wines: Fleur de Carneros Pinot Noir, Merlot, Mahoney Estate Chardonnay and Pinot Noir, Cabernet Sauvignon. Owners: The Mahoney Family. Winemaker: Melissa Moravec. Cases: 35,000. Acres: 187.
Carneros Creek Winery, 1285 Dealy Lane, Napa 94559; phone (707) 253–9463, fax (707) 253–9465, e-mail wineinfo@carneros-creek.com, Web site www.carneros-creek.com. Open from 10:00 A.M. to 5:00 P.M. daily. MasterCard, Visa, American Express, and Discover. Wheelchair-accessible.

As you leave Carneros Creek, turn left onto Dealy Lane to visit ARTESA WINERY (formerly Codorniu Napa), an architectural and artistic heaven. After a curve in the road, turn left onto Henry Road and drive for about 0.5 mile. Turn left into Artesa's long driveway, well marked with gate and gray cement walls. No—the cute old house on the left is not it. Keep going. Notice the

ARTESA'S ENTRANCE AND WINERY
UNDER NATIVE GRASSES

peaceful lake just below what appears to be a knoll topped by a mound of long
grass. *That* is Artesa.

Designed by Barcelona architect Domingo Triay and assisted by Napa
Valley architect Earl R. Bouligny, this local landmark features water cascading
down the building and staircase edges, reflecting pools, smoky quartz–colored
windows, an art gallery featuring exceptional Spanish and American artists
(including the decorative glass and sculpture of permanent resident artist
Gordon Huether), and winemaking artifacts. Barcelona craftspeople designed
and built the custom furniture and fittings to express contemporary Catalan
culture.

With their abundant resources the Raventos family built this remarkable
winery. Part of a hill was removed and set aside while the production facility,
offices, and visitor center were constructed. Then the complex was re-covered
with the reserved earth, and the new winery's height was matched with the top
of the original hill. Native grass was planted over the top so that the exterior
changes with the seasons in tune with the surrounding hills, with the grass drip-
irrigated from ponds on the estate. Talk about environmental sensitivity!

The family made the first *méthode champenoise* sparkling wine in Barcelona
in 1872 and began making elegant and delicate California sparkling wine here
in 1991. They have been making still wines in Spain since the 1500s and today

GRILLED RACK OF LAMB DINNER
from Artesa Winery

INGREDIENTS FOR THE RACK OF LAMB:

rack of lamb, approximately 2 lb
2–3 Tbs olive oil
1–3 cloves of garlic, split

PREPARATION:

Rub meat with olive oil and garlic. Arrange barbecue to achieve a hot, indirect open fire. Place lamb in center with coals around outside, or place opposite side of grill from coals. (Lamb should not be directly over coals.) Grill 10–15 minutes on each side. Serves 4.

Make batter for zucchini pancakes while the barbecue coals are heating, and start the herbed potatoes. Brown pancakes during the last 20 minutes that the lamb is grilling.

INGREDIENTS FOR THE HERBED POTATOES:

12 small red potatoes
2 Tbs butter
1 tsp crumbled dried rosemary

PREPARATION:

Wash potatoes, trim, and remove eyes. Cut in half. Melt butter in skillet. Add potatoes and sprinkle with rosemary. Pan roast, covered, 35–40 minutes, lifting cover from time to time to turn potatoes and prevent overbrowning. Serves 4.

INGREDIENTS FOR THE ZUCCHINI PANCAKES:

1 lb fresh zucchini
½ cup flour
½ cup grated Parmesan cheese
1 tsp garlic salt
1 egg, beaten

PREPARATION:

Coarsely grate zucchini, discarding juice. Mix with remaining ingredients. Twenty minutes before dinner is to be served, spoon batter onto preheated, nonstick griddle to make 2 ½–3-inch-diameter pancakes. Brown 10 minutes on each side. Serves 4.

are Spain's foremost maker of Cava. The renaming of Artesa signifies a winery move toward still wines, which they will certainly make successfully.

 Fine points: The Raventos family also own Bach, Bodegas Bilbainas, Rondel, and Raimat wineries. Featured wines: Sauvignon Blanc, Chardonnay, Pinot Noir, Brut, Reserve Cuvée. Tasting fee: $6.00 for five wines or $2.00 for two ounces, $8.00 for three reserve wines or $3.00 per taste. No picnicking. Owners: The Raventos Family. Winemakers: sparkling wines–Steven Tebb; still wines–Don Van Staavern. Cases: 15,000 still wines, with 150,000 expected in 5 years, and 5,000 sparkling wines. Acres: 350.

Artesa Winery, 1345 Henry Road, Napa 94559; phone (707) 224–1668, fax (707) 224–1672, Web site www.artesawinery.com. Open from 10:00 A.M. to 5:00 P.M. daily. Tours at 11:00 A.M. and 2:00 P.M., or call ahead. MasterCard, Visa, and American Express. Wheelchair-accessible by elevator at southern entrance.

SOUTH OF NAPA

As you approach Napa on Highway 29 coming from Berkeley/Oakland or the East Bay, you may want to detour east for a mile to the new Kirkland Ranch Winery or stop at three interesting places that most people miss: Hakusan Sake Gardens, Seguin-Moreau Napa cooperage, and Napa Ale Works. Kirkland is on Highway 12 (Jamieson Canyon Road) and Kirkland Ranch Road, while the other three, and a Lafitte cork production facility, are all in a newish industrial complex in a triangle formed by the Kelly Road cutoff between the junction of Highways 12 and 29. First we'll go to Kirkland Ranch Winery, certainly the most exciting new tasting room in the Napa Valley.

KIRKLAND RANCH WINERY is one of the few Napa Valley wineries where you are actually greeted by family members who host and work the property, and have for five generations. Brothers Larry and Lonnie Kirkland bought the land, still a working cattle ranch and vineyard, in 1978 and became the second owners of the actual deed from General Mariano Vallejo.

As you approach this dramatic edifice atop a hill along Highway 12 (Jamieson Canyon Road) you will be struck by the dramatic stone, water fountain and tumbling waterfall, and lovely landscaping. Just wait until you get inside. It appears that no expense was spared to create a tasteful Wild West cattle ranching theme, with giant murals of the Kirkland family working the cattle on horseback and with a covered wagon coming out of the downstairs mural into the reception room.

Take the elevator or stairs made of logs split by one of the Kirklands up to

WILDFLOWER HONEY LOAF
from Debi Kirkland, Kirkland Ranch Winery

INGREDIENTS:

   2 cups flour

   2 tsp baking powder

   ½ tsp baking soda

   1 tsp salt

   2 Tbs butter

   1 egg

   ½ tsp vanilla

   ¾ cup Kirkland Ranch Wildflower Honey

   1 cup milk

   ¾ cup toasted walnuts (or half nuts/half dates)

PREPARATION:

Sift together dry ingredients in bowl. Melt butter and cool slightly. Beat egg until light; add honey, milk, and vanilla, and beat well. Add melted butter. Pour the liquid ingredients into the dry and mix until blended. Fold in the nuts or fruit and nuts. Place dough in pan and bake for about 20 minutes. Serve with honey and butter. For honey butter, mix one cube of butter with ¼ cup Wildflower Honey. Cream until light and fluffy.

the tasting bar, and don't miss the viewing hall's three large windows through which you can see the bottling line, German tanks (wine, that is), and barrel rooms. The walls are lined with real family photos depicting local modern cattle ranching history. On the third floor is the Cedar Room, a corporate entertainment venue whose walls are covered with cedar.

Next, head back to the bar, made of rare reddish wood and surrounded by cowhide-covered chairs, red cedar tree trunks from Astoria, Oregon, for posts, and a veranda with tables and chairs for sipping and viewing the 2,600-acre ranch and beyond. Lots of barn siding lines the room, the central chandelier is made of forty pairs of naturally shed elk antlers, and all of the antiques are family heirlooms. There's even a large television, because Larry and Lonnie don't want to miss their favorite sports programs and assume you don't want to either.

Daughter Debi Kirkland selects products, which include jams and honey from bees used for pollinating the vineyards and herbs grown for erosion control. Signs instruct Cowboys leave your guns at the bar. These people have thought of everything. A must visit, if only for the Wild West experience. Debi suggests you check out the Web site for a virtual shop and tour of the winery.

   Fine points: Tasting fee: $5.00. Featured wines: Chardonnay, Pinot Grigio, Rosato di Sangiovese, Cabernet Sauvignon, Merlot. Owners: The Kirkland Family. Winemaker: Rick Tracy (formerly of Far Niente). Cases: 32,000. Acres: 140 planted of 2,600.

Kirkland Ranch Winery, 1 Kirkland Ranch Road (formerly Lynch Road) at

Highway 12–Jamieson Canyon Road, Napa 94558; phone (707) 254–9100, Web site www.kirklandwinery.com. Open from 10:00 a.m. to 4:00 p.m. daily. Visa, MasterCard, American Express, Diners Club, and Discover. Wheelchair-accessible.

To get to the other attractions, take Kelly Road off Highway 12 or 29 and follow the signs into the complex. Take the northern road (Camino Dorado) entrance to Seguin-Moreau and Napa Ale, and the southern entrance (Executive Way) to Hakusan Sake.

Directly across from HAKUSAN SAKE GARDENS' parking lot and past the cherry trees is an unusual tasting room with plenty of tables and garden views. Here you can taste at least seven sakes, served warm or cold in small glasses that resemble shot glasses. Made from California's finest rice, these premium sakes contain no sulfites, which reduces the possibility of headaches (if you limit intake).

If you sit in the tasting room, you can also take in the beauty of the Japanese gardens and American sculpture just south of the building and also facing the brewery. Because Hakusan is owned by Kahnan Inc., holders of a large Coca-Cola franchise in Japan, it is not a sake maker with etched-in-stone traditions that can't be broken. With such independence, Hakusan has experimented and

HAKUSAN SAKE GARDENS ENTRANCE
WITH SPRING CHERRY BLOSSOMS

SESAME SPROUT SALAD AND FRESH APPLE MIRIN CUPS
from Hakusan Sake Gardens

INGREDIENTS FOR SESAME SPROUT SALAD:

1 tsp Hakusan Sake	_1 tsp sugar_
2 tsp Hakusan Mirin	_1 tsp sesame oil_
½ cup soy sauce	_1 tsp sesame seeds_
½ cup rice vinegar	_1 lb bean sprouts_

PREPARATION:

Mix everything but the bean sprouts together. Rinse bean sprouts in colander. Drain. Heat a saucepan of water to a boil, then add sprouts. Cook for 1 minute, then drain. In a bowl, toss the bean sprouts with the dressing until thoroughly mixed. Served chilled. Serves 4.

For variety, use the dressing over a salad of noodles, cucumber slices, and shredded chicken. Serve with chilled Hakusan Premium Sake.

INGREDIENTS FOR FRESH APPLE MIRIN CUPS:

8 Tbs Hakusan Mirin	_cinnamon powder_
½ cup butter sliced in 8 pats	_8 large red apples, sliced and peeled_
8 tsp raisins	

PREPARATION:

Prepare apples and arrange one apple each in a dessert dish. Add 1 pat of butter, 1 Tbs of Hakusan Mirin, a dash of cinnamon, and 1 tsp raisins to each dish. Microwave on high, 4 dishes at a time, for 5–7 minutes or to desired tenderness. Serve chilled with Hakusan Sweet Blossom (dessert) Sake. Serves 8.

---

created sake six-packs as well as sake-filled chocolates and dessert sakes—moves disdained in Japan as being too American. When we visited, we suggested Hakusan infuse some sake with gas to make a carbonated sake to compete in the beer market.

When founder Toyokichi Hombo introduced Coca-Cola to Japan, he met resistance because the Japanese thought it looked suspiciously like soy sauce. Eventually overcoming that problem, he decided that the next-hardest project might be to talk Americans into liking sake.

Take the self-guided tour of the adjoining brewery, where you can view the process through windows and read excellent explanations of the brewing steps. If you buy some sake, you can take a sake recipe booklet.

Fine points: Perhaps sake should be called "the other white wine." Tasting fee: $1.00 total. Featured sakes: Premium Sake, Napa Hakusan, Mild Draft Sake, Sweet Blossom and Plum dessert sakes, Cooking Sake (Mirin), three kinds of sake-filled chocolates ($1.00 per piece), and assorted gift baskets and sake sets. Owners: Kohnan, Inc. (Toyokichi Hombo). Brewmaster: Hirotaka (Hiro) Sugiura. Cases: 200,000. Acres: Sacramento Valley.

❧ *Hakusan Sake Gardens, One Executive Way, Napa 94558; phone (707) 258–6160 or (800) HAKUSAN, Web site www.hakusan.com. Open from 10:00 A.M. to 5:00 P.M. daily. MasterCard, Visa, Discover, and JCB. Wheelchair-accessible.*

We highly recommend that you visit the Seguin-Moreau Napa cooperage to view the craft of making wine barrels in the French tradition from American oak. In the cooperage across from Seguin-Moreau's offices, you can watch from a walkway so close to the process that you can feel the heat of the flames and inhale the smoke and sawdust.

Huge signs explain the process, from cutting wood and stoking the fires with oak chips to the cooper's art of using water and dancing flames to mold the barrels. Like witches' cauldrons, the flames seem to toast the barrels and the coopers' hair, sending a vanilla aroma into the air. Watch the hammer blows shape the metal bands in the "barrel-maker's dance."

Fine points: T-shirts, books, and other souvenirs are available here. Barrels: 80 per day.

❧ *Seguin-Moreau Napa, 151 Camino Dorado, Napa 94558; phone (707) 252–3408. Open from 8:00 A.M. to 6:00 P.M. Best time to watch: 9:00 and 11:00 A.M., 1:00 and 3:00 P.M. MasterCard and Visa. Wheelchair-accessible.*

If you turn right as you leave Seguin-Moreau, then left onto Camino Ortega, you'll find Napa Ale Works on your left. In a truly symbiotic environmental relationship, Napa Ale saves its shredded paper and gives it to neighbor Seguin-Moreau to start its fires.

Dwayne Mathews and Elaine St. Clair started making beer at home in 1988, a natural result of Elaine's Scottish heritage and UC Davis Fermentation Studies. While an assistant winemaker at Domaine Chandon, Elaine joined

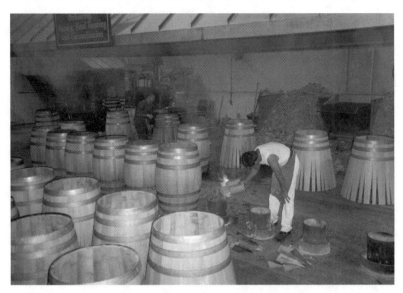

SEGUIN-MOREAU NAPA COOPER HEATS WOOD
SO IT CAN BE FORMED INTO BARRELS

with John Wright, chairman of Domaine Chandon, to build this brewery.

Napa Ale makes beer "faithful to the German Rhenheitsgebot," an ancient Bavarian purity law that allows only malted barley or wheat, yeast, hops, and water as ingredients, with hops from Washington's Yakima Valley.

Fine points: Be sure to call ahead for an appointment to visit this hands-on brewery for a down-and-wet experience. Be sure to check out the NAW merchandise. Featured beers: Napa Red Ale, Napa Wheat Ale, Napa Oatmeal Stout. Owners: Dwayne Mathews, Elaine St. Clair, and John Wright. Brewmaster: Elaine St. Clair. Barrels: 2,000.

🍇 *Napa Ale Works, 110 Camino Ortega, Napa 94558; phone (707) 257–8381, fax (707) 257–2436, e-mail aleworks@aol.com, Web site www.aleworks.com. Open from 8:00 A.M. to 5:00 P.M. Monday–Friday. Tours by appointment. No credit cards. Wheelchair-accessible.*

CHAPTER 2

IN THE CITY OF NAPA ITSELF

ood news, folks. Downtown Napa is undergoing an extensive makeover—a Mondavi-style makeover.

The Napa County seat, complete with historic courthouse, big post office, and excellent new library, has suffered predictably from the development of outlying shopping centers and discount chains in ticky-tacky big boxes, to say nothing of the Yountville earthquake. To the rescue, riding white stallions and wearing twenty-five-gallon white hats, have come Robert Mondavi and friends, including many city of Napa residents.

Until recently, private redevelopment of downtown storefronts and historic buildings had been slow, because the Napa River has flooded drastically a few times in recent years, making any new investments vulnerable to disaster. In June 1998 Napa voters decided to spend $155 million to control the river's flooding. This is great news for everyone because investors feel that they can safely put money toward the redevelopment of the downtown without fear. Napa is turning itself around, with historic buildings renovated as attractive galleries and restaurants.

Even before the people of Napa cast this life preserver into the water, Robert Mondavi's powerful safety net had begun to spread. When the restoration of the Napa Opera House seemed to have bogged down, for example, he and his wife, Margit Biever Mondavi, pledged millions of dollars to finish the project. (Mondavi also pledged support to create the Oxbow School, a residential art school that opened in 1999.) And, aware that the "Up Valley" towns of Yountville, St. Helena, and Calistoga really couldn't bear any more tourism and that the city of Napa was dying on the vine, Mondavi inspired, organized, and hired staff to raise funds to develop the enormous and fascinating **American Center for Wine, Food and the Arts.**

Located on thirteen acres on the banks of the Napa River on First Street, the center already enjoys support from the biggest names in American food and

DOWNTOWN
NAPA

wine, including Julia Child. Its purpose is to promote the best of American culture and play a significant role in the advancement of America's achievements in wine, food, and the arts. There will be exhibitions and educational programming to cover traditional and experimental programs in viticulture, enology, agriculture, cuisine, artistic and literary expression, the study of history, the science and politics of food, nutrition and health, sustainable agriculture, and the world food supply. Watch for Julia's Kitchen programs for home-cooks, The Food Forum, The Wine Learning Center, including The Wine Spectator Tasting Table, and the American Market Cafe. Mondavi has already brought in as affiliated organizations the American Institute of Wine and Food, the University of California at Davis, and the Cornell University School of Hotel Administration. The center is scheduled to open in November 2001, call (707) 257–3606 for more information.

All of this activity suggests a very exciting future for Napa.

Of course, the present isn't all that bad, either.

MAIN STREET, FIRST STREET, AND NAPA TOWN CENTER

Most of what you will want to visit on foot or wheelchair is along Main Street, First Street, and adjoining Napa Town Center, a collection of mall stores that snake around older buildings. Here is where most of Napa's interesting shops and restaurants are clustered, along with the Napa Firefighters Museum and some intriguing import shops.

Beginning at Main Street's south end, visit the new Napa Valley Inn in the redeveloped old Hatt Market building. Geezers Pub and Restaurant moved here from Main Street in 2000. Then, from Second Street on Main heading north, you might want to try one of several small restaurants, such as Pico Rio, P. J.'s at the corner of First Street, Peking Palace, and Downtown Joe's.

DOWNTOWN JOE'S, named for owner Joe Peatman, has been voted "Best Outdoor Dining," "Best Bar," "Best Night Spot," and "Best Place to Meet the Opposite Sex" by Napa residents. Downtown Napa's only microbrewery/restaurant, the restaurant and outdoor dining area look out over the river, a Napa park lawn, and Main Street action (such as it is). We enjoyed the best brew pub grub we've ever had here, ranging from a roasted-garlic Caesar salad and pulled pig, to burgers, grilled veggie pannini, flank-steak sandwich, pastas, and pizzas.

 Fine points: Featured beers: Lickety Split Lager, Ace High Cream Ale, Dancin' Feet Red Wheat Beer, Past Due Dark Ale, Golden Thistle Bitter Ale, and Slipknot Stout. Owner: Joe Peatman. Brewmaster: Lance McLaughlin. Chef: Paul Croshal. Barrels: 1,000.

❧ *Downtown Joe's, 902 Main Street, Napa 94559; phone (707) 258–2337, fax (707) 258–8740. Open from 11:00 A.M. to 11:00 P.M. daily, Sunday brunch from 8:30 A.M. Full bar. Visa, MasterCard, American Express, Discover, and JCB. Wheelchair-accessible.*

A couple of doors north on Main Street is Napa's best coffee place, the NAPA VALLEY COFFEE ROASTING COMPANY, where you can inhale the mouth-watering aromas of roasting coffee, sit and read while you enjoy a cup, nibble on light foods, and feel slightly urban.

Our only complaint is that the place closes at 6:00 P.M. Perhaps when downtown development is further along it will stay open later.

Fine points: Enjoy the Roasting Company's other cafe in St. Helena, at Oak and Adams Streets, 1 block west of St. Helena's Main Street (Highway 29).

❧ *Napa Valley Coffee Roasting Company, 948 Main Street, Napa 94559; phone (707) 224–2233. Open from 7:00 A.M. to 6:00 P.M. daily. No credit cards. Wheelchair-accessible.*

Just up the street is the Main Street Exchange Building, through or around which you can walk to our favorite Napa restaurant, CELADON, which hangs over the creek. Owner/chef Greg Cole considers Philippe Jeanty, formerly of Domaine Chandon and currently of his own Bistro Jeanty in Yountville, to be his mentor. And are we lucky! You can also get to Celadon over the footbridge from the public parking lot (home to downtown Napa's Farmers' Market) adjacent to the Cinedome Movie Theater.

In what was once the Cecil Hotel, built in 1905, Greg and his wife, Elizabeth Fairbairn, have created an extremely comfortable dining room with industrial angles and celadon colors. There are blond floors and celadon-colored chairs, trim, ducts, even vases and pitchers. Those lucky patrons who sit in the padded high chairs at the slate-covered counter get to watch all of the kitchen action in a small corner of the room. David Goines' Chez Panisse posters decorate the walls.

A graduate of the Culinary Institute of America, Greg worked for Jeanty at Domaine Chandon, opened Piatti's Sonoma restaurant in 1990, and served as chef at Robert Sinskey Vineyards for five years, having started at Sinskey working in the wine cellar. In March 1998 (Celadon's first year), *Wine Spectator* named Greg one of "America's Hottest Young Chefs."

Besides serving some of the best, most honest food in Napa Valley, Celadon's menu is extremely reasonably priced. Maine crab cakes are perfect ($9.50), as is the grilled cheese and porcini-mushroom polenta with chard and

MAINE CRAB CAKES WITH SWEET CORN AND PEPPERS AND GRAINY MUSTARD SAUCE
from Chef Greg Cole, Celadon

INGREDIENTS FOR THE CRAB CAKES:

½ lb Maine crab meat, cleaned

¼ cup mayonnaise

2 eggs

1 ½ cups fresh white-bread crumbs

1 tsp Worcestershire sauce

½ tsp Tabasco sauce

½ tsp salt

pinch black pepper

PREPARATION:

Combine all the ingredients and mix well. Divide the crab-cake mixture into 12 even portions. Pan fry in salad oil until golden brown on both sides. Remove onto absorbent paper and drain. Serve with Grainy Mustard Sauce. Serves 4.

INGREDIENTS FOR THE SWEET CORN AND PEPPERS:

2 Tbs salad oil

1 Tbs olive oil

1 medium onion, finely diced

2 celery ribs, finely diced

1 ear white corn, husked, cut off cob

1 tsp garlic

1 red bell pepper, finely diced

1 Tbs Italian parsley, chopped

zest of ½ lemon

PREPARATION:

Heat the olive oil in a small skillet and sauté the onion, celery, and corn kernels for 3 minutes. Add the garlic and cook for 1 minute. Add the red bell pepper and cook for an additional minute. Remove from heat and add the Italian parsley and lemon zest. Allow to cool. Serves 4.

INGREDIENTS FOR THE GRAINY MUSTARD SAUCE:

1 cup sour cream

¼ cup white wine

3 Tbs whole grain mustard

pinch salt and black pepper

PREPARATION:

Combine all ingredients and mix well.

balsamic glaze ($8.00). Salads are perfect and filling; the Caesar is available in both $4.00 and $7.00 sizes. The fish sandwich of the day could be soft shell crab ($10.00), and the achiote pork tender loin ($15.50), flash-fried calamari ($9.00), and grilled salmon ($17.00) are great. The steak frites ribeye with perfectly crisp fries is $16.50, while the horseradish-roasted half chicken with vegetables and saffron broth is succulent and delectable ($13.50).

❧ *Celadon, 1040 Main Street, Napa 94559; phone (707) 254–9690, fax (707) 254–9692. Open for lunch from 11:30 A.M. to 2:00 P.M. Monday–Friday, dinner from 5:00 to 9:00 P.M. Monday–Saturday. Visa, MasterCard, and American Express. Wheelchair-accessible.*

You might want to try TUSCANY restuarant, across Main Street, which is the newest show in town, having opened in June 2000. Chef Aram Chakerian, most recently head chef at Piatti's, offers a full page of antipasti, from steamed Prince Edward Island clams to romaine lettuce leaves stuffed with fried Dungeness crab ($8.00). Sample the spit-roasted rabbit ($16.00), veggie platter ($12.00), or sliced veal roast ($18.00). The open kitchen, counter seats, and windows overlooking Main Street add to the fun. Choose beer and wine from an extensive list.

❧ *Tuscany, 1005 First Street, Napa 94559; phone (707) 258–1000. Open from 5:00 to 11:00 P.M. daily. Visa, MasterCard, and American Express. Wheelchair-accessible.*

Just across a narrow part of Napa Creek, Greg and Elizabeth Cole recently opened COLE'S CHOP HOUSE, a Napa version of the old American steak house. More elegant than anything your parents habituated, Cole's Chop House was an instant hit in the renovated 114 year-old native stone Williams-Kyser building, which features a Douglas fir floor and vaulted ceiling.

Open only for dinner, Cole's offers a great Caesar salad ($6.00), portobello mushroom caps entree ($15.00), and an array of finest quality beef, veal, lamb, and pork chops, with filet mignon ($26.00) and salmon ($16.00). This is a great complement to the Coles' Celadon.

❧ *Cole's Chop House, 1122 Main Street, Napa 94559; phone (707) 224–6328. Open from 5:00 to 10:00 P.M. Tuesday–Saturday, 5:00 to 9:00 P.M. Sunday. Full bar. Visa, MasterCard, and American Express. Wheelchair-accessible.*

Continue up Main Street to explore exciting new Napa additions. Linda Kloos' NAPA VALLEY TRADITIONS AND FUTONS & FURNITURE is a fabulous treasure trove of funk and imaginative furniture, some of which is old, painted, practical, and whimsical. Great prices.

❧ *Napa Valley Traditions, Futons & Furniture, 1138 Main Street, Napa 84559; phone (707) 252–3626. Open from 10:30 A.M. to 6:00 P.M. Monday–*

Saturday (until 6:00 P.M. Thursday for Farmers' Market), noon to 5:00 P.M. Sunday. Visa and MasterCard. Wheelchair-accessible but crowded.

You must make absolutely sure to stop in at Anneka de Laat's cheerful IMANI GALLERY. Anneka, who used to manage the fine Shona Gallery in Sonoma, now exhibits paintings and prints of Sonoma and Napa's finest artists including those of our cover artist, Judy Theo Lehner.

❧ *Imani Gallery, 1144 Main Street, Napa 94559; phone (707) 224–7886, fax (707) 224–8872, e-mail: imanigallery@cs.com, Web site www.imanigallery. com. Open from 11:00 A.M. to 6:00 P.M. Monday–Saturday, noon to 5:00 P.M. Sunday. Visa and MasterCard. Wheelchair-accessible.*

At the corner, don't miss new HOUSE OF BREADS, Anne Evanish-Yungling's baby. Anne and friends mill their own Montana wheat flour right inside the door every morning and make chemical-free breads and goodies without fat, dairy products, or preservatives. Enjoy the choice of free bread samples cut to your request, along with a slab of room-temperature butter. Coffees are available in canisters. House of Breads bakes some breads daily, and also makes a full daily schedule of specialty breads.

❧ *House of Breads, 1146 Main Street, Napa 94559; phone (707) 257–0989, e-mail ayungling@cs.com, web site www.houseofbread.com. Open from 7:00 A.M. to 6:00 P.M. Monday–Friday, 8:00 A.M. to 5:00 P.M. Saturday, 8:00 A.M. to 4:00 P.M. Sunday.*

If you like Mexican food, take a chance on TAQUERIA ROSITA one door up in the next block of Main Street. Chef Daniel Lopez Pelayo of El Grullo Jalisco, Mexico, creates reliable, hearty Mexican food that is a favorite of Napans. The place is always packed, and locals line up next door at Rosita's take-out annex. You can have a great lunch for $5.00, $6.95 for an entree, including carne asada with pico de gallo.

❧ *Taqueria Rosita, 1210 Main Street, Napa 94559; phone (707) 253–9208. Open from 10:30 A.M. to 8:00 P.M. Monday–Wednesday, 10:30 A.M. to 9:00 P.M. Thursday–Saturday. Beer and wine. Visa and MasterCard. Wheelchair-accessible.*

Be sure to take the time to cross Main Street and visit the NAPA FIREFIGHTERS MUSEUM, which really should be called the International Firefighters Museum. A volunteer staff has collected donations of antique fire engines, equipment, uniforms, photos, carriages, badges, hats, and stories from around the world. The collection grows constantly as firefighters from everywhere hear of the museum and send contributions. This is a great place for families and anyone who ever followed a fire engine.

❧ Napa Firefighters Museum, 1201 Main Street, Napa 94559; phone (707) 259–0609. Open from 11:00 A.M. to 4:00 P.M. Friday–Sunday. No admission fee. Wheelchair-accessible.

Now go back to First Street, heading west from Main Street. Significant places to stop include Rod Covington's Napa Wine Merchants (1146 First Street), where you can find the best wines of the Napa Valley, in case you don't have time to explore the wineries yourself, and Bookends Bookstore at 1014 Coombs street between First Street and the Napa Town Center.

Continuing our walk north on Main Street, a little Berkeley-style import shop called INTI, named for the Peruvian sun god, sells pottery, jewelry, tapestry bedspreads, candles, incense, scarves, beads, and masks.

❧ Inti, 1139 First Street, Napa 94559; phone (707) 258–8034. Open from 11:00 A.M. to 6:00 P.M. Monday–Saturday; 11:00 A.M.–5:00 P.M. Sunday. Visa and MasterCard.

On the south side of First Street, check out the Napa Valley Historical Society's Research Library and Museum in the historic Goodman Building; Napa Children's Book Company with toys, stuffed animals, books and author readings; Copperfield's Books, an excellent North Bay independent book chain featuring used and new books; and Anette's Chocolate and Ice Cream Factory for Bud's Ice Cream, old-fashioned handmade candies, and espresso drinks. Venture up the block to the pink Neighborhood Collective Antiques, where fifty dealers offer their best.

SIGNIFICANT OTHERS

The immediate downtown center is not the only place in the city of Napa for good shopping and dining.

ALEXIS BAKING COMPANY AND CAFE is a hidden treasure in downtown Napa. Few visitors find it, but it is worth searching for. Alexis is a popular place to drop in for breakfast pastries and breads, tea-time pastries and cakes, lunchtime daily special salads and soups, and adventurous burgers (love that gorgonzola!). The same informal goodies and two tasty specials ($10–$11) are offered for dinner Thursday and Friday. Alexis is a great place to stop before or after a movie at the downtown Uptown Theater.

❧ Alexis Baking Company and Cafe, 1517 Third Street, Napa 94559; phone (707) 258–1827. Open from 6:30 A.M. to 6:00 P.M. Monday–Wednesday; 6:30

*A.M. to 8:00 P.M. Thursday–Friday; 7:30 A.M. to 3:00 P.M. Saturday; 8:00 A.M. to
2:00 P.M. Sunday. No credit cards. Wheelchair-accessible.*

The ATLAS PEAK GRILL is everyone's favorite secret steakhouse, especially for
those of us who claim that we no longer eat meat. At the northeast side of old
Napa and near the Silverado Country Club, Atlas Peak is in a charming storybook cottage surrounded by flowers and greenery. Here you can sink your teeth
into juicy, corn-fed beef that reflects another era, when Americans cared about
whether their steak cuts were in the New York or Chicago style. Everything car-
nivorous here is perfect, from pork loin to filet mignon. Famous also for its
perfect martinis, Atlas Peak provides an excellent chance to enjoy the best of
Napa Valley's wines.

❧ *Atlas Peak Grill, 3342 Vichy Avenue at Monticello Road (Highway 121),
Napa 94559; phone (707) 253–1455. Open for dinner only at 5:30 P.M. daily,
summer; Wednesday–Sunday, winter. Full bar. Visa and American Express.
Wheelchair-accessible.*

Often voted "Most Romantic Restaurant in the Napa Valley,"
CHANTERELLE is reliable, pleasant, and plush. There are huge upholstered
chairs, lots of room to spread out, and plenty of space between tables. Located
on First Street at Soscol (near the Napa Valley Wine Train's terminus),
Chanterelle offers no surprises and very good food, warranting its strong local
following.

Sunday Champagne Brunch is sumptuous, with a full range of entrees—
from omlettes and pasta to Petrale sole, calamari steak, leg of lamb, and eggs
Florentine with Hanns Kornell Extra Dry—at about $17. Here the Caesar sal-
ads actually have anchovies. The pastas are excellent, the Dungeness crab risotto is memorable ($15.95), and you might want to try the pork tenderloin with
cognac-soaked currants ($15.75). Or how about crispy roasted duck ($18.50),
herb-crusted filet of venison with sun-dried apricots and cranberries ($23.50),
seabass ($16.75), or the hazelnut-crusted rack of lamb with wild mushrooms
($21.50). All entrees are available prix fixe at $35, with appetizer, soup or salad,
entree, dessert, and coffee or tea.

❧ *Chanterelle, 804 First Street, Napa 94559; phone (707) 253–7300. Open
lunch and dinner daily. Full bar. Visa, MasterCard, and American Express.
Wheelchair-accessible.*

The DEPOT HOTEL is something else entirely. The "longest continuously
serving restaurant in Napa," this Depot Hotel (in contrast to the elegant one in

Sonoma) is a T-shirt and elbows-on-the-table, after-work-on-Friday-night kind of place. The main dining-room walls have olive-green, floral-print wallpaper above fake wood paneling, and green-squares linoleum on the floors. Waitresses who have been serving and living for a while engage in brief, matter-of-fact conversation and bring your dinner Italian "family style," which here means bowls of thick minestrone accompanied by Parmesan cheese, a bare-bones salad, a choice of pastas (try the malfatti or paper-thin ravioli, or both), and an entree (choices range from veal marsala to chicken livers, lamb chops, and steaks). And the whole dinner costs just $12.

You can't miss here if you want to run into lots of locals mixed with winery owners having a good time. The wine list is local, limited, and inexpensive, offering Robert Mondavi Pinot Noir at $18.00, Louis M. Martini Cabernet Reserve at $10.00, and Sutter Home White Zinfandel at $9.50.

❧ *Depot Hotel, 806 Fourth Street, Napa 94559; phone (707) 252–4477. Open for dinner daily. Full bar. No credit cards. Not wheelchair-accessible.*

Many locals go to Jerry Shaffer's FOOTHILL CAFE for his baby-back ribs, said by many Napa and Sonoma chefs to be the best in the country. But everything on the menu is tantalizing. Located in an unlikely little strip mall northeast of many Carneros wineries on Old Sonoma Road, Foothill Cafe is open only for dinner, alas, and is "closed for therapy Monday and Tuesday."

Jerry's humor shows everywhere, from decor to menu. The walls are bright mustard yellow with silver grape leaves. Round mirrors seem to enlarge the tiny room, and a red-framed window hangs free just inside the door. The total effect is to suggest you are going to have fun here. Jerry suggests in print, "If our food, drinks and service aren't up to your standards...please lower your standards."

Be sure to try the "world renowned baby back ribs" ($13.50), half smoked chicken ($11.50), or braised lamb shank ($14.50). The Thai spinach and Caesar salads are excellent ($6.50 each). Desserts such as crème brûlée, cobblers, crisp, and chocolate indulgences are each $5.00. Enjoy—but be sure to call for reservations in advance.

❧ *Foothill Cafe, 2766 Old Sonoma Road, Napa 94559; phone (707) 252–6178. Open from 4:30 to 9:30 P.M. Wednesday–Sunday. Wine and beer. "We like cash and take Visa, MasterCard, American Express, and checks that don't bounce." Wheelchair-accessible.*

GENOA DELICATESSEN & RAVIOLI FACTORY is one of our favorites and has been ever since Kathleen was growing up in Berkeley and her mother used to go to the original Genoa Deli in Oakland (here since 1926) to get ravioli. Located in a strip mall on Trancas Boulevard, Genoa is worth tracking down for picnic supplies or an informal lunch or dinner. Here you will find the best in deli salads, minestrone and other soups, roasted chicken with garlic bread ($4.29), pastas, an excellent espresso and juice bar, and a wine shop with Napa Valley's best. Oh yes, and huge sandwiches ranging from $4.50 to $5.25, featuring maple turkey, Virginia baked ham, crab salad, head cheese, domestic prosciutto, bresaola, beef tongue, coppa Veneziana, and just about anything else you can imagine (but no peanut butter). Delivery is available.

Genoa is also a great place to buy dried pastas and olive oils, and it sells its famous pastas and sauces, frozen, in a case against the wall. Long live the DeVincenzi family, please!

Genoa Delicatessen & Ravioli Factory, 1550 Trancas Street, Napa 94558; phone (707) 253–8686, fax (707) 253–2487. Wine and beer. Open from 9:00 A.M. to 6:30 P.M. Monday–Saturday, 9:00 A.M. to 5:00 P.M. Sunday. Visa, MasterCard, Diners Club, and JCB. Wheelchair-accessible.

OLD ADOBE BAR AND GRILLE is in the second-oldest adobe building in Northern California (1840), with 3-foot-thick walls, low ceilings and beams, loads of character and characters, and surprisingly good food thrown in. Locals go for the steaks and prime rib, and Reuben and French dip sandwiches. We also enjoy the Mexican food, like Lupe's Puerco Verde ($9.95), prawn fajita enchiladas ($10.95), and the Santa Fe Taco Salad ($8.95). Maybe you'll like the grilled pork-loin chops with rosemary-merlot butter ($13.95). Sunday brunch ranges from omelettes to French toast with ham, bacon, or sausage ($6.25), Tom's Prospector Scramble ($5.50), filet mignon and eggs ($14.95), and Crepes à la Reine ($7.25). The Old Adobe also has an interesting wine list.

Old Adobe Bar and Grille, 376 Soscol Avenue, Napa 94559; phone (707) 255–4310. Open for lunch and dinner daily. Full bar. Visa, MasterCard, American Express, and Discover.

You might want to stop at the RED HEN CANTINA and Red Hen Antiques, which you can't miss on the west side of Highway 29 between Napa and Yountville. Turn west on Oak Knoll, then immediately right on Solano (Frontage Road). Despite its glitz and large chicken on top of the roof, the Red Hen Cantina is a locally popular Mexican restaurant, where the bar and patio are after-work gathering places. Nachos and other ample appetizers go well with margaritas and salads, omelettes, and enchiladas. The Pollo Mexicano ($11.50), Chili Colorado ($9.50), Steak Rancheros ($11.50), and Red Hen Burger ($8.50) are all enormous and satisfying.

Red Hen Cantina, 5091 St. Helena Highway (Highway 29) via west turn on Redwood (or Oak Knoll to Solano), Napa 94559; phone (707) 255–8125. Open for lunch and dinner daily. Full bar. Visa and MasterCard. Wheelchair-accessible.

While you're at the Napa Valley Airport, don't miss JONESY'S FAMOUS STEAK HOUSE and its sidekick cafe. Often rated the "Best Beef in the Napa Valley" (read: steaks) by locals, Jonesy's takes us fifty years back to another era, when it was cool to smoke and drink Manhattans. You can actually order a cottage cheese and peaches salad (small or large), shrimp Louies, Caesar salads, shrimp cocktails, or calamari ringers.

So many locals come here for lunch that tables in the lounge are reserved for the cafe's overflow crowd. For a real steak-house experience, eat in the dining room, where you'll find linen tablecloths. Jonesy's Famous Steak Dinners are "Hand-carved on Premises." Top sirloin steak, "service for two," starts at $19.75, including tossed green salad with Jonesy's Bleu Cheese Dressing or soup, choice of potato or rice pilaf, and a "½ service" for one of top sirloin for $10.50. There are other steak meals on the menu, as well as chicken and seafood dishes. The children's menu is equally generous, from grilled cheese sandwiches ($3.75) to steak ($5.75) with salad or soup, french fries, and Jello included.

A short but well-selected local wine list ranges from Hakusan Sake ($6.50) and Beringer Gamay Beaujolais ($12.00) to exceptional Silver Oak Cabernet Sauvignon ($45.00).

❧*Jonesy's Famous Steak House, 2044 Airport Road (in the airport building), Napa 94558; phone (707) 255–2003. Open from 11:30 A.M. Tuesday–Sunday. Full bar. Visa, MasterCard, and American Express. Wheelchair-accessible.*

CHAPTER 3

HIGHWAY 29 (THE ST. HELENA HIGHWAY)

e will now take you up Highway 29—known locally and more fashionably as the St. Helena Highway. Road signs say 29, but merchants prefer to use St. Helena Highway in their addresses. Try not to be confused by the fact that Highway 29 is also called South St. Helena Highway, Main Street in St. Helena, St. Helena Highway North, and North St. Helena Highway. It's all the same road. If you don't want to explore the Napa Valley's wineries, restaurants, towns, and galleries quite this thoroughly, and decide to cut the tour short and head down the other side, just leap ahead in the book to the winery or restaurant you want.

We must emphasize the danger of turning left across Highway 29. Please make the crossing as few times as possible.

NAPA TO YOUNTVILLE

Four and a half miles north of the intersection of Highways 121 and 29, you'll come to a stoplight at an intersection, announced on overhead signs as Trancas Boulevard. What it doesn't tell you is that Trancas goes east from Highway 29, and Redwood Road heads west.

Take Redwood Road to the fabulous HESS COLLECTION—the ultimate expression of owner and Swiss entrepreneur Donald Hess's two passions, wine and art. Get into the left lane so that you can ease left in 0.9 mile. Continue up Redwood about 4.5 miles and turn left into The Hess Collection and Mont La Salle Christian Brothers Monastery and Retreat House. The Hess Collection is just beyond the monastery. It belonged to the Christian Brothers until Donald Hess bought the facility in 1985.

ENTRANCE TO THE HESS COLLECTION

The Hess Collection is an *absolutely do not miss!* destination. The architecture, the art collection, and the wines are among the best in California.

There's a bike rack for cyclists in the upper parking lot. Follow the wide brick path lined with oleander trees to the Visitors Center entrance on the right at the back of the courtyard. You will be struck by the elegant vestibule, with white walls and railings and blond wood floors. The round window in the stairway between the second and third floors evocatively frames the round tops of the punch-down fermentation tanks, and the windows in the shop and tasting room frame the wine barrels.

Explore the art collection, which rotates, showing about 25 percent of Hess's private collection at a time. It includes works by Francis Bacon, Robert Motherwell, Georg Baselitz, Magdelena Abakanowicz, Franz Gertsch, Bruce Robbins, Henri Michaux, Emilio Vedova, Frank Stella, and many other great artists.

Hess Holding has an extended family of prominent wineries on other continents, including Glen Carlou and Impala in South Africa, Castello Vicchiomaggio in Italy, and Bodega Norton in Argentina.

 Fine points: You *must* visit the shop here; it is the best in the wine country. The tasting fee is $3.00. Featured wines: Chardonnay, Cabernet Sauvignon, Merlot, Meritage, Zinfandel; from South Africa, Merlot, Chardonnay, and Classique Reserve. Owner: Hess

Holding. Winemaker: Randle Johnson. Executive Chef: Katie Sutton. Cases: 240,000. Acres: 400.

✳❧ *The Hess Collection, 4411 Redwood Road, Napa 94558; phone (707) 255–1144, fax (707) 253–1682. Open from 10:00 A.M. to 4:00 P.M. daily. Visa, MasterCard, and American Express. Wheelchair-accessible.*

As you leave The Hess Collection driveway, turn right down Redwood Road to Highway 29, and turn left (north).

Now we have you traveling northward on Highway 29, barely out of town, and if you're already hungry for lunch, stop immediately at one of our favorites, BISTRO DON GIOVANNI. As soon as you see the mud-colored building on the right, turn off Highway 29 into the driveway. As you walk onto the restaurant's deck from the parking lot, you can decide whether to choose an outdoor table or to walk inside. The deck wraps around the northern and eastern sides of the building, away from highway traffic. Wine-industry locals hang out here to see who's arriving with whom.

When we ask locals for their favorite restaurants, nearly everyone starts the list with Don Giovanni, and for good reason. When you walk in, you're greeted by unpretentious hosts in an unpretentious atmosphere that reeks of confidence in taste and style. Don't miss the large painting on Italian newspapers of a cutlery set hanging against soft yellow walls in one corner of the dining room. Gigantic arrangements of blue, yellow, and white flowers set the tone.

Owners Donna and Giovanni Scala were opening chefs at the original Piatti in St. Helena and basically set the chain's standard for Claude Rouas and his partners. Here at their own bistro, they have the luxury of doing it their own Italian–French way. What a relaxing pleasure! The staff is terrific, too.

The wood-burning oven and pantry fill one corner in the room, with the mesquite grill and rest of the kitchen behind glass, off to the side. Donna serves the perfect Caesar salad ($7.50), complete with an actual anchovy and large enough to share as an appetizer; and the beet and haricots verts salad ($6.95) is always a memorable treat. The Maine crab cakes ($8.75) are elegantly light—topped with avocado salsa and accompanied with a fennel slaw dressed in oil and vinegar. Even if you usually don't like clams, try Donna's Spaghetti Clams ($13.95), a dish she prepared for Giovanni's mother in Naples—who exclaimed that they were actually better than her own! All pastas and breads are house-made. We have friends who come here for drinks in the evening and happily make a meal of appetizers with terrific celebrity sightings.

✳❧ *Bistro Don Giovanni, 4110 St. Helena Highway, Napa 94558; phone (707) 224–3300. Open for lunch and dinner daily. MasterCard, Visa, and American Express. Wheelchair-accessible.*

GRILLED PORTOBELLO WITH BRAISED GREENS AND BALSAMIC JUS

from Giovanni and Chef Donna Scala, Bistro Don Giovanni

INGREDIENTS FOR THE BALSAMIC JUS:

2 cups balsamic vinegar	*1 bunch thyme*
3 cups chicken stock, reduced	*salt to taste*
4 shallots	*pepper to taste*
2 bay leaves	*2 tsp sugar*

PREPARATION:

Simmer balsamic jus ingredients 5–10 minutes until reduced by half.

INGREDIENTS FOR THE GRILLED PORTOBELLO:

4 portobello mushrooms,	*4 cloves garlic, sliced*
medium size	*¼ cup extra virgin olive oil*
5 bunches spinach, well washed	*salt to taste*
4 bunches broccoli rabe	*pepper to taste*
4 bunches chard, red or Swiss	

PREPARATION:

Lightly oil and salt and pepper portobello mushrooms, and grill, gill side down. Place a pot of salted water on high heat until boiling. Blanch spinach, broccoli rabe, and chard in the water and cook for 2–3 minutes.

Meanwhile, place a sauté pan on medium-high heat. Add the extra virgin olive oil and sliced garlic, and cook until garlic is lightly browned—approximately 1–1 ½ minutes. When garlic is browned, reduce heat, strain greens, and add to the sauté pan. Cover the pan, turn heat to low, and cook greens for 3 minutes.

To serve, place greens on the plate and the portobellos on the greens. Spoon the balsamic jus over the mushrooms and garnish with onion rings and chopped chives. Serves 4.

TREFETHEN ESTATE VINEYARDS is the first winery you come to north of here; it is also one of the most congenial and fun. To get here, turn east onto tree-lined Oak Knoll Avenue off Highway 29. One-half mile later, turn left onto Eshcol Drive, named for the Eshcol Ranch vineyard and winery located here from 1886 to 1940. Notice the labels on vineyards to help you know what varietals you're passing and the one hundred newly planted sycamore trees, whose shade we will welcome someday. Turn left at the large oak tree onto Trefethen Lane, and continue until you reach the pink wood winery with brown trim.

As you get out of your car, enjoy the large, 500-year-old valley and cork oak and the gardens full of old farming equipment, along with marked and identified plants and rows of herbs, from anise to rosemary. Built by James and George Goodman and designed by Captain Hamden McIntyre in 1886, the winery is listed in the National Register of Historic Places.

While Gene Trefethen was still president of Oakland's Kaiser Industries, he and Katie spotted this run-down old treasure and couldn't resist. Gene had only overseen construction of Hoover Dam and the San Francisco–Oakland Bay Bridge—that's all! So what was a mere 600 acres to replant, rebuild, and organize? After son John got his MBA at Stanford, he and his wife, Janet, joined the winery. Both serve as managing director, making Trefethen the largest contiguous family-owned and -operated vineyard acreage in the Napa Valley.

The brick floors and cedar walls in the tasting room set the mood, framing an excellent selection of cookbooks and guidebooks. The Trefethens attract cooking celebrations and classes, and Julia Child even cooked Thanksgiving dinner here for "Good Morning America" in 1992. Reflecting the Trefethens'

TREFETHEN ESTATE VINEYARDS

SHRIMP IN DRY RIESLING SAUCE
from Janet Trefethen, Trefethen Estate Vineyards

INGREDIENTS:

> 3 Tbs Trefethen olive oil
> 3 Tbs butter
> 2 slices fresh gingerroot (approximately the size of a quarter)
> 4 large cloves fresh garlic, cut in half lengthwise
> 1 cup Trefethen Dry Riesling
> 2 Tbs Dijon-style mustard
> 2 lb shrimp, shelled and deveined
> 2 Tbs fresh cilantro, chopped

PREPARATION:

In a large skillet heat oil and butter until a haze forms. Add garlic and ginger; cook until they start to brown. Remove and discard. Add wine and bring to a boil.

Lower the heat to medium and whisk in mustard; stir well. Add shrimp and simmer until they turn pink (approximately 3–5 minutes); garnish with the chopped cilantro.

Serve over pasta or rice, or enjoy with plenty of fresh sourdough bread for dipping into the wonderful sauce. Serves 2–4.

---

community and political involvement, their wines were served at Reagan and Clinton White House dinners for Queen Elizabeth II, the queen of Thailand, and a French president. Trefethen remains the only wooden gravity-flow winery and the largest estate-vineyard winery in the Napa Valley.

Aside from the wine biz, John is a pilot and motorcyclist. Once a Miss Rodeo California, Janet is an expert in food and wine matching, a leader of the quest for a local appellation designation, and an occasional speaker at the Culinary Institute of America's Hyde Park, New York, campus.

Under Janet Trefethen's leadership, the Napa Valley Cooking Class, featuring great chefs from around the United States, has taken place at the winery for more than twenty-five years. For Trefethen's thirtieth anniversary, in 1998, Trefethen held a cooking class given by four thirty-year-old chefs teaching thirty students, sponsored a Club 30 Recipe Contest for culinary professionals, and celebrated dinners honoring some of the country's top chefs' thirty-year-old protégés, with all proceeds from the dinners benefiting charitable causes fighting world hunger.

Oh yes, the wine. To hint at the quality, Trefethen's 1976 Chardonnay ranked number one in the world at the 1979 World Wine Olympics, sponsored by the French magazine *Gault Millau*. The next year Burgundy winemaker Joseph Drouhin challenged the '79 results, resulting in a second competition, this time at the esteemed Hospice de Beaune. Guess what? Trefethen won again, much to the disappointment of Monsieur Drouhin (who also once challenged the results when Oregon's Eyrie Pinot Noir finished in the top three at a Paris blind tasting. After Eyrie's wine finished a close second in retasting, Drouhin opened his own winery in Oregon's Dundee Hills.)

 Fine points: Featured wines: Chardonnay, Dry Riesling, Cabernet Sauvignon, Cabernet Franc, Merlot. Tasting fee: complimentary; charge for reserve wines. Owners: The Trefethen Family. Winemaster: David Whitehouse, Jr. Winemaker: Peter Luthi. Cases: 110,000. Acres: 650.

Trefethen Estate Vineyards, 1160 Oak Knoll Avenue, Napa 94558; phone (707) 255–7700 or (800) 556–4847, fax (707) 255–0793, e-mail winery@ trefethenwine.com, Web site www.trefethen.com. Open from 10:00 A.M. to 4:30 P.M. daily. MasterCard, Visa, and American Express. Wheelchair-accessible.

Back to Highway 29. Just north of Trefethen and on the other side of Highway 29 you will find NEWLAN VINEYARDS & WINERY on Solano Avenue, which parallels the highway. Newlan is definitely a family affair, with founder Bruce Newlan and winemaker Glen Newlan almost always available to talk about their exciting wines.

To get here, turn left across Highway 29 at Oak Knoll (or straight across the divided highway, ½ highway at a time please, from Trefethen) and turn north (right) onto Solano Avenue. Or turn west (left) from Highway 29 onto Darms Lane and left again onto Solano.

Bruce told us, "It doesn't take a rocket scientist to make wine," with an enticing twinkle in his eye. Yes, he is a rocket scientist for Lockheed Missiles in Sunnyvale. He worked on the *Polaris, Poseidon,* and *Trident* programs. Ultimately, his family's farm roots grow deeper, though. Bruce and son Glen used to buy grapes near Gilroy and ferment them in the garage. After working as a computer whiz in Santa Clara, Glen moved to Napa with his wife, Jerri-Lynn. Their young son, Ryan, is "a train fanatic who watches the Wine Train ride by the vineyard every day."

The Newlans bought their first acreage in Napa Valley in 1967 and turned the thirteen-acre mess of a walnut orchard into a Cabernet Sauvignon vineyard. Bruce took courses at UC Davis, read viticulture texts, and soon began selling his grapes to Inglenook, Clos du Val, and Robert Mondavi. When he discovered that his grapes usually ended up in the wineries' reserve or cask bottlings, he decided that he should make his own wine, if they were that good.

As you enter the California-style stucco building, you immediately run into a railing, which overlooks the small winery and the cozy tasting room. You are at eye level with wine barrels. Walk down the few stairs to the left to see everything.

Fine points: Newlan's Cabernet Sauvignon and Zinfandel have been rated in the 90s by Robert Parker, Jr., and Jerry Mead, creating a great demand nationally. Bruce and Glen manage their own vineyards and make their own wine from their own grapes. Simple and slow. No tasting fee. Featured wines: Chardonnay, Pinot Noir, Cabernet Sauvignon, Zinfandel, Late Harvest Riesling, Merlot. Owner: Bruce Newlan. Winemaker: Glen Newlan. Cases: 10,000. Acres: 30.

🍇 *Newlan Vineyards & Winery, 5225 Solano Avenue, Napa 94558; phone (707) 257–2399 or (800) 500–9463, fax (707) 252–6510, e-mail napa wine@wine.com, Web site www.winecom/nvw. Open from 10:00 A.M. to 5:00 P.M. daily. MasterCard and Visa. Not wheelchair-accessible.*

Your next stop could be Yountville, or you can just drive north 2.7 miles on Solano Avenue and cross California Drive at the Veterans' Home to visit Domaine Chandon.

YOUNTVILLE

Just over 4 miles north of the Highway 29–Trancas Boulevard intersection, take the Yountville exit for elegant small-town wine-country shopping, dining, wine tasting, and the new Napa Valley Museum on the grounds of the California Veterans' Home. As you turn off the highway to the right, turn right again and then immediately left at the stop sign and Washington Street to tour "downtown" Yountville. New resort hotels abound, as Yountville has made a decision to welcome visitors with open arms.

A historic town along the wine trail, Yountville is now known for its outstanding restaurants, such as The French Laundry, Bistro Jeanty, Bouchon, Livefire, Bocconcini, Domaine Chandon, Pacific Blues Cafe, the Napa Valley Grille, Gordon's Cafe and Wine Bar, and Campadres. The California Veterans' Home was established here in 1882 by veterans of the Mexican and Civil wars as a home for all veterans west of the Rocky Mountains. In 1900 the state of

YOUNTVILLE
AREA

NAPA CELLARS

COSENTINO
WINERY

YOUNTVILLE MILL RD.

YOUNTVILLE

GOOSECROSS CELLARS

NAPA
RIVER
ECOLOGICAL
RESERVE

STATE LANE

SILVERADO TRAIL

ROBERT
SINSKEY
VINEYARDS

YOUNTVILLE CROSS RD.

S. ANDERSON
WINERY

SHAFER
VINEYARDS

LA CONA RD.

MAYACAMAS
VINEYARDS

CALIFORNIA
VETERANS'
HOME

DOMAINE
CHANDON

CALIFORNIA DR.

SILVERADO
VINEYARDS

MOUNT VEEDER
ESTATE

PINE RIDGE
WINERY

STELTZNER
VINEYARDS

PLAM
VINEYARDS

HOFFMAN LN.

HAVENS WINE CELLARS

STAG'S LEAP
WINE CELLARS

29

REGUSCI
WINERY

THE HESS
COLLECTION
WINERY

MOUNT VEEDER RD.

CRICHTON HALL

DARMS LN.

WASHINGTON

CHIMNEY ROCK
WINERY

CLOS DU VAL

REDWOOD RD.

DRY CREEK ROAD

NEWLAN VINEYARDS
& WINERY

SILVERADO TRAIL

TREFETHEN ESTATE
VINEYARDS

OAK KNOLL AVE.

N

W   E

S

SOLANO AVE.

MONTICELLO
CORLEY FAMILY
VINEYARDS

ANDRETTI
WINERY

BIG RANCH RD.

SIGNORELLO
VINEYARDS

29

DARIOUSH
WINERY

REDWOOD RD.

TO NAPA

California bought it for a twenty-dollar gold piece. You can visit the Veterans'
Home Museum as well as the Napa Valley Museum here.

On the west side of Highway 29 in Yountville is the new open-to-the-pub-
lic golf course and restaurant called **LAKESIDE GRILL.** Locals say the grill's breakfast is the best in Yountville, with large portions, fresh ingredients, and great
views of the small lake, golf course, and mountains that line the Napa Valley.

Lunch and dinner include burgers, steak sandwiches, grilled fresh albacore
on focaccia with chipotle aioli, a club sandwich, a BLT of applewood-smoked
bacon and crab salad, a Southwestern Caesar salad with blackened chicken and

shaved Parmesan cheese, a jumbo prawn and crab Louie, and Lakeside fritos of everything from calamari to deep-fried jalapeño peppers and garlic Parmesan fries. Everything is under $10.

The golf course is lush and the fees are inexpensive, ranging from $10 early bird (before 8:00 A.M.) and $12 for Napa Valley residents to $18 to play nine holes, $16 to $24 for eighteen holes. Golf carts range from $12 to $24.

✤ *Yountville Golf Course and Lakeside Grill, 7801 Solano Avenue, Yountville 94599; phone (707) 944–1992, fax (707) 944–1993. Open from 7:00 A.M. to 8:00 P.M. daily. Full bar. Visa, MasterCard, and American Express. Wheelchair-accessible.*

Yountville's new Yountville Inn and Villagio Inn and Spa are among Napa Valley's most convenient and pleasant accommodations. (see Chapter 5, *Where to Stay in the Napa Valley.*)

We will take you up the right (east) side of Yountville's Washington Street, and then back down the west side.

Between the two palm trees on the right just as you enter Yountville from the south end jumps out THE DINER, decorated with Coca-Cola signs on the outside and Fiesta ceramic pitchers on the inside, ceiling fans and brown and beige linoleum floors. Choose the counter, with its round wooden seats, or the booth or table seating.

While locals swear by this place, we were slightly disappointed. It may be the best breakfast at this end of Yountville (try Gordon's at the north end), but we found the highly recommended portobello mushroom plate a bit dry, the cheeseburger flavor-free, and the fries limp. But the shakes are so thick they don't stir (yum!), and you get to finish off what's left in the metal glass it was blended in. The apple crisp, flan, sundaes, and banana splits are all great, as is the Mexican food, cooked by Mexicans. Here's an unusual chance to try Mexican eggs and German potato pancakes all in one meal.

This place served as the local Greyhound Bus Station and diner in the 1950s, and local adults and kids have been hanging out here ever since.

✤ *The Diner, 6476 Washington Street, Yountville 94559; phone (707) 944–2626. Open for breakfast all day, lunch, dinner daily. Beer and wine. No credit cards. Wheelchair-accessible.*

Right next door is the original RISTORANTE PIATTI, the first in Claude Rouas's vast and successful upscale chain, contrasting drastically with The Diner in appeal, design, food, and price. This is where Donna and Giovanni Scala set the menu and formula before they went on to their own Bistro Don Giovanni.

LEMON CREAM SAUCE
from Claude Rouas,
Ristorante Piatti

---

13 oz heavy cream

1 lemon, zest and juice

½ cup grated Parmesan cheese

⅛ tsp white pepper

½ tsp kosher salt

Bring all ingredients to a boil and strain through a fine strainer. Pour immediately over ravioli or other pasta.

The fabulous mesquite wood aroma you smell from the street and as you enter the dining room emanates from the open kitchen and oven, where Piatti pizzas toast. The California–Italian decor soothes, as does the food. Always reliable and innovative are Piatti's salads and pastas (here's that light lemon creme sauce on ravioli again), and the roasted chicken is exceptional. We also enjoy the Dungeness crab salad when it's available. The tiramisu is always good, as is the amaretto cheesecake with warm chocolate sauce. Entrees usually range from $12.50 to $20.00.

☙ *Ristorante Piatti, 6480 Washington, Yountville 94599; phone (707) 944–2070. Open for lunch and dinner daily. MasterCard, Visa, and American Express. Wheelchair-accessible.*

The local phenomenon RANCH MARKET supplies locals and transients with basic food needs such as blood oranges and a few veggies, brooms, soap, etc. Many office workers slip in the side door facing Bistro Jeanty's parking lot for a deli sandwich ($3.65) and Bud's ice cream. A true country store with red-and-white checked curtains, Ranch Market makes you feel as if you're really on vacation.

☙ *Ranch Market, 6498 Washington Street, Yountville 94599; phone (707) 944–2662. Open from 6:00 A.M. to 10:00 P.M. No credit cards. Wheelchair-accessible.*

One door up the street is BISTRO JEANTY, the creation of former Domaine Chandon executive chef Philippe Jeanty, who enjoys one of the greatest followings in the Napa Valley. The Champagne native shed the corporate umbrella to strike out on his own and give birth to a "homey place where my little daughter can come in anytime." Philippe is back in the tiny kitchen, to the good fortune of his new and loyal customers. Auberge du Soleil and Piatti co-founder Claude Rouas's daughter, Bettina, came from Niebaum-Coppola Winery to Bistro Jeanty to manage the dining room.

One of the greatest benefits of this bistro is that we can enjoy Philippe's food at prices lower than at Domaine Chandon. He truly wants you to come by regularly, be comfortable, and greet your friends. On the door facing Washington Street, Philippe has hand-written the hours and specials, making the whole greeting reminiscent of a Paris neighborhood bistro, with half curtains and little floor tiles. Outdoor tables face south and the parking lot, while French antiques fill the dining rooms. Terracotta flower pots planted with miniature roses decorate the tables. Framed French posters hang on the walls, and recorded Edith Piaf warbles reach even the patio tables, creating an even greater allure to us than spraying garlic into the fans.

You enjoy the same menu at lunch and dinner, featuring appetizers of smoked trout and potatoes in olive oil ($7.50), rabbit pâté and salad ($6.00), grilled quail and salad ($7.50), beet salad with feta and asparagus ($6.50), and tomato soup in puff pastry ($5.00). Main courses may include mussels in white-wine pastis and frites ($12.00), tuna steak au poivre ($23.50), and cassoulet ($16.50). Desserts and dessert wines, ports, cognacs, and brandies are all very special.

❦ *Bistro Jeanty, 6510 Washington Street, Yountville 94599; phone (707) 944–0103, fax (707) 944–0370. Open for lunch and dinner daily. MasterCard, Visa, and American Express. Wheelchair-accessible.*

Next door, to the north of Bistro Jeanty, is the ANTIQUE FAIR, a collection of interesting French antiques and furnishings, some from estates in Lyon and Paris. This is a great spot to find interesting old beds, silverware, armoires, jewelry, and figurines. Locals and visitors have found the antiques here intriguing for almost thirty years. Browse with care. Be sure to catch the Noel Française here from Thanksgiving to December 31, 10:00 A.M. to 9:00 P.M., during Yountville's Festival of Lights.

❦ *Antique Fair, 6512 Washington Street, Yountville 94599; phone (707) 944–8440, Web site www.antiquefair.com. Open from 10:00 A.M. to 5:00 P.M. daily. MasterCard, Visa, and American Express. Wheelchair-accessible.*

LIVEFIRE is Fred Halpert's latest great effort in the Napa Valley, where he has Brava Terrace north of St. Helena and Napa Valley Ovens bakery in Calistoga. A favorite of Paul Bocuse and the late James Beard House director Peter Kump, Fred has created another fabulous, fun dining experience here with Chef Terry Morrow.

Livefire is still underdiscovered, so we highly recommend that you scoot right over there for delectable herb-crusted calamari with lemon mustard sauce ($7.95), fried capers with tarragon oil and black pepper crisp ($11.50), and a baby spinach, portobello mushroom, bacon, corn, and garlic walnut vinaigrette salad ($8.95 lunch, $10.95 dinner). We like the grilled lamb sirloin with tapenade mayo sandwich ($12.95); the vegetable melt is sensational ($9.95), and the half-pound burger ($8.95) should satiate carnivores for a long time. Entrees range from wild mushroom risotto with white truffle oil ($12.95) and spit-roasted half chicken ($12.50 lunch, $15.50 dinner), to slabs of ribs, marinated New Zealand grouper with bok choy, shiitake mushrooms, and ginger broth ($20.50), steaks, and Moroccan spiced lamb sirloin with couscous, pearl onions, and garlic-infused olive oil ($18.50). Side dishes include mashed potatoes, cauliflower gratin, sautéed Swiss chard, and grilled asparagus ($3.50–$4.50), and we have dined on a combination of all four with great pleasure.

❧ *Livefire, 6518 Washington Street, Yountville 94599; phone (707) 944–1500, fax (707) 944–1504. Full bar. Open from 11:30 A.M. daily. Visa, MasterCard, American Express, Diners Club, and Discover. Wheelchair-accessible.*

Wine fans should not miss GROEZINGER'S WINE SHOP for the very best of rare French and local wines. You can taste at the tasting bar in back, after you have wound your way through the Old World–feeling shop, which sells 96 percent of its wine by phone orders. Owners Martin and Rick have built a reputation and private lists for fifteen years. Groezinger's also sells old issues of the *Wine Spectator* for 99 cents. If you live too far from the Napa Valley to purchase wine in person, you can rely on Groezinger's to provide the best of small-lot wines. Get on their mailing list.

❧ *Groezinger's Wine Shop, 6528 Washington Street, Yountville 94599; phone (707) 944–2331. Open from 10:00 A.M. to 6:00 P.M. Monday–Saturday. MasterCard, Visa, and American Express. Wheelchair-accessible.*

BOUCHON was created by the Keller brothers of The French Laundry (Yountville) and Fleur de Lys (San Francisco) as a bistro where people in the restaurant business could go for great food after work, but we are not sure just how often restaurant staff could actually afford to dine here.

Be sure to try Bouchon if you can't get into The French Laundry, which usually requires reservations months ahead. The food is sublime and less formal than its parent's, but equally adventurous. The menu is the same day and night.

Hors d'oeuvres range from garlic sausage with French green lentils ($9.75) and a charcuterie of Petit Jesus, Basquaise, and pâté maison ($8.50) to excellent onion soup ($6.75) and a terrine de foie gras de canard with toasted baguette ($35 for 5 ounces).

Select from a whole *fruits de mer* menu featuring six shellfish or a *petit* or *grand plateau* combination ($36.00–$70.00), truly French salads, six cheeses, and entrees from an open-faced sandwich or *croque madame* ($12.95), pan roasted trout with almonds ($15.50), and roasted skate wing with lyonnaise potatoes ($18.50) to white sausage with potato puree and sautéed prunes ($14.95), steak frites ($17.50), or leg of lamb with red beans and pearl onions ($18.50).

Here, too, you can combine sides of french fries, cauliflower gratin, potato puree, sautéed spinach, and olives, all in the $3.50 range.

✤ *Bouchon, 6534 Washington Street, Yountville 94599; phone (707) 944–8037. Open from 11:30 A.M. to 2:30 P.M., 5:30 to 10:30 P.M., with limited menu to 1:30 A.M. daily. Full bar. Visa, MasterCard, and American Express. Wheelchair-accessible.*

North of Bouchon, wander among a small complex of shops and galleries in Beard Plaza, including Images Fine Art, Artistry in Gold, Raku Ceramics, Raspberry's Art Glass Gallery, and Visions-Nature's Art.

Just for the heck of it, visit fun and charming Peggy Murray at her MOSSWOOD, a shop to enhance your garden. Peggy left the fast-paced world of public relations to own Mosswood, where she offers exquisite garden sculpture and statuary.

✤ *Mosswood, 6550 Washington Street, Yountville 94599; phone (707) 944–8151. Open from 10:00 A.M. to 5:30 P.M. daily. MasterCard, Visa, American Express, and Diners Club. Wheelchair-accessible.*

If you're ready for a splurge, make reservations to have lunch or dinner at THE FRENCH LAUNDRY, another block north on Washington Street at Creek Street, in a century-old, two-story stone house with no sign. The James Beard Foundation named owner/chef Thomas Keller the best chef in the United States in 1997. Keller's wry humor means to deceive and intrigue with occasional simplified names attached to complex dishes.

Originally a bar and brothel and then (yes) a French laundry, the building and exquisite tranquil gardens with raised beds of daffodils and vegetables melt away any anxiety if you have to wait for your table. Reservations are mandatory for the eleven-table dining room.

Lunch is served only Friday through Sunday. Both lunch and dinner consist of five courses and cost $90 prix fixe. The five-course orgy forces you to make several decisions, so you must come back to try other possibilities. First-course choices range from wild watercress soup to Tongue-in-Cheek braised beef-cheek-and-veal tongue. Second courses may include Atlantic skate wing or Maine lobster "pancake," followed by Hoffman Farm *poussin* with herbed risotto cake, liver and onions, lamb saddle with ravioli of *ris d'agneau et joue d'agneau*. Sweet treats could be "coffee and doughnuts" with cappuccino semifreddo, mango sorbet with Maui pineapple and sauce *l'impiratrice*, followed by a tasting of vegetables.

Dinner might include Dungeness crab salad, pan-roasted calf's brain, or

THE FRENCH LAUNDRY

cream of Savoy cabbage soup. Next, taste herb-roasted monkfish, filet of spiny lobster, or Maine diver scallop, followed by filet mignon of veal, Hoffman Farm squab, or Elysian Fields Farms lamb chop. Fruits and salads follow, finishing with desserts, which may include crème de farine, or a "floating island" of Swiss meringue with vanilla-bean custard sauce and bittersweet-chocolate "salad."

As an alternative, you may want to try the Chef's Tasting Menu ($105) of nine dishes that add up to a full meal of orgasmic pleasure.

The French Laundry, 6640 Washington Street, Yountville 94599; phone (707) 944–2380. Open for lunch Friday–Sunday, dinner daily. MasterCard, Visa, and American Express. Wheelchair-accessible.

On a more economical but still high culinary level, don't miss GORDON'S CAFE AND WINE BAR, another block north on Washington. The sign says GORDON'S MARKET.

Sally Gordon first visited the store run by the Tenaci family in 1967. She moved to the Napa Valley in 1977. We first met her as the public relations director at Domaine Chandon when we accompanied M. F. K. Fisher there for lunch every year to celebrate her birthday and Bastille Day.

Gordon's is immensely popular with locals at breakfast and lunch, and its Friday dinners sell out every week. When you walk in you feel as if you're entering a cozy country store. On your right, Chef Mari Tola, formerly of Mustards Grill and Table 29 (now Bistro Don Giovanni), and friends cook right in the room, and to the left shelves of well-selected delicacies line the wall. You will find Tazo teas, Potluck Studios bowls, V. G. Buck olive oils, The French Press Virgin Filbert Oil, Sparrow Lane vinegars, the *San Francisco Chronicle,* and the *New York Times.* Along the back of the left wall is an admirable collection of local wines for sale. And, miracle of miracles, when you select a bottle to accompany your Friday dinner, Sally sells it to you at the shelf price, without the customary restaurant increase.

Gordon's sells and uses our favorite della Fattoria and Acme breads and serves elegant sandwiches and salads ($7.50). If it happens to be on special, try the sandwich of roasted eggplant with sweet red peppers; Italian tomato, sausage, and lentil soup; corned beef and Gruyère on rye; and always the genuine croque monsieur at $5.95. The homemade raspberry lemonade is a must-try. Locals play chess or cards while eating huge bowls of oatmeal at 1:30 *P.M.*, and we love the espresso bar beyond the kitchen. Sally cooks and bakes on weekends.

Fine points: If you need a stiffer drink than wine, there's always Pancha's bar next door. Book reservations for Gordon's Friday Cafe supper ($35) for three exquisite courses.

❧*Gordon's Cafe and Wine Bar, 6770 Washington Street, Yountville 94599; phone (707) 944–8246. Open from 7:30 A.M. to 6:00 P.M. Tuesday–Saturday, later Friday, 7:30 A.M. to 5:00 P.M. Sunday. Beer and wine. MasterCard, Visa, American Express, and Discover. Wheelchair-accessible.*

At this point, Washington Street veers leftish and back to Highway 29. If, instead of going left with it, you decide to go straight ahead (north) on Lincoln, you can explore YOUNTVILLE PARK and a bit of Yountville history at the George C. Yount Pioneer Cemetery & Ancient Indian Burial Grounds.

Yountville Park offers colorful children's play equipment, good barbecues, public rest rooms, and lots of grass to play or lounge on.

❧ *Yountville Park, Washington and Lincoln Streets, Yountville 94599. Open from 6:00 A.M. to 10:00 P.M. No pets or motor vehicles.*

Just beyond the park, GEORGE C. YOUNT PIONEER CEMETERY & ANCIENT INDIAN BURIAL GROUNDS gives a short and fascinating history of Yountville, as do most old cemeteries. Ironically, George Yount was the first white settler in the Napa Valley and is buried here with Napa and Pomo Indians and some much more current immigrants.

❧ *George C. Yount Pioneer Cemetery & Ancient Indian Burial Grounds, Lincoln and Jackson Streets, Yountville 94599.*

Back toward Yountville proper (we're talking a total of about 5 blocks) and across from Gordon's Cafe & Wine Bar, you might want to take the kids to FRANKIE & JOHNNY & LUIGI TOO, a good, solid Italian restaurant with pastas, pizzas, veal, and fun for the kids. Featuring "homestyle Southern Italian cooking," FJ&L serves big portions, family-style dinners, all food to go, and lots of outdoor seating in good weather.

✤ *Frankie & Johnnie & Luigi Too, 6772 Washington Street, Yountville 94559; phone (707) 944–0177. Open from 11:30 A.M. to 10:00 P.M. daily. MasterCard, Visa, American Express, Diners Club, and Discover. Wheelchair-accessible.*

Just south of Frankie etc. is the intriguing Burgundy House five-room inn. Once a brandy distillery built in 1891, the rich little building's 22-inch thick local stone walls keep it cool in the summer, perfect for sipping the decanter of wine that greets you in your antiques-furnished room on arrival. (See Chapter 5, *Where to Stay in Napa Valley*.)

The Washington Square shopping center's primary attraction is the renowned NAPA VALLEY GRILLE, which is part of a group of California grill–style restaurants, but Chef Bob Hurley has total independence to use his massive talents, previously enjoyed at San Francisco's Masa's and Domaine Chandon.

This is a nonsnooty California-cuisine delight, with an openness of both decor and menu selections. Plan time to wait for your meal, but we found the wait worthwhile. The Thai chicken salad is the best anywhere, the fish is usually grilled over a wood fire and yummy, if occasionally dry. Hamburgers are great, and the polenta is sumptuous. Be sure to try the specials to experience Bob's substantial talents. Enjoy the patio in good weather.

✤ *Napa Valley Grille, Madison and Highway 29 (approach from Washington Street), Washington Square shopping center, Yountville 94599; phone (707) 944–8686. Open for lunch and dinner daily, Sunday brunch. MasterCard, Visa, and American Express. Wheelchair-accessible.*

COMPADRES MEXICAN BAR & GRILL is the only Mexican restaurant in Yountville, so if you truly have the urge, this is it. Campadres bills itself as "A Great Place to Party" for breakfast, lunch, and dinner, and it is. If that's your goal, go for it. This place is super-California and huge, with loads of indoor and outdoor seating. Watch for the daily fish specials, seafood tacos, enchiladas galore, and several Jaliscan specialties. Margarita variations abound, but we prefer the originals.

Yountville's Farmers' Market takes place in Campadres' parking lot Wednesdays from 4:00 to 6:00 P.M.

✤ Compadres Mexican Bar & Grill, *6539 Washington Street, Yountville, 94599; phone (707) 944–2406. Open from 8:00 A.M. to 10:00 P.M. Sunday–Thursday, 8:00 A.M. to 11:00 P.M. Friday–Saturday. MasterCard, Visa, and American Express. Wheelchair-accessible.*

Before we get you inside the Vintage 1870 complex, we want to introduce you to PACIFIC BLUES CAFE, named "Best New Restaurant of Napa Valley" in 1997.

Jeff Steen, formerly of Piatti and Compadres, and Frank Cox have created the most fun casual restaurant in the Napa Valley. They serve consistently hearty "maverick American" taste surprises in what was once the train station. Hence the train and blues themes, which carry into the old train posters on the walls and train names on the menu, while blues music pipes softly through the restaurant and deck facing Vintage 1870 during the week, replaced by live blues bands on the weekend. Portions are large and prices small.

Breakfasts are classic and innovative, from Flatcar Flapjacks with whipped orange butter and hot maple syrup ($1.00 each), buttermilk biscuits and Frank's gravy ($3.95), and vanilla-cinnamon French toast with bananas and walnuts ($5.75), to the Rocky Rail Scramble of turkey, spinach, onions, and egg whites ($6.25), the Healthy Car Scramble with poached veggies and egg whites ($5.25), and the Engineer's Hearty Breakfast of grilled New York steak with eggs and hashbrowns ($10.25).

Lunch and dinner share the same menu, with ribeye and other excellent steaks, several veggie specialties (from fancy baked potatoes to dim sum and hot veggie chili and veggie pastas), humungous double-layered, tricolored nachos ($6.95), grilled cheese ($3.95), Hobo's Red Beans and Rice ($5.75), Caesar and spinach salads, a fab iceberg-lettuce wedge with thick, creamy, chunky bleu cheese dressing ($4.50), burgers galore, finger-licking ribs, and Kathleen's favorite—the Blues Burger, with ground turkey, bleu cheese, and jalapeño jam, served with perfect slaw or french fries (go for the garlic ones with fresh, crushed garlic). Outlandish desserts and a children's menu make this a place we come back to again and again. Pacific Blues also has one of the best-selected local wine lists and good espresso drinks.

✤ Pacific Blues Cafe, *6525 Washington Street, Yountville 94599; phone (707) 944–4455, fax (707) 944–2453. Open for breakfast (6:30 to 11:00 A.M.), lunch, and dinner. Beer and wine. MasterCard, Visa, and American Express. Wheelchair-accessible.*

The large brick building across the patio is VINTAGE 1870, loaded with specialty shops and art galleries. Originally the Groezinger Wine Cellars, the building is listed in the National Register of Historic Places and is built on the original land grant made to Salvador Vallejo by the Mexican government in 1838. In 1870 G. Groezinger purchased it from George C. Yount's estate for $250 in gold coins, and it was used as a winery to 1954.

Vintage 1870 offers refreshingly high-quality businesses, one of the most tempting of which you encounter just to the right of the door. GILLESPIE'S ICE CREAM & CHOCOLATES serves Double Rainbow ice cream and made-before-your-eyes chocolates, including sugar-free peanut clusters. Smoothies, shakes, and sundaes steel you for shopping till you drop. CRAVINGS GOURMET & COOKWARE sells wine stuff such as drip stoppers, cookbooks, cool drinks, and picnic baskets. KINYON! RESTAURANT invites you in with hardwood floors, colored napkins, and cobalt-blue glasses, to say nothing of the Thanksgiving turkey sandwich ($9.75), Holy Cow roast beef on French roll, a grilled chicken sandwich called Last Mango in Paris, a veggie Griller Thriller, To Brie or Not to Brie, salads galore, and a Here's the Skinny menu.

Notice the plaque marking the old Chutney Kitchen's cutting board. You can still get the once-famous chutney at Cravings. TILTON'S RENDEZVOUS 1870 has attractive turquoise jewelry, pottery, and beaded leather, while MIRA BOUTIQUE sells replica jewelry (also in Sonoma). THE TOY CELLAR carries trains, stuffed Breyer bears and other animals, toys, Beanie Babies, yo-yos, everything Madeline, and a 1-cent box of goodies. GALLERY 1870 features Thomas Kinkade paintings (he's all over the wine country).

We especially like GENERATIONS, a fine art gallery, with interestingly designed space and involvement in the community. Generations features art of the West, Judith Gaulke's (former food editor of *Sunset* magazine) French waiter series, Mikki Senkauk, and other Northern California artists. Also on the first floor are ROSALIA'S FOR SHOES and TOUCH OF GOLD BATH SHOP.

We particularly encourage you to visit the WORKING ART STUDIOS (upstairs) of Eric Christensen and Steven Gordon, who is married to Sally Gordon of delightful Gordon's Cafe and Wine Bar at the other end of town.
❧ *Vintage 1870, 6525 Washington Street, Yountville 94599; phone (707) 944–2451. Open from 10:00 A.M. to 5:30 P.M. daily. Credit cards vary by shop.*

Jeff Steen, of Pacific Blues Cafe, has created another light-hearted success with BOCCONCINI, his new Italian restaurant in the back of the Vintage 1870 complex. It's worth the trip there to visit the fabulous wine shop next door, as well.

Bocconcini merans "little bites," according to Jeff, although he offers much larger portions than the name would suggest, thankfully. In one large room, you can enjoy the open kitchen with lots of copper and a take-out counter of Italian delectables. Jeff certainly offers the best list of Italian wines (and some Napa stars) in the valley, and the pastries are truly Italian.

The fettuccine, pappardelle, gnocchi, and ravioli are all made here, and don't miss the black truffle risotto with Parmesan cheese ($13 lunch, $14 dinner). You can also enjoy loads of salads, meats, and chicken, and the pizzas are substantial ($10–$12).

✻✷ *Bocconcini, Vintage 1870, 6525 Washington Street, Yountville 94599; phone (707) 944–9780. Open from 11:30 A.M. to 9:00 P.M. daily. Beer and wine. Visa, MasterCard, and American Express. Wheelchair-accessible.*

Just south of Vintage 1870, and across the street at the junction of Oak Leaf and Washington, stop at the Whistle Stop Center, a collection of shops in another train station beside a collection of railroad cars that make up the Napa Valley Railway Inn (see Chapter 5, *Where to Stay in Napa Valley*). If you like leather, the OVERLAND SHEEPSKIN COMPANY is a must-see for waxed coats, sheepskin pelts, purses, briefcases, bicycle-seat covers, suede skirts and vests, slippers, Western belts, and wallets. While it is one of twelve stores, this Overland at least feels local.

✻✷ *Overland Sheepskin Company, 6505 Washington Street, Yountville 94599; phone (707) 944–0778. Open from 10:00 A.M. to 7:00 P.M. Monday–Thursday, until 8:00 P.M. Friday, and until 6:00 P.M. Sunday. MasterCard, Visa, and Discover. Wheelchair-accessible.*

Upstairs, visit Galerie Bacchus for vintage posters from La Belle Epoque and heirloom tapestries.

Go under the highway at the south end of Yountville and up California Drive to the Veterans' Home, Napa Valley Museum, and Domaine Chandon winery and restaurant, all of which are off this main road and within pea-shooting distance of one another. While only a chainlink fence separates the Napa Valley Museum and Domaine Chandon, their staffs rarely visit each other in this cozily nestled complex.

Just before the Veterans' Home entry post, you will see DOMAINE CHANDON'S arch over California Drive. Turn right and follow the signs to the parking lot. You can either park in the first lot, cross the little bridge over peaceful ponds with waterfalls and lilies, and walk into Domaine Chandon's dramatic entrance, or you can drive to a lot above and enter at the restaurant level. Ramps and elevators help you get from floor to floor.

Domaine Chandon deserves attention for both its winery and the restaurant. California's early Champagne wine prospects turned sharply better in 1973, when Moët-Hennessy of France built this dramatic, state-of-the-art sparkling-wine facility, which it now owns with Louis Vuitton. Moët & Chandon, the French Champagne house founded in 1743 and parent company of Domaine Chandon, uses the same methods that the monk Dom Perignon discovered as cellarmaster at the Benedictine Abbey in Hautvillers in 1690. Domaine Chandon has integrated modern innovations with those traditional methods, including sustainable agriculture in its Carneros and Mt. Veeder vineyards. According to the 1920 Treaty of Madrid, which the United States did not sign during Prohibition, only sparkling wines made from Chardonnay, Pinot Noir, and Pinot Meunier grapes grown in Champagne and using *méthode champenoise* could be called Champagne. "Sparkling wine" applies to all wines containing effervescence created by natural fermentation. Out of deference to its French founders, Domaine Chandon calls its California product sparkling wine, even though it is made by the same methods as are their Moët & Chandon French Champagnes and legally can be called Champagne.

As you enter the winery, you can enjoy a vast shop of Domaine Chandon wines, beautiful books, aprons, glasses, wine goodies, mustards, shortbread cookies, and shirts even in kids' sizes. Along the hallway is a museum-style, lighted instructional display of the Champagne-making process, and stairs or elevators take you up to the next level.

On the mezzanine visit the Pavillion, an elegant, glassed-in tasting bar and the restaurant. Chef Robert Curry continues the cuisine he mastered as sous-chef to Philippe Jeanty, who left after twenty years to start his own Bistro Jeanty, "downtown" in Yountville. After graduating from the Culinary Institute of America in Hyde Park, New York, Robert also worked as sous-chef at Citrus in Los Angeles.

The menu changes weekly and may include mesquite appetizers of grilled asparagus ($9.00), duck foie blond pâté ($10.00), home-smoked salmon tartare ($11.00), or Maine crab salad ($14.00). Entrees can be pan-seared yellowfin tuna ($21.00 lunch, $27.00 dinner), rack of local lamb, Black Angus steak or beef tenderloin, mesquite-grilled squab ($27.00/$29.00), Laura Chenel goat cheeses ($9.00), or French cheeses ($18.00 for two). You might enjoy the seven-course tasting menu ($65 or $100 with paired wines).

Winemaker Dawnine Dyer graduated from UC Santa Cruz with a degree in biology, worked at Robert Mondavi Winery and Inglenook Vineyards, and studied enology at UC Davis. She joined Chandon in 1976, makes regular visits to Moët & Chandon in Epernay, France, and consults to Moet's Australian winery.

DOMAINE CHANDON

Fine points: In the restaurant, you may want to try the Tasting Menu, at $60 or $80, which includes four ounces each of five wines. In 1998 Domaine Chandon released its first still wines— Pinot Meunier, Pinot Noir, and Pinot Blanc—all made in small lots and available only in its shop, restaurant, and by direct mail. Featured wines: Brut Cuvée, Carneros Blanc de Noirs, Reserve Cuvée, Etoile Cuvée, Chandon Fleur de Vigne, Chandon Pinot Meunier, Pinot Noir, and Pinot Blanc. Owners: Moët-Hennessy-Louis Vuitton. Winemaker: Dawnine Dyer. Executive Chef: Robert Curry. Cases: 450,000. Acres: 1,600.

Domaine Chandon, 1 California Drive, Yountville 94599; phone (707) 944–2280, fax (707) 944–1123, e-mail dchandon@napanet.net, Web site www.dchandon.com. Winery open from 10:00 A.M. to 7:00 P.M., tours on the hour from 11:00 A.M. to 5:00 P.M., departing from the bottom of the stairs in the entry hall. Tasting fee: three for $8.00 or five for $12.00, complete with logo glass. Restaurant open for lunch from 11:30 A.M. to 2:30 P.M. daily May–October, dinner seatings from 6:00 P.M. Wednesday–Sunday year-round. Winery and restaurant are closed Monday and Tuesday November–April. MasterCard, Visa, American Express, Diners Club, and Discover. Wheelchair-accessible.

Just up the tree-lined divided road, about half a block from Domaine Chandon's entrance, is the NAPA VALLEY MUSEUM. The state-of-the-art edifice,

Black Mussels Steamed in Chandon Brut and Rabbit Terrine with Sliced Apples and Baguette

from Robert Curry, Executive Chef, Domaine Chandon

Ingredients for Black Mussels Steamed in Chandon Brut:

4 ½ lb black mussels
3 cups dry sparkling wine
3 shallots, diced
3 garlic cloves, chopped
½ bunch thyme, chopped

1 cup Italian parsley, chopped
½ cup tomatoes, peeled, seeded,
*   and diced*
2 lemons
⅛ lb butter

Preparation:

Sweat the shallots and ⅔ of the garlic in a little butter. Add the thyme. Add the mussels and the sparkling wine. Cover and steam until mussels open, about 2 minutes. Remove the cooking liquid from the mussels. Bring the liquid to a simmer and whisk in the butter. Add the parsley and tomatoes. Adjust the flavor with the lemon juice and chopped garlic. Pour the liquid over the mussels and serve. Serves 4.

Ingredients for Rabbit Terrine with Sliced Apples and Baguette:

2 lb 3 oz boneless rabbit meat
1 Tbs + 2 tsp salt
1 tsp pepper
3 garlic cloves, peeled and sliced

1 bunch thyme, washed and dried
2 oz virgin olive oil
2 baguettes
4 of your favorite apples

Preparation:

In a bowl, mix the rabbit, garlic, thyme, and olive oil. Cover and refrigerate overnight. The next day, remove the garlic and thyme.

Season the rabbit with salt and pepper and grind the meat through a meat grinder. Line a 5-cup terrine mold with plastic wrap and pack the ground meat into the mold. Fold over plastic wrap to cover. Place the cover on the terrine mold. Place terrine in a water bath and bake in a 300° F oven for 1 hour 20 minutes. Refrigerate overnight.

Slice and serve terrine with thinly sliced apples and baguettes. Serves 8.

designed by architects Fernau and Hartman to resemble two-thirds of a farm shed, serves as a regional museum that features wine-industry history, art, and local culture. This 10,000-square-foot vaulted structure represents the first phase of the 40,000-square-foot museum project.

Here you can visit the $1.5 million "California Wine: The Science of an Art" exhibit, which was moved here from the earthquake-unsafe California Museum of Science and Industry in Los Angeles and redesigned by Academy Studio for the Industry Gallery of the Napa Valley Museum. Explore the information provided on twenty-six video disc players, nine microcomputers, twenty-four monitors, and eleven audio speakers for a definitive wine-history experience.

Collections include works of Napa Valley painter Sofia Alstrom Mitchell, The Johnson Collection of Minerals and Fossils, Native peoples of the Napa Valley including Wappo relics and folk culture, local viticultural materials, and historical and contemporary works by artists who live or have lived in the Napa Valley or use the Napa Valley as subject matter. We particularly enjoy the work of Earl Thollander, a favorite book illustrator for *Gourmet* and *Sunset* magazines.

Fine points: Be sure to visit the museum shop downstairs. It has one of the best collections of Napa history books and souvenirs anywhere.

❧ *Napa Valley Museum, 55 Presidents Circle, Yountville 94599; phone (707) 944–0500, fax (707) 945–0500, Web site www.napavalley museum.org. Adults $4.50; seniors 60 and up and students over 17, $3.50; children 7–17, $2.50; under 7 free; free 5:00 to 8:00 P.M. first Thursday of the month. Free admission every Monday. Open from 10:00 A.M. to 5:00 P.M. Wednesday to Monday; closed Tuesday and major holidays. Wheelchair-accessible.*

As you visit the museum, you are surrounded by the CALIFORNIA VETERANS' HOME, established in 1882 by veterans of the Mexican and Civil Wars as "a home for all veterans west of the Rockies." Sold in 1900 to the state of California for a $20 gold piece, the vast home has been remodeled and updated (sort of) and has served veterans of the Mexican, Civil, Indian, Spanish-American, Korean, and Vietnam Wars, as well as World War I and World War II.

Fine points: The fascinating little museum behind the main building, south of the Napa Valley Museum is open only on Friday afternoon from noon to 2:00 P.M. If you plan lunch around those hours, you might see interesting rotating exhibits of historic uniforms, weapons, documents, models, and photographs.

❧ *California Veterans' Home, 180 California Drive, Yountville 94599; phone (800) 404–8387, fax (707) 944–4542, e-mail vets@fcs.net, Web site www. blink.com/vets.*

As you work your way northward on Highway 29 from Yountville, four interesting stops on the west side of the highway break our first recommendation of not turning left across this two-lane highway. Brix, Mustards Grill, Cosentino Winery, and Napa Cellars all tempt.

General Manager Curtis Jones and the Brix staff set the casually elegant tone in a restaurant where warm, comforting yellows and woods with beamed ceilings and large windows frame vegetable gardens, vineyards, and the Mayacamas Mountains. Brix makes olive oil from its trees' olives, grows vegetables and herbs for your meal, and maintains ten acres of Chardonnay and Cabernet Sauvignon grapes (which it sells to Caymus Vineyards).

At lunch, starters may include crunchy coconut seafood cigars with sweet 'n' sour pineapple-chili sauce ($8.50), prosciutto-fennel sausage, cambozola, spinach-and-roasted-garlic pizza ($9.00), or chopped romaine hearts with creamy lemon Parmesan dressing ($6.50). Main courses include pepper-seared tuna salad with Ponzu vinaigrette ($12.00), smoked-salmon spaghettini with fennel, capers, Maui onions, and orange gremolata ($12.00), Kasu grilled salmon with soba noodles and miso sauce ($13.50), and loads of Angus beef possibilities.

Dinner offers the same appetizers plus some others, a warm macadamia nut–crusted goat cheese salad ($8.00), Hawaiian mahi mahi with roasted-banana-and-coconut curry sauce ($21.50), Thai pesto smoked rack of lamb with spicy peanut saté and zinfandel glacé ($23.50), fennel-dusted bay scallops with Meyer lemon beurre blanc and truffle oil ($23.50), plus the Angus beef options.

 Fine points: The wine list is exceptional. Be sure to stop in at the interesting gift shop with wine-country goodies and excellent travel and cook/food books. Feel free to stroll through the vegetable gardens and vineyards.

❧ *Brix, 7377 Highway 29, Yountville 94599; phone (707) 944–2749, fax (707) 944–8320. Open lunch and dinner daily. MasterCard, Visa, American Express, Diners Club, Discover, Carte Blanche, and JCB. Wheelchair-accessible.*

Practically next door to mustard-colored Brix, the better known and noisier white MUSTARDS GRILL, is the original outpost of the Real Restaurants group, which now includes Fog City Diner, Tra Vigne and Tomatina in St. Helena and elsewhere, and the Buckeye Roadhouse in Mill Valley. The group just opened Miramonte at what was Showley in Miramonte next to Terra in St. Helena.

Mustards' roadside signs claim COCKTAILS, PORK CHOPS—ALMOST A MILLION SOLD, WAY TOO MANY WINES, GARDEN PRODUCE, CHOPS, RIBS. Just to the left of the front door is a small patio labeled MUSTARDS CIGAR & WILDLIFE PRESERVE, so park your stogies and stogie smokers here.

A fast-paced, clanking restaurant with attractive art, Mustards serves good-sized portions of hearty and occasionally healthy comfort food (speaking of which, you must try the off-the-diet stacks of crisp, thin onion rings with home-made ketchup). White walls, dark wood, and white tile floors give the feel of a city bistro.

The Caesar salad is good at $7.50, the lemon-and-garlic chicken with mashed potatoes ($15.75) and the Big Thyme chicken and morel pot pie ($14.95) are better, and the half-slab of barbecued baby back ribs with crispy yams and creamy slaw ($18.95) can be terrific. If you eat such things, try the grilled Mongolian pork chop with garlic mashed potatoes ($17.95) or the calf's liver Diablo with applewood-smoked bacon with griddled polenta ($13.95). The wild-mushroom "burger" with creamy potato salad and the regular ham-burgers are deals at $9.95, as is the ahi tuna steak sandwich with basil mayon-naise and ginger for $11.50.

 Fine points: The "New World" wine list includes 12 pages of fun reading and excellent wines, even some of Oregon's best Pinot Noirs. No photos of the restaurant without permission from manager Michael Kim Wolf personally.

✿ *Mustards Grill, 7399 St. Helena Highway, Napa 94558; phone (707) 944–2424, fax (707) 944–0828. Open lunch and dinner daily. Full bar. MasterCard, Visa, Diners Club, Carte Blanche, and Discover. Wheelchair-accessible.*

Immediately next door, to the north, is charming and small COSENTINO WINERY, the pride and joy of onetime assistant golf pro and wine distributor Mitch Cosentino. Possibly the only vintner to sell golf balls in his tasting room, Mitch plays golf in the Napa Valley with pals and pros, including Miller Barber and Walter Morgan.

Cosentino's Pinot Noir and Chardonnay are highly rated by most critics. Its 1995 The Poet Meritage red blend and the 1996 Reserve Merlot both won dou-ble gold awards at the Tasters Guild International Wine Judging, and its 1996 Cabernet Franc garnered a gold medal. It is one of the few wineries that prints and offers visitors the whole list of its *Wine Spectator* ratings and wine awards so that you can learn other people's opinions of its wines.

Taste for yourself. Oh yes, you might also enjoy the autographed Steve Young football in Cosentino's ribbon and trophy case.

 Fine points: Cosentino's "Rare Art Series," which include "The Sculptor," "The Poet," and "The Novelist," are all "stylistically more 'old world' European than the California wines of that day. Each name was chosen to honor a type of artist whose approach to his medium best reflected the winemaker's approach to the development of these individual wine types." Tasting fee: $5.00 (you keep the glass). Featured wines: Chardonnay, White Meritage/Sauvignon Blanc, Gewürztraminer, Viognier, Nebbiolo, Tenero Rosa, Pinot Noir, Merlot, Il Chiaretto, Tenero Rosso, Il Tesoro Sangiovetto, Cabernet Sauvignon, Zinfandel, Cigarzin, Cabernet Franc, Cabernet Franc Port, Zinfandel Port, Francesca d'Amore aperitif/dessert wine. Owner and winemaker: Mitch Cosentino. Cases: 30,000. Acres: 163.

❧ *Cosentino Winery, 7415 St. Helena Highway, Yountville 94599; phone (707) 944–1220, fax (707) 944–1254, Web site www.cosentinowinery.com. Open from 10:00 A.M. to 5:30 P.M. Visa, MasterCard, and American Express. Wheelchair-accessible.*

Now, walk next door to NAPA CELLARS in the interesting six-sided wooden building. As you enter, you face a corner of the tasting counter. Permanent Christmas-tree lights and dried flowers dangle over the six-sided bar. Enjoy the excellent book selection on the table to the left as you enter as well as the new Cabernet Sauvignon Vineyard around the tasting room.

Napa Cellars is a new endeavor of Koerner Rombauer of Rombauer Vineyards and former Academy of Motion Pictures president Richard Frank, who are also involved in ownership of Hanns Kornell Champagne Cellars. Frank-Rombauer suffered a horrible warehouse fire June 15, 2000, and lost its rare vintages. They are back making all of their wines again, fortunately. Try the wines and stay tuned.

Fine points: Marc Chagall and Guy Buffet posters decorate the walls. Tasting fee: $5.00. Featured wines: Chardonnay, Sauvignon Blanc, Merlot, Petite Syrah, Sangiovese, Cabernet Sauvignon, Zinfandel, Muscat Canelli. Owners: partnership including Koerner Rombauer and Richard Frank. Winemaker: Matt Cookson. Cases: 10,000. Acres: 50.

❧ *Napa Cellars, 7481 St. Helena Highway, Oakville 94562; phone (707) 944–2565 or (800) 535–6400, fax (707) 944–0250. Open from 10:00 A.M. to 6:00 P.M. daily. Visa, MasterCard, and American Express. Wheelchair-accessible.*

Across Highway 29, just north of Napa Cellars, visit CARDINALE/PEPI WINERY, home also to Pepi, Atalon, Lokoya Cabernets, and Artisans & Estates wines. All are owned by Jess Jackson of Kendall-Jackson Winery. To get there, turn right (east) at the Cardinale sign, proceed for 0.4 mile, and turn right up the hill to cement-block and then stone buildings. (You enter the tasting room from the parking lot.) Jackson is filling in his own reservoir to build winery with barrels underground.

Jess Jackson established Cardinale to make Cabernet Sauvignon and Merlot

NAPA CELLARS

in Oakville, in the heart of the Napa Valley, to use the exceptional hillside and benchland vineyards in Napa and Sonoma counties. Cardinale's handcrafted and unfiltered wines are aged 100 percent in French oak barrels.

Since 1966, Robert Pepi has grown and produced outstanding Sangiovese and Sauvignon Blanc from Pepi's original cuttings of Sangiovese Grosso, brought from Italy's Tuscany region. Pepi's Colline di Sassi comes from the "Hill of Stones" on the Pepi property. Jess Jackson bought Pepi in 1994 from Robert Pepi.

Fine points: The new tasting room will be spectacular, with fabulous views of the Napa Valley. Tasting fees: $5.00 to $8.00; a souvenir glass $2.00. You will find a limited but excellent selection of wine and cookbooks here, as well as handsome hand-carved wooden bottle stoppers. In *The Wine Advocate*, Robert M. Parker, Jr., rates Cardinale's Cardinale a 90–92. Featured wines: Cardinale: Royale Meritage, Cardinale Meritage, White Meritage, Due Baci. Cases: 3,000. Robert Pepi: Sauvignon Blanc, Arneis, Malvasia Bianca, Pinot Grigio, Tocai Friulano, Barbera, Sangiovese, Colline di Sassi Sangiovese, Teroldego. Winemakers: Cardinale: Charles Thomas; Robert Pepi: Marco DiGiulio. Cases: 30,000. Acres: 450+, and is the largest purchaser of Cabernet Sauvignon grapes in Napa Valley.

❧ *Cardinale/Pepi Winery, 7585 Highway 29, Oakville 94562; phone (707) 945–1391, Web site www.pepi.com. Open for retail sales from 10:30 A.M. to 4:00 P.M. MasterCard, Visa, and American Express. Wheelchair-accessible.*

DUNGENESS CRAB CIOPPINO
from Eric Markson, Napa Cellars

INGREDIENTS:

2 whole fresh crabs, cracked and cleaned

1½ lb fresh firm white fish (cod, snapper, sole) cut into 2-inch cubes

6–8 clams in shell, scrubbed and cleaned

½ lb fresh shrimp (prawns), cleaned and deveined

2 cans clams with juice

2 cans bay shrimp, drained

1 8-oz bottle clam juice

3 Tbs oilive oil

1½ cup onions or shallots, chopped

2 16-oz cans whole tomatoes

1 16-oz can tomato sauce

1½ cups Napa Cellars Chardonnay

1 bay leaf

3 Tbs fresh parsley, finely chopped

3 Tbs fresh basil, finely chopped (or 1 Tbs dried basil)

3 cloves garlic, minced (more if you like)

3 drops Tabasco (more if you like)

salt and pepper to taste

PREPARATION:

Remove the meat from the crab bodies and a few legs, and set it aside with the clams, fish, and shrimp.

Sauté the onions in oilive oil for about 8 minutes, and add the garlic. Cook together for another 2 minutes, then add tomatoes, tomato sauce, clam juice, herbs, and wine. Cover and let cook for 25–30 minutes at medium heat. Stir occasionally.

Add the crab legs and meat, fish, canned clams, and canned shrimp, and let simmer on low heat for 25 minutes.

Add fresh shrimp, clams, and let cook for 10 more minutes, discarding any unopened clams.

Add salt, pepper and Tabasco to taste. Serve with tossed green salad, lemon wedges, and lots of French bread to soak up the sauce. Serves 6.

North of Cardinale and Pepi, the Oakville Grade heads west from Highway 29 and winds almost treacherously to Glen Ellen in Sonoma County. There are several good reasons to make this turn: Pometta's Deli, an Episcopal church, the Carmelite House of Prayer and Religious Shop, and La Famiglia di Robert Mondavi Winery and Italian Marketplace. Many more signs guide you to the Carmelite mission than to any of the other attractions.

At **POMETTA'S DELICATESSEN AND CATERING**, owner Susan Potgeter and staff make sandwiches and picnic lunches for locals and tourists and cater most Robert Mondavi Winery staff lunches (a hint of the high quality of food here). Pometta's serves down-home Italian and Napa Valley specialties, barbecue

POMETTA'S DELI, OAKVILLE

chicken, salads, soups, and huge portions of good humor.

Sandwiches range from the Pometta Club and Muffaletta to the Sicilian, with salami, pastrami, sautéed zucchini, Swiss cheese, olive oil, and wine vinegar. You might try the vegetarian sandwich or the barbecued chicken or beef, the Hot Texan, or Mama's Homemade Meatloaf.

Picnic box lunches include such choices as roasted chicken or boneless chicken breast with pesto, salads, cheese, fruit, cookies, and other goodies. Prices range from $12.50 to $15.00 for each.

Be sure to pick up a jar of Pometta's highly rated Special Garlic Sauce or pasta sauces (which are also sold at Oakville Grocery). Don't miss a walk into the "dining rooms" with their red-and-white-checked tablecloths to see the chickens in the shower, then head outside to play horseshoes or enjoy your lunch on the lawn.

❧ *Pometta's Delicatessen and Catering, Highway 29 and Oakville Grade, Oakville 94562; phone (707) 944–2365. Open from 9:00 A.M. to 6:00 P.M. Beer and wine. MasterCard and Visa. Wheelchair-accessible.*

As you continue westward on the flat part of the Oakville Grade through acres of vineyards, notice the historic little St. Stephen's Episcopal Church on the right. It's worth getting out of the car if you're interested in local history. The next stop is also religious: the Carmelite House of Prayer and Carmelite Religious Store. Turn right up Mount Carmel Drive, and Stations of the Cross shrines lead you up the mission's driveway. Park at the top, respect the quiet, and explore the historic chapel to your left, the mosaics, and the popular shop.

Another 500 feet up the winding grade, turn left into LA FAMIGLIA DI ROBERT MONDAVI WINERY AND ITALIAN MARKETPLACE. As of 1998, Tim Mondavi, part of La Famiglia di Robert Mondavi, took over this winery and tasting room from another Robert Mondavi enterprise, Vichon, which moved to the Languedoc-Rousillon region of France. La Famiglia specializes in "Cal–Ital" wines—Italian in origin and Californian in style.

As you approach the winery overlooking the Napa Valley, picnic tables and bocce-ball courts are to your left, the tasting room to your right. (If you buy some wine, you can use the bocce-ball courts and picnic tables.) As you wander around the building, you can soak in the views and enjoy the beautiful flower beds.

Inside the newly remodeled marketplace and tasting room, you will find the most engrossing collection of Italian cookbooks and travel books we have seen gathered in one place, as well as the most attractive souvenir shirts around. There's an expansive mural by San Francisco painter Jennifer Ewing.

 Fine points: Tastes of these new Italian-style wines are real treats, as are the good humor and vast knowledge of the hosts. Some tasting is free; $5.00 for Reserves. Featured wines: Bocce Rosato, Bianco, and Rosso; La Famiglia Malvasia Bianca, Moscato Bianco, Pinot Grigio, Tocai Friulano, Barbera, Nebbiolo, Rosato, Sangiovese, and Sangiovese Riserva. Owners: Robert Mondavi Family. Winemaker: Heather Pyle. Executive Chef: Annie Roberts. Cases: 65,000. Acres: 4.5 here, many elsewhere.

❧ *La Famiglia di Robert Mondavi Winery, 1595 Oakville Grade, Oakville 94562; phone (707) 944–2811, fax (707) 944–2607, Web site www.robertmondavi.com. Open from 10:00 A.M. to 4:30 P.M. daily. Tours by appointment. MasterCard, Visa, American Express, and Diners Club. Wheelchair-accessible.*

OAKVILLE

As you come into Oakville, please slow down, both for your safety and for that of pilgrims gathering at the Oakville Grocery Mecca.

At the southern end of this three-building metropolis is NAPA WINE COMPANY, which is not in most books but is fun to visit. Turn right onto the Oakville Crossroad just before the Oakville Grocery, and right again into the winery's driveway.

The original winery on this site was built in 1877 by Adolph Brun and Jean Chaix as Nouveau Medoc Winery and California Bonded Winery No. 9. After passing through many winemaking hands before and after Prohibition, the property was bought by Heublein in 1986 and turned into Inglenook's Chardonnay Cellar. It closed three years later. The northwest corner building was built in 1892 for the Bartolucci Brothers' Modanna Winery, also passing through several hands and ending up with Heublein. The Andrew Pelissa family bought the whole works in 1993 and reopened under the name Napa Wine Company.

This is an unusual, custom-crush facility to which fifty small wineries bring their own winemaker, grapes, and barrels and use the equipment and space to crush, ferment, age, and bottle their wines. Here in the newly remodeled tasting room you can sample and buy hand-crafted wines from family wineries whose wines are rarely available in stores or restaurants, including a 1985–1994 vertical Marilyn Merlot for a mere $4,000. In this case, "vertical" refers to one bottle of each vintage, and not to Ms. Monroe.

 Fine points: If you have ever fantasized about starting your own small winery, check this out. It's full of learning opportunities. Tasting fee: $5.00. Wines from wineries you might sample and purchase in the salesroom here include Fife Vineyards' Cabernet Sauvignon, Merlot, Petite Syrah, and Zinfandel; Lanborn Family Vineyards' Zinfandel; Mason Cellars' Merlot and Sauvignon Blanc; Napa Wine Company's Sauvignon Blanc; Nova Wine Group's Marilyn Merlot and Marilyn Cabernet Sauvignon with luscious Marilyn portraits on the labels; Oakford Cellars' Cabernet Sauvignon; Pahlmeyer & Co. Chardonnay, Merlot, and Red Table Wine; Philippe Lorraine Cellars' Chardonnay and Cabernet Sauvignon; Tria Winery's Pinot Noir, Zinfandel, and Port; Staglin Family Vineyards' Cabernet and Chardonnay; and Madrigal's Petite Syrah, Merlot, and Cabernet. Owners: Andy Hoxsey, Dawne Dickenson, and the Harris family. Winemaker for Napa Wine Company: Randy Masonn. Acres: 650.

Napa Wine Company, 7840 St. Helena Highway, Oakville 94562; phone (707) 944–1710, fax (707) 944–9749, e-mail retail@napawineco.com, Web site

PORK SCALOPPINI
WITH PINOT GRIGIO, CAPER SAUCE
from Executive Chef Annie Roberts, La Famiglia
di Robert Mondavi Winery

INGREDIENTS:

1 ½ lb boneless pork tenderloin

3 Tbs olive oil

3 Tbs butter

½ cup flour

½ cup Pinot Grigio

2 Tbs capers, rinsed and drained

1 Tbs Italian parsley, chopped

¼ cup green onions, white part only, chopped

salt

freshly ground black pepper

PREPARATION:

Slice the pork across the grain into ½-inch slices. Place the slices between 2 sheets of waxed paper or parchment paper. With a meat pounder, lightly and evenly pound the pieces of meat to ¼-inch slices.

Heat all the oil and 1 Tbs butter in a large sauté pan. Coat the meat in flour and, when the oil is hot, brown the meat on both sides, then remove and set on a warm plate. Add the green onions to the pan and cook for about 1 minute. Add the wine and reduce slightly. Add the capers and the remaining butter and return the meat and any juices back to the pan.

Season with salt and pepper and cook just until the meat has been heated through. Sprinkle with Italian parsley and serve with Pinot Grigio. Serves 4.

www.napawineco.com. Open from 10:00 A.M. to 3:30 P.M. daily. MasterCard, Visa, and American Express. Wheelchair-accessible.

Next door to Napa Wine Company is the **OAKVILLE GROCERY**, a fabulous place for food lovers and lovers of food lovers. Built in 1881 by James and Jennie McQuaid as the "mercantile" for the bustling town of Oakville, Oakville

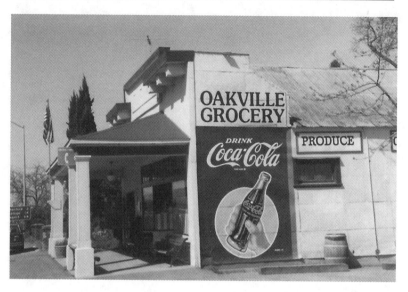

OAKVILLE GROCERY AND U.S. POST OFFICE, OAKVILLE

Grocery supplied essentials to locals for generations. Listed in the National Register of Historic Places, the store was owned from 1978 to 1980 by vintner Joseph Phelps, who sold it to current CEO Steve Carlin and partners.

It is worth braving the crowds for tastes of oils and della Fattoria, Artisans, and Acme breads; classic sandwiches to go, from Mediterranean chicken and smoked turkey and brie to Ozark peppered ham, vegetarian, curried turkey salad, and mom's tuna salad; or focaccia sandwiches of turkey pesto, roast beef and blue cheese, or house-roasted pork loin. All are under $7.00. Feast your eyes upon eight Italian pastas, Chinese noodle salad, citrus chipotle salsa, twenty kinds of olives, crab cakes with remoulade sauce, and chocolate-covered apricots, cherry pies, hazlenut mousse chocolates, and Graffeo coffees.

Be sure to notice the wines in the back, especially the unusual collection of splits of local wines, as well as Oakville Grocery's own oils, vinegars, mustards, preserves, honeys, and wines.

Fine points: The Oakville U.S. Post Office is still in the building, as are public telephones.

Oakville Grocery, 7856 St. Helena Highway, Oakville 94562; phone (707) 944–8802. Open from 9:00 A.M. to 6:00 P.M. daily; espresso bar open from 7:00 A.M. to 6:00 P.M. Monday –Friday, 7:30 A.M. to 6:00 P.M. Saturday, 8:00 A.M. to 6:00 P.M. Sunday. Beer and wine. MasterCard, Visa,

OAKVILLE POLENTA CROSTINI
WITH SUN-DRIED TOMATO PESTO
from Executive Chef Richard Hoff, Oakville Grocery

INGREDIENTS:

3 cups water
1 cup milk
1 tsp salt
1 cup Oakville Grocery Organic Polenta
2 Tbs McEvoy Ranch extra virgin olive oil
¼ cup grated Vella Dry Jack cheese (can substitute Parmesan cheese)
2 Tbs Italian parsley, chopped
pinch of freshly ground black pepper
1 9½-oz jar Bella Cucina Sun-Dried Tomato Pesto

PREPARATION:

In a medium-size saucepan, combine the water, milk, and salt and bring to a boil. Sprinkle the polenta slowly into the boiling liquid and stir with a whisk until fully incorporated to avoid lumps. Lower the heat so that the mixture simmers slowly rather than boils. Switch to a wooden spoon and stir frequently for 20–25 minutes. The polenta should be very thick and smooth and free of lumps. When the grains are tender, add ¼ cup of cheese, olive oil, parsley, and pepper to taste. Stir until incorporated.

Carefully pour the polenta into a rectangular 8-by-12-inch cake pan that has been brushed lightly with olive oil. Spread polenta with a spatula until it is about ½ inch thick. Cover with plastic wrap and allow to cool for 2 hours.

Cut into 24, 2-inch squares and arrange on lightly oiled cookie sheets. Brush tops with oil and set under preheated broiler until the tops brown lightly. Top each square with a dollop of pesto and sprinkle with reserved cheese. Place back in broiler to warm and serve immediately. Serves 6–8.

and American Express. *Wheelchair-accessible, but difficult to get around due to closeness of aisles.*

The greatest concentration of wineries is between Oakville and St. Helena, which means that you might want to plan your route carefully, with full awareness that some of your favorites might be between St. Helena and Calistoga or on the Silverado Trail.

OAKVILLE TO RUTHERFORD

OPUS ONE WINERY is the perfect child created by Robert Mondavi and the late Baron Philippe de Rothschild of Bordeaux's Chateau Mouton-Rothschild, combining France's best with California's champion of wine. Open for tasting and tours by appointment only, Opus One's secrecy and mystery, and Robert Mondavi's unequaled skills at promotion, have contributed to wine fans' heightened desire to gain admission to this shrine. To get here, turn east (right) off Highway 29 into Opus One's driveway, 0.4 mile north of Oakville.

Designed by Johnson, Fain & Perreira of Los Angeles, who also designed San Francisco's once controversial TransAmerica Pyramid, the building resembles a cross between a Mayan temple and a spaceship. Partially buried by grasses and plantings, the redwood and limestone winery was built in 1991 for about $26.5 million. It has a dramatic courtyard entrance and a breathtaking open pavilion overlooking Napa Valley's finest vineyards.

Fine points: Old World traditional gravity flow methods merge with advanced California technology here to produce some of the finest wines anywhere. This is one appointment worth making ahead to plan your trip around. While the tasting fee is the highest we know of ($25), it is also worth it. (The wines you taste here sell for about $65 per bottle.) Featured wines: Opus One (Cabernet Sauvignon, Cabernet Franc, and Merlot blends) and Overture. Owners: The Mondavi and Baron Philippe de Rothschild families. Winemakers: Tim Mondavi and Patrick Leon. Cases: 30,000. Acres: 144.

❧ *Opus One Winery, 7900 St. Helena Highway, Oakville, 94562; phone (707) 944–9442. Web site www.opusonewinery.com. Open from 10:30 A.M. to 3:30 p.m. by appointment only. MasterCard, Visa, and American Express. Wheelchair-accessible.*

The next winery as we progress northward on Highway 29 is ROBERT MONDAVI WINERY, on the west side of the road. Robert Mondavi is both the man and the winery. He is completely tied to his winery's image, because he promoted it and developed it, while also warning loudly of his perception of a new Prohibition coming from America's political right. His sons Michael and Tim now run the winery, while Robert continues, in his late eighties, to educate consumers and promote wine.

SMOKED SALMON AND CAPER CROSTINI
from Executive Chef Annie Roberts, Robert Mondavi Winery

INGREDIENTS:

¼ lb smoked salmon, sliced thinly into strips

2 Tbs capers

¼ cup red onion, chopped

¼ cup Italian parsley, chopped

2 Tbs mayonnaise

1 long, thin baguette

PREPARATION:

Combine ingredients in a bowl. Transfer to a food processor and pulse briefly until chunky-smooth.

Slice baguette into ¼-inch slices, brush lightly with olive oil, season with salt and pepper, and bake in 375°F oven until golden. Spread salmon mixture on toasted baguette and serve with Chardonnay. Makes 12 appetizers.

Upon leaving the Mondavi family–owned Charles Krug Winery, Robert Mondavi built and began his own winery in what was, in 1966, an avant-garde California–Italian building that stood out dramatically from the undeveloped, natural surrounding landscape. The winery now includes an elegant art gallery and dining rooms, reserve tasting room, and learning rooms, in addition to winemaking facilities. The layout resembles a California mission.

Besides its vast array of interesting wines, special events here are exceptional and well worth your attention. Robert and Margrit Mondavi and family work constantly to fulfill their goal of educating the public about wine and "its role as a mealtime beverage of moderation and to promote a gracious way of life." The summer music series has included the biggest names in American music. Kathleen particularly likes The Great Chefs at Robert Mondavi Winery series, which since 1976 has included Simone Beck, Jean Troisgros, Roger Verge, Gaston Lenotre, Julia Child, Paul Prudhomme, Larry Forgione, Paul Bocuse, Wolfgang Puck, Barbara Kafka, Alice Waters, Diana Kennedy, Paula Wolfert, Martha Stewart, Jeremiah Tower, Joyce Goldstein, Giuliano Bugialli, Lydia Shire, Marion Cunningham, Marcella Hazan, Charlie Trotter, Joachim Splichal, Roy Yamaguchi, and Jacques and Claudine Pepin.

Mondavi Picnics in the Vineyards begin at 10:00 A.M. on Mondays from May to October. They require reservations forty-eight hours in advance. The picnics are limited to ten people ($30 each) and include a four-hour tour and tasting, focusing on viticultural practices and tastings of wines selected to complement the day's picnic lunch.

Fine points: Mondavi has added two lovely new tasting rooms for your tasting pleasure: The To-Kalon Room for reserve-wine tasting, cigars, and Riedel Sommelier crystal stemware and the Appellation Room for district wines. Enjoy the Rose Garden for new releases outdoors (weekends June–October). Call the winery for tour information and reservations. Tasting fees range from $5.00 to $15.00. Featured wines: Chardonnay, Fumé Blanc, Sauvignon Blanc, Cabernet Sauvignon, Merlot, Zinfandel, Pinot Noir, Moscato d'Oro, and the La Famiglia di Robert Mondavi wines. Owner: Robert Mondavi. Winemaker: Genevieve Janssens. Cases: 600,000. Acres: information not available.

Robert Mondavi Winery, 7801 St. Helena Highway, Oakville 94562; phone (707) 226-1335 or (800) MONDAVI, Web site robertmondavi.com. Open from 9:00 A.M. to 5:00 P.M. daily May–October, 9:30 A.M. to 4:30 P.M. November–April. MasterCard, Visa, and American Express. Wheelchair-accessible.

Just north of the Oakville Cross Road on the east side of Highway 29, in a building with striking vertical redwood siding, is TURNBULL WINE CELLARS, founded in 1979 by famed architect William Turnbull, who died in 1997. Turnbull sold the winery in 1993 to publisher Patrick O'Dell, who rotates exhibits of his vast personal collection of works by Ansel Adams, Edward and Brett Weston, and other photographers in the tasting room.

A 1998 addition to the winery on its southwest side was designed in the same style as the winery in homage to Bill Turnbull. Don't miss the small old Ford truck collection in the parking lot. On the first Sunday of April–June, winemaker Jon Engelskirger hosts a preview of soon-to-be-bottled wines, from 1:00 to 4:00 P.M.

Fine points: There is a tasting fee of $3.00, which is refundable with a purchase. Featured wines: Old Bull Red (Cabernet Franc and Syrah blend), Sauvignon Blanc, Cabernet Sauvignon, Syrah, Zinfandel, Merlot. Owner: Patrick O'Dell. Winemaker: Jon Engelskirger. Cases: 25,000. Acres: 380.

Turnbull Wine Cellars, 8210 St. Helena Highway, Oakville 94562; phone (707) 963–5839 or (800) 887–6285, fax (707) 963–4407, Web site www.turn bullwines.com. Open from 10:00 A.M. to 4:30 P.M. daily. Tours and tastings by appointment only. Visa, MasterCard, American Express, Discover, and "checks that don't bounce." Wheelchair-accessible.

As you leave Turnbull, turn right and go 0.4 mile to CAKEBREAD CELLARS, one of the most upbeat and friendly wineries in the entire Napa Valley. Turn into Cakebread's driveway when you see vertical redwood siding like

TURNBULL WINE CELLARS

Turnbull's, but where the address number 8300 is written in red on a stone wall. There is no Cakebread sign.

Having left their mechanics garage in Oakland for greener vineyards, charming Jack and Dolores Cakebread bought the Sturdivant Ranch and started this winery in 1973. Bunches of friends helped them pound nails, trim roses, and generally build and fix up the place. Dolores cooked dinner for the weekend volunteer troops for several years, as the list of food and wine enthusiasts grew. Seven Cakebreads are now involved with the winery.

Now Chef Brian Streeter of Cakebread, who formerly worked at Domaine Chandon with Philippe Jeanty, gives four cooking classes a year. Culinary Director Dolores Cakebread hosts the annual fall American Harvest Workshop, featuring five chefs giving public classes. A winery with five kitchens and the tiny Cakebread Cellars Produce Center (which sells the extras from Dolores's one-and-a-half-acre vegetable and herb garden), Cakebread produces excellent wines. Instead of selecting a wine to go with food, the Cakebreads prefer to choose a wine and "cook to it."

As you walk into the barrel room, the tasting bar is to your left.

Fine points: The Cakebreads have assembled two exquisite binders containing Napa Valley restaurants' menus and chefs' histories for the convenience of visitors and staff. The binders are placed on two wine barrels in the back of the tasting room. Be sure to get on the mailing list for cooking classes, new wines, and special events. Cakebread's own

GRILLED POLENTA WITH WILTED GREENS AND SAUSAGE
from Cakebread Cellars Kitchen

INGREDIENTS:

3 cups polenta
10 cups water
1 Tbs kosher salt
½ cup Parmesan Reggiano, grated
2 links Italian Sausage, removed from casing
2 bunches spinach, Swiss Chard, or Escarole, washed and roughly chopped
2 cloves garlic, minced
2 Tbs olive oil
salt and pepper to taste
Pecorino Romano cheese

PREPARATION:

Bring salted water to rolling boil in a heavy-bottom pot. Whisk in polenta. Bring back to a boil, and turn to low heat. Cook for 25 minutes, stirring often. Stir in Parmesan cheese, and remove from the heat.

Spread polenta on an oiled sheet tray with a rim. Cover with plastic wrap, and press another sheet tray on top to flatten. Refrigerate until cool. When cool enough to handle, cut into 2-inch triangles.

In a medium-size pan, sauté sausage in olive oil. Using the back of a wooden spatula, break sausage up into small pieces. When sausage is cooked through, add garlic and greens and toss to wilt. Season with salt and pepper and reserve.

To serve: Grill polenta triangles over a barbecue or a well-seasoned griddle with ridges. Top with a small spoonful of sausage with greens, and garnish with a shaving of Pecorino Romano cheese. Enjoy with a glass of Cakebread Cellars Rubaiyat. Serves 15–18.

little cookbook, created to celebrate their first 25 years, is yours free for the asking. Cakebread enthusiastically serves alternative beverages to designated drivers. Tasting fee: $5.00 cellars tastings; $10.00 "vintners' tasting." Featured wines: Sauvignon Blanc, Chardonnay, Cabernet Sauvignon, Rubaiyat, Merlot.

Owners: Jack and Dolores Cakebread. Winemaker: Bruce Cakebread. Chef: Brian Streeter. Cases: 85,000. Acres: 82.

❧ Cakebread Cellars, 8300 St. Helena Highway, Rutherford 94573; phone (707) 963–5221 or (800) 588–0298, fax (707) 963–1067, e-mail cellars@cakebread. com, Web site www.cakebread.com. Open from 10:30 A.M. to 5:00 P.M. daily. Cellar tours: 10:30 A.M. and 2:00 P.M. Visa, MasterCard, and American Express. Wheelchair-accessible.

Just 0.1 mile up the line is SEQUOIA GROVE WINERY, the baby of Jim Allen, who holds degrees in psychology and political science; mined gold in Alaska; served as an interpreter for the United Nations in Germany, Australia, and Greece; worked as a correspondent for UPI in Europe; and taught at a college in Santa Fe, New Mexico.

Having thoroughly sipped and researched wine everywhere his travels took him, Jim is joined in this adventure of the soul by his brother, Stephen, and their wives, children, and mother. Turn right at the carved redwood burl sign.

The "sequoia grove" consists of seven trees surrounding the modest barn, a contrast to the flamboyant style of the Robert Mondavi Winery. Walking into the barn/tasting room, you will find the tasting bar to the right, barrels and hoses everywhere, and a welcoming committee of a couple of house dogs waddling through.

SEQUOIA GROVE WINERY

The personality and sociology of a winery really do contribute to the wine and aura of the endeavor—to say nothing of the local "Rutherford Dust" believed to yield the outstanding Cabernets grown on this Rutherford bench. (Hence the local effort to get the Bureau of Alcohol, Tobacco and Firearms to establish a Rutherford Bench appellation.)

With his robust, earthy energy, Jim transformed a more than century-old farmhouse into a winery whose wines have received platinum, gold, and silver medals throughout France and the United States. He also built "the first completely underground cellar in the floor of Napa Valley" to create perfect conditions for aging his wines—enduring criticism because of Napa's high water table, but resulting in excellent wines stored and cooled naturally at 55°F.

Fine points: Wine writer and critic Dan Berger named Sequoia Grove the 1988 American Winery of the Year, just twenty years after the winery's beginning. Wine writers from *Wine Spectator* and from Berger to Jerry Mead, Joe Pollack, and Bob Thompson rave about Sequoia Grove's Cabernet Sauvignon and Chardonnay. Tasting fee: $3.00 for four tastes. Featured wines: Cabernet Sauvignon, Chardonnay, Red Table Wine, Gewürztraminer. Owners: Jim and Steve Allen. Winemaker: Jim Allen. Cases: 30,000. Acres: 25.

❦ *Sequoia Grove Winery, 8338 St. Helena Highway, Rutherford 94573; phone (707) 944–2945, fax (707) 963–9411, Web site www.sequoiagrove.com. Open from 10:30 A.M. to 5:00 P.M. daily; tours by appointment. MasterCard, Visa, and American Express. Wheelchair-accessible.*

Just north of Sequoia Grove, don't miss what looks like an old barn and is— SAWYER CELLARS. When you walk in the door, you immediately smell the elegant old Inland Cedar walls used to restore the barn and set a cool, calm, and delightful ambience and creative environment.

Joanne and Charlie Sawyer started coming to the Napa Valley from Jacksonville, Florida, in the 1980s, enjoying the Napa Valley Wine Auction almost every year. Like many other wine aficionados, the Sawyers began spending more and more of their time here, and realized that they had to farm and make wine in the valley to "chase our dream." Sawyer is one of the few winery owners whom you might see working the vineyards with the crew.

After purchasing the property from Jaeger Vineyards in 1994, Sawyer, in one of his smartest moves, hired twenty-eight-year Robert Mondavi veteran Brad Warner as vice president and winemaker. Brad is often in the tasting room and will gently answer any questions you may have with deep knowledge of the Napa Valley.

You will also find terrific prices on hats, shirts, and leather totes, to say nothing of sensational wines.

Fine points: Tasting fee: $5 for three tastes. Featured wines: Estate-grown Cabernet Sauvignon, Merlot, Sauvignon Blanc. Tours and tastings available by appointment. Owners: Charles and Joanne Sawyer. Winemaker and Vice President: Brad Warner. Cases: 4,500. Acres: 50.

❦ *Sawyer Cellars, 8350 St. Helena Highway, Rutherford 94573; phone (707) 963–1980, fax (707) 963–3410, Web site www.sawyercellars.com. Open by appointment from 10:00 a.m. to 5:00 p.m. daily. Visa, MasterCard, and American Express. Wheelchair-accessible.*

Next up the line is the ST. SUPERY VINEYARDS & WINERY DISCOVERY CENTER, 0.2 mile north of Sequoia Grove. In stark contrast to Sequoia, St. Supery is a highly technical and marketed establishment owned by French agri-businessman Robert Skalli, who bought the property once owned by Edward St. Supery. Skalli built the winery next to Atkinson House, the white Queen Anne Victorian house built by Joseph Atkinson more than a hundred years ago.

As you drive into St. Supery, the Victorian and an educational vineyard are to your right, and the winery and Discovery Center are straight ahead. Offices are in a charming old wood pump house to your left. Notice wine bottle collection dating to 1884 just inside the front door of the Winery Discovery Center.

St. Supery's self-guided and guided tours are famously popular—including the SmellaVision Tour, where you can learn to discern those elusive "cherry" and "chocolate" flavors that cause wine writers to rhapsodize. Galleries of panoramic murals, photos, models, and interactive displays illustrate wine lore, to the delight of children and grown-ups alike.

CEO Michaela Rodeno came to St. Supery in 1988 after fifteen years

CRISPY & TANGY LEMON CHICKEN
from CEO Michaela Rodeno, St. Supery

INGREDIENTS:

4 cloves garlic, minced

1 Tbs minced fresh ginger

2 tsp soy sauce

2 tsp lemon juice

½ cup nonfat yogurt

1 tsp ground coriander

2 tsp ground cumin

1 tsp turmeric

1 tsp ground pepper

4 whole (including thigh) chicken legs, skinless

2 cups breadcrumbs

PREPARATION:

Combine the first 9 ingredients in a bowl, stirring to blend thoroughly. Cover the chicken legs with the marinade and refrigerate for 1–2 hours, or overnight for stronger flavor.

Preheat oven to 375°F. Remove chicken legs from marinade and coat in breadcrumbs. Bake chicken legs on a rack for 40–50 minutes until the juices run clear. Serves 4. Serve with Sauvignon Blanc.

Note: Removing the skin of the chicken eliminates about half of the fat. The lemony yogurt marinade replaces the fat with flavor.

with Domaine Chandon. Michaela is founder of Women for WineSense. She chaired the 1998 Napa Valley Wine Auction, holds an M.A. in French literature, and an M.B.A. from UC Berkeley. She lives on a vineyard in Oakville with

ST. SUPERY VINEYARDS & WINERY

her husband, Gregory, and their two children, and grows grapes in Pope Valley. Michaela's mission is to take the snobbishness out of wine and make it fun.

In one of the busiest tasting rooms anywhere, you will find not only great wines but also olive oils, dipping sauces, mustards, aprons, Gil's olives, Elena's pastas, books galore, corks, and videos. You can sit outside on the patio on green iron tables and chairs and check out St. Supery's booklet "Techniques for Living Well," available in the tasting room.

 Fine points: Besides its St. Supery and Bonverre labels, St. Supery's Mount Maroma wines are the only certified kosher for Passover and mevushal wines made in the Napa Valley. Be sure to get on the winery's mailing list for the funniest newsletter in the wine business. Tasting fee: One taste complimentary; $5.00 for "lifetime tasting pass." Guided tour with tasting $2.50, wine by the glass $2.50. Featured wines: St. Supery Sauvignon Blanc, Chardonnay, Semillon, Merlot, Cabernet Sauvignon, Meritage Red, Meritage White, Moscato; Bonverre Chardonnay, Semillon, Merlot, Cabernet Sauvignon, Viognier, Syrah, Zinfandel; Mount Maroma kosher Chardonnay, Cabernet Sauvignon. Owner: The Skalli Family. CEO: Michaela Rodeno. Winemaker: Michael J. Scholz. Chef: Sunny Cristadoro. Cases: 160,000. Acres: 485.

St. Supery Vineyards & Winery Discovery Center, 8440 St. Helena Highway,

Rutherford 94573; phone (707) 963–4507, fax (707) 963–4526, e-mail divinecab@stsupery.com, Web site www.stsupery.com. Open daily from 9:30 A.M. to 6:00 P.M. summer, 9:30 A.M. to 5:00 P.M. winter. Guided and self-guided tours. Visa, MasterCard, and American Express. Mostly wheelchair-accessible.

Next door, to the north, is PEJU PROVINCE, a lovely garden and winery that make you feel as if you have just walked into a home winery in Provence. What do you know? Madame Peju calls the trees down the driveway "Peju sycamores" because her husband trims the sycamores to look like a strong mistral wind blew the leaves and branches off one winter.

Notice Mendocino sculptor Welton Rotz's statuary in the parking lot and throughout the grounds. Enter through the brass-and-iron gate and enjoy the fountain and bell, Herta Peju's much-photographed, multicolored flowers, and French sculptured gardens.

Named the "Top Artisan Winery of the Year" in 1994 by *Wine & Spirits* magazine, its 1994 Cabernet Sauvignon was in the "100 Best Wines of the Year" at the 1997 World Wine Championships, and among the "50 Best American Red Wines" chosen by *Wine & Spirits Buying Guide–1998*; Peju should be on your must-stop list.

Anthony Peju grew up in Aix-en-Provence, studied film direction at UCLA, and owned an extremely successful nursery and garden supply business in Los Angeles. Tony and his wife, Herta, from Salzberg, Austria, scoured California

PEJU PROVINCE

PEJU BREADED TURKEY SLICES AU CABERNET
from Herta Peju, Peju Province

INGREDIENTS FOR THE MARINADE:

> *juice of 1 large lemon or ¼ cup lemon juice concentrate*
> *¼ cup Cabernet Sauvignon (optional)*
> *1 small onion, shredded*

INGREDIENTS FOR THE BREADED TURKEY:

> *1 lb turkey-breast slices, pounded flat*
> *3 whole eggs, lightly beaten (add salt)*
> *1 cup breadcrumbs, unflavored, spread on wax paper*
> *½ cup flour*
> *vegetable oil (should measure ⅜ inch up the side of a skillet)*
> *salt and pepper to taste*

PREPARATION:

Prepare marinade by mixing the ingredients in a bowl.

Pound turkey pieces very thin, and place in the bowl with marinade; add salt and pepper. Leave for at least 2 hours in the marinade.

Dredge each turkey slice in flour to coat well. Dip each slice in the egg mixture. Coat with breadcrumbs. As you turn each slice over, place a piece of wax paper over the slice and tap it into the breadcrumbs with the palm of your hand to get a better adherence of the crumbs to the meat. (You may prepare slices up to this point a few hours ahead of time.)

Heat the oil, preferably in a heavy skillet, over medium-high heat. Make sure oil is hot enough—it should sizzle—before you begin cooking. Cook as many slices at one time as will fit loosely in a single layer in the skillet. Remove them just as soon as they are brown and crisp on both sides, which will be very quickly because they are so thin.

Place the browned meat on paper towels, to absorb any excess oil. Serve piping hot with lemon wedges and cranberry sauce. Serves 4–6.

---

from Mexico to Napa Valley. They selected this site, finding it perfect.

We found an outstanding selection of wine and cookbooks, Jacques Pepin's pepper sauce, Sparrow Lane vinegars, and Scharffen Berger chocolate. Check out the elegantly sexy painted label on the $250 Cabernet bottle.

Fine points: If you are lucky, Events Coordinator Alan Arnopole, who considers every visit to be an event, might yodel or perform impromptu rap for you in the barrel room. Claiming to have learned to yodel by jumping over cactus, he sings to the wine and claims it just may be what makes Peju's wines so exceptional. Tasting fee: $3.00, $5.00 holidays. Featured wines: Chardonnay, Cabernet Sauvignon, Merlot, Cabernet Franc, Provence table wine, Karma Rosé, and Carnival (French Colombard). Owners: Anthony and Herta Peju. Winemaker: Anthony Peju. Cases: 12,000. Acres: 30 planted.

❧ ***Peju Province, 8466 St. Helena Highway, Rutherford 94573; phone (707) 963–3600, fax (707) 963–8680, Web site www.peju.com. Open from 10:00 A.M. to 6:00 P.M. daily.Visa and MasterCard. Wheelchair-accessible.***

Before you get into "downtown" Rutherford, Francis Ford Coppola's NIEBAUM-COPPOLA ESTATE is on your left. *Do not* turn west on Niebaum Lane. This is a road that does not lead to any wineries. Take the next left (west) off Highway 29 at the signs.

Flush with earnings from *The Godfather,* Eleanor and Francis Ford Coppola went to the Napa Valley to find a one-acre retreat, a place perfect for writing and creating. Instead they found this elegant estate, planted with vines in 1872 and acquired in the late 1870s by Finnish sea captain and Alaska fur trader Gustave Niebaum, who named the estate Inglenook. Niebaum's property was subdivided in 1969. Eventually, Heublein produced mass-market Inglenook wines in the winery facility. Coppola bought the Victorian estate home in 1975 and began to lust after the Inglenook Chateau to reunite the properties.

With *Bram Stoker's Dracula* profits, he paid most of the $10 million for the winery parcel in 1995, fulfilling his dream. The Coppolas turned the chateau into the Niebaum-Coppola Estate Winery and the Centennial Museum to showcase both the history of winemaking and Coppola's film career.

As you walk toward the chateau from the parking lot, you just know you have entered a movie set, complete with expansive walkways, decorative columns, and fountains. Once inside the heavy, cool building, notice the sweeping staircase made of exotic woods Coppola brought from Belize, where he owns a resort, Blancaneaux Lodge, in a remote rain forest. To the left facing the front of the building is a small shop, where you can buy a glass of wine, imported sodas, and apparel from both Neibaum-Coppola and Blancaneaux Lodge. The Coppola-conceived stained-glass window over the staircase depicts the historic estate's reunification.

As you turn right inside the front doorway, first you come to the tasting room, then to the retail shop. We were struck with the warm elegance of the Belize woods in these two vast rooms, as well as with the casual friendliness of the entire Niebaum-Coppola staff. You are welcome to sit at the long tables, sip wine, and enjoy the atmosphere and music, the latter of which comes from a player piano that sounds out songs written for *The Godfather* by Coppola's father, music publisher Carmine Coppola. The retail shop has such things as excellent Coppola herbed olive oils and pastas, Italian ceramics, linens, candles, copperware, cigars and accessories, and the best selections of French and Italian food books we have seen.

Be sure to pick up a copy of Coppola's *Zoetrope: All Story* magazine of short fiction, as well as a video or poster of Sofia Coppola's *The Virgin Suicides* movie.

Not incidental to all the movie jazz are some of America's finest vineyards and wines. Winemaker Scott McLeod (a well-known Italian name) received his B.S. in fermentation sciences at UC Davis and worked at Fattorie Isole e Olena in Tuscany's Chianti region and as winemaker at Fattorie Badia a Passignano in Tuscany, Robert Mondavi, Cain Cellars, and Charles Shaw and now Niebaum-Coppola.

 Fine points: Academy Award statues for *Patton, The Godfather,* and *The Godfather, Part II,* Coppola's 1948 Tucker from the film *Tucker,* Don Corleone's desk and chair from *The Godfather,* and Oscar-winning costumes from *Bram Stoker's Dracula* are all on display. Tasting fee: $7.50 (you may keep the glass). Featured wines: Niebaum-Coppola Estate wines, Rubicon (mostly Cabernet Sauvignon), Francis Ford Coppola Diamond Series including Chardonnay, Merlot, Zinfandel, Claret, Syrah, and Francis Coppola Presents: Talia Rosé, Bianco, and Rosso. Owners: Francis and Eleanor Coppola. Winemaker: Scott McLeod. Cases: 40,000. Acres: 195 planted of 1,654.

✣ *Niebaum-Coppola Estate, 1991 St. Helena Highway, Rutherford 94573; phone (888) COPPOLA, fax (707) 967–4178, e-mail rosso@aol.com, Web site www.niebaum-coppola.com. Open from 10:00 A.M. to 5:00 P.M. daily; tours at 10:30 A.M. and 2:30 P.M. Visa, MasterCard, American Express, and Discover. Wheelchair-accessible.*

Cross Highway 29 very carefully when you leave, turning left to go north only when it is clearly safe. Almost immediately you come to the Rutherford Cross Road, Rutherford Grill, and Beaulieu Vineyards on the right (east) side of the highway.

From the outside the RUTHERFORD GRILL looks like an ordinary roadside plastic-menu kind of place. It sits in front of Beaulieu Vineyards. Drive in

TONI'S MARINATED OLIVES
from Rutherford Grill

INGREDIENTS:

½ cup fresh tarragon leaves
¼ cup fresh thyme leaves
5 flat anchovy fillets
2 cups drained brine-cured black
   olives such as Kalamata or
   Niçoise
2 cups drained brine-cured green
   olives such as picholine
1 cup extra virgin olive oil
½ cup thinly sliced fennel bulb
   (anise)
¼ cup fresh lemon juice
2 Tbs minced onion
2 Tbs minced garlic
1 Tbs anise seeds
2 tsp fennel seeds
2 tap dried basil, crumbled
1 tsp freshly ground black pepper
2–4 Tbs balsamic vinegar

PREPARATION:

Chop tarragon and thyme, and mince anchovies. In a deep bowl stir together all ingredients except vinegar. Marinate olive mixture, covered and chilled, stirring occasionally, at least 6 hours and up to 3 days. Bring olive mixture to room temperature before proceeding.

To serve olives, transfer to a bowl with a slotted spoon and drizzle with vinegar to taste. Makes about 4½ cups.

Beaulieu's driveway and park either in its parking lot or behind the restaurant in a small lot shared with the tiny U.S. Post Office. Walk between the buildings to the patio and a bar (a poolside feeling without the pool), and on the right you will come to the dining-room entrance. Are you in for a surprise! Dark wood, comfy leather booths, leather-covered counter stools, and beamed ceilings with skylights set the tone. Opened linen napkins serve as "tablecloths" at the counter, where many singles drop in and enjoy a hearty, adventurous lunch or dinner. Expect lots of noise and action, with waiters and cooks shouting and repeating orders. Refresh with the milk bottles of chilled water.

The food is California hearty with a twist, and they "take rotisserie cooking very seriously." Try the roasted chicken with mashed potatoes ($13) or sliced leg of lamb ($17). You can get the same chicken as a chicken dip sandwich ($10) with cole slaw or in a "very wild rice" salad, or ask for a little of both for a unique salad orgy. Knife and Fork Barbecue Ribs are grilled over hardwood and basted with Texas Hill Country BBQ sauce and served with cole slaw and chips ($20). Rare tuna fans should try the Sashimi Tuna Salad ($15).

"This and Thats" include house-smoked-salmon appetizer ($11), Chicago Style Spinach and

Artichoke Dip ($8), and Blue Cheese Potato Chips ($7). The menu warns that "the California legislature has determined that eating is a dangerous endeavor. At Rutherford Grill we serve rare tuna, use raw eggs in our Caesar salad and grind chuck roast in house for all burgers. Upon request, we will be happy to change what we feel is a safe and delicious presentation and serve your food consistent with California Codes 113995, 113996, and 113998." Roast prime rib bones for your dog are available.

Vegetarians also enjoy the Napa Valley Vegetable Platter or club sandwich. The Caesar Salad (with raw egg) comes with homemade cornbread croutons. The Grill has a good Napa and Sonoma wine list.

✦↳*Rutherford Grill, 1180 Rutherford Road, Rutherford 94573; phone (707) 963–1792. No reservations accepted. Web site www.rutherfordgrill.com. Open from 11:30 A.M. to 9:30 P.M. daily summer, 11:30 A.M. to 9:00 P.M. daily winter. No reservations accepted. Visa, MasterCard, and American Express. Wheelchair-accessible.*

Seemingly behind the Rutherford Grill is the original champion of California Cabernet Sauvignon, BEAULIEU VINEYARDS, known in the local vernacular as "B.V." which, to some people, confuses it with Sonoma's Buena Vista Winery. Beaulieu is the oldest continuously producing winery in the Napa Valley.

The tasting room is in the newish, peaked-roof octagon building at the southeast corner of the Beaulieu complex. To the left of the entrance is a tree donated and planted by *Wine Spectator* in memory of Beaulieu's longtime winemaker and Napa wine guru, Andre Tchelistcheff.

Georges de Latour immigrated from Bordeaux, France, in the late 1800s to San Francisco, where he developed a successful cream of tartar business. After he and his bride, Fernande Romer, began their four-acre vineyard and named it Beaulieu ("beautiful place"), the dreaded phylloxera lice invaded, sending Georges back to France to find resistant rootstock. He brought some back to the Napa Valley, establishing a nursery and selling healthy vines to other vintners.

Surviving Prohibition by selling sacramental wines to the Catholic church in San Francisco, Georges switched from hard-to-get French oak barrels to American oak for his Cabernet Sauvignon, and he recruited Russian-born enologist Andre Tchelistcheff from Paris's Pasteur Institute in 1938. Two years later, Georges de Latour died, having won a gold medal and Grand Sweepstakes Award at the 1939 Golden Gate International Exposition for his 1936 Cabernet Sauvignon.

Having worked side by side with her husband, Madame de Latour took over management of the winery and named the Cabernet "Georges de Latour Private Reserve" in his honor. Relying on Tchelistcheff's expertise, she ran the winery until her death in 1952, expanding its prominence to the tables of

BEAULIEU VINEYARDS

Franklin D. Roosevelt and Winston Churchill.

Tchelistcheff gained worldwide fame and taught many prominent Napa winemakers, including Joseph Heitz, Miljenko Grgich, and Tom Selfridge. In 1963 he planted B.V.'s original Carneros vineyard, one of the first to realize the Carneros region's potential for fine grapes.

Beaulieu was sold to giant Heublein in 1969, which sold it in 1998 to United Distillers & Vintners (IDV Wines), which also owns Glen Ellen Winery in Sonoma Valley.

 Fine points: You can see Madame de Latour's influence in wine-making through the photos of Beaulieu Vintners' women and the placard honoring the "Women of Beaulieu." Tasting fee: $5.00 in Visitor Center; $25.00 in Reserve Room. Featured wines: Georges de Latour Private Reserve Cabernet Sauvignon, Tapestry Reserve Red Table Wine, Reserve Chardonnay, and Pinot Noir; the Signet Collection of Zinfandel, Ensemble (Rhone blend of Mourvedre, Grenache, Carignan, and Syrah); Napa Series of Cabernet Sauvignon, Merlot, Chardonnay, Pinot Noir, and Sauvignon Blanc; and Coastal Cabernet Sauvignon, Merlot, Zinfandel, Sauvignon Blanc, Chardonnay, and Pinot Noir. Many older vintages available. Owner: United Distillers & Vintners (UDV). Winemaker: Joel Aiken. Cases: 1,000,000. Acres: 1,100 Napa Valley.

❧ *Beaulieu Vineyards, 1960 St. Helena Highway South, Rutherford 94573; phone (707) 967–5200, Web site www.bvwine.com. Open from 10:00 A.M. to 5:00 P.M. daily; Reserve Room open from 10:00 A.M. to 4:30 P.M. Tours are from 10:00 A.M to 4:00 P.M. on the hour in winter, every half hour after 1:00 P.M. in summer. Visa, MasterCard, and American Express. Wheelchair-accessible.*

Just behind Beaulieu on Rutherford Road are nestled The Rancho Caymus Inn and La Toque.

Absolutely the most brilliant addition to the Napa Valley is Ken Frank's LA TOQUE IN the Rancho Caymas Inn, one of the valley's most lovely, and across Rutherford Road from La Luna Market.

Ken left his toque in Los Angeles to "take it easy" in the Napa Valley, but as creative people do, he couldn't help getting his juices going again. The cozy and calming decor in the dining rooms includes Spanish tile and fireplaces with candles burning in summer, and an elegant homelike deck that partly faces the inn's luxurious courtyard.

La Toque's menu changes weekly and frames a prix fixe ($72) six-course dinner with coffee and San Pellegrino and Evian waters included. The menu might include courses such as: white asparagus soup with duck prosciutto or seared Diver scallops with pea curry sauce; sugar drop tomato and fava bean risotto or corn flan in a savory lobster broth with spring vegetables; Niman Ranch shortribs braised all day in Rutherford red wine or seared rare tuna and foie gras with lentils and bacon; crispy-skinned salmon on rice beans with red pepper, balsamic onions, and red wine sauce or New Zealand venison with mustard spinach spaetzle and cabernet pissaladière with morels, ramps, and morbier; a selection of ripe cheese with toasted walnut bread; and for dessert, toasted coconut profiterolles with hot fudge sauce or Meyer lemon and huckleberry tart with crème fraîche sorbet.

❧ *La Toque, 1140 Rutherford Road, Rutherford 94573; phone (707) 963–9770; e-mail chefkenfran@latoque.com, Web site www.latoque.com. Beer and wine. Open for dinner Wednesday–Sunday. Visa, MasterCard, and American Express. Wheelchair-accessible.*

Just across the highway, in a slightly run-down, long wooden building, try Dione Carston's HACIENDA HARDWARE—COLECCION MEXICANA, where you will find a labyrinth of rooms crammed with great old peasant Mexican furnishings and home accessories, from huge, heavy wooden doors to light fixtures, furniture, a wooden highchair, an antique brass crib that swings, enormous pottery, and general house and garden doodads.

≫ Hacienda Hardware–Coleccion Mexicana, 1989 St. Helena Highway, Rutherford 94573; phone (707) 963–8850, fax (707) 963–8877, Web site www.haciendahardware.com. Open from 10:00 A.M. to 6:00 P.M. daily. Visa, MasterCard, American Express, and Discover. Not wheelchair-accessible.

Try to visit both Hacienda Hardware and Grgich Hills when you are driving south, so that you stay on the same side of Highway 29.

On the west side of the highway is GRGICH HILLS CELLAR, the baby of Miljenko (Mike) Grgich, a native of Croatia and champion of its independence from the former Yugoslavia, and Austin Hills of San Francisco's Hills Brothers Coffee family and fortune. As you turn across the railroad tracks, notice the Croatian flag flying. You will also see the Croatian shield on Grgich Hills wine labels.

Mike Grgich brought to this 1977 wine marriage a degree in viticulture and enology from the University of Zagreb, as well as long stints as chemist at Beaulieu Vineyards; chief enologist at Robert Mondavi Winery; and limited partner, winemaker, and vineyardist at Chateau Montelena, where he created the Chardonnay that won "Best Chardonnay" at the 1976 Paris Tasting and put Grgich firmly on the world wine-celebrity map. As a result of this triumph, his

GRGICH HILLS CELLAR

Chardonnay has been served to President Bill Clinton at the California Cafe in Los Gatos, Queen Elizabeth II, King Juan Carlos of Spain, and President Jose Sarney of Brazil. President Ronald Reagan took four cases to Paris for French President François Mitterrand.

For his contribution to the wine marriage, Austin Hills brought money, a fine coffee taster's palate, a refined sense of business management, and a reserved manner that allows Grgich to create and promote great wines. Hills's wife, Erika, owns Erika Hills Antiques, just south of St. Helena.

Together, Grgich and Hills agreed on the European tradition of concentrating on quality instead of quantity of their wines, and it has paid off. Their Chardonnay is often called the best in the world, the Cabernet Sauvignon consistently receives high ratings, and the Fumé Blanc has won several gold and silver medals. The Violetta, named for Grgich's daughter and manager, Violet, is a late-harvest dessert wine of Riesling and Chardonnay that received a 95 from *Wine Spectator* in 1997.

 Fine points: Enjoy the Old World feeling in the tasting room, with its dark wood, and take time to peruse the vast literature reprints and Croatian travel posters. You can also buy wooden boxes here for just $6.00 that are ideal for storing CDs. Tasting is free, but there's a $3.00 glass charge on weekends and holidays, because they can't get them all washed! Featured wines: Chardonnay, Fume Blanc, Cabernet Sauvignon, Zinfandel, Violetta Late Harvest. Owners: Mike Grgich and Austin Hills. Winemaker: Mike Grgich. Cases: 70,000. Acres: 200.

❧ *Grgich Hills Cellar, 1829 St. Helena Highway, Rutherford 94573; phone (707) 963–2784 or (800) 532–3057, fax (707) 963–8725. Open from 9:30 A.M. to 4:30 P.M. Visa, MasterCard, and American Express. Wheelchair-accessible.*

Recognizable by its bright pink, white, and purple petunias visible from Highway 29, RUTHERFORD GARDENS'S "Chateau Tomato" is a classically elegant vegetable stand featuring herb, flowers and veggie plants, snowball cauliflower, bok choy, cabbage, fennel, cut flowers, and whatever else is in season. The shade is pulled down when the outdoor stand is closed, and you pay your money in the honor box.

Rutherford Gardens, 1796 South St. Helena Highway, Rutherford 94573; phone (707) 967–8122. Open when they're open. No credit cards. Wheelchair-accessible.

North of Beaulieu, on the east side of Highway 29 just 0.9 mile away, is QUAIL RIDGE CELLARS & VINEYARDS, whose ponds and gardens offer one of the most peaceful of winery settings. Turn right onto Mee Lane.

QUAIL RIDGE'S DECK AND POND

Barrels line the cream-colored winery's eastern wall. Walk around to the western side of the building and onto the deck facing the lake and Highway 29 to get to the tasting room's entrance.

Inside the small, fun remodeled tasting room, you will find wine, juices, and water for picnicking on the deck. Notice Quail Ridge's new Fox Brook Chardonnay and Merlot, made from Jim Fetzer's biodynamically grown grapes from Mendocino.

 Fine points: Tasting fee: $4.00 for five tastes; $5.00 for four reserves, both refunded with purchase of wine. Featured wines: Sauvignon Blanc, Cabernet Sauvignon, Merlot, Cabernet Franc. Owners: Rutherford Benchmarks. Winemaker: Anthony Bell. Cases: 30,000. Acres: 10.

❧ *Quail Ridge Cellars & Vineyards, 1155 Mee Lane, St. Helena 94573; phone (707) 963–9783. Open from 11:00 A.M. to 6:00 P.M. daily summer; 10:00 A.M. to 5:00 P.M. daily winter. Visa and MasterCard. Wheelchair-accessible.*

On the west side of Highway 29, BEAUCANON NAPA VALLEY sports a new look with new paint, lots of red roses, shade trees around the parking lot, a bus turnaround, and huge lawns for picnicking. Even if you don't see any cars and the small window sign reads CLOSED, try the door.

The de Coninck family has been producing fine wines in St. Émilion,

Bordeaux, France, for more than 250 years. They bring part of the family and its knowledge and background to the Napa Valley. Intertwining French wine-making expertise with Napa Valley grapes, Jacques de Coninck established their La Crosse and estate Beaucanon labels in the 1980s.

 Fine points: No tasting fee. Featured wines: La Crosse and Beaucanon Chardonnay, Merlot, Cabernet Sauvignon. Owners: The de Coninck Family. Winemaker: Louis de Coninck. Cases: 30,000. Acres: 250.

❧ *Beaucanon Napa Valley, 1695 St. Helena Highway South, St. Helena 94574; phone (707) 967–3520, fax (707) 967–3527, e-mail beaucanon_winery@ msn.com. Open from 10:00 A.M. to 5:00 P.M. daily. Visa, MasterCard, American Express, and JCB. Wheelchair-accessible.*

To get to FRANCISCAN VINEYARDS, just north of Quail Ridge, turn east onto Galleron Road. Turn left immediately into Franciscan's driveway and parking lot. (Galleron Road will also take you to Sullivan Vineyards, the next stop after Franciscan.) Enjoy the brand-new elegant Visitors Center with a view looking up the Napa Valley.

The real story of Franciscan is far greater than just this winery, which has never had any relationship to Franciscan orders of the Catholic church. Until recently, Franciscan was owned by Germany's Eckes Family and its vintner/pres-

FRANCISCAN VINEYARDS

ident, Chilean Agustin Huneeus. (Huneeus owns other impressive properties, including the Quintessa Estate in Rutherford, huge Veramonte in Chile's Casablanca Valley, Mount Veeder Winery on the western slopes of Napa Valley, and Estancia Alexander Valley in Sonoma and Monterey counties.)

In 1998, Huneeus sold Franciscan to the huge Canandaigua Brands, which also owns Simi Vineyards in Asti. Huneeus stills serves as CEO.

As you approach the winery's entrance, enjoy the humor of the cement "Rutherford Bench," a pun on the Rutherford bench (land section) where the winery is located; the purple, lavender, and mustard banners; and a gigantic fountain, along with an eighteenth-century wine press in front. A peaceful, enclosed patio planted with roses, off the tasting room, provides a relaxing place to sample Franciscan wines and your picnic lunch.

 Fine points: Terylinn Buchanan manages both the Simi and Franciscan tasting rooms, turning them into warm, friendly havens. Be sure to notice prize-winning artist David Lance Goins designs for the Mount Veeder Winery labels. He also did graphics for Ravenswood Winery in Sonoma. Tasting fee: $4.00 regular wines, $10.00 reserves. Featured wines: Franciscan Chardonnay, Zinfandel, Merlot, Cabernet Sauvignon, Cuvée Sauvage Chardonnay, Magnificat; Quintessa; Veramonte Casablanca Estate Chardonnay, Cabernet Sauvignon, Merlot, and Primus Merlot; Mount Veeder Winery Cabernet Sauvignon, Merlot, and Zinfandel; Estancia Alexander Valley Estate Meritage, Cabernet Sauvignon, Merlot, and Duo; and Estancia Monterey County Estate Bottled Chardonnay, Pinot Noir, Reserve Chardonnay, and Reserve Pinot Noir. Owners: Canandaigua Brands. Winemaker: Larry Levin. Cases: Franciscan 120,000; Mount Veeder 10,000. Acres: nearly 4,000 worldwide.

✒ *Franciscan Vineyards, 1178 Galleron Road, St. Helena 94574; phone (707) 963–7111, fax (707) 963–7867, Web site www.franciscan.com. Open from 10:00 A.M. to 5:00 P.M. daily. Visa, MasterCard, American Express, and Discover. Wheelchair-accessible.*

If you leave the Franciscan parking lot by the southern exit onto Galleron Road, turn left (east) to SULLIVAN VINEYARDS. Turn left into Sullivan's gravel driveway. On your right will be the family's interesting two-story home with rolling lawns and a refreshing duck pond. The winery is to your left. Drive around to the south side of the winery and park. Zsa Zsa, the blond Lab, greets you with a green tennis ball firmly planted in his mouth.

You taste Sullivan's estate-grown wines with Sean Sullivan, co-winemaker and son of the founder, right in the middle of the winery with the inventory and barrels. Sean's sister, Kelleen, is obviously a talented painter, as her winery poster demonstrates. The Sullivans have been growing grapes here since 1978, and Jim Sullivan has been making wine since Sean was born in 1962. You can picnic at the table in the vegetable garden by appointment.

Fine points: Check out the elegant etched-crystal glasses ($32) as well as the tasteful shirts and well-priced hats ($20). Custom etched bottles are also available. Sullivan's special wines are all in the Bordeaux style and are promoted solely by word of mouth. The prized Coeur de Vigne is aged thirty-two months in oak. No tasting fee. Featured wines: Cabernet Sauvignon, Coeur de Vigne (80 percent Cabernet Sauvignon, 20 percent Merlot blend), Merlot. Owners: Jim and JoAnna Sullivan. Winemakers: Jim and Sean Sullivan. Cases: 3,700. Acres: 26.

❧ *Sullivan Vineyards, 1090 Galleron Road, Rutherford 94573; phone (707) 963–9646 or (877) BIG–REDS, fax (707) 963–0377, e-mail sean@fes.com, Web site www.sullivanwine.com. Open from 10:00 A.M. to 5:00 P.M. daily. Visa, MasterCard, and American Express. Wheelchair-accessible.*

As you leave Sullivan, turn right (west) onto Galleron to Highway 29. Turn right (north) to continue our tour.

The next three wineries moving north are on the west side of Highway 29.

RUTHERFORD GROVE WINERY AND NAPA VALLEY GRAPESEED OIL COMPANY is tucked back in a grove of century-old eucalyptus trees that envelop a lush expanse of lawns and gardens, protected from highway traffic and noise. This is just part of the reason it is the home of the Napa Valley Shakespeare Festival. Walking into Rutherford Grove is a cool, peaceful experience, thanks to its dark redwood walls, cement floors, rattan chairs, fireplace, and wrought-iron foot rail at the tasting bar. Vaulted ceilings and large windows showcase rotating art shows.

Rutherford Grove is worth a visit if only as a lesson in total-use recycling. In back of the winery, they make naturally cold-pressed grapeseed oil and compost residue from fifty vineyards, and sell back to vineyards for organic fertilizer. You can taste the grapeseed oils in the tasting room (but not the compost) and purchase Merlot Coffee chocolate sauce and Napa Valley Cabernet Salsa.

Founded by German-born Bernard Skoda, Rutherford Grove was eventually purchased by the Pestonis, originally a Swiss-Italian family from Monte Carasso. They have been in the Napa Valley since Albino Pestoni arrived four generations ago. Monte Carasso's thirteenth-century monastery appears on some of the red table wine labels. Bob and Marvin Pestoni carry on the family tradition at Rutherford Grove.

CAPONATA

Rutherford Grove Winery's Napa Valley Grapeseed Oil Company

Caponata is an excellent appetizer served with toasted baguette rounds or as a topping for pasta.

INGREDIENTS:

¾ cup Napa Valley Grapeseed Oil

¼ cup olive oil

1½ lb eggplant, peeled and cut into 1-inch cubes

2 large green peppers, cut into 1-inch pieces

1 onion, chopped

2 large cloves garlic, minced

1 28-oz can solid pack tomatoes, undrained

⅓ cup red wine vinegar

2 Tbs sugar

2 Tbs capers

2 Tbs tomato paste

2 tsp salt

½ cup fresh chopped parsley

½ cup pimento-stuffed green olives, rinsed, sliced thickly

½ tsp freshly ground pepper

2 tsp crumbled dried basil or ¼ cup loosely packed fresh basil leaves, sliced into ribbons

½ cup pine nuts sautéed in Napa Valley Grapeseed Oil

PREPARATION:

In a large heavy saucepan, combine ¾ cup Napa Valley Grapeseed Oil and ¼ cup olive oil, eggplant, green peppers, onion, garlic, and tomatoes. Cook for about 20–30 minutes or until just tender. Add wine vinegar, sugar, capers, tomato paste, salt, parsley, basil, green olives, and pepper. Cover and simmer for 15 minutes. Add pine nuts and serve warm or at room temperature. Makes 12 appetizers. Serve with Cabernet Sauvignon.

Fine points: Available only in fine restaurants and wine shops, Rutherford Grove's wines can be found at Domaine Chandon's restaurant, Dean & DeLuca, and Mustards, Viognier in Palo Alto, and Chasen's in Beverly Hills. The tasting fee of $3.00 ($5.00 for

WHOLE ROASTED PORK LOIN WRAPPED WITH PANCETTA
AND STUFFED WITH DRIED FRUIT
*from Rutherford Grove Winery and Napa Valley Grapeseed
Oil Company*

INGREDIENTS:

4–5 lb pork loin, center cut, trimmed of fat
½ lb pancetta, sliced thinly
20 dried apricots
¼ lb golden raisins
1 750-ml bottle dry red wine
1 small bunch sage, finely chopped
1 small bunch thyme, finely chopped
salt and pepper to taste

PREPARATION:

Macerate until soft (approximately 1 hour) the apricots and golden raisins in separate bowls in enough of the red wine to cover. Preheat oven to 325°F.

Lay the pork loin onto a cutting board. Keeping the knife parallel to the board, slice lengthwise, leaving a 1/2-inch thickness unsliced on the other side (don't slice all the way through). Open up the pork loin like a book.

Place a layer of apricots down the center of the butterflied loin, then cover with a layer of raisins. Close the loin back to its original shape, tie in 3 or 4 places with string, and season thoroughly with sage, thyme, salt, and pepper. Wrap the strips of pancetta around the width of the entire loin until it is completely covered.

Roast in a 325°F oven, turning once while cooking to brown both sides, until medium doneness (about 40 minutes). Remove from oven and let rest in a warm spot. Serves 8.

reserves) is refundable with purchase. Featured wines: Sauvignon Blanc, Chardonnay, Helena Rosé (Rosé of Cabernet Franc), Petite Sirah, Merlot, Sangiovese, Cabernet Sauvignon. Owners: Bob and Marvin Pestoni. Winemakers: Andy Pestoni and Bob Pepi. Cases: 6,000. Acres: 30+.

⁂ *Rutherford Grove Winery and Napa Valley Grapeseed Oil Company, 1673 St. Helena Highway, Rutherford 94573; phone (707) 963–0544, fax (707)*

963–3150, e-mail seedoil@fes.net, Web site www.Rutherfordgrove.com or seedoil. com. Open from 10:00 A.M. to 4:30 P.M. daily. Visa, MasterCard, and American Express. Wheelchair-accessible.

WHITEHALL LANE WINERY has created a new state-of-the art tasting and winemaking facility with adventurous angles and gift and logo-wear merchandise.

The Leonardini family of San Francisco bought the estate in 1993 and have been at work updating the wine and facilities ever since, first with winemaker Gary Galleron and now with Dean Sylvester. Sylvester comes to Whitehall Lane from Newton Vineyard, Chimney Rock Winery, and Mario Perelli-Minetti Winery. Besides being readily accessible at the winery, you might catch Sylvester playing guitar as his therapy "outlet" on the nightclub circuit with musician Gary Yoder. Their olive oil and balsamic vinegar are excellent.

Fine points: Don't miss the barrel tasting tours at 1:00 and 4:00 P.M. or the characters who work here. Tasting fee: $5.00, and you can keep the glass or apply fee to a purchase. Featured wines: Sauvignon Blanc, Chardonnay, Merlot, Cabernet Sauvignon, Belmuscato. Owner: Thomas Leonardini. Winemaker: Dean Sylvester. Cases: 25,000. Acres: 90.

❧ *Whitehall Lane Winery, 1563 St. Helena Highway, St. Helena 94574; phone (707) 963–9454, fax (707) 963–7035, Web site whitehalllane.com. Open from 11:00 A.M. to 6:00 P.M. daily. Visa, MasterCard, and American Express. Wheelchair-accessible.*

For a little side trip, turn right (east) onto Zinfandel Lane to RAYMOND VINEYARD & CELLAR. At 0.6 mile east of Highway 29, turn right (south) at Raymond's signs, go through the gates, and go another 0.2 mile.

On the outside, Raymond looks like a large California ranch house with gray vertical wood siding and stone walls and gorgeous renunculas in the garden. Inside, the tasting room, with its carpeting and dining table, make you feel as if you're in someone's home. You will find green-and-burgundy aprons, pastas, VinTea, Vintners Kitchen food products, Vine Village and French Press oils, and a Raymond Vineyard 550-piece puzzle.

Roy Raymond, Sr., began working in the barrel room of Beringer Winery in 1933, married winemaker Otto Beringer's daughter, Jane, worked his way to manager, and left Beringer when Nestlé Corporation bought it. Raymond bought ninety acres here on Zinfandel Lane in 1971, with the first grapes harvested in 1974, developing highly revered Cabernet Sauvignons. Even though the late Roy Sr. had sold the winery to Kirin Beer of Japan, he was often seen

WHITEHALL LANE NAPA CABERNET RED RISOTTO
from Whitehall Lane Winery

INGREDIENTS:

1 bottle Whitehall Lane Napa Cabernet
¼ cup butter
2 Tbs chopped fresh thyme
1½ cups Arborio rice (risotto)
3 cups canned vegetable broth
¼ cup grated Parmesan cheese
1 14-oz can cannellini beans, rinsed and drained (any white bean will work)
1½ cups red onion, chopped
4 cups thinly sliced radicchio
1¾ cups Whitehall Lane Napa Cabernet
1 cup toasted walnuts, chopped
salt and pepper to taste

PREPARATION:

Uncork the Cabernet, pour a glass for taste approval and for yourself! Remember, do not get too carried away in the enjoyment of the wine—you need 1¾ cups for the recipe itself, leaving approximately 2 glasses for dinner.

Melt the butter in a large saucepan over medium heat. Add onion and saute until soft and just beginning to brown, about 5 minutes. Mix in 1½ Tbs thyme. Add the sliced radicchio and the rice. Sauté until the radicchio wilts, about 3 minutes.

Meanwhile, begin to simmer the vegetable broth in a separate pot. Slightly increase heat and add the beans and 1 cup of wine to the mixture. Simmer until the wine is absorbed and stir. Add remaining ¾ cup of wine, while continuing to simmer, for about 3 more minutes.

When all of the wine is absorbed in the risotto, add the vegetable broth to the mixture. Stir to combine, cover, and simmer until the liquid is absorbed and the rice is tender but firm in the center. Stir in the remaining ½ Tbs thyme, the cup of walnuts, and add the ¼ cup Parmesan cheese. Season with salt and pepper and stir to combine. Transfer to a bowl, ready to serve with additional Parmesan at the table. Serves 4.

on his tractor mowing the winery's lush lawns, right up until his death in 1998. Roy Jr., Walter, and Craig Raymond, great-grandsons and great-great-grandson of Beringer, continue to manage Raymond.

Fine points: Tastings free except $2.50 for limited-production or hard-to-find wines. Featured wines: Sauvignon Blanc, Chardonnay, Pinot Noir, Cabernet Sauvignon, Merlot; Amber Hill Chardonnay, Cabernet Sauvignon, Merlot; Generations Chardonnay and Cabernet Sauvignon. Owner: Kirin Beer. Winemakers: Walter Raymond, Kenn Vigoda. Cases: 300,000. Acres: 600.

Raymond Vineyard & Cellar, 849 Zinfandel Lane, St. Helena 94574; phone (707) 963–3141 or (800) 525–2659, fax (707) 963–8498, Web site wwwray mondwine.com. Open from 10:00 A.M. to 4:00 P.M. daily. Visa, MasterCard, American Express, and JCB. Wheelchair-accessible.

MILAT VINEYARDS is one of the few remaining old wineries still run by the original owner family. Bob and Mike Milat and their wives, Joyce and Carolyn, run the whole show; in fact, they are the show. Bob and Mike grew up on the property where their family has been growing and selling grapes since 1949, eventually realizing that their high-demand grapes might just make good wine for them, too. They started making wine in 1986, and you can buy these personal and reasonably priced vintages only here in the tasting room. Be sure to stop and enjoy stories about Croatian food and wine.

MILAT VINEYARDS

Fine points: The Milat family also offers three guest rooms in cottages in the vineyard and a converted loft in the barn, with queen beds, full baths and patios, coffeepots, and refrigerators from $90 to $105. Tasting fee of $2.00 for logo glass. Featured wines: Chardonnay, Chenin Blanc, Sweet Chenin Blanc, Zivio blush table wine, Zinfandel, Merlot, and Cabernet Sauvignon. Owners: The Milat Family. Winemakers: Bob and Mike Milat. Cases: 3,000. Acres: 22.

❧ Milat Vineyards, 1091 St. Helena Highway South, St. Helena 94574; phone (707) 963–0758 or (800) 54–MILAT, fax (707) 963–0168, Web site www. milat.com. Open from 10:00 A.M. to 6:00 P.M. daily. Visa, MasterCard, American Express, and Discover. Wheelchair-accessible.

As we approach the city of St. Helena, the winery and specialty food forests thicken. Winery buildings range from expensive cement blocks to expensive charming old Victorian homes and wood barns. Locals refer to this area as St. Helena Highway South, with St. Helena as the center of the universe, of course. To mapmakers, it is simply Highway 29.

But whatever it's called, it is an engrossing (interesting as well as fattening!) food-and-wine mecca that even the most casual food-and-wine fans will enjoy.

On the left (west) side of Highway 29, heading north, FLORA SPRINGS WINE COMPANY has a brand new tasting room. To get to the tasting room, turn west into the driveway just past Zinfandel Lane and Inglewood Avenue.

Owner John Komes commissioned Richmond, Virginia, artist Happy the Artist to paint the cartoonish murals depicting wine growing and the winemaking process on the tasting-room walls. Enjoy the exhibits of well-known artists' work in the tasting room.

If you want to visit the first Flora Springs vineyard and wineries, head to 1978 West Zinfandel Lane in St. Helena. The Komes purchased the "old ghost winery and vineyard in the western foothills of the Napa Valley" in 1977. Komes' children, John and Julie, got caught up in the venture. John used his skills as a contractor and businessman to renovate the historic buildings and begin the winery, and Julie's husband, Pat Garvey, left his job as a college administrator to tend the vineyards. After two vintages of learning and making the wine themselves, the family invited Ken Deis to become winemaker, with impressive results.

Fine points: Tasting fee: $5.00 regular wines, $8.00 regulars and reserves. Flora Springs' 1991 Reserve Cabernet was selected #3 wine in the world in *Wine Spectator's* "Top 100 Wines of the Year." Flora Springs' featured wines: Chardonnay, Sauvignon Blanc, Soliloquy, Cabernet Sauvignon, Merlot, Pinot Grigio, Sangiovese,

Trilogy. Owners: Jerome and Flora Komes, Winemaker: Ken Deis. Cases: 55,000. Acres: 650.

❧ *Flora Springs Wine Company, 677 St. Helena Highway, St. Helena 94574; phone (707) 967–8032, fax (707) 963–5711, Web site www.florasprings.com. Open from 10:00 A.M. to 5:00 P.M. daily. Visa, MasterCard, and American Express. Wheelchair-accessible.*

Behind Flora Springs is 29 JOE'S COFFEE HOUSE, which also joins Dean & DeLuca by parking lot. Enjoy the mosaics at the cafe's entrance. This spot features good coffee, coffeebeans, Sweetie Pies cakes and pastries (the best!), sandwiches, salads, local art and music, checkers that you can pick up at the coffee bar and take to your table (chess is already set up), frozen drinks, and poetry readings. We particularly like the green chairs and tables right outside the cafe on the patio, on the non-parking-lot side. Use the drive-up window if you're in a hurry.

❧ *29 Joe's Coffee House, 677 St. Helena Highway, St. Helena 94574; phone (707) 967–0820. Open from 5:30 A.M. to 5:30 P.M. Monday–Friday, 6:30 A.M. to 3:30 P.M. Saturday, 7:30 A.M. to 3:30 P.M. Sunday. No credit cards. Wheelchair-accessible.*

Right next door, and in dramatic contrast to 29 Joe's, is famed DEAN & DELUCA, the Manhattan "Purveyors of Fine Food and Kitchenware" founded on Prince Street in SoHo by former publishing executive Joel Dean and former history teacher and son of a food importer Giorgio DeLuca. Leslie Rudd owns a controlling interest in Dean & DeLuca and is responsible for its successful expansion, with Giorgio DeLuca continuing day-to-day management and his global search for the finest food products.

You can enter Dean & DeLuca from the parking lot to the store's south; or through the southern front door, which takes you into the fresh local produce, breads, and delicacies sections; or through the northern front door into the wine shop, where Hyde Park CIA graduate John Hardesty oversees 1,200 California wines, cognacs, armagnacs, mezcals, and cigars in a walk-in humidor, where his best customers have their own lockers.

In the produce department you might find black trumpet or hedgehog mushrooms ($14.00 per pound), red and white Belgian endive ($5.95 per pound), and Della Fattoria and Artisan breads. The deli is like no other and offers cherry peppers stuffed with provolone and prosciutto ($1.25 each), Ozark and Serrano hams, salted capers, thirteen types of olives, duck confit ($11.95 per pound), foie gras, and various herrings.

Forty of the world's best olive oils, mustards, and other delicacies lead you

POLENTA WITH WILD MUSHROOMS
from Dean & DeLuca

INGREDIENTS FOR THE POLENTA:

1 cup polenta
¼ cup Parmesan cheese, grated
2 cups water

2 cups whole milk
2 oz unsalted butter
2 Tbs chives, finely chopped

PREPARATION:

Bring milk, water, and salt to a boil. Slowly whisk in polenta to avoid lumps. Cook approximately 30–45 minutes on low heat until polenta is soft. Remove from heat, stir in butter, cheese, and chives. Pour into molds or pour into a 1/2-sheet pan, then chill and cut into desired shapes. Reheat with roasted mushrooms on top.

INGREDIENTS FOR THE WILD MUSHROOMS:

8 shiitake mushrooms, stems removed and cut in quarters
12 oyster mushrooms, stems removed and cut in quarters
2 portobello mushrooms, stems removed, diced
3 cloves garlic, finely diced
1 sprig rosemary, cleaned, stems removed, chopped
1 sprig thyme, cleaned, stems removed, chopped
enough olive oil to lightly coat
2 tsp salt
1 tsp white pepper

PREPARATION:

Combine mushrooms, garlic, herbs, and olive oil. Season with salt and white pepper. Roast in 350°F oven approximately 7–9 minutes, or sauté.

Serve over polenta. Serves 4.

to the kitchenware section and finally to the cooked food case under the direction of Executive Chef Harold Imbrunetti and his highly qualified crew. You might find rotisserie pork loin with stoneground mustard and apricot preserves, chicken salad, yellow corn polenta with roasted mushrooms, or green-chile potato salad. You can even get elegant sandwiches to go for your picnic ($6.95).

The take-home dinner menu changes weekly.

The espresso bar offers fresh fruit smoothies, shakes, and coffees, with stand-up cafe tables, and excellent rest rooms down the hall.

❧ *Dean & DeLuca*, 607 South St. Helena Highway, St. Helena 94574; phone (707) 967–9980, fax (707) 967–9983, Web site www.deandeluca.com. Open from 9:00 A.M. to 7:00 P.M. daily, Espresso bar open at 7:30 A.M. Monday–Saturday, 9:00 A.M. Sunday. MasterCard, American Express, and Discover. Wheelchair-accessible.

THE SPOT, in all its glory, is next to Dean & DeLuca. You can't miss the pink arch, with the patio's turquoise railing and Coca-Cola umbrellas facing the parking lot and highway and neon signs everywhere. Posters of Elvis, *Leave It to Beaver,* and old movies welcome you to this retro joint where you order at the neon-lighted counter and choose between grease and grease. Thousands of Napa Valley locals stream in here daily for their burgers, fries, onion rings, and a pretty good salad bar (brought back from oblivion by public demand).

The floors are black-and-white-checked linoleum, and you can sit at red plush booths or on red-seated padded chairs at gray formica tables. Beef, turkey, chicken, emu, or veggie burgers come with fries or onion rings; and fried chicken, fries, and slaw in a basket cost a whopping $6.25. You can enjoy eight microbrews and local wines. Breakfast has its regulars, too.

❧ *The Spot*, 587 South St. Helena Highway, St. Helena 94574; phone (707) 963–2844. Open from 7:00 A.M. to 9:00 P.M. Sunday–Thursday, 7:00 A.M. to 10:00 P.M. Friday, Saturday. Beer and wine. Visa and MasterCard. Wheelchair-accessible.

On the east side of Highway 29 (here called St. Helena Highway South), you will find three great wineries right next door to one another. The first one you will come to going north is the venerable and fun V. SATTUI WINERY. Turn east onto White Lane and go over the railroad tracks to the winery's cool lawns and warm welcomes. If the parking lot is too crowded, drive farther east on White Lane to additional parking.

Sattui is under-known for its fabulous delicatessen, pastries, and, of course, prize-winning wines, which are sold only here at the winery.

Vittorio Sattui came to California from Carsi, near Genoa, Italy, and eventually made wine in San Francisco's North Beach Italian neighborhood—but who wasn't making their own wine then? Purchasing grapes from the Napa Valley, Sattui moved his operation to Bryant Street, then closed down during Prohibition.

Vittorio's great-grandson, Daryl Sattui, began to reestablish the family winery, this time in the Napa Valley, in 1975, with the goal of making "wines my

V. SATTUI WINERY

great-grandfather Vittorio would be supremely proud of." He even slept in a sleeping bag on the tasting room floor and took showers from the winery's hose, since he couldn't afford housing rent.

Opening the winery to the public on March 4, 1976, Daryl served wine tastes from a wooden plank bridging two barrels and kept the wine sales money in a wooden-box "cash register."

Daryl used a hand bottler and his great-grandfather's ninety-year-old corking machine to bottle his first wines, and traded several cases of wine to a college friend to modify the original, historic label. Having no money to advertise, he hoped the wine would sell itself, and it has. And, since all Sattui wines are sold here, a near-cult of devotees has developed of people who clamor to buy their wines directly from the winery.

In addition to the original winery building, where the delicatessen and tasting room are now, Sattui built a historically accurate, elegant stone winery building in 1985. It looks like one from the 1890s, with 3-foot-thick, hand-hewn stone walls and heavy rustic timbers. Be sure to take yourself on a self-guided tour of the stone building's underground cellars and small caves, where you will find a fascinatingly musty historical museum chronicling Sattui's and California's wine history.

Two acres of lawns, picnic tables. and century-old oak trees invite hundreds of picnickers to enjoy themselves daily. Kids run and scream, grandparents bask, and parents watch them all, eating and sipping wine all the way.

As you enter the old winery, the first thing you smell is cheese, not wine. And for good reason. An enormous Swiss Emmenthaler wheel and 200 varieties of imported and a few domestic cheeses greet you to the left of the door, along with Molinari salami, Sciambria and Acme breads, strawberries, apples, Dijon mustards, French cornichon pickles, Kalamata olives, Italian pepperoncini, and an entire wall of prepared-daily deli foods. Be sure to check out Sattui's own chocolate sauce and their Monastero Le Vallesi extra virgin olive oil from Tuscany. The charming staff offer you a choice of the day's cheese-tasting selections. Cheese Shop Manager Jean Varner came to Sattui from Oakville Grocery, where she served as assistant manager in charge of "charcuteries," specialty foods, and meats.

One of our most astounding food discoveries in the Napa Valley is Sattui's delicatessen, for which Daryl hired Executive Chef Charlotte Combe, the only American ever to apprentice (for nearly twenty years) under PBS television chef Jacques Pepin. Charlotte, whose delightful Scottish brogue surprises visitors to an Italian-American winery, ran the Charlotte Combe Cooking School in Woodside, California for many years. Charlotte trained primarily in Bologna in Italy's Emilia-Romagna province, thought by many to produce the finest food in Italy.

Charlotte told Kathleen that "Daryl Sattui gave me carte blanche to do it my European way." And has she ever. Feast your eyes upon fresh foods and reasonable prices of fresh artichokes ($2.95), oven-roasted salmon with remoulade ($4.95), smoked trout, Russian and American caviar, Gulf prawns with mustard sauce ($1.50 each or five for $6.95), steamed asparagus with olive oil ($6.95 per pound), and prosciutto di Parma.

If you attend one of Sattui's Harvest Balls, held two weekends in late September, often you can arrive three days early and participate in Charlotte Combe's cooking schools to learn how to prepare the dinner served at the balls.

Watch for annual Tax Relief and Crush Parties, full of music, fine foods, fine Sattui wines, and added discounts on case purchases. This is one mailing list you must get on.

 Fine points: Sattui's Preston Vineyard Cabernet Sauvignons often win medals, including a best Cab in California at the California State Fair. According to Sattui's brochure, *Wine Spectator* noted that V. Sattui has "garnered more gold medals in the big taste-offs than any other single winery in the Napa Valley." A must-stop! No tasting fee.

Featured wines: Chardonnay, Sauvignon Blanc, Johannisberg Riesling, White Zinfandel, Gamay Rouge, Suzanne's Vineyard Zinfandel, Howell Mountain Zinfandel, Merlot, Cabernet Sauvignon including three vineyard designates, Blanc de Noirs Champagne, and dessert wines Muscat, Madeira, Colli del Trasimeno, Felicita, and Vin Santo. Owner: Daryl Sattui. Winemaker: Rick Rosenbrand. Cases: 45,000. Acres: 750.

V. Sattui Winery, 111 White Lane, St. Helena 94574; phone (707) 963–7774 or (800) 799–2337, fax (707) 963–4324, Web site www.vsattui.com. Open from 9:00 A.M. to 6:00 P.M. daily, closes 5:00 P.M. November–February; Visa and MasterCard. Tasting room is wheelchair-accessible, museum is not.

Right next door, to the north, is HEITZ WINE CELLARS, which is now just the winery's tasting room, with the actual winery currently located in a restored, 1898 stone cellar originally built by Anton Rossi on a 160-acre property on Taplin Road, east of St. Helena. This is the original, where Alice and Joseph Heitz built a reputation and cult following for both Heitz's wines and his interesting personality.

Joe was from Illinois and Alice from South Dakota. They met in California in the 1940s. Joe earned two degrees in enology at UC Davis and spent seven years as understudy to the famed wine guru Andre Tchelistcheff at Beaulieu Vineyards. Joe and Alice purchased their first vineyard (eight acres) in 1961.

The three Heitz children grew up in the vineyards and business, and now David serves as winemaker, having made the 1974 commemorative bottling of Heitz Cellars' now famous Martha's Vineyard Cabernet Sauvignon as his first solo effort. Kathleen directs national and international sales and marketing, working with a biology degree from studies in Switzerland and at the University of Oregon. And Rollie oversees the company's finances and properties with his business degree from Santa Clara University.

When we visited the tasting room, our host's blue Rolls Royce Corniche was the lone automobile in the parking lot. The redwood structure looks like a mountain cabin on the outside and an elegant parlor on the inside. The teensy, carpeted, and subdued tasting room, with interesting corkscrews and calming classical music, focuses on a glass-topped table, where you are served.

In the Heitz's case, "Martha's Vineyard" refers to vineyards owned by Tom and Martha May near Oakville, while "Bella Oaks" refers to Barney and Belle Rhodes' vineyard abut 3 miles north of Martha's Vineyard, on the southwest side of Rutherford.

 Fine points: Joe Heitz actually pioneered single vineyard designation wines in California. He has been feted as one of the world's thirty top winemakers at La Tour d'Argent in Paris. No tasting fee. Be sure to get on this mailing list so you hear about the next

Martha's Vineyard Cabernet Sauvignon release, expected in January or February 2001, and get in line with other Heitz devotees. Other wine releases and tastings occur in February. Another must-stop. Featured wines: Chardonnay, Joe's White, Martha's Vineyard Cabernet Sauvignon, Napa Valley Cabernet Sauvignon, Bella Oaks Cabernet Sauvignon, Zinfandel, Grignolino, Ryan's Red (named for redheaded, first Heitz grandchild Ryan Thomas Heitz) and Grignolino Rosé, Grignolino Port. Owner: Joseph Heitz. Winemakers: Joseph and David Heitz. Cases: 40,000. Acres: 375.

Heitz Wine Cellars, 436 St. Helena Highway South, St. Helena 94574; phone (707) 963–3542, Web site www.heitzcellars.com. Open from 11:00 A.M. to 4:30 P.M. daily. Visa, MasterCard, American Express, Diners Club, and JCB. Wheelchair-accessible.

Just north of and next door to Heitz Cellars you will find LOUIS M. MARTINI, one of the oldest wineries in the Napa Valley. Three generations of colorful Martinis (men, that is) have dedicated themselves to finding the best land for growing grapes and matching soils and microclimates, following the old country Italian traditions.

In 1906, the year of the San Francisco earthquake and great fire, Louis M. Martini and his father, Agostino, made their first wine in San Francisco. They eventually built a 60,000-gallon winery in the Bayview District. Louis M. took his wine on his market wagon when he was selling clams and mussels on Polk Street and sold his first gallon to the fish-shop owner, who gave a taste to the chicken-shop owner. Then *he* bought a gallon and gave a sample to the butcher next door, who also bought a gallon, and off to the wine races went Louis M. Martini. He opened the L. M. Martini Grape Products Company in Kingsburg, California, in 1922, to make sacramental and "medicinal" wines and grape concentrates.

Anticipating the repeal of Prohibition, the Martinis moved to the Napa Valley in 1933 to build their winery, one of the first to use cold fermentation. Five years later Louis M. purchased the Goldstein Ranch in Sonoma Valley and made it Italian-American by renaming it Monte Rosso. By 1942 Louis M. owned the Stanley Ranch in Carneros, foreseeing the potential of the now-famous winegrowing region that flops on both sides of the Napa–Sonoma County border.

In the early 1950s Louis M. introduced wind machines to protect vineyards from winter frosts and worked with UC Davis enologists to pioneer clonal research on Chardonnay, Pinot Noir, and Riesling grapes. By 1954 Louis P. Martini became the second-generation Louis Martini winemaker, introducing gondolas for grape harvesting in 1957. In the late '60s he bot-

ROASTED CORNISH GAME HENS
from Carolyn Martini, Louis M. Martini

INGREDIENTS:

For the stuffing:
1 cup long-grain white rice
2 cups chicken stock
½ tsp salt
1 Tbs butter
¼ tsp. ground cinnamon
¼ tsp. ground cardamom
1 tsp freshly grated orange rind
½ cup pitted dates, chopped
½ cup pecans, chopped

FOR THE CORNISH GAME HENS:

6 Cornish game hens
6 Tbs butter, softened
½ cup orange marmalade
¼ cup Louis M. Martini Gewürtztraminer
salt and pepper

PREPARATION:

Stuffing: Bring chicken stock, salt, butter, cinnamon, cardamom, and orange rind to a boil. Add rice, cover, and reduce heat. Simmer 20 minutes, then let sit 5 minutes. Fluff with a fork and stir in dates and pecans. Preheat oven to 350°F.

Cornish game hens: Rinse game hens and pat dry. Salt and pepper cavity and stuff with a generous ½ cup of rice mixture. Secure legs with kitchen string, and place hens in a roasting pan. Brush the hens with softened butter and roast for 30 minutes.

Melt the orange marmalade with white wine and reduce slightly. Raise oven temperature to 400°F, baste hens with marmalade mixture, and continue roasting an additional 20–30 minutes or until juices run clear and hens are browned. Baste occasionally with the marmalade mixture, and if the hens start to darken too much, cover with aluminum foil. Serve chilled Louis M. Martini Gewürztraminer. Serves 6.

tled the first Merlot in the United States. (Sadly, Louis P. Martini died in September 1998.)

The Martini family continues the tradition. Louis M.'s granddaughter, Carolyn Martini, is now president. Louis P.'s son, Michael, graduated from UC Davis in enology and eventually became the third-generation Martini winemaker.

While the winery building itself has a slightly industrial look, it's what's inside that counts. Just as you walk in the door, stop for a minute before the historic cases in the vestibule. Placards in the cases give a quick, succinct course in winemaking. The Louis Martini "Food First" aprons tell the Martini story: Its wines are made to accompany food, to enhance its flavor, and to celebrate the sharing of mealtime among family and friends.

Pick up a wicker basket in the tasting room to load up with pasta sauces, salsas, olives, oils, vinegars, cherries, and the Louis Martini video.

LOUIS M. MARTINI'S CHRISTMAS EVE ZABAGLIONE
from Carolyn Martini, Louis M. Martini

INGREDIENTS:

For each person:
1 Tbs Louis M. Martini Cream Sherry
1 Tbs powdered sugar
1 egg yolk

PREPARATION:

Mix all ingredients together in the top of a double boiler (preferably heavy weight). Over simmering water, never allowing the water to touch the bottom of the pan, beat with an electric hand beater until thick and fluffy—10 or so minutes. Serve immediately in small glasses with freshly grated nutmeg over the top. Crisp, plain butter or walnut cookies, Italian anise bars, or ladyfingers make a nice accompaniment to the zabaglione.

Fine points: Ask about the Los Ninos Series, dedicated to the births of Michael's and Carolyn's children with labels designed by the kids. Enjoy a picnic (bring with you) and Martini wines in Martini Park, the winery's garden courtyard. No tasting fee for most wines; the $6.00 fee for reserves includes logo glass. Featured wines: Louis' White Blend, Sauvignon Blanc, Zinfandel Heritage Collection, Cabernet Sauvignon, Reserve Chardonnay, Barbera, Merlot, Gewürztraminer, Folle Blanche, Dry Sherry, and Cream Sherry. Owners: The Martini Family. President: Carolyn Martini. Winemaker: Michael Martini. Cases: 150,000. Acres: 1,200.

Louis M. Martini, 254 St. Helena Highway South, St. Helena 94574; phone (707) 963–2736 or (800) 321–WINE, fax (707) 963–8750, Web site www.louismartini.com. Open from 10:00 A.M. to 4:30 P.M. daily. Visa, MasterCard, and American Express. Wheelchair-accessible.

Between Heitz Cellars and Louis M. Martini, on the west side of Highway 29, you might want to try EDGEWOOD ESTATE WINERY. (In fact, we advise that you go into St. Helena proper, have lunch and shop, then come back south to visit Prager Winery Port Works, Trinchero Family Estates, and Edgewood Estate.)

Giant Golden State Vineyards (California is the Golden State), "California's largest vertically integrated grape growing and wine processing company," is developing its premium-wine division, Edgewood Estate Winery, by restoring what used to be the Napa Valley Cooperative.

Captain William Peterson, a New England sea captain, built the original winery on a forty-acre tract called Vineland, with the Vineland School in back of Edgewood Estate. For sixty years, beginning right after the end of Prohibition, the Napa Valley Cooperative served 128 growers and resurrected viticulture in the Napa Valley. Its purchaser, Golden State Vineyards, is now the largest grape grower and exporter of wines in the United States.

In 1985 many of the original vines were removed to create a parking lot. In 1998 Edgewood removed most of the parking lot and entry drive, replanted 2,880 Cabernet Sauvignon vines in front of the winery, and moved seventy-eight 20- to 40-foot-high mature trees around the property "to return the frontage to its agricultural beginnings and to create a grand entry to this historical site."

A gravel path leads from the parking lot to the newly remodeled tasting room, featuring resurrected wood from fifty-year-old wine storage tanks. Notice the high vaulted ceilings and the vegetable garden to the north. The actual winery is next door and encloses Captain Peterson's original winery building.

 Fine points: No tasting fee. All of Edgewood's wines are made in small lots of less than 1,500 cases, and many are available only in the tasting room. Featured wines: Chardonnay, Malbec, Cabernet Franc, Merlot, Cabernet Sauvignon, Zinfandel, Petite Sirah, Petit Verdot, and Zinfandel Port. Owner: Golden State Vineyards, Jeffrey O'Neill President and CEO. Winemaker: Jeff Gaffner. Cases: 12,000. Acres: 40.

✵ *Edgewood Estate Winery, 401 St. Helena Highway South, St. Helena 94574; phone (707) 963–7293, fax (707) 963–8537. Open from 11:00 A.M. to 5:30 P.M. daily. Visa, MasterCard, American Express, and Discover. Wheelchair-accessible.*

TRINCHERO FAMILY ESTATES (formerly Sutter Home Winery), dates from 1874, and the name Sutter Home from 1900, when pioneer John Sutter's daughter named it for him, although Italian immigrants John and Mario

TRINCHERO FAMILY ESTATES

Trinchero bought it in 1946 (still early by Napa standards) and majored in bulk wines until about 1970. They were well known for their mantra that, if you could bring it through the front door, they would fill it with wine.

Wine industry innovator Bob Trinchero eked a rosé-style wine out of some Zinfandel grapes and called it White Zinfandel, which, as an almost "pop" wine, became the best-selling wine in the United States. Bob also developed the single-service bottles you get on airplanes and Amtrak.

While the company has three vineyards in the Napa Valley, most of the grapes come from the Sierra foothills, the flat Delta area near Sacramento, and the hot Sacramento Valley. All Trinchero Family Estates' vineyards are farmed organically or by sustainable farming practices.

When you drive up to the winery, you will be struck by the lovely Victorian home and gardens with their hundred varieties of roses, forty varieties of day lilies, and a camellia at the Victorian Inn's entrance that was planted in 1876. The large palm tree was brought from the Canary Islands in the 1940s. Our late, great friend, landscape architect Bob Ernest, designed the current gardens, using all-natural fertilizers and predatory insects to control pests.

The spacious, wood-walled tasting room is to your left. Here there are lots of serious wines—and humorous other stuff and staff. You can take a "Blend

Your Own Wine" forty-five-minute seminar, discovering the differences among varietals and learning how to blend your own personalized wine, all for just $10.

Fine points: Trinchero Family Estates is one of the few wineries that produces alcohol-free wine; it is available here under the Fre label. The winery also announces special sale deals on the blackboard daily, so you have to be here to know about them. The company also makes fruit-flavored wines. Tasting fee: "zip, zero, nada;" $5.00 for better wines. Featured wines: labels Montevina, Sutter Home, Soleo, and M. Trinchero; various Zinfandels, Gamay Beaujolais, Sauvignon Blanc, Chardonnay, Chenin Blanc, Cabernet Sauvignon, Merlot, Gewürztraminer, Barbera, Sangiovese, Muscat Alexandria. Owner: The Trinchero family. Winemakers: Steve Bertolucci and Derek Holstein. Cases: 10,000,000. Acres: 5,500.

✣ *Trinchero Family Estates, 100 St. Helena Highway South, St. Helena 94574; phone (707) 963–3104, Web site www.tfe.com or www.sutterhome.com. Open from 9:30 A.M. to 5:00 P.M. daily. Visa, MasterCard, American Express, and Discover. Wheelchair-accessible.*

One of our favorite discoveries is PRAGER WINERY & PORT WORKS, which is actually right behind Trinchero Family Estates' Victorian house off Lewelling Lane, a narrow little one-lane street.

Prager's tasting room is the downstairs of an old wooden barn at the rear of a small parking lot. Originally a carriage house and the John Thomann Winery and Distillery, built in 1865, the building must be very happy with its current tenant.

Jim Prager presides over his realm from a wooden bar stool and sees the cobwebs holding bottles on the windowsill as "the original web site." He sees the secondary "web site" as the one draping the picture of "my father's father's grandson." Hello? It's also fun to study the paper money wallpaper chipped in by Prager's visitors from all over the world. A huge musty Oriental rug, well-worn wooden captain's chairs, classic cigars, and a truly old corkscrew collection complete the stage setting.

In a stroke of genius, Jim and his wife, Imogene, left Orange County for Napa, developed a small shopping center (now the St. Helena Premium Outlets) north of St. Helena, and settled on his other true love, wine, and even more specially, port. Imogene runs a small B&B adjoining their lovely home next to the winery, and their children, John, Jeff, Peter, and Katie, are all involved in this downhome and highly personal effort.

Fine points: Here you can taste at least three of the six styles of port that Jim produces, all a blend of sweetness and brandy. Jim talks of evaporation as something "the angels love," and of his ten-year-old Noble Companion Ultra Premium Port as "smooth as a baby's bottom." We recommend all of his ports for an elegant taste experience, smooth even on a hot day. Don't miss the Chocolate Drizzle, Chocolate Mousse Balls, and interesting cigars. Tasting fee: $5.00. Featured wines: Chardonnay, Zinfandel, Cabernet Sauvignon, Aria White Port, Royal Escort LBV Port, Madeline (late harvest Johannisberg Riesling), Noble Companion Ultra Premium Port, Alyssa, and Sweet Claire. Owner: James Prager. Wine and port maker: "God—we just tend the land," with the help of Pete Prager. Cellarmaster: Richard Lenney. Cases: 3,600. Acres: 15.

Prager Winery & Port Works, 1281 Lewelling Lane, St. Helena 94574; phone (707) 963–PORT or (800) 969–PORT, fax (707) 963–7679, Web site: www.pragerport.com. Open from 10:30 A.M. to 4:30 P.M. Visa and MasterCard. Wheelchair-accessible.

ST. HELENA

About 0.3 mile north of Sutter Home, on the same side of Highway 29, is Erika Hills's "THE PAINTED ILLUSION," one of the most fun and authentic emporia of antiques and collectibles in Northern California. The building, a converted early 1900s church, vibrates with memories. Austin and Erika Hills restored the building and put a new roof on top of the old one.

Don't miss the late-nineteenth-century Hills Bros. Coffee grinder, from Austin's family's business. He is now a partner in Grgich Hills Cellar.

Explore the seemingly unlimited niches and model living spaces full of eclectic period pieces. Lee Prosegger is the perfect guide around the shop, which includes painted furniture upstairs.

Erika Hills's "The Painted Illusion" Antiques and Furniture, 115 Main Street, St. Helena 94574; phone (707) 963–0919, fax (707) 963–8824. Open from 11:00 A.M. to 5:00 P.M. Thursday–Monday. Visa and MasterCard. Not wheelchair-accessible.

Almost a mile north of Trinchero Family Estates and Prager you will find what has become an interesting cluster of buildings, which include MERRYVALE VINEYARDS, the Real Foods group's Tra Vigne, Tomatina pizza restaurant, and The Inn at Southbridge. (You are still on Highway 29, which, as you noticed, was called St. Helena Highway and St. Helena Highway South, and is now called Main Street in St. Helena proper. Confused enough? We are.)

The Mondavi family's first wine venture began here in the lovely stone

ST. HELENA AREA

PETERSON DR.

LARKMEAD LN.

SILVERADO TRAIL

FRANK-ROMBAUER/HANNS KORNELL CHAMPAGNE

BALE LN.

SMITH-MADRONE VINEYARDS
BARNETT VINEYARDS

BIG TREE RD.

TUDAL WINERY

DOMAINE CHARBAY WINERY

29

SCHWEIGER VINEYARDS

SPRING MOUNTAIN RD.

ROMBAUER VINEYARDS

BURGESS CELLARS

VIADER VINEYARDS

STONY HILL VINEYARD

CASA NUESTRA WINERY

CHATEAU WOLTNER

DEER PARK WINERY

TO ANGWIN

LANGTRY RD.

ROBERT KEENAN WINERY

EHLERS GROVE

CHATEAU BOSWELL

HOWELL MOUNTAIN RD.

DUNN VINEYARDS
SUMMIT LAKE VINEYARDS
LA JOTA

FOLIE À DEUX WINERY

DUCKHORN VINEYARDS

FREEMARK ABBEY WINERY

LODI LN.

N

W   E

S

BALLENTINE VINEYARDS
ST. CLEMENT VINEYARDS

SPRING MOUNTAIN RD.

MARKHAM VINEYARDS

DEER PARK RD.

CHARLES KRUG WINERY

PRATT AVE.

HOWELL MOUNTAIN RD.

SULPHUR SPRINGS RD.

BERINGER VINEYARDS

MEADOWOOD LN.

FULTON LN.

ST. HELENA

MEADOWOOD RESORT

MADRONA ST.
SPRING ST.

POPE ST.

29

NOTE:
In St. Helena is
Highway 29 is
Main Street.

MERRYVALE VINEYARDS

SILVERADO TRAIL

SULPHUR SPRINGS RD.

LEWELLING LN.

LOUIS M. MARTINI

ROSS RD.

PRAGER WINERY & PORT WORKS
TRINCHERO FAMILY ESTATES
EDGEWOOD ESTATE WINERY

JOSEPH PHELPS VINEYARDS

ANDERSON'S CONN VALLEY VINEYARDS

INGLEWOOD AVE.

HEITZ WINE CELLAR

TAPLIN RD.

MILAT VINEYARDS

V. SATTUI WINERY

W. ZINFANDEL

ZINFANDEL LN.

WILLIAM HARRISON VINEYARDS/
MARIO PERELLI-MINETTI WINERY

FLORA SPRINGS WINE COMPANY

RAYMOND VINEYARD & CELLAR

structure that now houses Merryvale Vineyards. The first Napa Valley winery built after Prohibition, the Sunny St. Helena Winery was purchased and founded in 1983 as Merryvale by San Francisco developer Bill Harlan and friends, who renovated it and, in 1996, sold 60 percent to Jack Schlatter and his son Rene from Switzerland, who again renovated the winery, while preserving its historic look.

When Harlan first bought the winery, the wine was made at Rombauer Vineyards, whose winemaker, Bob Levy, is now winemaker at Merryvale. World-renowned winemaster Michel Rolland, owner of Chateau Le Bon Pasteur in Pomerol, serves as consultant.

 Fine points: Don't miss the Tank Room, with its 22,000-gallon wooden cask, and the Cask Room, lined with two stories of century-old 2,000 gallon casks, usually used for private and group parties. Book reservations to take the Wine Component Tasting Seminar, offered at 10:30 A.M. on Saturday and Sunday in the Cask Room ($10 per person). The tasting fee is $3.00 for Classic selections, $5.00 for Reserve wines, and $10.00 for prestige wines. Featured wines: Semillon, Chardonnay, Merlot, Antigua (Muscat de Frontignan); Connoisseur Vignette, Reserve Chardonnay, Reserve Merlot, and Profile. Owners: Jack and Rene Schlatter, Bill Harlan and partners. Winemaker: Bob Levy. Cases: 50,000. Acres: buy in Napa County.

Merryvale Vineyards, 1000 Main Street, St. Helena 94574; phone (707) 963–7777 or (800) 326–6069 outside California, fax (707) 963–3018, Website www.merryvale.com. Open from 10:00 A.M. to 5:30 P.M. daily. Visa, MasterCard, American Express, and Discover. Wheelchair-accessible.

If you're famished, you're in Californian–Italian heaven, right within short-walking distance of Merryvale. Across Charter Oak Street you will find TOMATINA, an upscale pizzeria that tries to fill the financial gap by offering reasonably priced food for both locals and visiting wine fans, including soups, salads, pastas, and desserts.

You'll notice the place by the huge red-tomato metal sculpture on the front porch. As part of the Real Foods group, Tra Vigne's well-known chef Michael Chiarello serves as executive chef.

The yummy piadine are un-rolled-up roll-ups made from pizza dough, with Caesar salad, lettuce, tomatoes, and other veggies combined with skirt steak, grilled chicken, or gorgonzola piled high. Just try to eat this politely! They even bring you a diagram of eating directions.

Pizzas and pizza crusts for the piadine are baked in a giant wood-burning brick oven. Be sure to notice that pizza prices start with a base of six slices

($7.95, or twelve for $12.95; all toppings are additional).

Order with the computer host at the counter just as you walk in the door, then sit at a table and wait for your food and beverages to arrive. Enjoy your meal indoors or on the west-facing patio with black-and-white-striped umbrellas. Even the counter stools, shaped like screw-top tomato vines, keep the theme.

This is a great place for groups and kids. Cokes come with free refills if you go up to the bar/counter.

Tomatina, *1016 Main Street at The Inn at Southbridge, St. Helena 94574; phone (707) 967–9999. Open from 11:30 A.M. to 10:00 P.M. daily. Beer and wine. Visa and MasterCard. Wheelchair-accessible.*

Just up Main Street at its intersection with Charter Oak Avenue is TRA VIGNE, one of the Napa Valley's best-known restaurants. Real Foods group has succeeded in creating the feeling of a small Italian village with Tra Vigne, its courtyard, and the smaller Cantinetta Tra Vigne in an old sherry winery. Flowers brighten tables and spirits inside and out, even on rainy days.

Tra Vigne itself feels Italian the minute you walk in, with 30-foot ceilings, heavily draped entry, a hand-carved bar, and Italian beaded light fixtures. Helen Berggruen's colorful paintings and Cinzano red posters decorate the walls. Service is meticulous, while the feeling is elegantly casual. The restaurant makes its own mozzarella and prosciutto, presses its own olive oil, and grows its own table grapes.

Some of Chef Michael Chiarello's signature dishes include appetizers, such as an antipasto of seafood–fried crisp in arborio rice flour ($7.95), oven-roasted polenta with wild mushrooms and Bellwether Crescenza cheese ($8.50), and renowned risottos and salads. Smoked Nieman-Schell beef short ribs with garlic soft polenta ($18.95), grilled Sonoma rabbit ($17.50), or yellowfin tuna ($19.95) are all exquisite. Passing of plates around the table and sharing are expected here. Do not leave without trying the Tiramisu do Cioccolata ($5.95).

Although there is a full bar, be sure

TRA VIGNE AND CANTINETTA
TRA VIGNE ENTRANCE FROM
PARKING LOT

ROASTED POLENTA AND BALSAMIC SAUCE
from Executive Chef Michael Chiarello, Tra Vigne

INGREDIENTS FOR THE ROASTED POLENTA:

3 cups chicken stock   *1 cup polenta meal*
3 cups heavy cream   *1 cup semolina*
pinch nutmeg   *½ cup grated Fontina*
¼ tsp ground white pepper   *1 cup Parmesan*
1 tsp salt

PREPARATION:

Combine stock, cream, grated nutmeg, salt, and pepper in a large, heavy-gauge pot. Bring liquid to a boil, then add the polenta and semolina gradually while stirring. Continue to cook over moderate heat while stirring constantly. Polenta is ready when it begins to pull away from the sides of the pot (approximately 10–15 minutes).

Remove from heat and stir in all the Fontina and ¾ cup Parmesan cheese until well incorporated. Spread polenta evenly on oiled sheet trays. Be sure to use trays that are not warped, and spread to a thickness of approximately ¾ inch.

Cool trays to room temperature, then cover with parchment and refrigerate. These may be prepared 48 hours in advance.

INGREDIENTS FOR THE BALSAMIC SAUCE:

1 pint balsamic vinegar   *6 peppercorns*
1 chopped shallot   *2 bay leaves*
2 quarts stock (roasted chicken, veal,   *1 stick sweet butter*
   rabbit, or canned; if using a canned
   broth, do not salt any portion of the recipe)

PREPARATION:

Reduce the vinegar with the chopped shallots to a syrup consistency. Add the stock, bay leaves, and peppercorns. Reduce to a sauce consistency and strain.

TO ASSEMBLE:

Cut polenta into squares or triangles. Put on a buttered sheet pan, sprinkle generously with leftover Parmesan cheese, and put in a 500°F oven until golden brown. Remove from oven and finish sauce.

Bring reserved sauce to a simmer and whisk in butter, adjust salt and pepper to taste, and pour on plates before polenta. Serves 4.

Notes from Chef Michael Chiarello: "This is the very best recipe for polenta I have ever used. The ratio of liquid and dry ingredients is 3 to 1. For soft polenta, try a ratio of 5 or 6 to 1. I encourage you to change the recipe as you see fit."

to check out Tra Vigne's exceptional Italian and California wine list, with an exclusive selection of 1987 Cabernet Sauvignons commemorating the restaurant's tenth anniversary. Take time to venture downstairs (under the guise of finding the rest room, if necessary) to see the interesting historic photos, including a locally famous train derailment. Chiarello has opened a multimedia, Napa food-oriented business across Highway 29, called Napa Style, which should be well worth a drop in.

If you're in the mood for a less formal and less expensive lunch or dinner, try CANTINETTA TRA VIGNE for excellent panini (sandwiches), including a tasty roasted vegetable one with eggplant, peppers, goat cheese, arugula, and garlic vinaigrette, smoked turkey, or warm corned beef (all $5.75); Pasta Fabioli soup ($4.25); salads from Caesar to roasted balsamic onions; veggie lasagna; spring tarts; stuffed focaccia; or five pizzas, all under $7.00.

Pastries, from the Tra Vigne kitchen, are divine. You can also purchase Tra Vigne's fresh mozzarella ($8.00 per pound) as well as its fresh stocks, sauces, and dressings. What a treat!

✢ *Tra Vigne* and *Cantinetta Tra Vigne, 1050 Charter Oak Avenue, St. Helena 94574; phone (707) 963–4444, fax (707) 963–1233. Visa, MasterCard, Discover, Carte Blanche, and Diners Club. Wheelchair-accessible from patio.*

We want you to take the time to drive another block down Charter Oak behind Tra Vigne to Allison Street and the NAPA VALLEY OLIVE OIL MANUFACTORY. Leonora and Ray Particelli and Policarpo (Pol) Lucchesi are the current generation nurturing the family olive-oil business founded by Guillermo Guidi in 1930. As you might guess by their names, the owners are all from Lucca, Italy.

Surprisingly enough, when you walk into the old white-clapboard barn, you smell salami, seemingly tons of loose Molinari salami. Heaven! The two rooms' walls are covered with thousands of business cards, including ours on the door-frame. Wander through barrels and barrels of dried mushrooms, tubs of dried beans from French flageolet to Lupini and canellini, pickled everything, prosciutto bones for $10.00, bag of herbs, and containers of anchovies from small ($2.75) to major ($25.00). Check out the freezer in the front room full of delectable crab or lobster ravioli ($4.50), veggie or cheese tortellini or ravioli ($3.00), and lasagna ($6.75).

Be sure to notice the olive press brought from Lucca more than seventy years ago. The tracks in the wooden floor were caused by the cart (now filled with salami) that was used to move olives brought in from Napa fields by Carmelite nuns for pressing. The olive oil is now made in the Sacramento Valley and bottled here. It is available in regular or extra virgin, in sizes ranging from pints to generous gallons. The Extra Virgin (blue label) is quite potent, and Leonora recommends the regular Pure Olive Oil (white label) for most purposes.

❧ *Napa Valley Olive Oil Manufactory, 835 Charter Oak Avenue, St. Helena 94574; phone (707) 963–4173. Open from 8:00 A.M. to 5:30 P.M. daily. No credit cards. Wheelchair-accessible.*

Across Main Street (Highway 29) from Charter Oak Avenue and Tra Vigne is one of St. Helena's local favorites, TAYLOR'S REFRESHER. Taylor's new diner look extends to the great food with ultimate burgers including the Western Bacon Blue Ring ($6.99), the California Chicken with Jack cheese, guacamole, and veggies ($6.99), and an Ahi burger ($8.99). Thick spoon-needed shakes may include Oreos or Snickers, and the tacos and onion rings still stand out.

❧ *Taylor's Refresher, 933 Main Street, St. Helena 94574; phone (707) 963–3486. Open from 11:00 A.M. to 9:00 P.M. daily. No credit cards. Wheelchair-accessible.*

We will walk you up the right (east) side of Main Street as far north as Pairs Restaurant and Tivoli. Then we will cross Main Street and walk back down the west side, guiding you into every shop, bakery, and restaurant along the way.

St. Helena's few blocks of downtown are elegant yet homey, and the city is trying hard to keep it from becoming too touristy, while maintaining its usefulness to locals and allure to visitors. It feels like a step back several decades, with a gracious, relaxed ambience and elegant boutiques to suit most needs, mixed with a pharmacy and hardware store, important parts of a functioning downtown.

The first shop you encounter walking north is ST. HELENA CYCLERY. Here you can rent tandem bikes, road, mountain, or hybrid bikes, as well as helmets and maps. Be sure to make a reservation for ten or more riders.

❧ *St. Helena Cyclery, 1156 Main Street, St. Helena 94574; phone (707) 963–7736. Open from 9:30 A.M. to 5:30 P.M., Sunday 10:00 A.M. to 5:00 P.M. Visa, MasterCard, and American Express. Wheelchair-accessible.*

The CREATIVE NEEDLE sells anything and everything you need for knitting, darning, and crocheting projects, including Adrienne Vittadini yarns.

❧ *Creative Needle, 1210 Main Street, St. Helena 94574; phone (707) 963–7533. Open Tuesday–Friday from 10:00 A.M. to 5:00 P.M., Saturday 10:00 A.M. to 1:00 P.M. Visa, MasterCard, and JCB. Wheelchair-accessible.*

Just two doors up, CALLA LILY sells elegant fine linens and gifts.
❧ *Calla Lily, 1222 Main Street, St. Helena 94574; phone (707) 963–8188. Open Monday–Saturday from 10:00 A.M. to 5:00 P.M., Sunday 11:00 A.M. to 4:00 P.M. Visa, MasterCard, and American Express. Wheelchair-accessible.*

Two doors farther on, CRICKET sells playclothes versions of Reel, Avalon, Workshop, Citron, and Flax for luxuriating at resorts and San Francisco Hat Co. hats. Everything looks very comfortable.
❧ *Cricket, 1226 Main Street, St. Helena 94574; phone (707) 963–8400. Open from 10:00 A.M. to 5:30 P.M. daily. Visa, MasterCard, and American Express. Wheelchair-accessible.*

D. CHAMPAIGN, "Where you can relax your style," purveys elegant casual men's resort wear, including designers such as Barry Bricken, Haupt, North 44, Java Lava, Columbian, Lazo, Tallia, Tommy Bahama, and Axis shirts, and Teva and H.S. Trask shoes.
❧ *D. Champaign, 1228 Main Street, St. Helena 94574; phone (707) 963–1782. Open from 10:00 A.M. to 6:00 P.M. daily. Visa, MasterCard, American Express, and Diners Club. Wheelchair-accessible.*

Next door, AMELIA CLAIRE offers elegant ladies' shoes, bags, and belts.
❧ *Amelia Claire, 1230 Main Street, St. Helena 94574; phone (707) 963–8502. Open from 10:00 A.M. to 6:00 P.M. daily. Visa and MasterCard. Wheelchair-accessible.*

The next storefront was recently enlivened with the arrival of BERGMAN'S, the hottest new restaurant in St. Helena. "Serving good food since 1998," this is where the best Napa Valley restaurant staffs end up for a good meal after a long day of cooking so that they too can sit down and be served in a fun atmosphere.

Bergman's took over the space of Trilogy, a longtime well-known California-French restaurant. Alexis and Bryan Bergman and Bryan's brother Andy have redone the place with bright colors, good music, and great food. You can now sit in a beautiful patio and enjoy the casual cafe atmosphere.

The Bergmans bring all the best local credentials, having cooked at Brava Terrace, Pinot Blanc, and Mustards, in addition to several top Atlanta establishments. Bryan and Andy handle the kitchen, while Alexis meets, greets, and delights.

The menu is simple and direct. Soups, such as chicken noodle and "the other soup," and large salads range from $5.00 to $7.00. Hot entrees come with your choice of three sides and range from All Vegetable Plate ($12 for five sides) and Andy's Meatloaf to A Piece of Salmon ($14), The Pork Chop ($12), and grilled sirloin steak ($14). Sides include mashed potatoes, egg noodles and tomato gravy, squash casserole, spinach, cabbage, stewed tomatoes, macaroni and cheese, string beans, carrots, and applesauce. Is my mother here?

Desserts may include chocolate cream pie, apple crisp a la mode, jelly sponge cake, or Grapenut custard, all at $4.00. Lots of soda and an excellent short, local wine list complete the scene. Corkage fee if you bring in your own bottle of wine: "A taste of wine for the house."

The fun and young message is loud and clear. Don't miss it.

Bergman's, 1234 Main Street, St. Helena 94574; phone (707) 963–1063, fax (707) 963–1569. Beer and wine. Open for lunch from 11:30 A.M. to 2:00 P.M. Thursday–Saturday, dinner 5:00 to 10:00 P.M. Monday–Thursday, 5:00 P.M. to midnight Friday–Saturday. No reservations. Visa and MasterCard. Wheelchair-accessible.

One of Kathleen's favorite shops in all of Napa County is Margaret Word's ON THE VINE, a food-and-wine-lover's clothing and trinket boutique at the corner of Main and Hunt Streets. The shop's design alone is worth going in to see.

Don't miss the wine-and-food-inspired jewelry and "wearable art," including silver asparagus pins, whisk earrings, and silverware picture frames, and the lighthearted casual clothes perfect for traveling in the heat. Visitors from other countries have been known to come in, be astonished at the appropriateness of the clothing, and purchase whole racks of a style.

Hand-painted wearable art "Field of Grapes" silk jackets are $725, ties $100. Garnet Merlot grape earrings are only $42. You can even find grape cluster cufflinks and tuxedo studs. Be sure to get on Margaret's mailing list to learn all the latest.

On the Vine, 1234 Main Street, St. Helena 94574; phone (707) 963–2209 or (800) 992–4339. Open from 10:00 A.M. to 5:30 P.M. daily. Visa, MasterCard, and American Express. Wheelchair-accessible.

Continue northward on the right (east) side of Main Street. Once the Wonderful Drug Store, according to brass letters in the sidewalk, REED'S offers comfortable ladies' clothing from Calvin Klein, Harari, Loose Threads, Kevo, Kathleen Sommers, and Joan Vass. This is a popular boutique both with locals and visitors.

Reed's, 1302 Main Street at Hunt, St. Helena 94574; phone (707) 963–0400. Open from 10:00 A.M. to 5:30 P.M. daily. Visa, MasterCard, and American Express. Wheelchair-accessible.

Next door to Reed's are two fun and wonderfully different (and differently wonderful) restaurants. The first one you come to is ᴀʀᴍᴀᴅɪʟʟᴏ's, serving fresh Californian-Mexican food. Fun primary colors permeate, with large murals, painted chairs and tables, and trademark mosaic-cornered tables. Copper palm trees greet you at the door.

Both Mexican and gringo food are served including breakfast, with a special children's menu and crayons available. Locals come in here constantly on their lunch breaks, which tells you something about Armadillo's prices and consistency.

We particularly enjoy the Enchilada Pollo con Mole, fresh shredded chicken covered with house-made mole sauce. The best! Lots of vegetarian specialties grace the menu, popular with the large Seventh-Day Adventist community in the area. The chips are warm and the salsa fresh, served in a metal ice cream dish.

*❧ *Armadillo's, 1304 Main Street, St. Helena 94574; phone (707) 963–8082. Open from 11:00 A.M. to 9:00 P.M. Sunday–Thursday, 11:00 A.M. to 10:00 P.M. Friday–Saturday. Beer and wine. Visa and MasterCard. Wheelchair-accessible.*

Just one door up the street from Armadillo's is a small, narrow restaurant that is so good, popular with Napa Valley residents, and under-discovered that we hesitate to tell you about it. We don't want it spoiled.

Tʀᴀᴛᴛᴏʀɪᴀ Gʀᴇᴇɴ Vᴀʟʟᴇʏ ᴀɴᴅ Gʀᴇᴇɴ Vᴀʟʟᴇʏ Cᴀғᴇ & Tʀᴀᴛᴛᴏʀɪᴀ (both are on the front signs) is/are all the same Italian bistro.

International investment consultants drive from Calistoga for a weekly "best burger in the Napa Valley," members of local bocce-ball teams (with names like The Olive Oilers) come in for a pasta lunch, and winemakers sneak in without letting outsiders know that this is one of the best restaurants in the Napa Valley. Locals bring in the *St. Helena Star* and sit on green padded stools at the green marble counter, soaking up the gossip, printed and verbal.

Turandot, Othello, and Verdi posters decorate the walls, and deals are made in the larger back room. Be sure to check the daily specials blackboard to the left of the door as you enter.

At lunch you can have exceptionally flavorful fresh salads and sandwiches, hot sandwiches such as a North Beach Burger, Italian sausage, or vegetarian grilled eggplant (drippy gooey and wonderful) with tomatoes, cheese, peppers, onions, and olives (with small salad for $6.95), and outrageously divine pastas. The cannelloni stuffed with chicken, mushrooms, spinach, and artichokes is $9.95. If crudeola is on the specials board, it is a compulsory try ($10.00), as is the portobello, prosciutto, and provolone sandwich ($8.50) with salad. Otherwise, try the spaghetti aja e ojho—spaghetti with fresh garlic, virgin olive oil, red-pepper flakes and parsley, gnocchi with Gorgonzola cheese sauce

($8.75) said to be the "best not in Italy," or ricotta-filled spinach tortellini with smoked salmon, tomatoes, mushrooms, and cream. The fried calamari with garlic mayonnaise is mouth-watering ($9.00).

Dinner features some of the same salads and pastas, plus linguini with fresh clams ($12.75), braised chicken ($10.75), grilled New York steak ($16.00), braised lamb shank with polenta ($11.95), marinated and grilled lamb top sirloin ($16.00), and mussels steamed in white wine and garlic ($10.75). Espresso drinks are available, and you can split an entree for an extra $2.00. Local and Italian wines, of course.

Trattoria Green Valley, 1310 Main Street, St. Helena 94574; phone (707) 963–7088. Wine and beer. Open lunch and dinner. Visa and MasterCard. Restaurant is wheelchair-accessible; rest room is not.

FIDEAUX has quickly become a destination "outfitter for cats and dogs" like no other, except for its new sister store in Carmel. A former teacher, proprietor Jennifer Blevens certainly knows how to catch your eye and your passion for pets. You can spoil yours with bracelets, collars, Fideaux Futons washable beds, locally made pottery bowls, a wine barrel doghouse, dog clocks with tongues wagging, and guidebooks for traveling pets and the owners. Visiting dogs are welcome but must be on a leash.

Fideaux, 1312 Main Street, St. Helena 94574; phone (707) 967–9935, Web site www.fideaux-bestselections.com. Open from 9:30 A.M. to 5:30 P.M. daily. Visa, MasterCard, and American Express. Wheelchair-accessible.

KELLER'S MARKET is St. Helena's good old stand-by local grocery store, with green-and-white-checked linoleum floors. You can still see the lighted Stornetta's dairy picture across the back wall. You can also get decent deli sandwiches and warmable meals, and indulge in the latest Acme breads or the *New York Times.*

Keller's Market, 1320 Main Street, St. Helena 94574; phone (707) 963–2114. Open from 8:00 A.M. to 8:00 P.M. daily. Visa, MasterCard, and Discover. Wheelchair-accessible.

As you walk by the *St. Helena Star* newspaper offices next door to Keller's, pick up a copy of the visitor edition, a tremendous wealth of local information, including wine and food transitions and developments.

For an evening of cinema, the Cameo Theatre at 1340 Main Street is a classic theater providing a classic American movie-going experience. Enjoy it for what it was and is.

Marc Robbins and Wayne Bradshaw own and preside over both PATINA

FINE JEWELRY, just north of the Cameo Theatre, and Paladium, between David's and Buchanan's on the west side of Main Street. Their personal delight and passion for their jewelry shows the minute you walk in the door. At Patina they sell estate jewelry, including platinum and diamonds, objets d'art, and antiques, ranging from the late 1700s through the 1960s and costing from $150 to $25,000.

꙳ꙮ *Patina Fine Jewelry, 1342 Main Street, St. Helena 94574; phone (707) 963–5445. Open from 10:00 A.M. to 5:30 P.M. Monday–Saturday, 10:30 A.M. to 5:00 P.M. Sunday. Visa, MasterCard, American Express, and Discover. Wheelchair-accessible.*

SHOWPLACE NORTH, just one door north of Patina, feels like the elegant extension of San Francisco's wholesale furniture houses that it is. The ceilings are high, the rooms are large, and the furniture is massive in both size and impact. Ralph Lauren upholstery, leather armchairs from $1,000, mosaic dining tables at $2,625, beds, and lamps are enticing to look at or perhaps even to purchase to furnish your home.

꙳ꙮ *Showplace North, 1350 Main Street, St. Helena 94574; phone (707) 963–5556. Open from 10:00 A.M. to 5:00 P.M. Monday–Saturday, 11:00 A.M. to 5:00 P.M. Sunday. Visa, MasterCard, and American Express. Wheelchair-accessible.*

One of the most professional and elegant galleries in the Napa Valley is I. WOLK GALLERY, which features dramatic large paintings, works on paper, photography, and sculpture.

꙳ꙮ *I. Wolk Gallery, 1235 Main Street, St. Helena 94594; phone (707) 963–8800, fax (707) 963–8801, Web site www.iwolkgallery.com. Open from 10:00 A.M. to 5:30 P.M. Wednesday–Monday. Visa, MasterCard, and American Express. Partially wheelchair-accessible.*

STEVES' HARDWARE AND HOMEWARE, INC., at the corner of Main Street and Adams, is a fine social and business institution whose existence reminds us all of what life was like in Napa and Sonoma Valleys before big wine came. If you are lucky, Carol Rutherford (yes, as in the town of Rutherford) or co-owner Louise Menegon will be presiding over the counter to the left of the entrance. They and the Steves family have the longevity and knowledge to tell you anything you could possibly want to know about the Napa Valley.

Steves' moved here in 1991 from next door, where they had been for 107 years in a store 2,000 feet smaller than this one. You will find Good Housekeeping's *Household Encyclopedia* on a James Graham stove with Le Creuset and Calphalon cookware. Rifles, guns, warnings, and ammo are sold along with Winchester sign replicas, paint, nails, sandpaper, copper cookware, ceramic animal salt-and-pepper shakers, tiles, canisters, pepper grinders, and wooden salad bowls. Well-selected cookbooks, toasters, tool belts, plumbing and garden supplies, glassware, and live fishing bait add to the good old hardware-store quality, disappearing at the hands of the chain stores but lovingly preserved at Steves'.

❧ *Steves' Hardware and Homeware, Inc., 1370 Main Street, St. Helena 94574; phone (707) 963–3423. Open from 7:30 A.M. to 6:00 P.M. Monday–Friday, 7:30 A.M. to 5:30 P.M. Saturday, 9:30 A.M. to 4:00 P.M. Sunday. Visa, MasterCard, American Express and Discover. Wheelchair-accessible.*

We highly recommend that you go another half-block up Main across Adams Street, passing the most expensive gas station (Chevron) in the wine country, and have a look at Lolo's Consignment Shop and Tivoli.

Lᴏʟᴏ's Sᴇᴄᴏɴᴅ ᴛᴏ Nᴏɴᴇ Cᴏɴsɪɢɴᴍᴇɴᴛ Sʜᴏᴘ, is funky, with used clothing, furniture, and eclectica.

❧ *Lolo's Second to None Consignment Shop, 1424 Main Street, St. Helena 94574; phone (707) 963–7972. Open from 10:30 A.M. to 5:30 P.M. Tuesday–Saturday, 10:30 A.M. to 4:00 P.M. Sunday–Monday. Visa, MasterCard, American Express, and Discover. Wheelchair-accessible.*

Go one shop farther and walk down the driveway to Tɪᴠᴏʟɪ, in what used to be the town meeting hall and then funeral home. Dottie Richolson manages Tivoli for owner Tom Scheibal, who also owns Bale Mill Pine Furniture, south of Calistoga.

Tom designs and builds iron-and-pine furniture and carries handmade mosaic tables made with Moroccan tiles, huge iron chandeliers, and unusual Ira Yaeger paintings. (He also has luxurious vacation accommodations available near Calistoga.) Tivoli is a great place to browse and escape to another world in just a few steps.

❧ *Tivoli, 1432 Main Street, St. Helena 94574; phone (707) 967–9399, fax (707) 967–9397. Open from 10:00 A.M. to 5:00 P.M. daily; closed Tuesday in winter. Visa and MasterCard. Wheelchair-accessible.*

Here we cross Main Street and, contrary to our nature, we suggest you walk the few steps back to the crosswalk and light. Traffic along Main Street is heavy, and crossing mid-block creates confusion and infuriates local drivers.

It's worth it to drop into Vᴀɴᴅᴇʀʙɪʟᴛ & Cᴏᴍᴘᴀɴʏ–Nᴀᴘᴀ Vᴀʟʟᴇʏ, a shop and gallery of home and personal accessories, including Vietri Italian ceramic dishes and paintings, place settings, tablecloths and napkins, interesting cookbooks, Phoebe Ellsworth's St. Helena paintings and white flower scene collection, and Vanderbilt's Napa Valley Collection of hand-painted platters, flower dinner plates (inspired by the rich colors and textures of the Napa Valley), all work of local artists such as Sherman Nobleman, John Nyquist, and Charles Gautreaux. The colors of the ceramics and the bed, bath, and table linens make us happy. Be sure to check out the closeout table in the back corner of the back room.

❧ *Vanderbilt & Company–Napa Valley, 1429 Main Street, St. Helena 94574; phone (707) 963–1010. Open from 9:30 A.M. to 5:30 P.M. daily. Visa, MasterCard, American Express, and Discover. Wheelchair-accessible.*

As you come out of Vanderbilt's, turn right and go south on Main past the bank and turn right on Adams Street to Tantau, Tapioca Tiger, Sportago, Pat Quigle–Paper Tiger–Napa, and the Napa Valley Coffee Roasting Company, for a minor but interesting diversion.

TANTAU is an intriguing little boutique featuring "accents for living," from glorious French poster originals ($1,200), cards, ceramics, beautiful accessories for kids' rooms, personal shopping treats, and bridal registry, to coffee cups and quilts.

❧ *Tantau, 1220 Adams Street, St. Helena 94574; phone (707) 963–3115. Open from 9:30 A.M. to 5:30 P.M. Monday–Saturday, 11:00 A.M. to 5:00 P.M. Sunday. Visa and MasterCard. Wheelchair-accessible.*

Next door, TAPIOCA TIGER appeals to kids of all ages, with Madeline Tea Sets, Curious George everythings, children's books, clothes, and shoes.

❧ *Tapioca Tiger, 1224A Adams Street, St. Helena 94574; phone (707) 967–0608. Open from 10:00 A.M. to 5:30 P.M. Monday–Saturday, 10:30 A.M. to 4:00 P.M. Sunday. Visa and MasterCard. Wheelchair-accessible.*

One of our great surprise finds in St. Helena is SPORTAGO for great outdoor clothes and emergency sports equipment. Forget your tennis racket? This is the place.

Christine Miller and Christina Stephens converted what had been an automobile dealership into the most appealingly abstract designed shop we have ever seen. Sportago is an authorized Patagonia dealer and also sells Prince and Wilson tennis rackets, balls, books, clogs, and jazzy Arnelle sunglasses.

❧ *Sportago, 1224 Adams Street, St. Helena 94574; phone (707) 963–9042. Open from 9:00 A.M. to 5:30 P.M. Monday–Saturday, 9:00 A.M. to 4:00 P.M. Sunday. Visa, MasterCard, and American Express. Partially wheelchair-accessible.*

Just beyond Sportago, women especially might want to venture into PAT

QUIGLE–PAPER TIGER–NAPA for B Country Clothes, Sigrid Olsen, Pringle and Ballentine sweaters, Foxcroft Blouses, Bagit raincoats, Mari sweaters, and other fine wear from Nancy Rogers, Catherine Stewart, Mishi, and Corbin. We just had fun talking to the staff, all from the larger outside world and graduates of UC Berkeley.

❧ *Pat Quigle–Paper Tiger–Napa, 1234 Adams Street, St. Helena 94574; phone (707) 963–4336. Open from 10:00 A.M. to 5:00 P.M. daily. Visa and MasterCard. Wheelchair-accessible.*

Local coffee lovers hang out at the NAPA VALLEY COFFEE ROASTING COMPANY. Since not too many visitors venture to the end of this single block off Main Street, this is a great place to find out what's happening locally. Sister to the store in Napa, it has the best coffee in town and is worth the extra steps. All your favorite espresso drinks, scones, and biscotti are here. Enjoy!

❧ *Napa Valley Coffee Roasting Company (with entrances on both Adams and Oak), 1400 Oak Avenue, St. Helena 94574; phone (707) 963–4491. Open from 7:30 A.M. to 6:00 P.M. Visa and MasterCard with $5.00 minimum purchase. Wheelchair-accessible.*

Around the corner and half a block down Oak Street from the coffee roastery, dip into THE BIG DIPPER ("Ice Cream Parlor with an Old-Fashioned Flavor"), across from St. Helena Elementary School. (Is this location or what?) More than an ice cream parlor, this place is an informal shrine and museum to ice cream parlor and Coca-Cola memorabilia. Be sure to look up at the stuff covering the walls, from huge ice cream cone displays and a 1908 ice cream dipper, a 1920 ice cream sandwich maker, and early milkshake blenders. Return to your childhood or earlier at the penny candy counter, games, and a jukebox you can play with all those oldie favorites.

❧ *The Big Dipper, 1336 Oak Avenue, St. Helena 94574; phone (707) 963–2616. Open from 11:30 A.M. to 8:00 P.M. Monday–Saturday, noon to 6:00 P.M. Sunday. Cash only. Wheelchair-accessible.*

We highly recommend that you return to Adams Street, follow it across Main Street for 2 blocks (or if you are on Main, turn east on Adams), and turn north on Library Lane to both the Silverado Museum and the George & Elsie Wood Public Library and Wine Library.

SILVERADO MUSEUM is a near shrine to onetime Napa Valley resident Robert Louis Stevenson, established in 1969 by Charlotte A. Strouse and Norman H. Strouse, a former executive with J. Walter Thompson advertising.

The Silverado Museum is the largest of five museums dedicated to Stevenson (although Yale University has the largest collection of his manuscripts). In 2000, the museum acquired the Stevensons' marriage license issued in San Francisco on May 19, 1880, a diary written by Fanny Stevenson, and Stevenson's drawings between ages 6 and 18. There are loads of copies of various editions of his work for sale at the museum, which certainly heightened our interest in the author. Director Ed Reynolds and Associate Director Ann Kindred are treasures of knowledge about the author, his works, and his life.

❧ *Silverado Museum, 1490 Library Lane, St. Helena 94574; phone (707) 963-3757, Web site www.napanet.net/vi/silverado. Open from noon to 4:00 P.M. Tuesday–Sunday. Visa, MasterCard, and American Express. Wheelchair-accessible.*

Beside and behind the Silverado Museum is the GEORGE & ELSIE WOOD PUBLIC LIBRARY and the Napa Valley Wine Library, an unusual effort resulting from private and public funding.

Two things that make this library worth a trip are the Wine Library and its accompanying food-book collection. For visitors deeply interested in California wine-industry history and gossip, this is the place. The library attempts to collect every book worth its salt on wine, and also has a substantial collection of food literature. A real treat to browse are the transcribed oral interviews done with all of the Napa Valley's prominent wine pioneers, from Maynard Amerine to Robert Mondavi, and many in between. To see these volumes, ask the librarian to unlock the glass doors. She might ask for your youngest child as a deposit, but it's only for a little while!

❧ *George & Elsie Wood Public Library, 1492 Library Lane, St. Helena 94574; phone (707) 963-5244 or call the Napa Valley Wine Library Association at (707) 963-5145. Open from noon to 9:00 P.M. Monday–Wednesday, 10:00 A.M. to 6:00 P.M. Thursday–Friday, 10:00 A.M. to 4:00 P.M. Saturday, 1:00 to 5:00 P.M. Sunday. Wheelchair-accessible.*

Resuming our walk or roll down the west side of Main Street, at the corner of Adams you will find VASCONI'S DRUGS, a local Valu-Rite pharmacy, for all your emergency prescription and associated health needs, cards, trinkets, great postcards, and film and film processing. If you have the kids along, they can get crayons and other fun stuff to keep themselves occupied.

❧ *Vasconi's Drugs, 1381 Main Street, St. Helena 94574; phone (707) 963-1444. Open from 9:00 A.M. to 7:00 P.M. Monday–Saturday, from 10:00 A.M. to 5:00 P.M. Sunday. Visa and MasterCard. Wheelchair-accessible.*

CLAUDIA "K" FLORIST specializes in exquisite orchids, gifts and flowers to go, and metal garden decorations.

❧ *Claudia "K" Florist, 1375 Main Street, St. Helena 94574; phone (707) 963–3101, Web site www.ftd.com/claudiakflorist. Open from 9:00 a.m. to 5:00 p.m. Monday–Saturday, noon to 4:00 p.m. Sunday. Visa and MasterCard.*

At ALAN'S FRAMES & PHOTOGRAPHY, you can get film, picture frames, photos developed in one hour, and chat with the owner, who restored and recently sold his house, which had been M. F. K. Fisher's home for two decades here in St. Helena.

❧ *Alan's Frames & Photography, 1371 Main Street, St. Helena 94574; phone (707) 963–9294, e-mail alans@fcs.net. Open from 9:00 A.M. to 6:00 P.M. Monday–Saturday. Visa and MasterCard. Wheelchair-accessible.*

If you're thinking of taking home a colorful painting to remember your wine-country experience forever, be sure to stop at THE GALLERY ON MAIN STREET. Bright and cheerful colors depict local vineyard scenes, painted primarily by local artists. We also like the classic French art posters. English wine-bottle stoppers cost only $9.50.

❧ *The Gallery on Main Street, 1359 Main Street, St. Helena 94574; phone (707) 963–3350. Open from 10:00 A.M. to 5:00 P.M. daily. Visa, MasterCard, and American Express. Wheelchair-accessible.*

South just one door from the gallery is a local favorite, THE MODEL BAKERY, a wonderful bakery-cafe where you can get fabulous Old World–style scones, muffins, croissants, breakfast pastries, and breads to go or eat here with teas or Spinelli espresso drinks. We love their oat bread. Light meals are also here to tempt, including daily specials such as fresh spinach soup ($3.75), meat or veggie brick-oven pizzas ($5.00), and a great sandwich special ($5.00).

Soft yellow walls, ceiling fans, and black-and-white-checked linoleum set the mood. If you're lucky, you can get a window table and alternate between people watching and newspaper reading.

❧ *The Model Bakery, 1357 Main Street, St. Helena 94574; phone (707) 963–8192. Open from 7:00 A.M. to 6:00 P.M. Tuesday–Saturday, 8:00 A.M. to 4:00 P.M. Sunday. Visa and MasterCard. Wheelchair-accessible*

South of the bar you will find GAIL'S CAFE, a funky step into the past complete with soda fountain and ice cream parlor, player piano, jukebox, antiques, and collectibles. Gail and John Marshek's cafe's walls are covered with original old signs, the counter's stools are vinyl-backed, and the oak back bar over the espresso counter was built in 1861 in Sacramento. The mahogany apothecary cabinets were built in the 1900s in Oakland in a building that burned in the

ST. HELENA HOME OF THE LATE M. F. K. FISHER

1960s riots, near where Gail grew up. *Sunset* magazine readers voted Gail's one of the best cafes and ice cream emporiums in the western United States and Napa residents voted it the Best Sweet Place in 1999.

Gail's features Bud's Ice Cream of San Francisco, unbelievable shakes, flavored Cokes (always liked those cherry Cokes), nonfat frozen yogurt, smoothies, daily special pastas, espressos, sandwiches, soups and salads, a killer grilled cheese ($5.95), and a tremendous half-pound hamburger ($6.50), with fries or homemade potato chips for $1.95 extra. Loads of locals pile in here for daily lunch specials, especially corned beef and cabbage. Oh yes, the fudge is made here—chocolate, cappuccino, maple, or rocky road.

Great spot downtown for a full breakfast too, ranging from eggs and their friends to thick French toast and pancakes. Nothing over $7.00.

❧ *Gail's Cafe 1347 Main Street, St. Helena 94574; phone (707) 963–3332, Web site www.napavalley.com/gails. Open from 8:00 A.M. to 8:00 P.M.; closes earlier in winter. Beer and wine. Visa, MasterCard, and American Express. Partly wheelchair-accessible.*

DAVID'S is St. Helena's authorized Rolex and Cartier jewelry dealer since 1976.

❧ *David's, 1343 Main Street, St. Helena 94574; phone (707) 963–0239. Open from 10:00 A.M. to 5:30 P.M. Tuesday–Saturday. Visa, MasterCard, and American Express. Wheelchair-accessible.*

BISON is Main Street's newest high fashion boutique featuring "American and European country life apparel" with a distinct western flare. Owner Michelle Newman designs fabulous leather bags, Norwegian sweaters, and belts made in Italy, and also sells Double D Ranchwear, Bavarian blouses, silk scarves, and Austrian suede pants, as well as custom-made boots from the United States and Italy.

Bison, 1341 Main Street, St. Helena 94574; hone (707) 963–8883. Open from 10:00 A.M. to 5:30 P.M. Monday–Saturday, 10:30 A.M. to 4:00 P.M. Sunday. Visa, MasterCard, and American Express. Wheelchair-accessible.

Wayne Armstrong and Marc Robbins, who own Patina across the street, have recently opened another fine boutique featuring contemporary jewelry. Stop in at PALLADIUM just to soak up the ultra contemporary design—of both the store and its jewelry. Most of the latter is so beautiful that just viewing it is a peaceful experience.

❧ *Palladium, 1339 Main Street, St. Helena 94574; phone (707) 963–5900, fax (707) 963–5757. Open from 10:00 A.M. to 5:30 P.M. daily. Visa, MasterCard, and American Express. Wheelchair-accessible.*

BUCHANAN'S STATIONERY sells fine letter papers, artists' materials (in case you left sketch pads, pencils, watercolors etc. at home), cards, gifts, and wrapping paper.

❧ *Buchanan's Stationery, 1337 Main Street, St. Helena 94574; phone (707) 963–3198. Open from 9:30 A.M. to 5:00 P.M. Monday–Saturday. Visa, MasterCard, and American Express. Wheelchair-accessible.*

Don't miss GOODMAN'S SINCE 1879, just south of Buchanan's. The clothing is resort, the wine-country souvenir shirts resemble Hawaiian, the ceiling creaks, and the place is loaded with local history. Joking aside, those wannabe Hawaiian shirts are the best available in the Napa Valley.

Check out the historic-clothing display case toward the back of the store, the Abraham, Cecelia, Jacob, and Julius Goodman photos, the original articles of the 1906 incorporation of Goodman–Lauter Company, and the bargain balcony.

The women's clothing is natural fiber, loose and lovely, some in ample sizes, including Cut Loose dresses.

❧ *Goodman's Since 1879, 1331 Main Street, St. Helena 94574; phone (707)*

963–1750. Open from 10:00 A.M. to 6:00 P.M. Monday–Saturday, 10:00 A.M. to 5:00 P.M. Sunday. Visa, MasterCard, and Discover. Wheelchair-accessible.

One door down, NATURE ETC. sells mood music, nature-learning toys and puzzles, and name bead bracelets in case you forget your name or your child's name.

❧ *Nature Etc., 1327 Main Street, St. Helena 94574; phone (707) 963–1706, Open from 10:00 A.M. to 5:30 P.M. Sunday–Thursday, 10:00 A.M. to 6:00 P.M. Friday–Saturday. Visa and MasterCard. Wheelchair-accessible.*

Even if you aren't a chocoholic, you must go into NAPA VALLEY CHOCOLATES for a sensuous experience. Candy Cane Dryer (yes, that is the owner's name) and her son Adam Burns and daughter Elizabeth Dryer have been making candy the old-fashioned way by roasting the cocoa beans. They make all the caramels by hand (occasionally assisted by their new machine).

Voted the "Best of Napa Valley Place to Get Something Sweet" in 1998, this family is a group of zany artists whose medium is chocolate. Adam makes chocolate sculptures, like the hand-painted white-chocolate Madame Mustard for the Napa Valley Mustard Festival, while Elizabeth puts tiny chocolate eyeballs with pupils on white-chocolate-covered gummy worms. Notice the collection of old chocolate cans and flour sifters on top of a shelf near the front window.

❧ *Napa Valley Chocolates, 1325 Main Street, St. Helena 94574; phone (707) 967–0808. Open from 10:00-ish to 6:00-ish daily. Visa, MasterCard, American Express, and Discover. Wheelchair-accessible.*

Wine fans should not miss the ST. HELENA WINE CENTER, where you can taste and purchase the finest and most rare wines made and sold in the Valley, often at discount prices. Many of the wines here are true collectibles.

The St. Helena Wine Center is primarily owned by the extremely knowledgeable and local Beringer family, founders of Beringer Vineyards. Recently the store began to offer high-end liquor, such as specialty tequilas, rums, vodkas, and single-malt scotches.

❧ *St. Helena Wine Center, 1321 Main Street, St. Helena 94574; phone (707) 963–1313 or (800) 331–1311, fax (707) 963–8069, e-mail shwc@aol.com. Open from 10:00 A.M. to 6:00 P.M. Monday–Saturday, 10:00 A.M. to 5:00 P.M. Sunday. Visa, MasterCard, American Express, Diners Club, Discover, and JCB. Wheelchair-accessible.*

Next door to St. Helena Wine Center, HEAVEN & EARTH majors in aromatherapy, essences and body, bath, and spirit goodies.

❧ *Heaven & Earth, 1313 Main Street, St. Helena 94574; (707) 963–1124. Open from 10:00 A.M. to 6:00 P.M. daily. Visa and MasterCard. Wheelchair-accessible.*

MAIN STREET BOOKS is one of the smallest and most charmingly independent book stores in the world. This is a real book-person's bookstore, featuring new and used books of literature, the classics, great children's books, and nice, warm people. Because of their space limitations, these folks have mastered the special-order process.

❧ *Main Street Books, 1315 Main Street, St. Helena 94574; phone (707) 963–1338. Open from 10:00 A.M. to 5:30 P.M. Monday–Saturday. Visa and MasterCard. Wheelchair-accessible.*

One of St. Helena's landmarks is GILLWOOD'S CAFE, a local institution and old-timey hangout for "homestyle cooking," even though it's only been here since 1990. Flowered vinyl tablecloths cover the tables, surprisingly comfortable wooden benches line the walls, and there's a "community table" down the middle of the dining room to "share with friends and neighbors." Locals sit reading books and newspapers as long as they want. Breakfast is better than standard and includes Dickinson's preserves to go with house-baked breads.

This is where you get those all-American reliables such as meatloaf with mashed potatoes, fresh vegetables, and mushroom gravy ($8.75), chicken fried steak with mashed potatoes and country gravy ($9.25), Yankee pot roast ($9.95), crispy boneless half chicken with creamed sweet Vidalia onions and country potatoes ($9.95), patty melts, BLTs, a good old tuna-salad sandwich ($6.40), and even a healthy apple, pecan, and Gorgonzola salad ($7.50). At lunch, all sandwiches come with green salad, french fries, or homemade soup. At dinner, salads are extra and come with a mini-loaf of multigrain bread.

❧ *Gillwood's Cafe, 1313 Main Street, St. Helena 94574; phone (707) 963–1788. Open for breakfast, lunch, and dinner. Visa, MasterCard, American Express, Discover, and Diners Club. Wheelchair-accessible.*

Eccola's women's resort clothing occupies the front of the St. Helena Hotel, a character of a small hotel whose lobby is packed with dolls, a pack-rat heaven. Once a flop house, St. Helena Hotel is now a Victorian bed and breakfast. Walk down the short alleyway just to check out the lobby, complete with spittoons.

The next shop down the street is Sweet Pea, a great place for kids of all ages with Brio toys, trains, cars, and clothes. Its neighbor to the south is I-elle, which sells professional women's clothing both here and in Sonoma. My Favorite Things is a delightful shop with table settings, picture frames, and home accessories, perfect to take home as gifts.

Plan to spend some time wandering through ST. HELENA ANTIQUES & OTHER FINE COLLECTIBLES, where you will find everything from old pots to huge and heavy statuary, a collector's treasure-hunt paradise.

❧ *St. Helena Antiques & Other Fine Collectibles, 1231 Main Street, St. Helena 94574; phone (707) 963–5878. Open from 11:00 A.M. to 5:00 P.M. Wednesday– Monday. Visa and MasterCard. Wheelchair-accessible.*

Just south of the antiques heaven is GIUGNI'S DELICATESSEN, an extremely local deli purveying everything from jawbreakers to great sandwiches. Papers tacked to the walls flap in the air conditioner's breeze, photos on the back wall are signed by Daryl Hannah and Joe Montana (yes, it's that popular), and decades of old memories are collected and posted for all to enjoy. Attention British candy fans: Giugni's has Violet Crumbles and loose candy.

The sandwiches are huge and varied with twelve bread and roll choices, plus twenty-three meats, from turkey pastrami to mild or hot coppa. Cheeses are just as abundant, and the service is cheerful and irreverent. But then we know owner Lonny Dunlap from when he had the same sort of deli across from the mission in Sonoma, a space now occupied by Cucina Viansa. Great pickups for picnics at the wineries, since very few of them are allowed to sell food.

❧ *Giugni's Delicatessen, 1227 Main Street, St. Helena 94574; phone (707) 963–3421. Open from 9:00 A.M. to 5:00 P.M. Beer and wine. No credit cards. Wheelchair-accessible.*

South of the OK Barber Shop, where the barber snoops behind a screen in the back so that he can see you if you come in (reminiscent of a confessional), is MARIO'S FOR MEN, a fashionable men's boutique with clothes from Jhane Barnes, Zanella, Nicole Miller, Mondo, Cole-Haan, Caruso sport coats, Trafalgar Braces, Equilibrio shirts, leather shoes and belts, and other elegant resort and dining wear. (This is a brother store to D. Champaign on the east side of Main Street.)

❧ *Mario's for Men, 1223 Main Street, St. Helena 94574; phone (707) 963–1603. Open from 10:00 A.M. to 6:00 P.M. daily. Visa, MasterCard, American Express, Diners Club, Discover, and JCB. Wheelchair-accessible.*

The next store down the street is San Francisco's splendiferous WILKES SPORT, a resort-wear child of Wilkes Bashford. Men and women will find the finest in fashion here from lots of Italian designers, including Zegna, Loro Piana, Biella, Piazza Sempione, Industria, and Yoshi Hishinuma. Wilkes Sport even provides treats for your dogs, who are most welcome here. How refreshing!

❧ *Wilkes Sport, 1219 Main Street, St. Helena 94574; phone (707) 963–4323. Open from 10:00 A.M. to 6:00 P.M. Visa, MasterCard, American Express, and Diners Club. Wheelchair-accessible.*

R. S. BASSO HOME FURNISHINGS (1829) is a great place to stop for dramatic French posters, cigar music (sexy jazz) CDs, interesting furniture, and mosaic objects.

❧ *R.S. Basso Home Furnishings, 1219 Main Street, St. Helena 94574; phone (707) 963–0391. Open from 10:00 A.M. to 6:00 P.M. Monday–Saturday, 10:30 A.M.–5:00 P.M. Sunday. Visa and MasterCard. Wheelchair-accessible.*

Now we come to ANA'S CANTINA, where El Salvador native Ana provides a unique hangout for bar regulars to spend their days and farm workers and winery owners to stop by for breakfast or come in after work to play pool, throw darts, listen to music from country to reggae, and dine on Ana's special food. Francis Ford Coppola drops in to sing karaoke in Spanish on Monday and Thursday nights under a huge canvas portrait of Freda Kahlo that hangs in "Ana's Gallery," which means the walls of the bar and restaurant. Coming partly from an Irish background, Kathleen was slightly alarmed by the regular "Black and Tan Night," but here it just means one night when they officially mix Guiness light and dark ales.

Music nights (Thursday, Friday, and Saturday) have featured Dana Hubbard and Philip Claypool, among others. The margaritas are famous, and the combination platillos range from only $5.95 to $7.95. Try the fajitas or Pollo Acapulco.

❧ *Ana's Cantina, 1205 Main Street, St. Helena 94574; phone (707) 963–4921. Open for breakfast and lunch daily, dinner 6:00 to 9:00 P.M. Thursday–Saturday. Visa, MasterCard, and Diners Club. Wheelchair-accessible.*

At VALLEY EXCHANGE we found wonderfully priced imitation Fiestaware dishes, pottery, and fun local products. The book selection, which you'll find toward the back of the store, includes *The Hot Flash Cookbook* and *Getting in Touch with Your Inner Bike*, both prominently displayed. You will also enjoy Graffeo coffee beans and chocolates, Annette's Napa Valley Truffles, Napa Valley Herbs (Kathleen finds these to be among the best and definitely best priced for the quality), Napa Valley Cabernet sauce, loads of pepper mills, great tea towels, and floor lamps.

❧ *Valley Exchange, 1201 Main Street, St. Helena 94574; phone (707) 963–7423. Open from 10:00 A.M. to 5:30 P.M. Monday–Saturday, open at 11:00 A.M. Sunday. Visa and MasterCard. Wheelchair-accessible.*

Some of the Napa Valley's best restaurants are on St. Helena's side streets, so now we will take you to them. Terra and Miramonte are next door to each other on Railroad Avenue, east of Main Street.

In what had been Showley's Restaurant for decades, Cindy Pawleyn and group have launched another delightful success called MIRAMONTE.

With a historic 1860 building, Miramonte looks like a country inn, indoors as well as on the pleasant brick patio. Simple linens cover the tables, and the excellent and unpretentious service contributes to a relaxing meal.

➳ *Miramonte, 1327 Railroad Avenue, St. Helena 94574; phone (707) 963–1200. Open for lunch and dinner Tuesday–Sunday. Visa, MasterCard, American Express, and Diners Club. Wheelchair-accessible.*

TERRA is one of California's finest and most creative restaurants, and one that gets lots of publicity. Hiro (Hiroyoshi) Sone and Lissa Doumani have created the perfect blend of history and culture in their restaurant in this historic 1884 Taylor, Duckworth & Company Foundry Building, dignifying the stone walls and large arched windows with a comfortable decor that immediately makes visitors feel at home.

Hiro developed and directed the kitchen at Wolfgang Puck's Spago in Los Angeles, and Lissa is earth mother and pastry chef, with deep roots in wine-

TERRA RESTAURANT ENTRANCE

country vineyards. The food they create speaks for itself in an unabashed California-Asian-French way, the definition of which you will experience by dining at Terra. The menu changes with the seasons.

Appetizers may include tartare of salmon and tuna ($11.00), terrine of Sonoma foie gras on fig endive salad ($13.50), or salad of heirloom beets, sweet corn, and yellow wax beans with blue cheese ($9.50). If you are lucky, main-course experiences may include one of our favorites, broiled sake-marinated Chilean sea bass with shrimp dumplings ($22), grilled ranch quail with wild-mushroom risotto and Pinot Noir sauce ($22), pan-roasted noix of sweetbreads on ragout of farro and wild mushrooms ($21), or grilled milk-fed veal chop with mashed potatoes and Pinot Noir sauce ($27). Our favorite dessert is the sautéed strawberries in black-pepper Cabernet Sauvignon sauce with vanilla-bean ice cream ($7.00); or maybe it's the plum almond kuchen with crème fraîche. Jerry likes the chocolate mousseline tart with pecan sablé and cof-fee granité.

Terra's wine list is exceptional, which should be no surprise.

❧ Terra, 1345 Railroad Avenue, St. Helena 94574; phone (707) 963–8931. Open for dinner Wednesday–Monday. Beer and wine. Visa, MasterCard, Diners Club, and Carte Blanche. Wheelchair-access down the alleyway to the back.

PINOT BLANC, just south of St. Helena proper, is the northern exposure of famed restaurateur Joachim Splichal's Patina Restaurant in Los Angeles. Sean A. Knight executes the orders as executive chef.

Pinot Blanc has one of the most soothing decors in the wine country, with its dignified dark wood walls, clublike bar, and private-feeling dining areas. Check out the great French magazine cartoons on the lounge walls and the wall-paper of actual wine labels on the walls down the hall to the rest rooms.

Pinot Blanc serves lunch and dinner, with daily specials. Some of the most popular dishes are the steak frites with Pernod butter ($22.95), Basque grilled farm chicken ($14.50), planked Atlantic salmon with French lentils ($19.95), a pot of mussels with Pernod broth ($15.95), and the Soup of Yesterday (always better) at $6.50. Lunch may feature endive salad with Roquefort cheese and caramelized walnuts ($7.95), French onion soup ($6.95), high-cholesterol (but oh so good) foie gras ($13.95), big salads, burgers and sandwiches including a good Niçoise salad ($13.95), creative pastas, exotic fish, and braised short ribs ($18.95).

Regular nightly specials include Tuesday's Scottish mallard duck, Wednesday's roasted local squab, Thursday's Scottish pheasant, Friday's grilled veal chop, Saturday's lamb shank, and Sunday's Calistoga pig.

❧ Pinot Blanc, 641 Main Street (Highway 29), St. Helena 94574; phone (707)

963–6191. Open for lunch and dinner. Visa, MasterCard, American Express, Discover, Diners Club, and JCB. Wheelchair-accessible.

St. Helena to Calistoga

As we head north on Highway 29 from St. Helena, the first two major stops are on your left (west). Beringer Vineyards comes up quickly on the left barely outside St. Helena, and the Culinary Institute of America's western campus and its *Wine Spectator* Greystone Restaurant appears 0.4 mile farther.

Amidst what our children called "the tree tunnel" and Napans call the "Row of Elms," you enter BERINGER VINEYARDS, "the oldest continuously operating winery in the Napa Valley." Beringer is the most spectacular winery setting in the Valley, with exquisitely cultivated gardens, vast lawns (no picnicking, please), preserved historic buildings, fun tours, and ample wine tasting in three places. But the wine is made across the road where you can't go, so enjoy showtime here.

In 1876 German immigrants Jacob and Frederick Beringer bought land and founded Beringer Winery. Chinese laborers returning to the San Francisco Bay Area, after completing the transcontinental railroad, hand-chiseled rock tunnels 250 feet into the hills. Wines are still aged and stored here.

After the winery was built, Jacob lived in an existing 1848 farmhouse on the property, now restored and expanded and called Hudson House, which serves as Beringer Vineyards' Culinary Arts Center and home of the School for American Chefs.

Frederick began construction of the seventeen-room mansion to re-create the family home on Germany's Rhine River. Frederick's Rhine House is now listed in the National Register of Historic Places and serves as Beringer's hospitality center. We recommend just walking into Rhine House to experience its opulence. An excellent collection of books on wine and food are available in what was Frederick Beringer's library. Notice the stained-glass windows.

Premium-wine tastings take place upstairs in the Private Reserve Room (regular tasting and souvenir purchasing is in the Old Bottling Room and the Rhine House toward the back of the property). Enjoy delicious tastes of breads, oils and sauces such as four dipping and marinade oils, olive and grapeseed oils, yummy mayonnaise, bread spreads (artichoke and garlic eggplant), and pasta sauces.

 Fine points: In September 2000, the Nestlé Corporation sold Beringer Wine Estates to Foster's Brewing Group, Ltd., of Australia and its Midara Blass international wine division. The Beringer family has the St. Helena Wine Center in downtown

CAESAR SALAD WITH GARLIC OIL
from Beringer Vineyards

INGREDIENTS FOR THE DRESSING:

1 Tbs Dijon mustard   *1 anchovy fillet*
1 Tbs lemon juice   *1 Tbs Parmesan cheese, grated*
1 tsp salt   *1 tsp ground black pepper*
1 Tbs red wine vinegar   *½ cup Infused Garlic Grape Seed Oil*
1 tsp garlic, minced

INGREDIENTS FOR THE CROUTONS:

1 cup sourdough bread cut into ¾-inch cubes
1 Tbs Infused Garlic Grape Seed Oil
salt to taste

INGREDIENTS FOR THE SALAD:

3 Tbs Parmesan cheese, grated
1 head romaine lettuce (washed and cut into 1-inch pieces)

PREPARATION:

Combine first 9 ingredients in a blender to make the Caesar dressing.

Toss the bread cubes with Garlic Grape Seed Oil and salt to taste. Bake croutons in an oven at 450°F for 4–5 minutes until lightly golden.

Toss the lettuce with the dressing. Add the croutons and the Parmesan cheese, and toss again. Serves 4.

St. Helena on Main Street. Tasting fee: three tastes for $3.00 with credit against purchase; with private reserve, tastes based on bottle cost. Featured wines: White Zinfandel, Johannisberg Riesling, Chenin Blanc, Gewürztraminer, Alluvium Blanc, Viognier, Chardonnay, Gamay Beaujolais, Pinot Noir, Zinfandel, Cabernet Sauvignon, and dessert wines. Recently inaugurated are White Merlot, and six "Founder's Estate" wines, which are lighter versions of Merlot, Syrah, Pinot Noir, Chardonnay, Cabernet Sauvignon, and Sauvignon Blanc, all at $10 or $11 a bottle. Owner: Foster's Brewing Group's Midara Blass. Winemaker: Ed Sbragia. Cases: Undefined. Acres: 600.

Beringer Vineyards, 2000 Main Street, St. Helena 94574; phone (707)

*963–4812, fax (707) 963–8129, Web site www.beringer.com. Open from 9:30
A.M. to 6:00 P.M. daily except Thanksgiving, Christmas, and New Year's. Tours
($5.00) are every half hour from 10:00 A.M. to 5:00 P.M. Visa, MasterCard,
American Express, and Discover. Old Bottling Room is wheelchair-accessible.*

As you progress northward you absolutely *must* stop at the CULINARY
INSTITUTE OF AMERICA AT GREYSTONE, the thirty-acre western campus for continuing education of the CIA–Hyde Park, New York, the foremost culinary educational institution in the United States.

While this campus welcomes professionals in a wide range of fields connected to food and wine (including writers), home chefs are welcome to indulge
in watching cooking demonstrations held in Greystone's exquisite Ecolab
Theatre ($5.00, and you get a hat to take home).

Built in the late 1880s for William Bourn and Everett Wise as a cooperative
winery where Napa Valley growers could make wine and circumvent San
Francisco's tightly controlled wine dealers, Greystone is built in the
Richardsonian–Romanesque style with 22-inch-thick walls of locally quarried
tufa stone. It is now listed in the National Register of Historic Places. Notice the
cathedral ceilings, grand arches, tasteful antiques, and massive hand-crafted furniture, combined with the latest state-of-the-art cooking equipment.

First known as the Bourn and Wise Cellar, Bourn sold the building in 1894
to Charles Carpy, a founder of the California Wine Association, which then
became one of the largest wine producers in California. At its peak under the
CWA, Greystone could make 1,349,000 gallons of wine with a marvelous gravity system. Eventually passing through several owners, the Christian Brothers
bought the property in 1950, making brandy and wine here for many years.

Heublein bought Christian Brothers' wine line and eventually closed down
the operation at Greystone. The Culinary Institute bought the building from
Heublein, which, in turn, made a magnificent donation to the nonprofit CIA,
enabling it to embark on a fabulous restoration project you can now enjoy.

Do not miss the De Baun Museum, where you can view Christian
Brothers' famed winery leader's Brother Timothy's fabulous corkscrew collections, winemaking artifacts, a Tuscan olive press, and an extensive collection
of oak cooperage. In front of the building and to the left, stroll through the
organic Cannard herb garden on little terraces and wander among culinary
herbs, onion and garlic beds, edible flowers and herbal teas, and the salad-
greens plot. This garden provides the teaching and restaurant kitchens with
more than 145 different types of vegetables, sixty varieties of culinary herbs,
twenty-seven types of fruit, and eleven varieties of berries.

The fifteen acres of Merlot grapes on the grounds result in custom-crushed

SPICY PORK KEBABS WITH MOORISH FLAVORS
from Wine Spectator *Greystone Restaurant* at the Culinary Institute of America in St. Helena

INGREDIENTS:

2 garlic cloves, sliced	¼ tsp crushed red pepper
salt to taste	1 tsp curry powder
freshly ground pepper to taste	4 Tbs olive oil
1 tsp coriander seeds	1 Tbs lemon juice
¾ tsp paprika	1 Tbs parsley, chopped
¾ tsp cumin seeds	1 lb lean pork, cut into ¾-inch cubes
½ tsp thyme, dried	1 lb red grapes

PREPARATION:

In a mortar, pound the garlic with a pinch of salt to make a paste.

In a dry skillet, heat the coriander seeds, paprika, cumin seeds, thyme, crushed red pepper, and curry powder until hot and aromatic, about 30 seconds. Remove from pan and put the mixture into a spice grinder or mortar and pestle. Grind to make a fine powder.

In a bowl, combine the garlic, spices, olive oil, lemon juice, parsley, ¾ tsp salt, pepper, and pork cubes. Toss well to coat completely and let marinate several hours, mixing occasionally.

Skewer the pork along with the red grapes and grill. Yields 12 skewers.

and custom-bottled Greystone Cellars wine, available at the Campus Store and in the *Wine Spectator* Greystone Restaurant. Ah, the Campus Store. Kathleen thought she had arrived in heaven: every cooking utensil imaginable, 2,000 cookbook titles including children's cookbooks, the CIA videotape series, all prices and colors of chef's uniforms and aprons, and a world market of unusual spices and ingredients. Check out the big stove imported from the Hyde Park campus.

A new exciting feature of the CIA is its Apple Pie Bakery Cafe, a real classroom for baking and pastry students where you can enjoy inexpensive lunches and snacks such as roasted portobello mushroom, salmon and cucumber, and even a turkey, lettuce, and tomato sandwich for under $6.00. Pizzas, soups, salads, and pastries complete the menu and allow you to enjoy CIA quality at low prices.

Now to experience the *Wine Spectator* Greystone Restaurant, where every Adam Tihany–designed table has a view of the restaurant's chefs (no students) at work. You can dine and sip in front of the roaring fireplace or bask in the sun on the terrace overlooking Charles Krug Winery and part of the Napa Valley.

An excellent eight-page wine list accompanies the creative menu, which offers you tastes of the Mediterranean from Spanish tapas, Italian antipasti, and eastern Mediterranean meze. With great pleasure we tried tempura soft shell crab ($12), venison carpaccio ($11), wild striped bass ($24), and sauteed squab ($27). Now you can purchase Greystone's sensational hearth-baked breads to take home for only $6.00.

There's even a cigar menu of fine and unique cigars. Servers provide cutters and matches so that you can indulge in the cigar in the terrace's designated smoking area. Be sure to enter the CIA's annual Apple Pie Recipe Contest.

❧ *The Culinary Institute of America at Greystone, 2555 Main Street, St. Helena 94574; phones: restaurant (707) 967–1010, continuing education (707) 967–0600; Web site www.ciachef.edu and www.digitalchef.com. Restaurant open from 11:30 A.M. to 9:00 P.M. Thursday–Monday, December 1–March 31, and daily April 1–November 30; Campus Store open from 10:00 A.M. to 6:00 P.M. daily. Demonstrations and Kitchen Viewings 10:30 A.M. and 1:30 and 3:30 P.M. Saturday and Sunday. Visa, MasterCard, American Express, Diners Club, and Discover. Wheelchair-accessible via parking lot and terrace at north end of building.*

As you leave the Culinary Institute, turn left to continue north on Highway 29 to Charles Krug, Markham, St. Clement, Freemark Abbey, Folie à Deux, Ehlers Grove, Frank-Rombauer/Hanns Kornell Champagne, and Stonegate wineries, plus an entrance to Sterling—all before you get to Calistoga.

Turn right (east) just north of the CIA to CHARLES KRUG WINERY, the "oldest operating winery in the Napa Valley," founded by Prussian-born Charles Krug. Krug died in 1892, and San Francisco banker James Moffitt bought the winery from Krug's heirs. (Remember, Beringer claims to be the "oldest continuously operating winery," the key word being *continuously*.)

Rosa and Cesare Mondavi purchased the property from Moffitt in 1943. Their son, Peter Mondavi, Sr., named one of twelve "Living Legends" by the Napa Valley Vintners' Association, took over the winery in 1966 and instilled cold fermentation and use of French oak barrels, passed management duties on to his sons, Peter Jr. and Marc. They all live on the family estate.

Olive trees line the driveway to the historic buildings and the separate tasting room (be sure to try the Charles Krug Peter Mondavi Family Extra Virgin Olive Oil, based on Krug estate olives). Catch the fabulous view of Greystone, and take time to picnic in the vineyards.

If you had any previous misgivings about Krug wines, try them again. They are contenders, particularly the Cabernets and Pinot Noir. You will find Krug wines under both Charles Krug and C. K. Mondavi labels. Their Generations blend won gold medals in 1998 competitions at the National Orange Show, Monterey Wine Competition, and *Dallas Morning News* Wine Competition. Enjoy bread squares to dip into Tuscan Hills grapeseed or olive oils, excellent herbes de Provence, and Scharffen Berger chocolates.

 Fine points: Featured wines: Chardonnay, Sauvignon Blanc, Sangiovese, Cabernet Sauvignon, Merlot, Zinfandel, Pinot Noir, and Generations (blend of Cabernet Sauvignon, Merlot, and Cabernet Franc. Tasting fee $3.00 for regular wines, $5.00 for family reserves. Owner: Peter Mondavi, Sr. Winemakers: John Maynier and Jac Cole. Cases: Charles Krug 100,000, C. K. Mondavi 1,000,000. Acres: 800.

⁂ *Charles Krug Winery, 2800 North Main Street, St. Helena 94574; phone (707) 967–2200, fax (707) 967–2291, e-mail www.charleskrug@pmondavi.com, Web site www.charleskrug.com. Open from 10:30 A.M. to 5:30 P.M. daily. Visa, MasterCard, American Express, and Discover. Wheelchair-accessible.*

MARKHAM VINEYARDS will be on your right going north. Look for a rather industrial new building at the front with flagpoles, dramatic dripping fountains filled with floating lilies, and lovely marguerites in the entrance patio.

The historic building was built as La Ronde Winery in 1874 by prospector Jean Laurent, and passed through various owners over the decades. Bruce Markham bought the winery in 1977 and sold it in 1988 to giant Mercian, Japan's largest wine importer.

The tasting-room entrance is to the left at the rear of the entrance patio, with the daily Tasting Menu posted on a tripod at the door. Mercian has put millions into elegant blond-wood floors, Alexander Calder prints, high ceilings, Robert O. Rowland ceramics, and jazz background music—obviously someone talented is in charge of display and color. Venture upstairs to the gallery for seasonal exhibitions.

You might be interested in the Oaxacan pottery and posters, Napa Valley Wine Auction posters, olive oils, cookbooks, lead-free pewter flatware and corkscrews, jewelry, and wine bottles of doggie treats called Chateau Pooche.

 Fine points: The Chardonnay, Sauvignon Blanc, and Merlot have all been rated tops in California by *Wine Spectator*. Tasting fee; $3.00 for whites, $5.00 for reds. Featured wines: Chardonnay, Merlot, Zinfandel, Cabernet Sauvignon. Owner: Mercian of Japan. Winemaker: Michael Beaulac. Cases: 285,000. Acres: 300.

⁂ *Markham Vineyards, 2812 St. Helena Highway North, St. Helena 94574;*

ST. CLEMENT VINEYARDS

phone (707) 963–5292, fax (707) 963–4616. Open from 10:00 A.M. to 5:00 P.M. daily. Visa, MasterCard, American Express, and JCB. Wheelchair-accessible.

The next winery going north is ST. CLEMENT VINEYARDS in a big yellow-and-white Victorian house up the hill to the left (west) of Highway 29. Leave Markham and turn right, ready to turn left almost immediately and carefully. Park in the lot below and hike up the path, climb the steps, and rest and recover at the patio's wrought-iron tables and chairs. If the hike didn't take your breath away, the view will. As you walk in the front door, turn right to the library and feast your eyes on a marvelous collection of wine books, which you are welcome to leaf through.

San Francisco glass merchant Fritz Rosenbaum built this elegant Gothic-Victorian in 1878 and lived in the house with his family while producing commercial wines in the stone cellar beneath the house, the eighth bonded winery in the Napa Valley.

Bill Robbins bought the property, restored the building, and started Spring Mountain Winery here. It was Robbins's Parrott Mansion, to which he moved Spring Mountain, that was the residence in the "Falcon Crest" night-time soap. The name St. Clement refers to an island at the mouth of the

Potomac River where interim owner Dr. Bill Casey, a Maryland ophthalmologist, loved to sail.

Japanese Sapporo beer company bought the property from Casey in 1987, and in September 1999, St. Clement was sold to Beringer Wine Estates. Both are now owned by Foster's Brewing Group Ltd. of Australia.

Fine points: Tasting fee: $2.00. Featured wines: Chardonnay, Sauvignon Blanc, Merlot, Cabernet Sauvignon, and Oroppas, a Bordeaux-style blend. Owner: Foster's Brewing Group Ltd. of Australia. Winemaker: Bill Ballentine. Cases: 20,000. Acres 3.

❧ *St. Clement Vineyards, 2867 St. Helena Highway North, St. Helena 94574; phone (707) 967–3033 or (800) 331–8266, fax (707) 963–1412, e-mail sclement@napanet.com, Web site www.stclement.com. Open from 10:00 a.m. to 4:00 p.m. daily. Visa, MasterCard, American Express, and Discover. Wheelchair-accessible, although slightly precarious, by parking in lot at top of driveway.*

With bumper stickers asking "Where the Hell is **BALLENTINE VINEYARDS?**" Betty and Van Ballentine launched their own winery in 1998 after growing grapes and making wines for others for decades. Look for Ballentine on the east side of Highway 29, north of Markham and south of Freemark Abbey. It has a tiny tasting room, well worth the stop for the fun and wine.

Ballentine's label is an interesting old survey map of Napa Valley showing the soil conditions exactly where their vineyards are. Give this one a chance.

Fine Points: No tasting fee. Featured wines: Zinfandel, Merlot, Syrah, Cabernet Franc, red table wine. Owners: Betty and Van Ballentine. Winemaker: Jim Moore. Cases: 12,000. Acres: 115.

❧ *Ballentine Vineyards, 2820 St. Helena Highway North, St. Helena 94574; phone (707) 963–3493 or 963–7919, Web site www.ballen tinevineyards.com. Open from 8:00 a.m. to 4:30 p.m. by appointment Monday–Friday. Visa and MasterCard. Wheelchair-accessible.*

To get back on our tour, head north on Highway 29. At your next stop, you can visit Freemark Abbey, Hurd's Bees Wax Candles and Gourmet, and the superb Brava Terrace restaurant.

FREEMARK ABBEY WINERY's name has nothing to do with the Catholic church, although many of us grew up believing there were monks wandering around in long brown robes. The name is actually a combo of Southern Californians Albert "Abbey" Ahern, Charles Freeman, and Markquand Foster, who bought Lombarda Cellars in 1939.

Founder Josephine Marlin Tychson became the first woman to build and operate a winery in California in 1886, which she called Tychson Cellars. San

FREEMARK ABBEY'S COMFORTABLY ELEGANT TASTING ROOM

Lorenzo, California, native Josephine and her Danish husband John Tychson, moved here in 1881 to cure his tuberculosis. They bought 147 acres, known as Tychson Hill, on the west side of Highway 29, for $8,500. He died, and Josephine built a 50-square-foot redwood winery and hired Nils Larsen as foreman to make wine, producing Zinfandel, Riesling, and a Burgundy blend. When phylloxera attacked, she sold the winery to Larsen, who sold it to Antonio Forni, a friend of Josephine's, who renamed it Lombarda Cellars in 1898.

A thinking man, Forni made Chianti and other Italian-style wines to sell to Italian immigrants working Barre, Vermont's marble and granite quarries. Using stones from nearby Glass Mountain, Forni expanded by building a new structure around the wooden one so he wouldn't have to move the tanks and later removed the redwood building. Prohibition shut Forni down, and along came the Freemark Abbey boys in 1939, who sold their wine primarily in San Francisco.

Freemark Abbey went through several owners, ending up with a group that included the late Chuck Carpy and Jim Warren, Dick Heggie, Brad Webb, and Laurie Wood. Carpy is generally credited with resurrecting the winery.

Enjoy the living room feeling in the tasting room with large upholstered chairs, elegant wood furniture, and a roaring fire in the walk-in fireplace. Freemark Abbey was named "Winery of the Year" by *Wine & Spirits* magazine in 1994, 1996, and 1997.

 Fine points: Tasting fee: $4.00 to $5.00 (you keep the glass). Featured wines: Chardonnay, Cabernet, Sauvignon-Bosche, Cabernet Sauvignon-Sycamore, Cabernet Sauvignon, Merlot, Sangiovese, Petite Sirah, Viognier, Johannisberg Riesling, Cabernet Franc, Merlot, and Edelwein gold late harvest Riesling. Owners: the group. Winemaker: Tim Bell. Cases: 40,000. Acres: 330.

Freemark Abbey Winery, 3022 St. Helena Highway North, St. Helena 94574; phone (707) 963–9694, fax (707) 963–9554. Open from 10:00 A.M. to 4:30 P.M. Visa, MasterCard, and American Express. Wheelchair-accessible.

Right next to Freemark Abbey, and in the same building complex about 2 miles north of St. Helena, don't miss HURD BEES WAX CANDLES AND GOURMET. The sweet, musty smell of candles-in-progress permeates the air in this rambling emporium of everything to do with candles, including encased buzzing bees, honey, and women making and dipping candles. This is an aesthetic and educational experience in a casual but professional atmosphere.

Hurd Bees Wax Candles and Gourmet, 3020 St. Helena Highway North, St. Helena 94574; phone (707) 963–7211, fax (707) 963–4358. Visa, MasterCard, American Express, and Discover. Partly wheelchair-accessible.

Just north of Hurd's is one of our favorite restaurants, the casually elegant and comfortable BRAVA TERRACE. Owner/chef Fred Halpert has worked with the best: Chapel, Senderens, Verge, Jacques Maximin, and Louis Outhier, for starters. His classic French training merges with California wine-country realities and peppers and vegetables from the back garden to treat you to some of the most refreshing real food to survive the puddle and stacking schools of California nouvelle cuisine. If you are in Yountville or San Francisco, try Halpert's hot Livefire, and Napa Valley Ovens's bakery in Calistoga.

As you walk in the front door, which actually faces the back of the property, the small open kitchen is right ahead for you to watch and enjoy. To your left down the hall to the rest rooms are framed letters to Fred Halpert from Paul Bocuse, James Beard House's late director Peter Kump, and a Man Ray sketch of Halpert. Hardwood floors, big windows, and an enormous stone fireplace make a cozy room, particularly on a rainy day. In good weather, enjoy the terrace with its white umbrellas.

For food starters, you absolutely must indulge Executive Chef Miguel

Franco's slightly salty homemade potato chips with melted Danish blue cheese and basil pesto ($4.75), the rock crab cake with pickled beet tartar sauce is different and intriguing ($10.95). The grilled vegetable melt sandwich was huge and yummy, with plenty of portobello mushroom, zucchini, eggplant, and cheddar ($8.75) and grilled salmon with lemon aioli sandwiches ($10.50) were better than perfect. Try the daily risottos or pastas ($13.95), the Cassoulet of lentil du Puy with chicken, spicy turkey sausage, and pork tenderloin ($16.95), the half slab of BBQ ribs with corn and garlic bread ($16.95), superb braised veal shank osso bucco with garlic mashed potatoes ($17.50), or the positively no oil or butter penne pasta with chopped tomatoes, garlic, balsamic vinegar, and basil ($12.50).

We blissfully tried all the "extras," including spicy fries, roasted potato cake, sautéed spinach, and garlic mashed potatoes—a potato lover's feast. Daily specials draw regular fans with fish on Monday, ribs and Zin on Tuesday, braised short ribs on Thursday, 20-ounce T-bone steak on Friday, coq au vin on Saturday, and crispy half chicken on Sunday.

➳ *Brava Terrace, 3010 St. Helena Highway North, St. Helena 94574; phone (707) 963–9300, fax (707) 963–9581. Beer and wine. Open from noon to 9:00 P.M. daily May–November, closed Wednesday December–April. Visa, MasterCard, and American Express. Wheelchair-accessible.*

On to more wineries and the St. Helena Premium Outlets. After you leave the Freemark Abbey complex, head north and over a little hill, at the bottom of which is the driveway to FOLIE À DEUX WINERY. Turn right (east) at the colored flags flying across from the St. Helena Premium Outlets, and right again at the oak tree. The little yellow century-old farm house and its new add-on serve as tasting room in this bucolic setting.

Enjoy your picnic at a table on the lawn under the old oak tree. You can even tour the new caves Friday and Saturday at 11:00 A.M. and 1:00 P.M. by appointment.

When the two psychiatrists who founded the winery told psychiatrist friends they were going to fulfill a mutual dream by starting a winery, their friends said the couple were showing classic symptoms of folie à deux, a term that refers to two "batty individuals [who] share the same delusional ideas or fantasies about the real world." In other words, they were both crazy. Indeed.

Folie à Deux began producing wine in 1981 with grapes from its twelve acres, winning "Best of Show" at the 1985 California State Fair for its 1983 Chardonnay. In 1995, renowned winemaker Dr. Richard Peterson and friends bought the winery and hired winemaker Scott Harvey, named by wine writer Dan Berger as one of the "Ten Best Winemakers in America" in 1990. Watch for the Amador Zinfandel from the 130-year-old Grandpère Vineyard. Be sure to taste St. Helena Olive Oil Company's flavored oils and their new Eggplant Marinara. Custom bottle etching is available ($20–$100).

Featured wines: Chardonnay, Chenin Blanc, Cabernet Sauvignon, Merlot, Zinfandel, Menage à Trois, and "fantaisie" sparkling wine. Owner: Winery Asset Management, Dr. Richard Peterson, CEO. Winemaker: Scott Harvey. Cases: 25,000. Acres: 13.

❧ *Folie à Deux Winery, 3070 North St. Helena Highway, St. Helena 94574; phone (707) 963–1160 or (800) 473–4454, fax (707) 963–9223, e-mail fantasy@ folie-a-deux.com, Web site www.folie-a-deux.com. Open from 10:00 A.M. to 5:00 P.M. daily in winter, to 5:30 P.M. in summer. Visa, MasterCard, and American Express. Not wheelchair-accessible.*

To get to EHLERS GROVE and CARTLIDGE & BROWNE wineries, turn right (east) on Ehlers Road off Highway 29, then left at the sign to the small pinkish beige stone building with planters full of colorful flowers and a black iron rocking chair near the tall sliding wooden door. Notice the gorgeous wildflowers growing beneath the grove of olive trees next to the winery. You are welcome to picnic here, reminiscent of some extremely romantic French scenes. If no one seems to be around, ring the bell by the door.

Bernard Ehlers built the wonderful stone winery in 1886, and it has since been inhabited by ghosts, Saintsbury (now in Carneros), Vichon (now in France), and Conn Creek. Now it is one of the most people-friendly wineries around. Paul Moser and British partner Tony Cartlidge moved here in 1993 and began to renovate, first naming their enterprise Stratford Winery, and later changing the name to fit its historical origins. Partly because of Tony's contacts, Ehlers exports loads of wine to England and Norway.

Be sure to stop at this highly personal and cozy winery. Many of Ehlers's wines have received ratings in the high 80s and 90s from all of the major critics and have started to win gold medals in several competitions. Ehlers Grove won Best Zinfandel at the California State Fair in 1996. Check out Jean's Wine Jellies made here ($3.95).

Fine points: No tasting fee. Featured wines: Ehlers Grove Sauvignon Blanc, Chardonnay, Dolcetto, Zinfandel, Cabernet Sauvignon, and Cartlidge & Browne Pinot Noir and Zinfandel. Owners: Glenn Browne and Tony Cartlidge. Winemaker: Paul Moser. Cases: 5,000. Acres: buy from others.

❧ *Ehlers Grove and Cartlidge & Browne, 3222 Ehlers Lane, St. Helena 94574; phone (707) 963–3200 or (888) 234–5377, Web site www.ehlersgrove.com. Open 11:00 A.M. to 5:00 P.M. daily. Visa, MasterCard, and JCB. Wheelchair-accessible.*

EHLERS GROVE AND CARTLIDGE & BROWNE

Three miles north of Brava Terrace and half a mile north of Ehlers Grove is
BALE GRIST MILL STATE HISTORIC PARK, a wonderful place to take kids of all
ages. Follow signs up the hill and park in the designated lot. Then walk down
an asphalt path (no dogs, please) through thick, luxuriant green growth. You
can hear the water in Mill Creek as soon as you get out of the car.

The mill was built in 1846 by Dr. E. T. Bale, Grantee, Carne Humana
Rancho. When settlers arrived in the Napa Valley in the 1830s and 1840s,
they planted corn and wheat to replace the oats they found growing wild. To
convert these grains to usable flour, they needed a mill, which also became the
local social center and gathering place. The miller was the local bigshot,
someone to whom everyone spoke, a collector of gossip, and an adviser on
banking and business.

A real character, Bale shot at Salvador Vallejo twice on a Sonoma street
during an argument. Bale barely escaped lynching, went to jail, and partly due
to untrue rumors that settlers were going to storm the jail and get him out,
the governor ordered him released. Somewhat sobered by the experience, Bale
settled down on his rancho and sold off some land to finance building this
mill. A subsequent owner of the mill and land, Mrs. Sara Lyman, deeded it all
to the Native Sons of the Golden West in 1923.

Now George Stratton is the miller, and he does his thing four times a day on the weekends at unspecified times. Sometimes he even makes bread on the wood stove in the granary. You can buy (and we did) all sorts of ground-here rye, whole wheat, cornmeal, and pastry flour, and polenta by the half or whole pound, as well as an excellent historic cookbook ($5.00). You can also follow a 1.02-mile trail from Bale Mill State Historic Park to Bothe Napa Valley State Park. The Culinary Institute of America at Greystone in St. Helena brings students here to learn the elementary process of making flour and bread.

⁂ Bale Grist Mill State Historic Park, 3369 Highway 29, St. Helena 94574; phone (707) 942–4575. Open from 10:00 A.M. to 5:00 P.M. daily. Admission fee: $2.00 adults, $1.00 children, which is also good to get into Bothe Napa Valley State Park up the road and state historic buildings on Sonoma Plaza the same day. Wheelchair-accessible on paths to the park. The historic mill is not wheelchair-accessible.

BALE MILL PINE FURNITURE on your left (west) going north is in a two-story old white structure that was actually an inn, but feels more like a whore house, with little rooms upstairs, escape routes, and creaky floors. Here you will find fabulous framed and large French posters, pine furniture made locally, wrought iron, iron canopy beds upstairs, and the world's best straw sun hats. Owner Tom Scheibal also has Tivoli on the north end of St. Helena proper, and Dottie Richolson is design consultant and elegant hostess. Be sure to stop in.

⁂ Bale Mill Pine Furniture (also known as Bale Mill Classic Country Furniture), 3431 St. Helena Highway North, St. Helena 94574; phone (707) 963–4595, fax (707) 963–4128. Open from 10:00 A.M. to 5:00 P.M. Wednesday–Monday. MasterCard and Visa. Not wheelchair-accessible.

BOTHE NAPA VALLEY STATE PARK entrance is just a mile north of Bale Mill, and you can walk between the two parks on a trail. Bothe is nearly 2,000 acres of lush laurel, madrone, and oak trees that afford quiet campsites and non-vineyard views from the top of Coyote Peak. You can swim in the natural spring pool ($3.00) near the Visitor Center or ride horseback with Napa Valley Trail Rides. Be sure to visit the Native American Plant Garden, Wappo People next to the Visitor Center. Enjoy Redwood Trail along Ritchey Creek Canyon and picnics under the towering Douglas firs.

⁂ Bothe Napa Valley State Park, 3801 St. Helena Highway North, Calistoga 94515; phone (707) 942–4575. Open from 8:00 A.M. to sunset. Admission fee: $5.00 per vehicle, $4.00 senior's car or $2.00 per adult and $1.00 per child. Parts of the park are wheelchair-accessible.

OLD BALE MILL CHEESE SPOON BREAD
from Bale Grist Mill State Historic Park

You can purchase a whole booklet of recipes from Bale Grist Mill State Historic Park, but we include here one of the miller's recipes that is not in that cookbook.

INGREDIENTS:

2 cups milk or buttermilk (buttermilk makes it even better)
2 Tbs butter
1½ cup cornmeal
2 eggs, separated
1½ cups grated cheddar cheese
½ tsp salt

PREPARATION:

Preheat oven to 375°F. Grease baking dish. Bring milk to just below boiling. Add butter. Gradually stir in cornmeal. Cook over medium heat, stirring constantly 2 minutes or until thick. Remove from heat, stir in egg yolks, cheese, and salt. Beat egg whites until stiff. Fold into mix.

Place dish in oven and bake 35 minutes.

Practically across the road is Larkmead Lane, which leads to FRANK-ROMBAUER CELLARS, formerly Hanns Kornell Champagne Cellars, one of Marilyn Monroe's wine-country hangouts. It was originally Larkmead Cellars from 1884–1938, when Hanns Kornell bought it. In the meantime, Treasury Department villains came in with sledge hammers during Prohibition and destroyed the wine tanks, sending a "river" of red wine flowing down the road. It is now owned by grape-grower Richard Frank and managed by Koerner Rombauer of Rombauer Vineyards. Rombauer brings their crushing pad to this partnership and Richard Frank is a former president of the Academy of Television Arts and Sciences.

Marilyn Monroe was a very close friend of Hanns Kornell. When she used to visit the Calistoga baths when hubby Joe DiMaggio was off playing baseball, she would plant herself on a couch in what is now the outer tasting room and spend the afternoon sipping Champagne and listening to Kornell's stories.

FRANK-ROMBAUER CELLARS—KORNELL CHAMPAGNE
TASTING ROOM ENTRANCE

Hence, the life-size portrait and Andy Warholesque series over the reserve wine bar in the back room. On June 15, 2000, Frank-Rombauer suffered a horrible fire in its warehouse. Much of the stock was lost but the winery is back in production.

 Fine points: Featured wines: Brut, Blanc de Blancs, Blanc de Noirs, Rouge, Extra Dry, Alexander Valley Cabernet. Owner: Richard Frank. No tasting fee. Champagne winemaker: Duane Dappen. Cases: 10,000.

⁂ *Frank-Rombauer Cellars—Kornell Champagne, 1091 Larkmead Lane, Calistoga 94515; phone (707) 942–0859 or (800) 574–WINE, fax (707) 942–0657. Open from 10:00 A.M. to 5:00 P.M. daily. Visa, MasterCard, and American Express. Tours are wheelchair-accessible, but the historic tasting room is not. The staff, however, is happy to help anyone needing assistance.*

To visit prized SCHRAMSBERG VINEYARDS, you must make an appointment ahead of time, according to Napa County regulations. It is well worth making the call ahead of time to experience its highly regarded sparkling wines. Turn left (west) off Highway 29 at Peterson Drive and wander through lush woods, turning onto Schramsberg Road and taking care around curves for about a mile, and watching for deer. Schramsberg's Blanc de Blancs was the first non-French champagne served in the White House.

German immigrants Annie and Jacob Schram founded the winery in 1862 as the first winery on the hillsides of the Napa Valley. Chinese laborers cleared the scrub oak and replaced them with vineyards, along with a network of 2 miles of tunnels and caves in the soft volcanic rock.

The Schrams built the large Victorian house as they prospered, and hosted Robert Louis Stevenson here in 1880. He later devoted a whole chapter to Schramsberg in his *Silverado Squatters*. The entire 200-acre Schram estate became a California Historical Landmark in 1957. Until his death in 1998, owner Jack Davies and his wife, Jamie Davies, with the influence of the Davies's friend and environmentalist Dorothy Erskine showing everywhere, dedicated themselves and Schramsberg to drawing on the best of the past to create premier sparkling wines in the *méthode champenoise*. Jamie continues that tradition today.

As you arrive at the sloped parking lot, you are greeted by handsome and huge Dalmatians and Irish setters, who lazily get up to welcome you to their home. The cozy tasting room is to the left of the parking lot, just beyond the elegant pond with its statue of a frog wearing a tuxedo and holding a champagne bottle and glass. Plan a little time to look at the fascinating photos and

SCHRAMSBERG POND AND TASTING ROOM ENTRANCE

letters on the walls, and enjoy the high quality of shirts, ice buckets, hats, champagne stoppers, and even a flashlight and a copy of Stevenson's *Silverado Squatters* ($6.00).

Schramsberg certainly takes the sweepstakes for prestigious pourings of their wines, including dinners at the White House for Presidents Reagan and Bush, for Queen Noor of Jordan, for Princess Grace of Monaco, for Prince Charles and Princess Diana, for Mikhail Gorbachev, for President Richard Nixon and Chou En-lai, and at the North Pole. Proceeds from sales of Quernica go to the Jack Davies Fund of The Community Foundation of Napa Valley.

 Fine points: Tasting fees: $7.50 or $10.00 to $15.00 for Reserve Library wines. Featured wines: Blanc de Blancs, Blanc de Noirs, Brut Rosé, Quernica Brut Rosé, Cremant, J. Schram. Owner: Jamie Davies. Winemaker: Mike Reynolds. Cases: 50,000. Acres: 200.

❧ *Schramsberg Vineyards, 1400 Schramsberg Road, Calistoga 94515; phone (707) 942–4558, fax (707) 942–5943, e-mail schramsbrg@aol.com, Web site www.schramsberg.com. Open from 10:00 A.M. to 4:00 P.M. daily by appointment only. Visa, MasterCard, and American Express. Wheelchair-accessible.*

Go back to Highway 29 and turn left (north) to go to Sterling Vineyards and STONEGATE WINERY, until recently one of the few small family wineries remaining in Napa Valley. The Spaulding family, who developed and ran Stonegate for more than twenty-five years, sold the winery to the California Wine Company.

Far less publicized than its glamorous neighbors Sterling and Clos Pegase, Stonegate concentrates on wines made from grapes best grown on hillsides, which happen to be cluttered with stones. First, they wanted to call it Stonewall, but it was Nixon time and they decided wisely on Stonegate for a name. Stonegate offers interesting wines in a very informal atmosphere. Enjoy the newly renovated tasting room and the Stonegate Guest House, where you get a free one-night stay if you buy forty-eight bottles in one year. Winemaker Gerard Zanzonico came to Stonegate in 1999 from renowned Chateau Montelena.

 Fine points: Tasting fee: none weekdays, $1.50 for the glass on weekends. Featured wines: Chardonnay, Fumé Blanc, Cabernet Franc, Merlot, Late Harvest Sauvignon Blanc, Sauvignon Blanc from Gunn Estate Vineyard in Calistoga, Cabernet Sauvignon, Merlot. Owners: California Wine Company. Winemaker: Gerard Zanzonico. Cases: 23,000. Acres: 200.

❧ *Stonegate Winery, 1183 Dunaweal Lane, Calistoga 94515; phone (707) 942–6500, e-mail SGNAPA@aol.com. Open from 10:00 A.M. to 4:30 P.M. daily.*

Visa, MasterCard, and American Express. Wheelchair-accessible.

The enormous white Moorish-looking structure you see on a hill to the east of Highway 29 is STERLING VINEYARDS, a remarkably striking structure built in 1973. It is not a monastery, as many of us have grown up believing. To find your way there, turn right on Dunaweal Lane for 0.4 mile, then turn right (south) at the white mausoleum-style arches. Even the divided driveway hints that something interesting is ahead.

Park in the parking lot and get in line to pay your tram fee ($6.00 adults). You cannot drive up to the winery, so you have to take the tram, except for handicapped visitors, who can ride in a van. The Disneyesque experience again contributes to the mood.

Brace yourself for a spectacular view, relaxing tasting, and glorious balcony seating where servers bring the wine to you, truly unusual in this stand-up-to-the-bar-and-have-a-sip wine country. Take yourself on an excellent self-guided tour and enjoy the Three Palms Art Gallery. This is a must-stop experience like no other.

Peter Newton, an English paper broker, started the winery in 1964 and sold it to Coca-Cola in 1977, which later sold it to the Joseph E. Seagram & Sons group in 1983. Tremendous investment is obvious, but you can't miss the Old St. Dunstan's Church bells Newton brought to chime every half hour to remind him of his English origins. This is one winery where you can also purchase film and Calistoga mineral water. Kids are served juices in the tasting room.

 Fine points: Tasting fee: included in $6.00 tram fee, with children given juice and "coloring packet" to keep them entertained. Featured wines: Chardonnay, Sauvignon Blanc, Cabernet Sauvignon, Merlot. Owners: Joseph E. Seagram & Sons Chateau and Estate Wines. Winemaker: Rob Hunter. Cases: 360,000. Acres: 1,200.

ℑ *Sterling Vineyards, 1111 Dunaweal Lane, Calistoga 94515; phone (707) 942-3344. Web site: www.sterlingvineyards.com or www.aboutwines.com. Open from 10:30 A.M. to 4:30 P.M. daily. Visa, MasterCard, American Express, and JCB. Winery is wheelchair-accessible, tram is not, and rest rooms at tram station are. A wheelchair-accessible van is available.*

For a nearby wildly different art and wine experience, visit CLOS PEGASE across Dunaweal Lane and eastward from Sterling. You can also get to Clos Pegase easily by turning west from Silverado Trail.

Jan and Mitsuko Shrem's shrine to art and wine is a must-see on the Napa wine trail. Here several senses will be pleased. Just driving into the parking lot

ONE OF THE MANY FIRST IMPRESSIONS AT CLOS PEGASE

is a pleasure, so be alert to large abstract sculptures in the fields and vineyards surrounding the winery.

The whole place celebrates Pegasus, the winged horse who brought us art and wine by releasing the Spring of the Muses. Water flowing from the spring gave new life to the vines, inspiring the gift of poetry in those who drank the wine.

A native of Colombia with Jewish heritage, Shrem made his first fortune importing technical books to Japan and then translating and publishing them there. He hired famed Princeton architect Michael Graves to design his wine and art gallery in 1984 and acquired outstanding works, including some by Dubuffet, Francis Bacon, Max Ernst, Tanguy, Miro, Kandinsky, Oscar Dominguez, Jacques Lipschitz, Matta, Auguste Herbin, and Appel. Many of the paintings in Shrem's collection, including his prized *Pegasus,* painted circa 1890 by French artist Redon, grace the winery and its wine labels.

Having broken out of a few accepted ruts himself, Shrem advocates that you break out of your wine rut and not allow yourself to be intimidated by wines or winemakers. Freeze good wine if you want to—Shrem does.

Fabulous sculptures greet you throughout the winery, including a sculpture at the end of the cave of Dionysus depicting his decision between wine and love. If you're really interested in art and wine, there's a free presentation on 4,000

MITSUKO'S LEG OF LAMB WITH VEGETABLE MEDLEY AND LENTIL–RICE MIX

from Mitsuko Shrem, Clos Pegase

INGREDIENTS FOR LENTIL–RICE MIX:

3 cups rice   1 cup lentils

1 Tbs olive oil   salt

INGREDIENTS FOR LEG OF LAMB:

1 6-lb leg of lamb   1½ cup chicken broth

6 bay leaves   olive oil

6 garlic cloves, 4 cloves slivered   salt and pepper
    and 2 cloves mashed

INGREDIENTS FOR VEGETABLE MEDLEY:

2 Spanish onions, large and chopped

3 lb potatoes; cut 2 lb in 1½-inch cubes, and 1 lb in ½-inch cubes

1½ lb carrots, cut lengthwise in 1½-inch strips

3–4 Tbs olive oil

2 pinches curry powder

chicken broth

4 pinches dried thyme

salt and pepper

PREPARATION:

Wash and soak lentils for 2 hours in water, then drain.

Preheat oven to 425°F.

Cut small slits in the leg of lamb and insert the 4 slivered garlic cloves. Mix the mashed cloves with 2–3 Tbs of olive oil and spread over meat with salt and pepper. Crush 3 bay leaves to cover bottom surface of the lamb. Place lamb in pan with fatty side up. Crush and sprinkle remaining bay leaves on the rest of the meat. Place lamb in hot oven for 15 minutes, then reduce heat to 350°F. Allow the lamb to cook for an additional 10 minutes per pound if you like it rare, 15 minutes for medium, and 20 minutes for well.

When the lamb has cooked to your liking, remove from oven and pour off excess fat. With a fork prick holes in lamb and pour chicken broth over it.

(continued on next page)

Mitsuki's Leg of Lamb with Vegetable Medley and Lentil–Rice Mix (continued)

Remove lamb to warm plate and cover with aluminum foil. Allow to rest for 20 minutes.

In rice cooker (or traditional) place rinsed rice and soaked lentils with olive oil and salt to taste. Fill with water to 4 cups and cook 15 minutes. Allow rice to rest an additional 15 minutes. Mix lentils and rice well before serving.

Meanwhile, put roasting pan on stove top and deglaze meat drippings. Season to taste, optionally adding lemon juice, and strain into sauce boat.

Heat pressure cooker (wok or heavy pan) and stir-fry onion and thyme in oil until translucent. Add additional vegetables and stir fry all, then add salt, pepper, and curry powder. Add broth to cover vegetables and cook for 15–20 minutes or until carrots are cooked. If liquid remains, reduce until almost dry. Mix so that small potato pieces crush to coat all the other vegetables.

Serves 12. Mitsuko says, "Dozo Meshiagate Kudasai—Please enjoy!" Serve with Clos Pegase Merlot.

---

years of art the third Saturday of every month at 2:00 P.M. Don't be so distracted by the art that you miss the fine wines, and they are.

Fine points: Tasting fee: $2.50 for whites, $5.00 for reds. Featured wines: Chardonnay, Pinot Noir, Merlot, Cabernet Sauvignon, Claret, Hommage series blends. Owners: Jan and Mitsuko Shrem. Winemaker: Steven Rogstad. Cases: 40,000. Acres: 450.

✦ *Clos Pegase, 1060 Dunaweal Lane, Calistoga 94515; phone (707) 942–4981, fax (707) 942–4993, e-mail jishrem@aol.com, Web site www.clospegase.com. Open from 10:30 A.M. to 5:00 P.M. daily. Visa, MasterCard, and American Express. Wheelchair-accessible.*

Let's head back west on Dunaweal Lane (turn right coming out of Clos Pegase and left out of Sterling) and turn right (north) on Highway 29 to Calistoga.

As you drive into Calistoga, you can choose. You can pass the intersection of Highway 29 and Lincoln Avenue, Calistoga's main street, and continue northward as Highway 29 turns onto Lincoln, goes through Calistoga, and turns left (north) to Clear Lake. Highway 128 (straight ahead) takes us to the Petrified Forest, Vigil Vineyards, and Tubbs Lane, where you will find Summers Winery, Old Faithful Geyser, and Chateau Montelena. If you take this route, you can easily continue 0.2 mile eastward to Highway 29 and turn right (south) back toward Vincent Arroyo Winery, Traulsen Vineyards, Calistoga, and the Silverado Trail. Or you can turn right (east) onto Lincoln Avenue at the flashing red light and enjoy downtown before continuing on to wineries and the Silverado Trail.

We will visit the wineries before strolling through town, taking you first to Vigil Vineyards, the farthest one north. At the flashing red light, continue straight ahead on Highway 128 instead of turning right (east) on Lincoln and Highway 29. You may want to stop 0.8 mile north of Lincoln at the Calistoga Pioneer Cemetery to learn a little local history.

If you want to take a 4-mile detour to the PETRIFIED FOREST, go ahead, following the signs west from Highway 128 1 mile north of Lincoln. "Petrified Charlie" Evans happened upon a petrified tree stump while wandering with his cows and thus discovered the pretrified forest covered with volcanic ash. Now you can drive in, take a tour of the important biggest and oldest trees, and visit the museum and store in the Ollie Bickee House for souvenirs

❧ *Petrified Forest, 4100 Petrified Forest Road, Calistoga 94515; phone (707) 942–6667. Admission fee $4.00 adults, $2.00 for children 12–17, $1.00 for children 4–11. Visa and MasterCard. Partially wheelchair-accessible.*

In 0.8 mile north of Highway 128's intersection with Petrified Forest Road, you come to Tubbs Lane, with the light green Mitchell's Drive-In on the right (southeast corner). To get to Summers Winery, Old Faithful Geyser, and Chateau Montelena, turn right at Tubbs Lane. To get to VIGIL VINEYARDS, go another 0.7 mile northward on Highway 128 and turn right at the Vigil sign to the peach stucco and peach tile roof winery off in the near distance to the east of the road. Trumpet vines climb the trellis covering the tiled patio, and a young lemon tree looks pregnant with heavy lemons hanging. The small tasting room feels like home.

Fluent in three languages, owner Jamie Pawlak graduated from Tulane in economics and is a California lawyer, with the good fortune to have been born the grandson of the founder of Champion Spark Plugs, and has both Irish and Apache ancestors. Jamie has succeeded quickly in several careers.

Jamie started making wine in law school, purchased and revitalized an abandoned fifty-year-old vineyard in 1989, and built his state-of-the-art winery in 1995. His Vigil Vineyards is a certified organic farm, in homage to the family's Apache respect for the land.

Pizza of the Day
from Zina Bower, Vigil Vineyards

INGREDIENTS:

> 1 frozen pizza dough
> 1 12-oz jar pasta sauce
> Firm cheese, such as Asiago, grated
> 1 large onion
> 4 sausages of your choice
> handful of fresh herbs, such as basil, oregano, and/or thyme
> olive oil
> garlic, crushed

PREPARATION:

Thaw pizza dough at room temperature until soft.

Sauté onion in a little olive oil until caramelized. Set aside.

Depending on which type of sausage you use, the preparation may differ. A smoked sausage just needs to be sliced. Uncooked sausage, such as mild Italian, needs to be released from its skin and cooked in a pan on top of the stove until browned.

Grate cheese. Preheat oven to 425°F. To assemble, pull and play with dough until it makes a circle large enough for your pizza pan. Spoon on tomato sauce, top with most of the grated cheese, lay on sausage slices, top with sautéed onion and fresh herbs, the remaining cheese, and some crushed garlic.

Bake for 10 minutes, then take a peek. Now is a good time to brush the outside edge of the pizza with a little olive oil. Bake another 2 minutes or so until the crust is nicely browned. Let cool for a minute, slice, and eat. Delicious with Vigil Vineyard's Tres Condados Zinfandel.

Or try creamed cheese, smoked salmon, onion, and capers with Vigil's Chardonnay.

Enjoy free wine tastes and check out Sonoma food products such as Adamson's excellent chutneys and Koslowski Farms dressings.

 Fine points: Tasting fee: none. Featured wines: Terra Vin (Zinfandel and Carignan), Meritage, Carignan Mourvedre; Bella Vigne Sauvignon Blanc, Merlot, Zinfandel, Tradiciòn Petit Sirah,

Late Harvest Zinfandel. Owner: Jamie Pawlak. Winemaker: Michael Loftus, Ph.D. Cases: 17,000. Acres: 10 and buy from others.

❧ *Vigil Vineyards, 3340 Highway 128, Calistoga 94515; phone (707) 942–2900 or (800) 94–VIGIL, fax (707) 942–2902, Web site vigilwine.com. Open from 10:30 A.M. to 4:30 P.M. daily. Visa, MasterCard, and American Express. Wheelchair-accessible.*

As you leave Vigil, turn left (south) on Highway 128, and then left (east) again at Mitchell's Drive-In, a light green grocery store, onto Tubbs Lane and head east to Summers Winery, Old Faithful Geyser, and Chateau Montelena.

The first winery you come to going east from Highway 128 on Tubbs Lane north of Calistoga is the new **SUMMERS WINERY,** also just west of Old Faithful Geyser. Jim and Beth Summers bought the old San Pietro Vara Winery in 1996, renamed the vineyard Villa Andriana after their young daughter, and began to make Merlot with their grapes that had previously produced acclaimed Merlots for other wineries.

Enjoy the intimate tasting room with its grapevine paintings, a small labeled vineyard just off the tasting room patio, and the new bocce court. You can even join Summers' Bacchus and Bocce Club, a guaranteed fun adventure.

Fine points: No tasting fee. Featured wines: Merlot, Chardonnay, Charbono, Cabernet Rosé, Zinfandel, New Viognier, Bianco, Rosso. Cases: 10,000. Acres: 28.

❧ *Summers Winery, 1171 Tubbs Lane, Calistoga 94515; phone (707) 942–5508, fax (707) 942–4039, e-mail: sumranch@aol.com, Web site sumwines.com. Open from 10:30 A.M. to 5:00 P.M. daily May–October, weekends remainder of year, some weekdays; call for appointment. Visa, MasterCard, and American Express. Wheelchair-accessible.*

OLD FAITHFUL GEYSER brings us a spectacle of nature every forty minutes right here on Tubbs Lane. Enter the parking lot and walk into the building to pay for your right to see the phenomenon. Now a private enterprise, free viewings are blocked by tall bamboo and pampas grass. This geyser is one of three legitimately called "Old Faithful"; the others are in New Zealand and Yellowstone National Park. This Old Faithful is also an official U.S. Weather Station.

Some parts of the year, somewhat unpredictably, the geyser spouts every ten minutes, varying by the weather, tides, earth stresses, and season. The water is always 350°F and shoots about 60 feet into the air. When the water erupts more frequently than every forty minutes, owner Olga Kolbek begins to be alert for earthquakes, since it has acted up before almost all of the major nearby earthquakes.

The little ticket and convenience store stocks film, postcards, drinks, microwave sandwiches, snacks, excellent brochures and information pamphlets in twenty-three languages, and lots of local lore and conversation from the family. You are welcome to bring picnics and use their tables near the geyser, just so you pay the admission price.

Old Faithful Geyser, 1299 Tubbs Lane, Calistoga 94515; phone (707) 942–6463. Open from 9:00 A.M. to 6:00 P.M. daily in summer, 9:00 A.M. to 5:00 P.M. in winter. Admission: $6.00 adults, $5.00 seniors, $2.00 children 6–12. Visa and MasterCard. Wheelchair-accessible.

As you leave Old Faithful, turn left (east) onto Tubbs Lane to CHATEAU MONTELENA, one of the Napa Valley's most majestic and respected wineries. It is an absolute must-stop on your personal wine tour. Six-tenths of a mile east of Old Faithful turn left (north) up Chateau Montelena's narrow paved driveway. Cyclists love the ride up here, but picnicking is by reservation only. The stone fountain rocks were cut out of the cliff now covered with moss, ivy, and ferns to the left of the winery entrance. To see the old chateau, go down the stairs to the right of the tasting room.

Along with Stag's Leap, Chateau Montelena was one of two Napa wineries to defeat the French in a blind Paris wine tasting in 1976. Chateau Montelena's

CHATEAU MONTELENA'S TASTING ROOM ENTRANCE

1973 Chardonnay beat the best from Burgundy. Upon winning the tasting, owner Jim Barrett said, "Not bad for kids from the sticks." It was only his second vintage since resurrecting the winery, which had stopped bottling fifty years earlier.

Humor pervades this elegant establishment, including a life-sized chessboard painted on the barrel room floor, where players walk around to move their men. Three generations of Barretts work at every level of production, and the winery's brochure features Mary Breiner, who runs the office/business side of the place and hosts the staff for big-deal sports events in "The Mary Dome," in front of her giant home television screen. Cats reign from bath towel perches on top of pedestals.

Alfred Tubbs began Chateau Montelena in 1882 by planting 254 acres of vines. By 1896 the winery was the seventh largest in the Napa Valley. The winery itself is carved into the north side of a hill, forming its own cave, with walls 3 to 12 feet thick. In 1960 Chinese immigrant Yort Franks built a "moat" called Jade Lake around the winery, which is now a beautiful fish and wildlife sanctuary inhabited by swans and geese and lucky picnickers. In 1972 James Barrett bought the chateau, brought in the latest winemaking equipment, and replanted the vineyard. You are welcome to explore the grounds and visit Jade Lake.

Be sure to indulge in this elegant experience. Robert M. Parker, Jr., in *The Wine Advocate*, said, "This is a splendid winery at the top of its game."

Fine points: Tasting fee: $5.00. Featured wines: Chardonnay, Riesling, Cabernet Sauvignon. Owners: James Barrett and family. Winemaker: Bo Barrett. Cases: 40,000. Acres: 120.

❧ *Chateau Montelena Winery, 1429 Tubbs Lane, Calistoga 94515; phone (707) 942–5105, fax (707) 942–4221, Web site www. montelena.com. Open from 10:00 A.M. to 4:00 P.M. daily. Visa, MasterCard, and American Express. Tasting room is wheelchair-accessible.*

Now you can either return to Highway 128 the way you came and turn left on 128 to Lincoln Avenue and downtown Calistoga, or you can complete the winery loop by turning left (east) as you leave Chateau Montelena, go 0.2 mile to Highway 29, and turn right (south) toward Calistoga. In 0.4 mile you cross the 1902 Garnett Creek Bridge, and in another 0.5 mile turn right at Greenwood Avenue to VINCENT ARROYO WINERY. Turn right at the sign and go down the gravel driveway past the house to the beige barn winery. Notice the beautiful roses, lawns, and picnic tables, all for your pleasure.

Vincent Arroyo is the owner's name, not the Spanish name of the Vincent Riverbed. Vince is a warm, earthy fellow who, fortunately, gave up life as a mechanical engineer in Silicon Valley to make wine here in the far north of

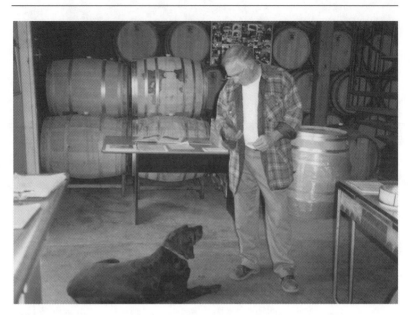

VINCENT ARROYO AND JOY IN THE WINERY AND TASTING ROOM

the Napa Valley. He learned to make wine hands-on from his Spanish father, who was a home winemaker. Always accessible to tasters, Vince teaches visitors about wine and loves to talk with young couples who are just venturing into the wine field. The entire winery is in one little room, so visitors can learn a lot from the source.

Joy, a black Labrador, greets you and quietly dominates the whole scene. Having shown up on the Arroyo's doorstep in 1990 sick and starving, she now has her own wine label, Joy's Choice, her own companion, J.J., and her own line of clothing (black shirts with white paws) available in the retail sales room. Vince says, "Joy sells more wine than anyone." Sample Vincent Arroyo's new estate olive oil.

Vincent Arroyo wines are sold only here at the winery, so get them while you can. The winery hosts an annual open house featuring vintage wines, food, and winemakers' dinners for $75. Be sure to get on the mailing list, because tickets usually sell out to loyal fans within five days. Because 80 percent of the wine is sold before it's bottled, you can now buy wine futures here.

      Fine points: Featured wines: Chardonnay, Melange (red blend), Cabernet Sauvignon, Merlot, Zinfandel, Petite Sirah. Owner: Vincent Arroyo. Winemaker: Vincent Arroyo. Cases: 5,000. Acres: 70.

★⌣ *Vincent Arroyo Winery, 2361 Greenwood Avenue, Calistoga 94515; phone (707) 942–6995. Open from 10:00 A.M. to 4:30 P.M. daily by appointment only. Call ahead. Visa, MasterCard, and American Express. Wheelchair-accessible.*

John and Sandy and Tony and Laura Zahtila needed to try something beyond roofing contracting and tech industries and purchased what used to be Traulsen Vineyards, now named **ZAHTILA VINEYARDS.** Be sure to notice the 300 rose bushes and paths winding through them.

This is one of the smallest, most intimate family wineries you will find, with its tasting room at a table just outside the barrel room and winery door. The Zahtilas feel extremely lucky that neighbor Vincent Arroyo and others have been so generous with time and knowledge.

Winemaker Corey Beck, assistant winemaker at Niebaum-Coppola Estate for years, is concentrating on making a truly fine Zinfandel, which was served to Francis Ford Coppola at his own restaurant for his birthday dinner.

 Fine points: Tasting fee: $2.00 (refunded with purchase). Featured wine: Zinfandel, both Zahtila and Traulsen. Owners: John, Sandy, Tony, and Laura Zahtila. Winemaker: Corey Beck. Cases: 1,100. Acres: 4.

Zahtila Vineyards, *2250 Lake County Highway, Calistoga 94515; phone (707) 942–9251, fax (707) 942–9241, e-mail sandy@zahtilavineyards.com, Web site www.zahtilavineyards.com. Open from 10:00 A.M. to 5:00 P.M. daily. Visa, MasterCard, and American Express. Not wheelchair-accessible.*

CALISTOGA

Calistoga tops off the Napa Valley 75 miles from San Francisco. Founded over 130 years ago as a hot springs resort, Calistoga still feels like a small western town where you might expect to see horses tied at the sidewalk's edge and guys swaggering up to the saloon's swinging door. Calistoga generously provides a parking lot for residents and visitors that runs behind all the shops on the south side of Lincoln Avenue.

We begin our walking tour of Calistoga at the western end of Lincoln Avenue, where Highway 29 turns east and Highway 128 goes north. (*Note:* In downtown Calistoga, Lincoln Avenue is Highway 29.) We will first take you up the south side of the street, then back down the north side of Lincoln Avenue, with a 1-block side track on Washington Street to Wappo Bar Bistro and the Sharpsteen Museum.

Coming from Chateau Montelena, Summers Winery, or Vincent Arroyo Winery, begin the walking tour by starting with the north side of Lincoln.

LINCOLN AVENUE, SOUTH SIDE

The first notable building you come to on your right is the venerable CALISTOGA INN AND RESTAURANT, whose dining room is everyone in town's favorite birthday celebration place, because "everyone knows and loves Rosie." Owner/chef/hotelier Rosie Dunsford is a member of the Calistoga City Council and hosts clusters of unofficial gatherings.

The 1882 hotel has eighteen reasonably priced upstairs rooms ($65 midweek and $90 weekends) with shared baths, a restaurant, and "one small brewery," and its office is around the corner on Cedar Street, between window boxes draped with bright red geraniums.

In the summer you can dine on the old, comfortable patio overlooking the river in front of the Napa Valley Brewing Company in the former pump house. The restaurant offers live music every night except Monday. Check out the collection of turkey platters rimming the dining room and dish towels hanging all over the place, along with Christmas lights that "go outside in summer." Try Napa Valley Brewing Company's Calistoga Pilsner, Wheat Ale, Red Ale, and Porter.

The reliables on the menu at lunch are the burgers with garlic fries ($9.25), spicy Mexi-Cal quesadillas ($7.25), Dungeness crab cakes ($9.50), a sausage-chop plate ($15.25), and lots of salads and vegetarian chili, curry, and sandwiches. Dinner is more

NAPA VALLEY BREWING COMPANY PATIO AT THE CALISTOGA INN

expansive, with a choice of chopped leaf or whole leaf Caesar salads, garlic crusted calamari ($7.95), filet mignon ($21.00), and Australian lamb chops ($18.25). Again, vegetarian specials are always on the menu.

CALISTOGA AREA

STORYBOOK MOUNTAIN VINEYARDS

HELENA VIEW JOHNSON

ROBERT PECOTA WINERY

CHATEAU MONTELENA

OLD FAITHFUL GEYSER

VIGIL VINEYARDS

BENNETT LN.

TUBBS LN.

SUMMERS WINERY

VINCENT ARROYO WINERY

29

TO SANTA ROSA

ZAHTILA VINEYARDS

128

GRAESER WINERY

29

LINCOLN AVE.

CALISTOGA WATER

SILVER ROSE CELLARS

SILVERADO TRAIL

CALISTOGA

128
29

CLOS PEGASE

CUVAISON WINERY

DUNAWEAL LN.

STERLING VINEYARDS

STONEGATE WINERY

DUTCH HENRY WINERY

PETERSON RD. TURNOFF

LARKMEAD LN.

SCHRAMSBERG RD.

FRANK-ROMBAUER/ HANNS KORNELL CHAMPAGNE CELLARS

SCHRAMSBERG VINEYARDS

29

WERMUTH WINERY

BALE LN.

BIG TREE RD.

N
W E
S

*꙰ **Calistoga Inn and Restaurant**, 1250 Lincoln Avenue, Calistoga 94515; phone (707) 942–4101, Web site www.calistogainn.com. Open for lunch and dinner. Full bar. Visa, MasterCard, and American Express. Restaurant is wheelchair-accessible; the hotel is not.*

As you progress eastward on Lincoln Avenue, the next interesting stop is the LEE YOUNGMAN GALLERIES, featuring national and Napa Valley artists, including Gene Zesch bronze sculpture, Neil Boyl, and Paul Youngman, local vineyard scenes, handmade paper, Navajo turquoise and silver jewelry, Betty Carr and Howard Carr, Joe Beeler bronze sculpture, and early California paintings. Youngman also has a frame shop just beyond the auto parts store next door.

*꙰ **Lee Youngman Galleries**, 1316 Lincoln Avenue, Calistoga 94515; phone (707) 942–0585. Open from 10:00 A.M. to 5:00 P.M. daily. Visa, MasterCard, Discover, and American Express. Wheelchair-accessible through the parking lot and back door.*

In this land of spas and mineral and mud baths, you will find many body care possibilities, including FREE TIME, which offers toys, lotions, soaps, walk-in massages and facials, and seasonal specials. Sonoma County *Independent* readers voted Free Time the "Best New Age Emporium" of 2000.

*꙰ **Free Time**, 1348 Lincoln Avenue, Calistoga 94515; phone (707) 942–0210. Open from 10:00 A.M. to 6:00 P.M. Sunday–Thursday, to 9:00 P.M. Friday–Saturday. Visa, MasterCard, and Discover. Wheelchair-accessible.*

Joel Guitron's very local TAQUERIA SANTA ROSA (SR Restaurant) has a spectacular chile relleño made from peppers roasted here. Beef and chicken dishes are made of hand-shredded meats, and the mole sauce is the restaurant's own. Try the parrillada for two cooked over charcoal in terra-cotta and including chicken, carne asada, carnitas, roasted pork, and shrimp ($24.95 for two). McDougall-style fat-free dishes are also available.

*꙰ **Taqueria Santa Rosa**, 1350 Lincoln Avenue, Calistoga 94515; phone (707) 942–6468. Open from 11:30 A.M. on. Visa, MasterCard, American Express, Diners Club, Discover, Carte Blanche, and JCB. Wheelchair-accessible.*

Next door is one of our favorites, and one voted Napa residents' favorites too, SOO YUAN CHINESE FOOD, serving Mandarin and Szechuan specialties. The owner had restaurants in Taiwan and Vallejo before moving here a few years ago and now boasts a "Best Asian Restaurant in the Napa Valley" award (1999). Lunch at under $6.00 is a healthful bargain, with no MSG, and includes a light soup and several selections from the menu of fresh entrees. Portions are so large,

two can almost share one lunch. Ironically, the narrow room and Chinese decor make us feel as if we are in a small restaurant in an Asian country. Napa residents drive for miles for the food, and Soo Yuan will deliver to your hotel room.
❧ *Soo Yuan Chinese Food, 1354 Lincoln Avenue, Calistoga 94515; phone (707) 942–9404. Open from 11:00 A.M. to 9:30 P.M. serving continuously. Beer and wine. Visa, MasterCard, American Express, and Discover. Wheelchair-accessible.*

BOSKOS RISTORANTE is definitely here, serving cafeteria style with windows open onto the sidewalk and a wheelchair ramp entry. A sign commands you to ORDER WITH CASHIER BEFORE TAKING A SEAT. Choices include pizza from a wood-burning oven in the back ($6.50–$9.95), loads of fresh pastas, a roasted garlic chicken and other salads ($5.95 and $7.95), and their own garlic bread ($1.75–$3.25). It's a good informal place to go with the kids and still have some creative food. There are lots of wines by the glass, or select a bottle from the rack across from the cashier and then pay for it at the register. Don't miss the historic photos in the hallway to the rest rooms.
❧ *Boskos Ristorante, 1364 Lincoln Avenue, Calistoga 94515; phone (707) 942–9088. Open from 11:00 A.M. to 10:00 P.M. daily. Beer and wine. Visa and MasterCard. Wheelchair-accessible.*

At the corner of Lincoln and Washington Streets, BRANNAN'S GRILL is named for Calistoga historical bigwig Sam Brannan, but it's owned by Ron Goldin and Mark Young, who also own Checkers up the street and in Santa Rosa. When Ron and Mark took on the building, which last housed the Silverado Restaurant and Tavern, they discovered huge beams beyond a false ceiling and created a meticulously restored American Craftsman interior and a new terraced dining space with windows opening onto Lincoln Avenue. The nineteenth-century Brunswick bar was discovered under layers of cigarette smoke and tar. Calistoga artist Carlo Marchiori created a trompe l'oeil mural as a backdrop for the dining room. Ron and Mark have also planted the Young–Goldin Truck Farm on their ranch to provide fresh produce for Brannan's year-round.

Chef Ron Lam loves to mix regional specialties, as Brannan's menu reflects. You might try the seafood minestrone ($8.00), Hoisin glazed baby back ribs ($8.00), salt and lemon baked chicken ($14.00) or curry poached salmon ($14.00 lunch, $19.00 dinner). Carnivores will love the house-smoked Niman Schell pork chop ($20) or the blue cheese and walnut crusted filet mignon ($25). Several excellent local wines are available by the glass at $6.00 or less. You can also enjoy an excellent bar menu and fabulous desserts at $5.50.
❧ *Brannan's Grill, 1374 Lincoln Avenue, Calistoga 94515; phone (707) 942–*

2233, fax (707) 942–2299, Web site www.brannansgrill.com. Open from 11:30 A.M. to 10:00 P.M. daily. Visa and MasterCard. Wheelchair-accessible.

One of our secret favorites we almost hate to tell people about is the under-heralded ALL SEASONS CAFE AND WINE SHOP, also on Lincoln right across Washington from Brannan's. Located in the Del Mar Building, the All Seasons seems hidden right on Calistoga's prime corner. The interior feels like an old, unpretentious big-city bistro, with black-and-white linoleum floors, wooden benches with restful cushions for your back, and views of the community's comings and goings. The lively paintings on the walls come from I. Wolk Gallery in St. Helena. Feel free to have fun sitting at the counter.

Owned by Alex Dierkhising, who also has Hydro Bar & Grill across the street, All Seasons has the mother of all wine lists in quality if not in quantity.

All Seasons's menu changes by seasons, which are even broken down as far as "Almost Spring." You must try the warm spinach salad with cafe-smoked chicken, crumbled bacon, and feta, which I praised beyond the ceiling to the server, who replied, "It's Robert Redford's favorite, too." Seems he was ensconced in a nearby home editing a movie, and is rumored to have bought a house near Calistoga. When in town, he comes in almost every night around nine and orders the warm spinach salad.

The roast leg of lamb sandwich is actually an elegant pile of sliced tender warm lamb laid ever so gently on a piece of thick rosemary toast, grilled onions, portobello mushrooms, red peppers, lamb jus, and feta cheese ($9.95). There are always choices of pizzas, risottos, and pastas, but try the roasted halibut on wilted baby spinach ($18.95), the oven-roasted rabbit with portobello mush-rooms, runner beans, and braised mustard greens ($18.50), or the roast half chicken ($15.75). Desserts at $7.00 are just as superior as the rest of the menu. For all this we have Executive Chef John Coss and friends to thank.

What is truly unusual about All Seasons is its wine shop to the left at the back of the restaurant. This is the finest restaurant wine shop anywhere, as we discovered by looking for a few obscure bottles that happened to be here. The wine shop sponsors Wine Basics—A Down to Earth Tasting and Discussion that includes family-style All Seasons lunch and tasting and primarily features Napa Valley and French wines.

❧ *All Seasons Cafe and Wine Shop, 1400 Lincoln Avenue, Calistoga 94515; phone (707) 942–9111, Web site www.allseasonswineshop.com. Open for lunch and dinner until 9:00 P.M. Beer and wine. Visa and MasterCard. Wheelchair-accessible.*

Just east of All Seasons is the GOOD N AIRY ANGEL espresso bar featuring Killer Brownies, Son of Killer brownies, and Beyond Killer brownies, loads of

candy, cool drinks, and breakfast treats baked here daily.
➵ *Good N Airy Angel, 1408 Lincoln Avenue, Calistoga 94515; phone (707) 942–0714. Open from 8:30 A.M. to 6:00 P.M. daily. Wheelchair-accessible.*

The Surfwood Bar is exactly what it says for lots of locals, with good weekend music from the likes of Philip Claypool.

Beyond the Surfwood is CHECKERS PIZZA & PASTA restaurant, which is a great informal place for pizzas, wonderful salads, huge calzones, and vegetarian and carnivore sandwiches served on focaccia bread with soup or salad. Pizza add-ons of goat cheese, sun-dried tomatoes, and others are only $1.00. Chef Douglas Wattson has added some protein to the menu in the form of seafood, such as scallops and mussels. Yes, this Checkers is related to the one in Santa Rosa.

Enjoy Chico sculptor Daniel Parks's flying monsters hanging from the ceiling and the Pasta Piper airplane hanging over the wine bar. Lots of humor and color keeps you going while you wait for your food. Checkers is owned by the same great team as Brannan's, Mark Young and Ron Goldin.

Try the roasted leg of lamb sandwich ($8.25), a great Caesar salad, or the butternut squash ravioli ($10.95).
➵ *Checkers Pizza & Pasta, 1414 Lincoln Avenue, Calistoga 94515; phone (707) 942–9300. Open from 11:00 A.M. to 10:00 P.M. daily. Beer and wine. Visa and MasterCard. Wheelchair-accessible.*

STEAMED CLAMS WITH PANCETTA, CHARDONNAY, APPLE JUICE, AND SAGE

from Executive Chef John Coss, All Seasons Cafe

INGREDIENTS:

> 3–4 lb Manila clams
> cold water
> 1 Tbs cornmeal
> ¼ lb pancetta, diced
> 3 Tbs chopped shallots
> 1 cup Chardonnay
> ¾ cup apple juice, fresh if possible
> ¼ cup unsalted butter
> 2 Tbs fresh sage, chopped
> 2 Tbs parsley, chopped

PREPARATION:

Place clams in cold water and add cornmeal. Refrigerate for 1–2 hours. Drain and rinse.

Sauté pancetta in a large pot until almost crisp. Drain away half of the fat. Add shallots and sauté for 1 minute. Add clams, Chardonnay, and apple juice. Cover and cook over high heat until clams open, shaking pan occasionally. Add butter, chopped sage, and chopped parsley. Serve immediately. Serves 4. Enjoy!

Note: Discard clams that don't open in cooking process.

Next to Checkers, Calistoga Natural Foods sells sandwiches, wheat grass smoothies, health books, lotions, and vitamin supplements. Moreno's offers quickie burritos, tostadas, hot dogs, and shaved ice, while the Smoke Shop and Liquor Store provides the obvious and emergency corkscrews.

CIN CIN is one of our great new culinary thrills in Calistoga. John Gillis and Gina Armanini, whose food we instantly loved when they were at The Girl and the Fig in Glen Ellen, completely revamped an old dive and created a lovely, peaceful rustic Italian dining room exhibiting local artists' work and truly old family photos.

Unlike many Napa Valley restaurants, Cin Cin has an excellent list of imported wines from France, Italy, Spain, and Australia, and a terrific selection of beers from Canada, Belgium, England, Germany, and California. Cin Cin also sautés with Napa Valley Grapeseed Oil, which is available for purchase here.

Weekend brunch ranges from Clive's blueberry and cream cheese scone ($3.50) and brioche French toast with fresh berries and cream or real maple syrup ($7.50) to an asparagus and brie omelette ($8.50) or a smoked salmon and mascarpone cheese omelette ($9.00) served with Yukon gold potatoes, crème fraîche, and chives. Alternatives include a Niman Ranch BLT, rainbow trout, salads, and divine burgers.

No lunch is served during the week, but dinner is exceptional. Unusual starters include grilled sweetbreads on arugula salad ($8.50), grilled "local" sardines ($8.50), a bagna cauda of warm anchovy and garlic fondue with fresh vegetables and Italian bread ($8.00), and an honest "classic raw egg Caesar salad" (7.50). Entrees to enjoy include risotto, which may feature English peas, fava beans, asparagus, and pesto ($14.50), house-made gnocchi in a ragout of Liberty duck, pancetta, and porcini with fava beans ($17.50), a rosemary-scented game hen schiaciatta ($15.50), seafood, steak, or short ribs braised in red wine vinegar with mashed potatoes and a fennel and red onion salad ($18.00).

Cin Cin, *1440 Lincoln Avenue, Calistoga 94515; phone (707) 942–1008, fax (707) 942–0230. Open from 5:30 to 10:00 P.M. Wednesday–Sunday, brunch 10:00 A.M. to 2:00 P.M. Sunday. Beer and wine. Visa and MasterCard. Wheelchair-accessible.*

Keep walking to the old Calistoga Depot built in 1886 by Sam Brannan, who brought the steam train and people to Calistoga. From 1912 to 1937 electric trains also came to Calistoga and terminated at what is currently the Calistoga Fire Station.

The Calistoga Depot was converted to historic exhibits and small specialty shops in 1976, and Greyhound Bus purchased the Napa InterUrban in 1936, took out the tracks, and started running diesel-spouting buses up Napa Valley.

The station's original waiting room is now the Smokehouse Café, which you enter off the parking lot, featuring smoked meats and sausages including Acadian bacon and eggs, flat iron steak, Sacramento Delta crawfish cakes ($13.80), and Arkansas Slow Pig Plate ($12.95). Also look for Adell & Adela Yarn Shop, Treasures of Tibet, The Flower Lady, interesting Calistoga Wine Shop in a Central Pacific Coach, Le Artisan Gifts, and several other goodies.

If you're dying for a superb hamburger or chicken sandwich with fries and a shake, or a decent Philly cheese steak sandwich, BIG DADDY'S DRIVE-IN is the place, just east of the Southern Pacific railroad cars next to the Calistoga Depot. It is now a northern branch of St. Helena's Taylor's Refresher. All hamburgers are huge and made from low-fat Harris Ranch beef (which is wonderful if you don't mind feed lots), and the beer-battered tempura onion rings are sensational and somehow seem less sinful than ones not called tempura. There are lots of flowers and umbrellas at picnic tables. Order at the window and wait to be called.

Big Daddy's Drive-In, 1522 Lincoln Avenue, Calistoga 94515; phone (707) 942–9503. Open from 11:00 A.M. to 6:00 P.M. daily (sometimes later in summer). No credit cards. Wheelchair-accessible.

You might also enjoy Tin Barn Antiques and Calistoga Gardens next to Nance's Hot Springs. Calistoga Gliders offers glider rides and truly majestic, breathtaking flights. (See Chapter 6, *Beyond Wine Tasting.*)

LINCOLN AVENUE, NORTH SIDE

A favorite coffee destination for both Calistoga locals and the *New York Times* is the CALISTOGA COFFEE ROASTERY coffee clinic. Aussie Clive Richardson and Terry Rich roast thirty-five kinds of coffee beans, six of which are decaf, and sell beans (whole or ground) as well as espresso drinks, poached eggs, sandwiches, bagels, and—surprise—Calistoga waters bottled right around the corner. They also make blends for the Culinary Institute of America's *Wine Spectator* Greystone Restaurant.

A sign on the wall quotes Clive: DRINK MORE COFFEE, YOU SLEEP WHEN YOU ARE DEAD. New customers ask if there's a charge for the entertainment (Clive). In a cozy side room facing the street kids can sit at their own table and play with a plastic toy espresso machine. Enjoy the shaded deck on the east side of the coffee clinic.

Calistoga Coffee Roastery, 1631 Lincoln Avenue, Calistoga 94515; phone

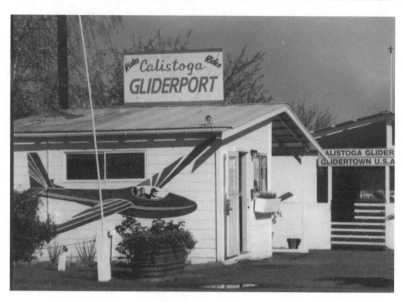

CALISTOGA GLIDERS

*(707) 942–5757 or (800) 879–5282. Open from 6:30 A.M. to 6:00 P.M. daily
(closed Christmas) No credit cards. Wheelchair-accessible.*

Heading back west on Lincoln Avenue, Calistoga Photography will develop
your film in one hour. Then we come to the wonderfully elegant MOUNT VIEW
SPA and MOUNT VIEW HOTEL, home of Jan Birnbaum's Catahoula Restaurant
& Saloon. In an attempt to bring the outside in, artists have painted ivy on the
hotel's art deco lobby walls, surrounding thick, soft sofas and soothing music.

Once called the European Hotel, the Mount View was built in 1919 and
now has a swimming pool and thirty-three rooms, suites, and cottages with hot
tubs, all extremely pleasant and ranging from $130 to $250.

❧ *Mount View Spa* and *Mount View Hotel, 1457 Lincoln Avenue, Calistoga
94515; phone (707) 942–6877. Visa, MasterCard, and American Express.
Wheelchair-accessible.*

Jan Birnbaum's CATAHOULA RESTAURANT & SALOON features Jan's personal brand of southern-inspired American food in an ambience somewhere
between Old West and Deep South. Named for the Catahoula hound dog, the
official dog of Louisiana and the only breed native to Louisiana, Jan says it is "a
cross between a Spanish war dog and a Native American Red Wolf." Hence, all

the photos, sculptures, and signage feature this spotted, webbed-foot loyal guard and hunting dog.

Jan is, thankfully, from Baton Rouge, Louisiana and began his culinary apprenticeship under Chef Paul Prudhomme at K-Paul's Louisiana Kitchen. He left to become head chef at New York's Quilted Giraffe Restaurant, worked as sous-chef at Denver's Rattlesnake Club, and served as executive chef at San Francisco's five-star Compton Place Hotel Restaurant. He is one of the most widely praised chefs in America. It's a real treat to have his humor and creativity available in the wine country. Watch for Jan's annual Seafood Boil & Fish Fry with microbrews, featuring blue crabs, braised brisket, and fried squid ($38).

Try the Bibb and arugula salad with teleme cheese, hot coppa, and perfectly ripe pears ($7.50), seafood filé gumbo ($5.00 or $7.00), thick pizza pies, real andouille sausage, pork Porterhouse steak with red eye gravy, soft sexy grits, and pickled cabbage ($21.00), southern fried rabbit with dirty rice and collard greens ($18.00), cornmeal fried catfish with Mardi Gras slaw ($18.00), or roast chicken fricassee with white beans, artichokes, and rosemary gremolata ($17.00). We love the spicy paella with clams, rock shrimp, and chorizo ($20.00).

Don't miss breakfast on the weekends for the usuals with a twist to crispy hominy cake with fried egg, Catahoula ham, and sauce piquant ($9.00), Bubble Squeak with poached eggs and jalapeño gravy ($9.50), and lots of eggs, grits, and southern smoked meats. The fresh lemonade and gin fizzes are out of sight. ❧ *Catahoula Restaurant & Saloon, 1457 Lincoln Avenue, Calistoga 94515; phone (707) 942–2275. Open for lunch-brunch from 10:00 A.M. to 3:30 P.M. Saturday–Sunday, dinner 5:30 to 10:00 P.M. Full bar. Visa, MasterCard, and Discover. Wheelchair-accessible.*

South of Mount View and Catahoula are Calistoga Jewelers (every town has one) and North Star, with T-shirts, bracelets, and trinkets. Alex's Restaurant serves prime rib, steaks, liver, and pastas, specializing in daiquiris and open for dinner only. The Evans Ceramics Studio Outlet branch sells ceramics at a discount, and Casa Design has interesting home furnishings.

L. FUNKE & SON DEPARTMENT STORE has been a great emporium of comfortable clothes serving Calistogans since 1904 and is located in the stone Fisher Building. Funke features New Options dresses, Blue Cactus, Caribe, and Jan Michaels designs for women, and Pendleton shirts, Levis, Dockers, Reyn Spooner, Paradise Found wild shirts, Back East, Johnny Cotton, and Tommy Bahama for men.

❧ *L. Funke & Son Department Store, 1417 Lincoln Avenue, Calistoga 94515; phone (707) 942–6235. Open from 9:30 A.M. to 6:00 P.M. Monday–Saturday,*

11:00 A.M. to 4:00 P.M. Sunday. Visa and MasterCard. Wheelchair-accessible.

Right next to L. Funke is fun CAFE SARAFORNIA, a name made of the leftovers of Sam Brannan's combination of Saratoga and California to get Calistoga. Cafe Sarafornia is a very informal restaurant that opens onto the sidewalk and features champagne mimosas, oatbran pancakes, healthy omelettes, special Five Alarm Chili, a good Thai chicken salad, a decent Caesar salad with extra anchovies, blue cheese pasta with grilled chicken, a Zinfandel burger (which you can also enjoy as turkey), and Jalisco club sandwiches. The cheese blintzes are to die for. Baked muffins and breads are really special. (Owner Drake Dierkhising is the brother of Alex, who owns Hydro Bar & Grill three doors down and All Seasons Cafe and Wine Shop across Lincoln Avenue.) Be prepared to wait in line on the sidewalk on weekends for breakfast. Locals love this place, as do we. ❧ *Cafe Sarafornia, 1413 Lincoln Avenue, Calistoga 94515; phone (707) 942–0555. Open breakfast, lunch, and dinner till closing. Beer and wine. Visa and MasterCard. Wheelchair-accessible.*

Thomas Kinkade presents his inevitable tourist gallery between the Dierkhising's restaurants. Alex Dierkhising's HYDRO BAR & GRILL at the corner of Lincoln and Washington is a locally popular pub and casual restaurant where you can enjoy hummus and veggies, steak sandwiches, burgers, and thick-crust pizzas. Try the housemade spicy beer sausage with garlic aioli or the fabulously different lasagna with goat's milk cheese, tomatoes, spinach, and roasted peppers. Hydro is handy because it serves a late-night menu until 11:00 o'clock after everyone else has closed, and its prices are reasonable, from $4.95 to $14.95. Those of you who need a beer break from all that wine can select from more than twenty microbrews. Hydro bills itself as "the place to party in Calistoga." So be warned. Breakfast too. ❧ *Hydro Bar & Grill, 1403 Lincoln Avenue, Calistoga 94515; phone (707) 942–9777. Open from 7:30 A.M. to closing. Full bar. Visa and MasterCard. Wheelchair-accessible.*

Take the time to walk west 1 block on Washington Street for a few minutes to the Wappo Bar Bistro and the Sharpsteen Museum. Don't miss Calistoga City Hall's honesty, with its decorative, band-aid approach.

The WAPPO BAR BISTRO is one of Calistoga's most interesting and widely publicized restaurants, with an exquisite patio-gathering place and a simple but elegant narrow dining room. Wappo is the anglicized version of Guapo, the name given by early Spanish-speaking settlers to local American Indians.

Flavors come from Latin America, Africa, and the Mediterranean, so have on your adventure hat when you try Wappo. There are also plenty of standards with a twist, such as roasted pork sandwich with sweet-and-sour cabbage ($12.00) or grilled eggplant sandwich on focaccia with baked goat cheese ($10.00), but try the pan-fried chicken livers on field greens salad with apple-smoked bacon ($10.50) or the sensational Vatapa stew, with scallops, shrimp, snapper, black beans, and feta topped with peanut sauce and sautéed bananas ($12.50).

At dinner roasted vegetables with polenta and persillade ($12.50), Ugandan peanut chicken with roasted yams, banana, and coconut ($15.50), and Hornada Ecuadoran braised pork with chile and beer with stuffed potato pancake and hominy ($15.75) are marvelous experiences, as is the osso bucco gremolata veal shanks with white wine and porcini mushroom sauce with risotto Milanese ($17.00). Caesar and local greens salads are also available for a little familiarity.

❧ *Wappo Bar Bistro, 1226B Washington Street, Calistoga 94515; phone (707) 942–4712, fax (707) 942–4741. Open from 11:30 A.M. to 2:30 P.M., 6:00 to 9:30 P.M. Wednesday–Monday. Full bar. Visa, MasterCard, and American Express. Wheelchair-accessible.*

CALISTOGA CITY HALL'S BAND-AID APPROACH

The city of Calistoga has done some very smart things. It moved one of Sam Brannan's cottages downtown and graciously allowed Bernice and Ben Sharpsteen, a major creator for Walt Disney, to build a museum of Calistoga and wine country history—the SHARPSTEEN MUSEUM—and threw in a senior center and police station to form an efficient and attractive small civic complex.

Ben Sharpsteen was an Academy Award–winning animator, producer, and director for Walt Disney Studios, who retired with his wife to their ranch in Calistoga, which his grandmother had acquired in the 1800s. The ultimate fan of Sam Brannan, resort builder, promoter, pioneer, publisher, entrepreneur, soldier of fortune, and the person who brought the railroad to Calistoga and put it on the map, Sharpsteen dedicated his creative energies in "retirement" to designing and building the Sharpsteen Museum.

A side benefit to the public is that we get to view Sharpsteen's Academy Awards and loads of memorabilia from the early Disney studios, as well as Sharpsteen's collections of California automobile license plates and hubcaps dating from wooden-spoke carriages. In a well-planned compact space you will also see dioramas of Sam Brannan's original resort, which he called "The Saratoga of the Pacific," and which he built in 1859 when he bought a square mile of land containing the hot springs at the foot of Mount St. Helena, beginning the fad of "taking the waters in Calistoga." California + Saratoga = Calistoga. At one time his resort had a hotel and thirteen cottages, a stable and racetrack, telegraph, bath house and pool, an observatory, a skating rink, riding trails, a distillery and winery, and a cooperage shop.

You can also learn from a Napa Valley Timeline, a beautifully restored stagecoach, and a simulated barn interior with a collection of period farming tools, then walk into the Brannan cottage to see what life was like, and experience the simulated interior of a general store, kitchen, and blacksmith shop from the 1800s. The little shop at the entrance also stocks the best collection of Napa Valley history books and pamphlets available anywhere.

❧ *Sharpsteen Museum, 1311 Washington Street, Calistoga 94515; phone (707) 942–5911. Open from 10:00 A.M. to 4:00 P.M. daily summer, noon to 4:00 P.M. daily winter. Admission fee: donation. No credit cards. Wheelchair-accessible.*

Walk back the short block to Lincoln Avenue and turn right (west) to continue your exploration of Calistoga's shops. Bella Tootsie sells Bass, Sam & Libby, and kids' shoes, sunglasses, and rain boots in what was a glorious bank building. Nature Etc. purveys its educational nature toys and books as it does in Sonoma and St. Helena. The Candy Cellar sells not-made-here salt water taffy, Jelly Bellies, and fudge from barrels, and Mr. Moon's offers a good kids' stop, or a stop for good kids, with Beanie Babies, souvenirs, shirts, and body lotions.

For a little local color, you might want to follow the in-ground train tracks and saunter back to SUSIE'S BAR, truly a working men's and women's bar with "no beer on draught" and Napa Fairgrounds (in Calistoga) Sprint Car Races posters and fans. Pool tables and pinball machines complete the picture. The old tracks used to bring flour bins from the street back to the ovens when Susie's was a bakery fifty years and more ago.

Susie's Bar, 1365 Lincoln Avenue, Calistoga 94515; phone (707) 942–6710. Open from 9:00 P.M. to 2:00 A.M. Full bar. No credit cards. Wheelchair-accessible.

Nicola's Delicatessen serves hot or cold deli sandwiches, low-cost breakfast, and hot dogs and chili if you order at the counter. Mostly local kids hang out here. The T-Shirt Shop is one of the best of those, and then, we come to a must-stop, Napa Valley Ovens, the pride and joy of Fred Halpert of Brava Terrace and Livefire (both discussed earlier in the chapter). NAPA VALLEY OVENS supplies most of the better restaurants and bed-and-breakfasts, and offers fabulous creative breads, focaccia, quiche, hot cross buns, ice cream, sundaes, and smoothies.

Napa Valley Ovens, 1352 Lincoln Avenue, Calistoga 94515; phone (707) 942–0777. Open from 7:00 A.M. to 3:00 P.M. Wednesday–Monday. No credit cards. Wheelchair-accessible.

In a town where many visitors come to pamper themselves and indulge in their bodies, WEXFORD & WOODS excels in offering pamper vehicles such as skin care products, including a whole section of products for men, meditation candles, lavender, natural herbal soaps, Hawaiian floral bath bars, and colorful paper flowers.

Wexford & Woods, 1347 Lincoln Avenue, Calistoga 94515; phone (707) 942–9729. Open from 10:00 A.M. to 6:00 P.M. Sunday–Thursday, 10:00 A.M. to 9:00 P.M. Friday–Saturday. Visa and MasterCard. Wheelchair-accessible.

Up some narrow stairs between Wexford & Woods and the Calistoga Bookstore a wooden butler beckons you to Upstairs Enoteca, Margaux Singleton's Wine Shop, and Lone Dog Fine Art & Antiques.

We especially enjoy the CALISTOGA BOOKSTORE, where you find great vacation reading and travel material, as well as school and art supplies, crayons, pads, and mood music.

Calistoga Bookstore, 1343 Lincoln Avenue, Calistoga 94515; phone (707) 942–4123. Open from 10:00 A.M. to 6:00 P.M. Sunday–Thursday, 10:00 A.M. to 9:00 P.M. Friday–Saturday. Visa, MasterCard, and American Express. Wheelchair-accessible.

Heading west, next comes the Lincoln Avenue Spa, Tammy's New Leaf ladies' clothes, and an extraordinary local art gallery, THE ARTFUL EYE. We loved the blown glass, hand-painted platters, Steven Dixon jewelry, salt and pepper chess sets, books, wearable art clothing, wild-looking home accessories, and hand-carved lamps. Don't miss it.

❧ *The Artful Eye, 1333A Lincoln Avenue, Calistoga 94515; phone (707) 942-4743. Open from 10:00 A.M. to 6:00 P.M. daily. Visa, MasterCard, and American Express. Wheelchair-accessible.*

As you walk across the little bridge opposite the Calistoga Inn, there's an interesting clothing store facing the creek with colorful clothes and flags luring you down the wooden deck to THE BIRD'S EYE, featuring women's wear "to escape the ordinary." Women will find mostly handmade natural fiber clothing including lean to generous sizes and one-of-a-kind Calistoga-made jewelry, casual vacation clothes to glitzy sequined evening wear, Japanese wedding kimonos, and autographed Parisian scarves.

❧ *The Bird's Eye, 1307 Lincoln Avenue, Calistoga 94515; phone (707) 942-6191. Open from 9:00 A.M. to 6:00 P.M. Monday–Thursday, 9:00 A.M. to 8:00 P.M. Friday–Sunday. Visa, MasterCard, and Discover. Wheelchair-accessible.*

Detour north on Cedar Street to CA'TOGA GALLERIA D'ARTE. Carlo Marchiori, self-proclaimed maestro d'arte, has built an unusual art gallery on Cedar Street, which exclusively shows his work created at his Palladian villa north of Calistoga. He opens his house and workshop for tours at 11:00 A.M. Saturdays, May–October ($20).

His gallery exemplifies his style, with a mural painted on the barrel-vaulted ceiling showing the Ptolemic constellations and a terrazzo floor that is a chart of the pre-Copernicus universe. Marchiori produces plates, cups, vases, and all sorts of collectibles.

Born in Italy, Marchiori studied classic art and academic design in Padua and Venice, left Italy for Canada, where he worked as an illustrator and film animator for CBC Television and the National Film Board of Canada, was nominated for a 1967 Academy Award for an animated short, and abandoned filmmaking and advertising for mural painting. Since 1978 he has lived and worked in San Francisco.

Ca'toga Galleria d'Arte, 1206 Cedar Street, Calistoga 94515; phone (707) 942-3900, fax (707) 942-3939, Web site www.catoga.com. Open from 11:00 A.M. to 6:00 P.M. Thursday–Monday. Visa, MasterCard, and American Express. Wheelchair-accessible.

Just across Cedar Street is PACIFICO RESTAURANTE MEXICANO, a refreshingly popular local Mexican restaurant that's best known for its signature fish dishes, particularly the grilled snapper or prawns sautéed several ways, and shrimp and fish ceviche ($8.75). You will find Oaxacan cheeses, grilled chicken tacos, red snapper tacos ($7.95), and even tamales stuffed with mushrooms, roasted poblanos, tomatoes, and tomato chile salsa ($7.25). And for the less adventurous, Salvador Gomez cooks good hamburgers served with a Caesar salad ($4.50), and carne asada burritos ($8.75).

The rooms are wide open and decorated with primary colors, with lots of Mexican masks; a fountain cools on hot days. The margaritas and Fiesta Hour (4:40–6:00 P.M. Monday–Friday) are famously good in this up-to-date spot owned by John Seeger of Boskos Italian restaurant down Lincoln.

❧ *Pacifico Restaurante Mexicano, 1237 Lincoln Avenue, Calistoga 94515; phone (707) 942–4400. Open from 11:00 A.M. to 10:00 P.M. Monday–Friday, 10:00 A.M. to 10:00 P.M. Saturday–Sunday. Full bar. Visa and MasterCard. Wheelchair-accessible.*

CHAPTER 4

THE SILVERADO TRAIL

*A*s *you turn down the Silverado Trail from Calistoga's Lincoln Avenue at the Trailhead Deli and Juice Bar, don't miss the old, overflowing water truck on a mound "announcing" the Calistoga Mineral Water Company. Luella Ackerman founded the company in 1916 and sold it to Enrichetta and Giuseppe Musante in 1920.*

Giuseppe had a soda fountain and candy store called The Railway Exchange, where he sold ice cream, phosphates, and other soda-fountain goodies. One day in 1920 he was drilling for a well at his Railway Exchange and tapped into a geyser that blew him off his scaffold and burned him so badly that he had to be hospitalized. Giuseppe had discovered the Calistoga geyser, and he soon began to sell the mineral water from the geyser in his fountain. In 1924 he set up a bottling line and began selling Calistoga Sparkling Mineral Water.

The company passed through many owners, and in 1971 a Pepsi Cola truck driver named Elwood Sprenger bought the company when it was in one of its sad shape phases. Soon thereafter Perrier started advertising the glories of mineral waters in the United States; Perrier bought the company from Sprenger in 1980. In 1991 the Nestlé Corporation bought the Perrier Group, and Calistoga Mineral Water is now the top-selling water in the western United States.

The old truck is as close as you can get to the plant, and there are no tastings or tours—just an interesting story.

The Silverado Trail vintners and resorts refer to themselves as being along "The Road Less Traveled" on "the quiet side" of the Napa Valley. And they are right! The Silverado Trail feels more like the Sonoma Valley than busy Napa Valley. The Trail feels less commercial, or at least less hustle-bustle, more rural, and more peaceful. Cyclists will enjoy the generous marked bike lanes on both sides of the road as well as the fewer cars and seemingly more polite drivers than on Highway 29. We love it.

Most of the attractions on the Silverado Trail are highly reputed wineries and resorts, so prepare to enjoy. All of the crossroads go all the way across Napa Valley to Highway 29.

SILVER ROSE CELLARS is one of our favorite new wineries and tasting rooms in the Napa Valley. J-Paul and Sally Dumont bought the neighboring bed-and-breakfast in 1985 along with twenty-two acres, rebuilt it in 1989, and eventually added eleven rooms and a conference center. They've now opened a multi-sided visitor center with restaurant space upstairs with spectacular views, including the Inn & Spa and its putting hole complete with sand trap. Unlike most Napa County wineries, Silver Rose is within the Calistoga city limits and is not governed by county regulations prohibiting wineries with restaurants. So watch for great things to happen here. You will enjoy the knowledge and grace with which Michael Chramko manages the visitor center.

The Dumonts put in the lake you see outside the tasting room, which performs several functions, including running hot air through the water to create air conditioning. Sally Dumont designed the unusual interior, including the rest rooms whose lights are motion sensitive and go on when you enter and off when you leave. Calistoga architect Bev Moore designed the building with radiant heating in the floor. We appreciate the extra roomy parking places in the lot, so that your car doesn't get dinged while visiting.

Check out J-Paul's twenty years' worth of bidding paddles from his community donations through the Napa Valley Wine Auction.

 Fine points: Featured wines: Chardonnay, D'Argent Chardonnay, Merlot, Cabernet Sauvignon, Dentelle (Bordeaux blend). Tasting fee: $8.00, including glass. Owners: J-Paul, Sally, and Derrick Dumont. Winemaker: Chuck Plomteaux. Cases: 3,000. Acres: 20.

❧ *Silver Rose Cellars, 400 Silverado Trail, Calistoga 94515; phone (707) 942–9581 or (800) 995–9381, Web site www.silverrose.com. Open from 10:00 A.M. to 5:00 P.M. daily. Visa, MasterCard, American Express, and Discover. Wheelchair-accessible.*

Half a mile south of the Calistoga Mineral Water Company, you come to Dunaweal Lane to your right, taking you to Clos Pegase, Sterling, and Stonegate wineries.

Just 0.2 mile past Dunaweal Lane (1.8 miles from Silverado Trail and Lincoln Avenue in Calistoga), don't miss CUVAISON WINERY on your left (east) side. Park and enter the homelike white-stucco building with a tile roof and Dutch door. The large parking lot and lush lawns—and gardens with plenty of picnic tables—encourage visitors to stay a while.

Founded in 1969 by two Silicon Valley engineers, Thomas Parkhill and

CUVAISON ON THE SILVERADO TRAIL

Thomas Cottrell, Cuvaison is now owned by one of Switzerland's wealthiest men, Thomas Schmidheiny of Holderbank (supposedly the world's largest cement company). Money and good taste show throughout. Schmidheiny wisely bought acreage in Carneros, and most of the winery's grapes come from his vineyards in that prime growing region straddling the Sonoma–Napa County line. Cuvaison's wines were served in the White House to residents of the Republic of China and Russia. The '97 Chardonnay was served on the papal jet. You might want to indulge in Curvaison's lovely pastel color-coordinated shirts and hats.

Fine points: Cuvaison's cozy and elegant tasting room features a wine bar and shop with excellent selections of silver jewelry and corkscrews, books, and shirts. Membership in Club Cuvaison brings extraordinary discounts. There is a winery tasting fee of $5.00, $7.00 Library wines. Featured wines: Chardonnay, Pinot Noir, Merlot, Cabernet Sauvignon, Zinfandel. Owner: Thomas Schmidheiny. Winemaker and President: John Thacher. Cases: 63,000. Acres: 400.

Cuvaison Winery, 4550 Silverado Trail, Calistoga 94515; phone (707) 942–6266, fax (707) 942–5732, Web site www.cuvaison.com. Open from 10:00 A.M.

to 5:00 P.M. daily. Visa, MasterCard, and American Express. Wheelchair-accessible.

As you leave Cuvaison, turn left onto the road very carefully and go south on the Silverado Trail, to DUTCH HENRY WINERY, a true family operation of Kendall Phelps and Scott Chafen. Dutch Henry is an almost two-story building, nestled against the hillside on the east side of the road.

A former administrator of San Francisco's late French Hospital (now Kaiser), Kendall Phelps says they had to make up a name for the winery because he's not related to either of the prominent Kendall or Phelps wine families. Pity.

The Phelps' Airedale, Buggsy, greets you. Rumor has it that there's a $5.00 fee to play with the dog. While there's a small tasting room at the northern end of the building, the real action is in the large winery room, where you may enjoy barrel tastings with one of the owners. Try the new bocce-ball court, as well as their certified virgin olive oil; 2,000 pounds of the winery's olives yields two cases of the delicacy.

 Fine points: Tours consist of standing in the middle of the tank room and spinning yourself around, hopefully with Kendall's accompanying words and wry humor. He gives barrel tastings during the week, especially in slow season. If you like the wine, buy it here because it's your only chance. No tasting fee. Featured wines: Chardonnay, Pinot Noir, Merlot, Rosé, Syrah, Cabernet Sauvignon, Zinfandel. Owners: Kendall Phelps, Les Chafen, and Scott Chafen. Winemaker: Scott Chafen. Cases: 4,000. Acres: 16 and buy locally.

❧ *Dutch Henry Winery, 4310 Silverado Trail, Calistoga 94515; phone (707) 942–5771, fax (707) 942–5512, Web site www.dutchhenry.com. Dog friendly. Open from 10:00 A.M. to 4:30 P.M. daily except Tuesday. Visa, MasterCard, American Express, and Discover. Wheelchair-accessible.*

Larkmead Lane comes in to your right 0.5 mile south of Dutch Henry. It will take you west to Frank-Rombauer/Hanns Kornell Champagne Cellars (see previous chapter). For now, continue another 0.7 mile to one of the two smallest wineries in the Napa Valley, WERMUTH WINERY.

When we visited Wermuth, owner/winemaker Ralph Wermuth came out to our car and apologized because there were so many cars (four) parked at his winery's entrance. His wife, Smitty, who designed their label and poster, had "a few of the ladies over to lunch today." Believe the sign that says IF I'M NOT HERE, HONK HORN, I'M AROUND.—RALPH.

A Canadian doctor with a few intriguing eccentricities and interests, Ralph uses an eighteenth-century wood basket press. He "can't stand automatic things" and likens his winemaking methods versus more modern ones to rowing across a pond instead of using a motorboat.

Wermuth's tiny tasting room has a slanting wood ceiling and windows facing west, yellow walls, a green cement floor, and a worn wooden counter—all resembling a sauna in the summertime. It's well worth a stop for this slightly eccentric and different winemaking experience. Ralph will gladly show you around with a little notice.

Fine points: Tasting fee: $1.00, refundable with purchase. Featured wines: Dry Colombard, Chenin Blanc, Gamay Beaujolais. Owner and winemaker: Ralph Wermuth. Cases: 4,000. Acres: 2.

➷ *Wermuth Winery, 3942 Silverado Trail, Calistoga 94515; phone (707) 942–5924. Open "loosely" from 11:00 A.M. to 5:00 P.M. daily. Visa and MasterCard. Wheelchair-accessible.*

Next, you might like to visit ROMBAUER VINEYARDS, 1.6 miles south of Wermuth and 1.1 miles south of the intersection of Bale Lane, on the right (west) side of Silverado Trail. Turn right at Rombauer's sign and the big American flag. Be sure to stay to the right as you wind up the steep and beautiful driveway to Rombauer's pink cement-block building in a small forest—a 0.3-mile drive well worth the trip just to see the view, even if you aren't interested in Rombauer's limited production wines. Notice the "R" metal gate leading down a flowered path to the winery's caves, gorgeous pink and orange impatiens, and the brown Rolls-Royce in the parking lot. Photos of Senator John McCain and Barbra Streisand line the walls, along with a Braniff poster.

Koerner Rombauer is a former Braniff International pilot who, with his wife Joan, bought this property in 1972. The grand-nephew of Irma Rombauer of *The Joy of Cooking* fame, Koerner spreads his "Joy of Wine" message through his wines, brochures, and T-shirts. The Rombauers' children, Koerner (K. R.) Rombauer III and Sheana, are both active in the winery. (Koerner Rombauer is owner and has an interest in Napa Cellars.) In June 2000 Rombauer suffered a tragic fire at the Frank-Rombauer/Hanns Kornell Champagne Cellars warehouse fire. The fire makes the remaining wines even more rare.

Fine points: Rombauer's retail sales room is cozy, and Jim Kozier and Harvey Posert are among the most informative hosts in Napa Valley. Tasting fee: $5.00. Featured wines: Chardonnay, Cabernet Sauvignon, Merlot, Zinfandel, Cabernet Franc, Le Meilleur du Chai ("The Best of the Cellar") Bordeaux blend, Zinfandel Port. Owners: Koerner and Joan Rombauer. Winemaker: Gregory Graham. Cases and acres: Undefined.

➷ *Rombauer Vineyards, 3522 Silverado Trail, St. Helena 94574; phone (707) 963–5170, fax (707) 963–5752, Web site www.rombauervineyards.com. Open*

from 10:00 A.M. to 5:00 P.M. daily. Visa, MasterCard, and American Express. The
tasting room is wheelchair-accessible.

As you leave Rombauer, turn right (south) onto the Silverado Trail. On your
left will be Chateau Boswell, a curious Elizabethan structure that is never open
to the public.

Just 0.3 mile south of Rombauer's driveway and slightly past Chateau
Boswell, turn right (west) into CASA NUESTRA WINERY. In this sublime setting
the winery blends in with the oak trees' leaves, as if you are sitting in someone's
picturesque yard.

Gene Kirkham is an amusing and committed civil-rights lawyer who mostly left the hustle and bustle in the mid-1970s for this once "remote" part of the
Napa Valley. He works to keep the county from paving his gravel road and practices sustainable agriculture without fertilizers, pesticides, or herbicides, and
using cover crops and hand labor. Go for the wines and to pick up the humorous and informative newsletter. After you read it once, you will want to be on
the mailing list.

Fine points: Tasting fee: $2.00. Featured wines: Chenin Blanc,
Johannisberg Riesling, Cabernet Sauvignon, Cabernet Franc,
Tinto and Quixote blends, Late Harvest Johannisberg Riesling.
Owners: Gene and Cody Kirkham. Winemakers: Gene Kirkham
and Shay Boswell. Cases: 1,000+. Acres: 20.

❧ *Casa Nuestra Winery, 3451 Silverado Trail, St. Helena 94574; phone (707)*
963–5783, Web site casanuestra.com. Open from 11:00 A.M. to 5:00 P.M.
Friday–Sunday. Visa and MasterCard. Not wheelchair-accessible.

A mile south of Casa Nuestra, DUCKHORN VINEYARDS is tucked away on
the west side of the Silverado Trail, just before Lodi Lane. Only open for the sale
of wine, Duckhorn's superb Merlot alone is worth many fans' whole trip to the
Napa Valley, as are the Cabernets and the fun, bargain Decoy label line. Enjoy
the new gray-and-white two-story Victorian-style farmhouse tasting room, with
its shaded, wraparound porch.

Fine points: Featured wines under Paraduxx, Decoy, and
Dudehorn: Merlot, Cabernet Sauvignon and King Eider
Vermouth. Owners: Margaret and Dan Duckhorn. Winemaker:
Mark Beringer. Cases: 50,000. Acres: 200+.

❧ *Duckhorn Vineyards, 3027 Silverado Trail, St. Helena 94574; phone (707)*
963–7108. Open for retail sales only from 11:00 A.M. to 4:00 P.M.
Monday–Saturday. Tours available Saturday by appointment. Visa and
MasterCard. Wheelchair-accessible.

As you leave Duckhorn, come back to the Silverado Trail and turn right (south). Cross the intersection with a stoplight at Deer Park Road, which to the east leads to Angwin. If you would like to try extremely fresh local fruit and vegetables, stop at the two little fair-weather produce stands on the western corners of the crossroads.

Along with Auberge du Soleil, just south of here, MEADOWOOD RESORT is one of the two most elegant places to stay in the Napa Valley, and even the whole of Northern California. To get there, turn left (east) onto Howell Mountain Road and then left onto Meadowood Lane. The resort's excellent signage is extremely helpful to first-time visitors. Follow the well-kept road past tennis courts, swimming pools, the golf course, and the perfectly manicured croquet courts. New England–style cottages and lodges dot the 250-acre wooded property, located at the foot of Howell Mountain. The resort's whole ambience feels like understated, elegant New England.

THE RESTAURANT AT MEADOWOOD and the Grill facing the golf course are legendary for the ultimate in sophisticated service, dining, and prices. The open beamed cathedral ceilings and bucolic views will enhance your dining experience. Most diners are guests at the resort, but the public is also welcome for Sunday brunch or dinner. Prix fixe dinner choices always include an excellent vegetarian dinner. Regulars usually indulge in the daily soufflé. Breakfast by

MEADOWOOD RESORT

the pool is especially exhilarating. The Grill is open for breakfast and lunch.

Fine points: All rooms have air conditioning, ceiling fans, private decks facing greenery, and every amenity imaginable, with the most expensive four-bedroom suites running about $2,000 per night. The spa and health facilities alone could keep you occupied for days.

✦ **Meadowood Resort** and *The Restaurant at Meadowood, 900 Meadowood Lane, St. Helena 94574; phone (707) 963–3646 or (800) 458–8080. Visa, MasterCard, American Express, and Diners Club. Wheelchair-accessible, but call ahead for details.*

Don't miss JOSEPH PHELPS VINEYARDS, which is on the east side of the Silverado Trail. If you have visited Meadowood, turn left (south) onto Silverado Trail, then turn left (east) onto Taplin Road and drive for 0.3 mile. If you didn't visit Meadowood, just go east on Taplin for 0.3 mile. Turn left through the wooden gate and take the paved road uphill for 0.5 mile. You have to make an advance appointment to tour and taste, but it's worth the effort to see the redwood barn and sophisticated wine production systems.

As you walk into the winery's courtyard, turn left to the barn and retail room. Take a whiff of the blooms from the wisteria covering the overhead trellis, which is made from century-old recycled bridge timbers. Just inside the door look to the left at the gorgeous Great Hall dining room. In good weather, tastings are held out on the deck overlooking the Napa Valley; in bad weather, you get to taste in the dining room.

Fine points: Knowledgeable and friendly hosts make the whole experience attractive. The entire place exudes Joseph Phelps's and his staff's love of what they are doing. Featured wines: Chardonnay, Gewürztraminer, Grenache Rosé, Sauvignon Blanc, Cabernet Sauvignon, Merlot; "Insignia" Bordeaux blends, "Vin du Mistral" Rhone Valley–style Syrah, Viognier, Le Mistral, Muscat Marsanne, Late Harvest Johannisberg Riesling. Owner: Joseph Phelps. Winemaker: Craig Williams. Chef: Scott Harding. Cases: 100,000. Acres: 600.

✦ *Joseph Phelps Vineyards, 200 Taplin Road, St. Helena 94574; phone (707) 963–2745 or (800) 707–5789, fax (707) 963–4831, Web site www.jpvwines. com. Open for sales from 9:00 A.M. to 5:00 P.M., Monday–Saturday, 10:00 A.M. to 4:00 P.M. Sunday. Tasting and tours by appointment. Visa, MasterCard, and American Express. Wheelchair-accessible.*

Leaving Joseph Phelps, go back down Taplin Road to the Silverado Trail, turn left very carefully, and head south past Zinfandel Lane.

For a Wild West Italian experience, try **WILLIAM HARRISON VINEYARDS/ MARIO PERELLI-MINETTI WINERY**, whose sign on the Silverado Trail proclaims that it is AMERICAN OWNED, lest someone suspect otherwise because of the name. Turn right off the Silverado Trail at the sign and pass the family home, sometimes with kids riding their bikes through puddles, to the two-story stone building with a window sign announcing PARKING FOR ITALIANS ONLY. Patio tables and chairs invite you to the deck, and geraniums in window boxes set the cheerful tone.

The Perelli and Minetti families have been making wine since 1250 in Italy, and, as Jeff says, they have been making wine for 90 years in this country "without a computer, so who needs one?" Mario still delivers wine at age ninety. Notice the accordion and piano (go ahead!), and the Perelli-Minetti family tree of four generations in the United States (and proud of it) on the door. William Harrison is Mario's nephew and has been making wine since 1992.

 Fine points: When the tasting room is full of tasters, this place almost sounds like an Old West bar. Host Yvonne Gray's father founded Jonesy's Steakhouse at Napa Valley Airport in 1946. The tasting fee of $3.00 is waived with purchase. Featured wines: All estate Chardonnay, William Harrison Cabernet Sauvignon, Rutherford Red

WILLIAM HARRISON VINEYARDS/MARIO PERELLI-MINETTI
WINERY

Meritage, Cabernet Franc. Owner: William Harrison and Mario Perelli-Minetti. Winemaker: Gary Galleron. Cases: 5,000. Acres: 9.

ॐ **William Harrison Vineyards/Mario Perelli-Minetti Winery,** *1443 Silverado Trail, St. Helena 94574; phone (707) 963–8310, fax (707) 963–8762. Open from 11:00 A.M. to 5:00 P.M. daily. Visa and MasterCard. Wheelchair-accessible.*

When you leave the winery, turn right (south) onto Silverado Trail and continue for about a mile to Rutherford Hill Road. Turn left (east) to visit Auberge du Soleil and Rutherford Hill Winery & Picnic Grounds.

Voted by *Gourmet* magazine readers in 1998 to be the ninth top hotel in the world, AUBERGE DU SOLEIL attracts the wealthy and famous from around the world. This is a modestly elegant resort where you can hide away in your cabin or mingle in the bar overlooking Napa Valley.

The atmosphere is Southern France/Mediterranean, and no wonder. Owner Claude Rouas, once of L'Etoile in San Francisco's Huntington Hotel and later of the successful Piatti Ristorante chain, hails from French Algeria. One brother, Maurice, co-owns Fleur de Lys in San Francisco; his other brother, Albert, created the late, great Le Beaujolais and now works at the Yountville (original) Piatti.

Check out the Auberge Boutique and the Gayle Houston Salon (by appointment). Tennis, swimming, massage, a new gym, and full spa treatments are yours for the asking—and, of course, paying.

No detail is overlooked, and it's as if the staff spend all their time trying to anticipate new human or culinary needs. While meals here are expensive, Executive Chef Andrew Sutton offers both healthy and not so healthy foods. Meals are available morning, noon, and nighttime, too. Asterisks on the menu indicate vegetarian dishes. Two asterisks signal spa cuisine.

At breakfast Valencia orange juice is a mere $5.00, while the continental breakfast is $12.75. The All American, with eggs, meats, potatoes, and toast, is $12.50. Assorted meats and cheeses, "European style," is $15, while the Hillside Benedict is $13. Chocolate waffles, pancakes, lemon brioche French toast, huevos rancheros, lox and bagels, and Starbuck's coffee are also on the menu.

Lunch gets interesting, with an extravagant Mediterranean platter ($26.00), warm asparagus with goat cheese flan ($9.00), pistou soup with calamari and white beans ($9.00), grilled tuna Niçoise salad ($15.00), or a foie gras and roast duck club with bleu cheese and apple-smoked bacon ($23.00).

For dinner you can indulge in the Prix Fixe "Sharing of the Senses" menu: $78 per guest for five courses; paired with wine the price is $118 per guest. Among your choices you might find chervil asparagus soup scented with imported white truffle oil, pancetta roasted monkfish tail, and warm chocolate-hazelnut fondue. There are less expensive three-course options and a vegetarian tasting menu ($57 for three courses with dessert) as well. All desserts are spectacular and under $8.00. For a more casual bistro menu of soups, salads, sandwiches, and pizzetta, try The Bar.

❧ Auberge du Soleil, 180 Rutherford Hill Road, Rutherford 94573; phone (707) 963–1211, Web site www.augergedusoleil.com. Open for breakfast from 7:00 to 11:00 A.M. daily, for lunch 11:30 A.M. to 2:30 P.M. daily; for dinner 6:00 to 9:30 P.M. Monday–Friday, 5:30–9:30 P.M. Saturday–Sunday. The Bar is open from 11:00 A.M. to 11:00 P.M. (no reservations). Visa, MasterCard, American Express, and Diners Club. The restaurant is wheelchair-accessible, as well as some of the rooms in the resort.

Just up the hill from Auberge du Soleil, enjoy RUTHERFORD HILL WINERY, set in what looks like a sophisticated, well-designed barn with rough wood walls. The windows frame perfect white clouds, and a century-old olive grove covers the hillside below to create the most romantic picnic grounds in Northern California. We once heard a young woman coming out the door of Rutherford Hill's tasting room remark, "I'm in heaven now" (to which her male companion responded, "You are?").

No wonder she felt so good. The tasting room is full of excellent wines (be sure to try the Merlot), Calistoga waters, iced tea, fudge and garlic sauces, chocolates, wine and food books, cigars, elegant leather cigar cases and cigar books, French Laguiole wine openers ($119.95), and marble ashtrays. Try to visit the largest man-made wine-aging caves in California, which go nearly a mile into the rock—the best part of Rutherford Hill's frequent tours.

Fine points: Founded by William P. Jaeger, Jr,. Charles Carpy, and Thomas Witter, Rutherford Hill was purchased in 1996 by the Terlato family of Chicago. The $5.00 tasting fee includes logo glass for regular wines, $10.00 for reserves. Featured wines: Chardonnay, Gewürztraminer, Sangiovese, Merlot, Cabernet Sauvignon, Zinfandel Port. Owners: The Terlato Family. Winemakers: Kevin Robinson and Kent Barthman. Cases: 120,000. Acres: Undefined.

❧ Rutherford Hill Winery, 200 Rutherford Hill Road, Rutherford 94573; phone (707) 963–7194 or (800) 726–5226, fax (707) 963–4231, e-mail rhw@nbn. com, Web site www.rutherfordhill.com. Open from 10:00 A.M. to 5:00 P.M. daily; free tours 11:30 A.M. and 1:30 and 3:30 P.M. daily; no reservations. Visa, MasterCard, American Express, and Discover. Wheelchair-accessible.

In case you've been enjoying yourself just a little too much in the tasting room, drive carefully back down Rutherford Hill Road. Pay special caution to guests leaving Auberge du Soleil; they sometimes forget to look up the hill for oncoming cars.

Back down at the Silverado Trail, turn left (south) and proceed to ROUND-HILL FAMILY OF WINES, which has one of the most interesting family stories in the Napa Valley. Turn into Roundhill's driveway and take the left side of the fork toward the retail-sales section. Check out the terra-cotta pot statues in the trees to the right of the parking lot.

A successful and popular buyer at Joseph Magnin's clothing stores in San Francisco, Virginia McInnis married Ernie Van Asperen and honeymooned at the Roundhill Resort in Jamaica. (Guess where the winery's name came from?)

A protégé of master marketeer and creative genius Cyril Magnin, Virginia applied her substantial skills to developing Roundhill Family of Wines, including Van Asperen and Rutherford Ranch wines. With the help of industry veteran Mike Hardy, Virginia is following her vision to cease production and sale of Roundhill's generic wines, so there are some real bargains available here. Virginia is developing the Van Asperen Signature wines, with the first release in 1997 of its 400-case Cabernet Sauvignon, in addition to selling Roundhill and

TERRA-COTTA POT SCULPTURES WELCOME VISITORS TO
ROUNDHILL FAMILY OF WINES

Rutherford Ranch wines. Be sure to enjoy Bill Hamilton's cartoons on the walls. The Van Asperens recently sold Roundhill to Marco and Theo Zaninovich, who produce bulk wines near Bakersfield in the San Joaquin Valley. Ernie and Virginia Van Asperen remain President and CEO of Roundhill.

Fine points: No wine tastings here. Featured wines: Van Asperen Chardonnay, Cabernet Sauvignon, Merlot, Signature Reserve, Cabernet, Rutherford Ranch Chardonnay, Sauvignon Blanc, Cabernet Sauvignon; Roundhill Chardonnay, Sauvignon Blanc, Cabernet Sauvignon, Merlot, White Zinfandel. Owners: Marco and Theo Zaninovich. Winemaker: Mark Swain. Cases: 400,000. Acres: 210.

✢✣ *Roundhill Family of Wines, 1680 Silverado Trail, St. Helena 94574; phone (707) 963–9503, Web site www.roundhillwines.com. Open from 10:00 A.M. to 4:30 P.M., sales only. Visa, MasterCard, American Express, and Discover. Wheelchair-accessible.*

If you're ready for a 10-mile round-trip detour adventure to the Rustridge Ranch & Winery, Bed & Breakfast, & Thoroughbred Home, with the Nichelini Winery thrown in, turn east up Conn Creek Road, which becomes Sage Canyon Road (Highway 128) opposite Villa Mt. Eden Winery.

If you want to continue on our tour without the long side trip, we offer a much shorter one here to Frog's Leap Winery and Caymus Vineyards on Conn Creek Road, which runs west along the side of Villa Mt. Eden Winery. Should you choose this alternative to the 10-mile trip, just skip the paragraphs below on Nichelini and Rustridge wineries.

If you want to go the long, exquisite, and winding way, after you pass Lake Hennessy on your left, take Chiles Valley Road (Pope Valley Road) northeastward, then turn back on Lower Chiles Valley Road (Highway 128) to RUSTRIDGE RANCH & WINERY, BED & BREAKFAST, & THOROUGHBRED HOME. (The easier but less scenic way is to go straight up Sage Canyon to Highway 128 and turn left to Nichelini Winery and Rustridge.)

You truly feel as if you have arrived at someone's home when you drive into Rustridge's wandering, bumpy road, and you have. As you pass the home and B&B, tennis court and swimming pool—going slowly of necessity—hostess Kirsten Niesar will jump into her car and tail you as you follow the signs through the horse paddocks to the winery. This is a very personal winery, with wine prizes and wines displayed on tables.

Winemaker Susan Meyer and her husband, Thoroughbred racehorse trainer Jim Fresquez, combine their interests and talents most successfully on Susan's family ranch to raise racehorses and make good wine. Old horse equipment decorates the rails around the winery in this heavenly meadow high in the Chiles

Valley. Picnics are encouraged on the lawns and at tables under a huge, shady oak tree. Try not to miss this experience!

 Fine points: The ranch has been breeding and training horses since the 1950s, with an occasional winner at Santa Anita. The winery has had several winners, too, especially its Cabernet Sauvignon. Tasting fee: $2.50. Featured wines: Chardonnay, Cabernet Sauvignon, Cabernet Zinfandel blend, Zinfandel, Late Harvest Riesling. Owners: Susan Meyer and Jim Fresquez. Winemaker: Susan Meyer. Cases: 2,000. Acres: 442 (50 in grapes).

❧ *Rustridge Ranch & Winery, Bed & Breakfast & Thoroughbred Home, 2910 Lower Chiles Valley Road, St. Helena 94574; phone (707) 965–2871 for winery, (707) 965–9353 for B&B, or (800) 788–0263, e-mail rustridg@napanet.net or rustridge@aol.com. Open from 9:00 A.M. to 5:00 P.M. daily. Visa, MasterCard, American Express, and Discover. Wheelchair-accessible.*

As you leave Rustridge, which you may not want to, turn left on Lower Chiles Valley Road to reach NICHELINI WINERY, one of the oldest in the Napa Valley. Founded in 1890, Nichelini is Bonded Winery No. 843, and the old Nichelini family home hangs over the edge of the hillside with the winery. Park in the gravel pullouts along the road (don't knock on the door of the white house—it's a private home). Walk down the steep driveway between the original dark, weathered wood winery and the house to the cellar level, where you will find a bar made of barrel wood and picnic tables on the grass near the creek. There's also a bocce-ball court for family and guests.

 Fine points: Nichelini is famous for its Old Vine Zinfandel from eighty-year-old vines and is now owned by the grandchildren of Anton Nichelini, who say that Nichelini "is the oldest winery owned by the same family in the Napa Valley." No tasting fee. Featured wines: Old Vine Zinfandel, Cabernet Sauvignon, Merlot, Petite Syrah. Owners: Vic Wainwright, Greg Boeger, Joe Nichelini, and Toni Nichelini-Irwin. Winemaker: Greg Boeger. Cases: 3,000. Acres: 100.

❧ *Nichelini Winery, 2590 Sage Canyon Road, St. Helena 94574; phone (707) 963–0717. Open from 10:00 A.M. to 6:00 P.M. Sundays, holidays, and by appointment. Visa and MasterCard. Not wheelchair-accessible.*

After enjoying the Nichelini Winery, go back down to the Silverado Trail to resume your tour. Carefully cross the Silverado Trail to VILLA MT. EDEN WINERY and CONN CREEK WINERY, a newly remodeled, pink-stucco, state-of-the-art edifice and winery just south of the Conn Creek Road/Rutherford Cross Road.

NICHELINI WINERY

(Or you can cross Silverado Trail to Conn Creek Road, which becomes Rutherford Cross Road, and visit Frog's Leap and Caymus Wineries, which are open by appointment.)

Villa Mt. Eden's origins date to the 1880s, when John Bateman planted the original eighty acres. Some of Bateman's original property was expanded by its next owner, George S. Meyer of Oakland, who began to make wine. California Wineries owned the No. 11 Bonded Winery in the early 1940s, and Jim and Ann McWilliams bought it in 1969 from Baron Constantine Ramsay. In 1995 Washington State winery giant Stimson Lane bought and moved Villa Mt. Eden here, to sister winery Conn Creek's facility, and completed the ultimate renovation in 1998.

The elegant tasting room and winery, with the property lined by olive trees, looks across the Silverado Trail toward Auberge du Soleil, up the hill. You will find a pleasant tasting bar to the right, as you enter and an attractive gift shop to the back. Colorful grapevine pottery and dishes rest on heavy wood furniture along with books and wining and dining accessories.

Villa Mt. Eden is in the process of acquiring Guenoc and McDowell wineries.

Fine points: Be sure to sample the Orange Muscat, only 4 percent alcohol and a great topping on ice cream or cheesecake or dribbled into champagne. We enjoy just sipping it. No tasting fee. Featured wines: Villa Mt. Eden Pinot Blanc, Chardonnay, Sauvignon Blanc, Syrah, Cabernet Franc, Pinot Noir, Zinfandel, Merlot, Cabernet Sauvignon, Orange Muscat. Owners: Stimson Lane (U.S. Tobacco). Winemakers: Mike McGrath for Villa Mt. Eden, Tom Montgomery for Conn Creek. Cases: 200,000 Villa Mt. Eden, 5,600 Conn Creek. Acres: 1,168 and buy from others.

❧ *Villa Mt. Eden Winery and Conn Creek Winery, 8711 Silverado Trail, St. Helena 94574; phone (707) 944–2414 or (800) 793–7960, fax (707) 963–7840, e-mail info@reserveclub.com, Web site www.villamteden.com Open from 10:00 A.M. to 4:00 P.M. daily. Visa, MasterCard, American Express, and Discover. Wheelchair-accessible.*

For a quick and delightful distraction, follow Conn Creek Road (also called Highway 128 and Rutherford Cross Road) down beside Villa Mt. Eden to the Napa Valley Grapevine Wreath Company, Frog's Leap, and Caymus wineries.

You come to brown-shingled NAPA VALLEY GRAPEVINE WREATH COMPANY on the first turn of Conn Creek Road off the Silverado Trail. The Wood family turns their Cabernet Sauvignon vines into other people's treasures, including baskets, hearts, crosses, wine holders, magic wands, and, by golly, wreaths. This is a wonderful recycling project, making the most of every part of the vine.

❧ *Napa Valley Grapevine Wreath Company, 8901 Conn Creek Road (Highway 128), Rutherford 94573; phone (707) 963–8893, fax (707) 963–3325. Open from 10:30 A.M. to 5:30 P.M. daily. Visa, MasterCard, and Discover. Wheelchair-accessible.*

Just around the bend west of the wreath company is FROG'S LEAP WINERY, in a big old barn built by C. T. Adamson in the late 1800s. Frog's Leap purposely doesn't have a sign on the road to make it a wee bit difficult to visit. Just turn off Conn Creek Road when you see the biggest barn around.

Adamson made and sold bulk wine here, and for ninety-six years the building served as a farming center to store and dry cherries and prunes. In 1994 Frog's Leap moved here from the "frog farm" where they started by leaps and bounds.

The leaping frog on top of the winery's roof doubles as a weathervane. Park in the lot and walk to the back of the property on the left side of the barn (facing it) to the Vineyard House retail room. If no one is there, venture through the raised vegetable and herb beds, and go past the lawn and barbecue to the office on the far side. The winery is only allowed to serve by appointment—so go right in and make one on the spot.

FROG'S LEAP WINERY'S LEAPING FROG
CHECKS WHICH WAY THE WIND BLOWS

 Fine points: Featured wines: Sauvignon Blanc, Chardonnay, Zinfandel, Merlot, Cabernet Sauvignon. Owners: Julie and John Williams. Winemaker: John Williams. Cases: 47,000. Acres: 40.

❧ *Frog's Leap Winery, 8815 Conn Creek Road (Highway 128), Rutherford 94573; phone (707) 963–4704, e-mail Ribbitt@frogsleap.com, Web site www.frogsleap.com. Open from 10:00 A.M. to 4:00 P.M. Monday–Saturday, wine tasting by appointment. Visa, MasterCard, and American Express. Wheelchair-accessible.*

Farther down Conn Creek Road is CAYMUS VINEYARDS, the world-renowned producers of Special Selection Cabernet Sauvignons, which *Wine Spectator* rates in its "Top 10" as often as it does Chateau Margaux's. To get there, drive south on Conn Creek from where the Rutherford Cross Road (Highway 128) intersects with it. Caymus is on the left (east) side of the street.

To enter, you must approach the gate, buzz, and inquire whether appointments are available. Or you can call ahead. Caymus schedules its appointments carefully so that all guests can be treated privately. Wines are served in the cream-colored dining room with brick floors to the right of the entrance.

The Charles Wagner family began farming here in 1906, and Chuck Wagner

was born and raised on the property, the son of Charlie and Lorna Wagner. The
Wagners named their winery in honor of the Caymus Indians. They show their
respect for the land by allowing their wines to develop primarily on their own.
Besides good wine you can purchase great logo hats ($13), corkscrews, shirts, and
the *Wine Spectator's Buying Guide and California Wine Book.*

Fine points: Featured wines: Special Selection Cabernet Sauvignon,
Conundrum dry white blend, Pinot Noir Blanc, Oeuil de Pedrille.
Owner and winemaker: Chuck Wagner. Cases: 54,000. Acres: 65.
*Caymus Vineyards, 8700 Conn Creek Road, Rutherford 94573;
phone (707) 967–3010. Open from 10:00 A.M. to 4:30 P.M. daily, wine tasting by
appointment. Visa and MasterCard. Wheelchair-accessible.*

If you're famished, rush west on the Rutherford Cross Road to Rutherford
Grill at Highway 29. Otherwise, we recommend that you retrace your tracks
back to Silverado Trail by turning right when you leave Caymus and continuing back northeastward. When you get to the Silverado Trail, turn right (south)
to continue.

Don't miss MUMM NAPA VALLEY, about a mile south of Villa Mt. Eden
Winery on the right (west) side of the Silverado Trail. Red flags hint that you
have arrived at the winery, which was modeled after an early 1900s barn with
screened porches. Cyclists enjoy the bike rack. When you enter the winery, a gift
shop is on the right. The tasting porch lies beyond, facing south and west and
overlooking sumptuous vineyards and the Mayacamas Mountains. Sit at a table,
and the champagne will be brought to you. Heaven!

The French Champagne maker Mumm gave original Mumm Napa
Valley winemaker Guy Deveaux, a native of Epernay in the heart of France's
Champagne district, carte blanche to develop this estate sparkling wine
works, and Mumm's vineyard along Highway 12 in Carneros between
Sonoma and Napa is named for him. Joseph E. Seagram & Sons owns the
French Mumm company as well as Mumm Napa Valley and Sterling
Vineyards.

Mumm provides a whole cultural and educational experience, with tours
through its demonstration vineyards and video monitors, as well as the fabulous
Ansel Adams "The Story of a Winery" permanent photo exhibit in the Art
Gallery. Adams's photo series resulted from his friendship with Otto E. Meyer,
president of the wine division of Joseph E. Seagram & Sons. Mumm Napa
Valley sparklings have been served in the White House to British Prime
Minister Tony Blair and French Prime Minister Jacques Chirac. You can but it
in all quantities, from splits. to Balthazars (12 litres).

The gift shop is a delight, with everything from books and maps to film and aspirin. The staff encourage individuality and fun. We found them to be the most friendly and helpful around.

Fine points: Try Mumm's special still wines, Chardonnay and Pinot Noir, which are only available here. The tasting fee of $3.75 to $6.50 will be applied to your purchase, or you can pay $7.50 for a sampler of three half-glasses. Featured wines: Blanc de Blancs, DVX, Brut Prestige, Blanc de Noirs, Chardonnay, Sparkling Pinot Noir, Pinot Noir, Rosé, Demi Sec, dessert wine. Owners: Joseph E. Seagram & Sons. Winemakers: Greg Fowler, Executive Winemaker; Rob McNeil, hands-on Winemaker. Cases: 200,000+. Acres: 1,200.

➤ *Mumm Napa Valley, 8445 Silverado Trail, Rutherford 94573; phone (707) 942–3434, fax (707) 942–3469, Web site www.mumm.com. Open from 10:00 A.M. to 5:00 P.M. daily. Free tours hourly from 10:00 A.M. to 3:00 P.M. Visa, MasterCard, American Express, and JCB. Wheelchair-accessible.*

When you leave Mumm, turn right (south) onto the Silverado Trail. Watch carefully for **ZD WINES** just 0.3 mile south. ZD's tile roof is what you see from the road. Turn right (west) at the sign and park in the lot. Follow the path beside the winery by the lawns and tree roses in the patio to the large wood doors and the tasting room. White walls highlight the many soft-colored woods in the room and its Mexican-tile floor.

ZD was founded in the Carneros District in 1968 by aerospace engineers Norman de Leuze and Gino Zepponi, with $3,000 each. They obtained the first Sonoma County winery permit issued in twenty years and purchased grapes from Rene di Rosa to make wine "in Sonoma from grapes grown in the Carneros region of Napa." Ten years later they moved the winery here. Since Zepponi's tragic death in an automobile accident, the de Leuze family has developed ZD alone, with mother Rosa Lee and son Brett handling marketing. Robert serves as winemaker, and Julie is administrative director—and a fabulous cook. In 2000 ZD poured its thirtieth release of Carreros Pinot Noir.

We encourage you to visit this happy and quietly elegant winery. Check out the tasteful and high-quality shirts and hats, ZD-logo cork pullers, and aprons.

Fine points: ZD provides small baskets of sliced bread to cleanse your palate between wines. The $10 tasting fee is refundable with purchase. ZD wines have been served at state dinners in the White House by three presidents. Featured wines: Chardonnay, Merlot, Cabernet Sauvignon, Pinot Noir. Owners: The de Leuze Family. Winemaker: Robert de Leuze. Cases: 30,000. Acres: 35.

➤ *ZD Wines, 8383 Silverado Trail, Napa 94558; phone (707) 963–5188, fax (707) 963–2640, e-mail info@zdwines.com, Web site www.zdwines.com. Open from 10:00 A.M. to 4:30 P.M. daily. Visa, MasterCard, and American Express. Wheelchair-accessible.*

Almost 1½ miles south of ZD and on the left (east) side of Silverado Trail, you might want to visit MINER FAMILY VINEYARDS (formerly Oakville Ranch Winery). Bob Miner, founder of the Oracle Corporation, and his wife, Mary, bought the initial acreage for this winery in 1989 and began making wines. In 1996 they purchased the adjacent property, the brand-new but never used Stratford Winery. After Bob Miner's death, Mary ran it for a while, then sold it to nephew David Miner, his wife, Emily, and his parents, Ed and Norma. The winery's Cabernets have received ratings of 90 or higher consistently since 1989.

Set slightly up the slope from the road, the winery has a towering, vanilla façade. The pleasant tasting room (on the second floor—an elevator is available) is beige with light hardwood floors covered with Oriental rugs. There is an excellent selection of books on a large dining table and a glassed-in humidor to keep cigars at the perfect temperature. Walk down the hall toward the rest rooms and look through the windows to the barrel room with pinkish-beige walls. Relax on the patio furniture and take in the spectacular Napa Valley view.

 Fine points: Tasting fee: $3.00 Oakville Cellars, $5.00 estate wines. Featured wines: Oakville Ranch and Miner Family Vineyards Chardonnay, Sauvignon Blanc, Pinot Noir, Merlot, Cabernet Franc, Sangiovese, Viognier, Zinfandel, Cabernet Sauvignon. Owners: Bob and Emily Miner, Ed and Norma Miner. President: David Miner. Winemaker: Gary Brookman. Cases: 12,000 estate wines. Acres: 80 of 300 in use.

❦ *Miner Family Vineyards, 7850 Silverado Trail, Oakville 94562; phone (707) 944–9500, fax (707) 945–1280, Web site www.minerwines.com. Open from 11:00 A.M. to 5:00 P.M. daily; tours by appointment from 11:00 A.M. to 3:00 P.M. Visa, MasterCard, and American Express. Wheelchair-accessible.*

We highly recommend a slight detour west on Oakville Cross Road to Plumpjack, Groth, and the prized Silver Oak wineries.

The first of the three that you come to from the Silverado Trail is PLUMPJACK WINERY, a venture of San Francisco's Plumpjack Cafe owners and thirty-something movers and shakers: Plumpjack managing director and San Francisco Supervisor Gavin Newsom and Bill and Gordon Getty. Plumpjack made news in 2000 by breaking with tradition and introducing a sexy-looking screw-top bottle (instead of cork), formerly thought of as a sacrilege by wine snobs.

Three-tenths of a mile from the Silverado Trail, turn north at the sign, take a sharp left in front of the winery building, then turn right into Plumpjack's

ASIAN CRAB CAKES WITH LIME-GINGER SAUCE
from Miner Family Vineyards

INGREDIENTS:

For crab mixture:
1 small yellow onion, finely minced
8 oz fresh crabmeat
2 slices white bread, broken into pieces
2 tsp fresh lemongrass, minced
1 Tbs gingerroot, grated
1 egg, beaten
6 Tbs butter, melted
mixed baby greens
salt and pepper to taste

FOR SAUCE:

3 Tbs lime juice
1 tsp lime rind
3 Tbs soy sauce
1 Tbs gingerroot, grated
⅓ cup peanut oil

PREPARATION:

Sauté the onion in 3 Tbs butter until soft and just golden on edges. Remove from pan and mix with crab, bread pieces, egg, gingerroot, and lemongrass.

Form crab mixture into small patties on a cookie sheet. Cover with plastic wrap and chill for at least an hour. In small skillet, brown cakes in melted butter until golden brown.

Arrange one cake just to one side on bed of greens and drizzle with the following sauce.

In a small bowl, whisk lime juice, lime rind, soy sauce, gingerroot, and peanut oil. Serve with Miner Family Vineyards Viognier. Serves 4.

parking lot. Walk on rose-colored gravel through herb gardens and olive trees to the tasting room on the left of the tank house. Admire the shiny copper "chandelier" in the middle of the room.

Located in what used to be Jim and Ann McWilliams' Villa Mt. Eden Winery (now Stimson Lane's Villa Mt. Eden), Plumpjack has great picnic tables, Henry IV Shakespearean decor, and a youthful irreverence unusual in these parts. The sign opposite the tasting room reads: IMPRESS YOUR DATE, IMPRESS YOUR FRIENDS. WHAT THE HECK—IMPRESS SNOOTY WAITERS NAMED MAURICE.

Fine points: The logo shirts and hats are highest quality, as are the emerging wines. Tasting fee: $5.00. Featured wines: Chardonnay, Merlot, Sangiovese, Cabernet Sauvignon. Owners: Gavin Newsom, Bill and Gordon Getty. Winemaker: Nils Venge. Cases: 8,000–10,000. Acres: 50.

✢ *Plumpjack Winery, 620 Oakville Cross Road, Oakville 94562; phone (707) 945–1220, fax (707) 944–0744, Web site www.plumpjack.com. Open from 10:00 A.M. to 4:00 P.M. daily. Visa, MasterCard, and American Express. Gravel makes wheelchair-access difficult.*

Practically adjoining Plumpjack is GROTH VINEYARDS & WINERY, the baby of Judy and Dennis Groth, former CPA with Ernst Young & Co., former executive vice president of Atari and president of Atari's International Division, and one of the wine industry's truly nice guys. You can't miss the enormous rose-stucco Mission-style structure with its blue tile fountain and sweeping steps, designed by Napa architect Bob Gianelli. The monumental building northeast of the winery is the Groths' new home.

When you enter the lovely cavernous rooms, the first thing you see are daughter Suzanne Groth's bold, colorful, and fun paintings, which also adorn the winery's posters and wine labels. Walk through the large dining room with its dramatic fireplace, Nino Barrucca serving platters and bowls, and seating for crowds. (Unfortunately, the dining room is used only for house and trade events.) Through the arched windows you can see the barrel aging room. Walk out onto the patio to enjoy the view of vineyards to the north.

Judy and Dennis met in the first grade in Sunnyvale and are still together. They introduced the concept of winemakers getting equity (10 percent) in the winery instead of just being employees. With great success they hired Villa Mt. Eden's winemaker, Nils Venge, to create the wines, since they knew nothing about the process. They now release their Reserve Cabernet Sauvignon the last Saturday before February 1, the same day Silver Oak releases theirs.

Fine points: In 1988 Robert Parker called Groth "one of California's hottest wineries" and gave Groth's 1985 Cabernet Sauvignon a rare "perfect" score, immediately spiking the demand for Groth's 400 cases. Tasting fee: $5.00, refundable with purchase. Featured wines: Chardonnay, Sauvignon Blanc, Cabernet Sauvignon, Merlot. Owners: Dennis and Judy Groth. Winemaker: Michael Weis. Cases: 40,000. Acres: 165.

✢ *Groth Vineyards & Winery, 750 Oakville Cross Road, Oakville 94562; phone (707) 944–0290, fax (707) 944–8932, Web site www.grothwines.com. Open from 10:00 A.M. to 4:00 P.M. Monday–Saturday. Visa, MasterCard, and American*

GROTH VINEYARDS & WINERY'S IMPRESSIVE EDIFICE

Express. Wheelchair-accessible by entrance to left of stairs and elevator to second floor.

Leaving Groth, turn right (west) onto Oakville Cross Road. Go about half a mile to the superb SILVER OAK WINERY. Turn left (south) into Silver Oak's double driveway, lined with olive trees and silver oaks, to what was once the Oakville Dairy. Silver Oak makes only Cabernet Sauvignon—and makes only the best Cabernet Sauvignon in the Napa Valley and possibly anywhere. Try to sneak a taste of its Meyer Family Port.

Partner, president, and winemaster Justin Meyer was once a teacher-coach member of the Christian Brothers religious order. He was "drafted" to work at Christian Brothers Winery instead of teaching. Experiencing every job in the winery, adding B.S. and M.S. degrees in viticulture and enology in addition to his M.S. in economics, Justin left the order after fifteen years to create his own winery, with the intent of making the best Cabernet in the world. He has. Having taught "Wine Appreciation" at Napa Valley College, he also wrote *Plain Talk about Wine*, a fun and user-friendly book about viticulture, enology, and wine appreciation. It is available in Silver Oak's tasting room.

Partner Raymond Duncan is an investor, Denver oilman, buffalo rancher, and co-owner of an art gallery. Ray and Justin began their endeavor in 1972 to plant and manage 750 acres that Ray owned in the Napa and Alexander valleys.

SILVER OAK WINERY

In 1975 they bought Franciscan Winery from bankruptcy. There they crushed and bottled Silver Oak's grapes from 1975 to 1981. They sold Franciscan to the Eckes Company of Germany in 1979.

So here they are in this elegant, stone monastery-looking winery. As you enter the dark tasting room, it might take your eyes a few moments to adjust from the sunlight outside. Tasters may sit on stone benches or upholstered black wrought-iron furniture.

Silver Oak also has a winery in Sonoma County's Alexander Valley in what was once the old Lyeth Winery facility. At both wineries Justin makes a masterful effort of creating a family among staff members. The results are readily apparent.

Fine points: Be sure to look into the glassed-in Library Room, where Silver Oak's finest bottlings are stored. Sliding glass doors lead to the barrel and tank rooms, where the Cabernets are aged at least thirty months in American oak barrels. Tasting fee: $10 including souvenir glass. Featured wines: Cabernet Sauvignon, Port. Owners: Justin Meyer and Raymond Duncan. Winemaker: Justin Meyer. Cases: 50,000. Acres: 220.

Silver Oak Winery, 915 Oakville Cross Road, Oakville 94562; phone (707) 944–8808, Web site www.SilverOak.com. Open from 9:00 A.M. to 4:00 P.M. Monday–Saturday. Visa and MasterCard. Wheelchair-accessible.

As you leave Silver Oak, we suggest that you turn right (east) onto Oakville Cross Road and go back to the Silverado Trail. Turn right (south) onto Silverado Trail and turn left (east) to visit **ROBERT SINSKEY VINEYARDS**, up the hill to the left (east). Nestled in soft hills, the winery has ivy-covered stone walls, rose gardens, interesting half-circle benches, a half-circle fish pond (no coins, please), and great views. Enjoy the vegetable and herb gardens in the summer.

Robert Sinskey is a graduate of the Parsons School of Design in New York. He designed the winery and does all the graphics. His father, Dr. Robert Sinskey, was a partner in Acacia Winery in Carneros when the Chalone group bought it.

As you enter the cavernous tasting room and kitchen, hosts greet you as if you have just arrived in their home. Because Robert Sinskey believes so strongly in the importance of food and wine, he has a gorgeous professional kitchen right in the tasting room—and a house chef. You will see both a historic wood stove and ultra-modern ovens, wood-burning ovens, a television/video screen, a full range of professional pots and pans, and a magnificent view of Silverado Vineyards across the road.

Robert brings in restaurant chefs from all over the country to conduct cook-

ROBERT SINSKEY VINEYARDS

ing classes, including Joseph Keller, Craig Stoll, Mark Sullivan, James Ormsby, and Maria Helm Sinskey of Plumpjack Cafe in San Francisco. Demonstration cooking classes cost $75 per person and include lunch paired with Robert Sinskey wines. Get on the mailing list if you might be interested in the Front Porch Dinners ($150).

Every year Robert Sinskey stages his fun Release Party so you can "hear the gospel according to Pinot," feast on "life-sustaining creations," listen to "down-home music," and "take The Pinot cure." It all takes place close to May 1 for $150 per person.

Robert Sinskey Vineyards becomes Certified Organic in 2001.

Fine points: You can purchase the best olive oils and books here. Tasting fee: $5.00. Featured wines: Chardonnay, Pinot Noir, Merlot, Cabernet Sauvignon, Cabernet Franc, Zinfandel, Claret, Pinot Blanc. Owner: Robert Sinskey. Winemaker: Jeff Birnig. Chef: Maria Helm Sinskey: 31,000. Acres: 205.

❧ *Robert Sinskey Vineyards, 6320 Silverado Trail, Yountville 94558; phone (707) 944–9090 or (800) 869–2030, Web site www.robertsinskey.com. Open from 10:00 A.M. to 4:30 P.M. daily. Visa, MasterCard, and American Express. Wheelchair-accessible.*

As you leave the winery, turn left (south) onto the Silverado Trail, and then turn right (west) on Yountville Cross Road, where you will find S. Anderson and Goosecross Cellars. (On your way south you will see Vine Cliff Cellars up the hill to the east, but it is not open to the public.) If you choose not to make this detour, just continue southward to Shafer and Silverado vineyards.

Head down the slight hill on Yountville Cross Road, then left into S. ANDERSON WINERY, a small family winery of great taste and flower-bedecked ambience. The exquisite lawns, rose-covered arbors, and gazebo with gravel patio made us want to move right in.

Owner Carol Anderson graduated from UC Davis's School of Viticulture and Enology and created S. Anderson Champagnes and Chardonnays. She still directs the winemaking. Her late husband, Stanley, supervised planting of the noble vinifera Chardonnay and Pinot Noir vineyards in the Stag's Leap and Carneros districts, as well as creation of the caves and winery. Son John oversees business and marketing, while his wife, Tracy, a graduate of the California Culinary Academy, is the winery's chef and chief entertainment organizer.

S. Anderson's caves hold 400,000 bottles of Champagne, Chardonnay, and Cabernet aging in the barrel. These are great places for candlelit parties and chamber-music concerts. The stone tasting room feels like a cave. Notice photographs of Stanley Anderson at the end of the bar.

LEMON TEA BREAD
from Carol Anderson, S. Anderson Winery

INGREDIENTS FOR THE BREAD:

¾ cup milk
1 Tbs lemon balm,
* finely chopped*
1 Tbs lemon thyme,
* finely chopped*
2 cups flour

1½ tsp baking powder
¼ tsp salt
6 Tbs butter, at room temperature
1 cup sugar
2 eggs, beaten
1 Tbs lemon zest, grated

PREPARATION:

Set out butter to come to room temperature. Butter a 9x5x3-inch pan. Preheat oven to 325°F. Heat the milk with the chopped herbs and let steep until cool.

Mix the flour, baking powder, and salt together in a bowl. In another bowl, cream the butter and gradually beat in the sugar. Continue beating until light and fluffy. Beat in the eggs, one at a time. Beat in the lemon zest. Add the flour mixture alternately with the herbed milk. Mix until the batter is just blended.

Put the batter into the prepared pan. Bake for about 50 minutes, or until a toothpick inserted in the center comes out dry. Remove from the pan onto a wire rack that is set over a sheet of waxed paper. Pour the lemon glaze over the still-hot bread. Decorate with a few sprigs of lemon thyme.

INGREDIENTS FOR LEMON GLAZE:

juice of 2 lemons
powdered sugar

PREPARATION:

Put the lemon juice in a bowl and add the sugar, stirring until a thick, but still pourable, paste forms. Pour the glaze over the hot bread.

Fine points: Get on their mailing list for the terrific "S. Anderson News." Tasting fee: $5.00. Featured wines: Chardonnay, Merlot, Cabernet Sauvignon, Brut Champagne, Blanc de Noirs, Rosé Champagne. Owner and Champagne Maker: Carol Anderson.

Winemaker: David DeSante. Cases: 12,000. Acres: 120.

✤✣ **S. Anderson Winery**, *1473 Yountville Cross Road, Yountville 94599; phone (707) 944–8642 or (800) 4–BUBBLY, fax (707) 944–8020, Web site www.4bubbly.com. Open from 10:00 A.M. to 5:00 P.M. daily. Visa, MasterCard, and American Express. Wheelchair-accessible.*

As you leave S. Anderson, turn left onto Yountville Cross Road, then turn right on State Lane to visit GOOSECROSS CELLARS, a fun, informal, and homey winery behind the old Gorsuch home. Goosecross is a rough translation of *Gorsuch*, an Old English name meaning "where the goose crosses the stream." Canadian geese cross the Napa Valley here in their migration north and south.

Two wooden geese in front of the house suggest that you go to the right and park beside the winery's tanks in back of the house. Ring the bell if you don't see anyone, and walk between the tanks to the tasting-room door, where Tyrone, a black Lab, used to greet visitors until the coyotes got him. Now you can meet Maidchen, another black Lab, and Humdinger, the winery cat. The tasting room, gift shop, and winery are all one, which makes this stop especially fun.

Patt and Rey Gorsuch founded the winery and passed it on to their son and winemaker, Geoff, whose business partner is David Topper. As director of hospitality, Colleen Tatarian Topper oversees the retail center as well as the popular "Wine Basics" classes. Colleen and David met "on the job" and got married right here at the winery.

 Fine points: You can purchase minor snacks such as Wisecrackers, chocolate turtles, and tapevades, and sample cheeses, pretzels, mustards, and a generous supply of Hershey's kisses. Check out

---

COLLEEN'S FLANK STEAK
from Colleen Topper,
Goosecross Cellars

INGREDIENTS:

1½ lb flank steak
meat tenderizer
½ bottle dry Vermouth
small bottle soy sauce
8 cloves garlic, chopped
⅔ cup parsley, chopped

PREPARATION:

Poke holes all over meat on both sides with fork. Put steak in 12-x2-inch glass dish. Sprinkle with meat tenderizer on both sides and refrigerate for 20 minutes.

Remove meat from refrigerator and add the Vermouth and soy sauce. Spread garlic and parsley over meat. Marinate ½ day to 8 hours. Barbecue. Serves 2–4.

the triple chocolate-dipped bottles of wine. Tasting fee: $4.00 for 4 wines. Goosecross rarely submits its wines to review by magazines or contests. Be sure to ask about the elegant Aeros Merlot. Featured wines: Chardonnay, Sauvignon Blanc, Syrah, Merlot, Cabernet Sauvignon. Owners: Geoff Gorsuch and David Topper. Winemaker: Geoff Gorsuch. Cases: 10,000. Acres: 50.

❧ *Goosecross Cellars, 1119 State Lane, Yountville 94599; phone (707) 944–1986 or (800) 276–9210, Web site www.goosecross.com. Open 10:00 A.M. to 5:00 P.M. daily. Visa, MasterCard, and American Express. Wheelchair-accessible.*

Back to the Silverado Trail to a series of interesting and excellent wineries. Turn right (south) from Yountville Cross Road onto the Silverado Trail. To get to SHAFER VINEYARDS, turn left (east) at the Shafer sign and turn left again in 0.2 mile, keeping to the right side so that you will be on the upper part of the divided road. Continue for 1 mile, passing sensuous rolling hills, a valley, and vines circling knolls all around. You arrive at what looks like a two-story ranch home with a large oak tree in front. The working part of the winery is on your left. Just looking at the earth-colored stucco, stone, and natural wood relaxes visitors.

John Shafer left the publishing business in Chicago in 1972 and moved his family to this rocky, hilly vineyard in the Napa Valley. He discovered that what looked like lousy soil and water conditions turned out to stress vines and produce prized intense flavors in his wines. John's son Doug studied at UC Davis, graduating in enology and viticulture, and became Shafer winemaker in 1983. He was soon joined by Elias Fernandez, as assistant winemaker. Now Elias is winemaker. Doug became president in 1994, when John became chairman of the board.

Dogs Jake, Rocky, and Charity form the welcoming committee. Be sure to collect the vast selections of printed information and recipes that Shafer makes available for free to visitors.

 Fine points: Shafer wines have been served at the White House to Queen Elizabeth II and Prince Philip of Britain and to President Hosni Mubarak of Egypt. Shafer's Cabernet Sauvignon outranked those of Chateau Margaux, Chateau Latour, and Chateau Palmer at a blind tasting in Germany in 1993. No tasting fee. Featured wines: Chardonnay, Merlot, Firebreak, Cabernet Sauvignon, Sangiovese, Port. Owner and CEO: John Shafer. President: Doug Shafer. Winemaker: Elias Fernandez. Cases: 30,000. Acres: 200.

❧ *Shafer Vineyards, 6154 Silverado Trail, Napa 94558; phone (707) 944–2877, fax (707) 944–9454, Web site www.shafervineyards.com. Open from 9:00 A.M. to 5:00 P.M Monday–Friday for retail sales. (Only one tasting appoint-*

ROASTED GARLIC MASHED POTATOES
from Shafer Vineyards

INGREDIENTS:

4–6 potatoes
1 medium head garlic
½ Tbs olive oil
2 Tbs butter
½ cup milk
salt and white pepper to taste

PREPARATION:

Slice off top of garlic head. Pour olive oil into opening and wrap in foil. Place garlic into 350°F oven for 30–45 minutes until soft. Remove from oven and allow to cool. Squeeze out garlic cloves. Remove any skins and mash into a smooth paste.

Bring 2–4 quarts of salted water to a boil. Peel potatoes and cut into ½-inch cubes. Add potatoes to boiling water and cook until soft (approximately 10 minutes). Drain and place in bowl with garlic and remaining ingredients. Mash until well incorporated and smooth. Serves 4.

---

ment allowed per day, so call ahead.) *Visa and MasterCard. Wheelchair-accessible by driving up behind the winery to the back.*

SILVERADO VINEYARDS is 2 miles south of the Yountville Cross Road and just south of the road to Shafer Vineyards. Turn right (west) up Silverado's driveway to its gorgeous Italian gardens and courtyard, fountain, flowers, benches, and Old World ambience. There are glorious views from the private knoll above the Napa Valley.

Long ago Lillian Disney, Diane Disney Miller, and Ron Miller set out to grow some of the best grapes in the Napa Valley and to "deliver the best wine the Napa Valley could produce at a fair price." Named for an abandoned silver mine, Silverado symbolizes the Disney family's commitment to Napa wine. They see themselves as "prospecting," as Robert Louis Stevenson suggested winegrowers do, seeking viticultural paydirt.

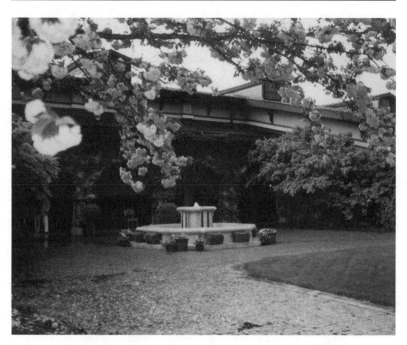

SILVERADO VINEYARDS' COURTYARD ENTRANCE

Toward that goal, the Disneys brought in John Stuart before construction to take charge of technical design and vineyard development. Highly regarded by colleagues and wine reviewers, Jack is a fifth-generation Californian with a literature degree from Stanford and graduate training in viticulture and enology from UC Davis.

Do not miss this informally elegant experience, in the new Visitors' Center and its phenomenal view of the Napa Valley and Mt. St. Helena. You can even sign in on the electronic guest list computer. Enjoy Merlot-filled chocolates ($1.25 each or $9.95 per box).

Join the club so you can attend Silverado Vineyards' fun Quicksilver Wine Club Grilling Festival and Contest.

Fine points: Tasting fee: $2.00 on weekends, free weekdays. Featured wines: Sauvignon Blanc, Chardonnay, Sangiovese Rosato, Sangiovese, Merlot, Cabernet Sauvignon. Owners: Diane Disney Miller and Ron Miller. Winemaker: Jack Stuart. Cases: 100,000. Acres: 348.

🍇 *Silverado Vineyards, 6121 Silverado Trail, Napa 94558; phone (707)*

SAGED SANGIOVESE VEAL CHOPS

from Silverado Vineyards' Quicksilver Wine Club Grilling Festival—1999
First Place Winner, Dave Ruegg

INGREDIENTS:

> 6 2½-inch fresh veal chops
> 1 pint extra virgin olive oil (Soda Creek Ranch)
> 2 bunches whole fresh sage
> 16 oz fine sea salt
> 1 whole bulb fresh garlic
> 1 pint balsamic vinegar
> 1 bottle Silverado Sangiovese
> 2 bunches fresh red Swiss chard

PREPARATION:

In marinade pan, place olive oil, chopped sage, chopped garlic to taste, 2 oz vinegar, and half the bottle of Sangiovese. Mix well, add veal chops to marinade, sprinkle with sea salt. Let stand for 2–3 hours. Before grilling, dredge veal chops on one side with sea salt to form crust.

Barbecue on medium heat until tender in center. Braise Swiss chard with garlic, wine, and balsamic vinegar to taste.

Serve chops on bed of chard and enjoy with the rest of the Sangiovese. Serves 4–6.

257–1770, fax (707) 257–1538, Web site www.silveradovineyards.com. Open from 10:30 A.M. to 5:00 P.M. May 15–September 15, 11:00 A.M. to 4:30 P.M. daily in winter; tours 11:00 A.M. and 2:00 P.M. weekends. Visa, MasterCard, and American Express. Wheelchair-accessible.

As you come back down Silverado's driveway, turn right (south) again onto the Silverado Trail to PINE RIDGE WINERY, 0.4 mile down the road. Turn right (west) at Pine Ridge's sign. As you approach the winery, you get a feel of the place from the adult tire swings hanging from pine trees, among which you are welcome to stroll, swing, or picnic. There are even barbecues for your use.

A former Olympic skier with a degree in organic chemistry and an MBA, co-founder Gary Andrus is a self-proclaimed "wine geek" who grew up Mormon in Utah and worked three harvests in Bordeaux studying enology at Montpellier. Gary's wife and Pine Ridge co-founder, Nancy Andrus, is executive vice president for marketing. Nancy runs the Napa Marathon and frequently rides her Harley Davidson through the wine country.

Be sure to walk through Pine Ridge's demonstration vineyard adjoining the south side of the parking lot and at the foot of the ridge covered with pines, and call ahead to make an appointment to tour the vast, enlarged caves.

A new financial relationship with Leucadia Cellars, an East Coast investment firm, has led to a total makeover of Pine Ridge's tasting room and processing, what Gary calls "reinventing ourselves." The Andruses even bought a vineyard in Dundee, Oregon, near Drouhin, where they built Archery Summit Winery. They actually made Archery Summit's first Pinot Noir vintages here before the winery was completed. Go ahead and be impressed with the etched bottles of wine they have done for Ferrari and Apple Computers.

 Fine points: Take home some of Pine Ridge's Extra Virgin Olive Oil, made from its estate-grown olives. Pine Ridge uses olive trees as active participants in organic farming, since they attract blue-green sharpshooters (like grasshoppers) and keep them busy so they

PINE RIDGE WINERY

VIETNAMESE FIVE-SPICE CHICKEN
from Pine Ridge Winery

Note: Marinate the chicken in the morning for dinner that night. In warm weather, you can grill the chicken over coals instead of broiling it.

INGREDIENTS:

6 cloves garlic, sliced
1 large shallot, coarsely chopped
1 Tbs ginger, minced
1 Tbs plus 1 tsp sugar
¼ cup soy sauce
¼ cup Thai or Vietnamese fish sauce
½ tsp Chinese five-spice powder
4 chicken thighs, bone in
3 chicken half-breasts, bone in
freshly ground black pepper

PREPARATION:

In a small food processor or by hand, mince garlic, shallot, ginger, and sugar to a paste. Transfer to a small bowl and whisk in soy sauce, fish sauce, five-spice powder, and several grinds of black pepper. Put chicken in a shallow dish and pour marinade over the pieces. Turn pieces in the marinade to coat. Refrigerate 8–12 hours, turning pieces several times in the marinade. Bring to room temperature before cooking.

Preheat broiler. Set broiler pan on a rack 7–8 inches from the heating element, and preheat pan so chicken doesn't stick.

Place chicken skin side down, on broiler pan. Broil until nicely browned, about 12 minutes, basting once or twice with marinade. Turn, baste again, and broil until skin is richly browned and chicken juices run clear, about 12 minutes, basting two or three more times with marinade. Adjust distance of chicken from broiler if needed to keep it from burning. Let chicken cool for about 5 minutes, then chop breasts in half.

Serve each guest a thigh and a piece of breast meat. Serves 4. Serve with Pine Ridge Chenin Blanc-Voignier.

don't attack the vines. You might also enjoy the elegant Nicole Miller wine-label shirts. Tasting fee: $5.00–$10.00. Featured wines: Chenin Blanc-Viognier, Eye of the Tiger, Chardonnay, Merlot, Cabernet Sauvignon, Cabernet Franc, Black Diamond Port, Archery Summit Vireton, Pinot Noir. Owners: Gary and Nancy Andrus. Winemaker: Stacy Clark. Cases: 90,000. Acres: 310.

❧ *Pine Ridge Winery, 5901 Silverado Trail, Napa 94558; phone (707) 252–9777, fax (707) 253–1493, Web site www.pineridgewinery.com or www.archery summit.com. Open from 11:00 A.M. to 5:00 P.M. daily. Visa, MasterCard, American Express, and Discover. Wheelchair-accessible.*

Just 0.2 mile south on the east side of Silverado Trail is STELTZNER VINEYARDS. The winery is set in a new California/Mediterranean stucco structure, in a flat valley within view of the road. Turn left at the sign. The tasting room is the long, narrow entrance to Steltzner's caves, which are dug into the hillside. The winery office building is topped with a three-story observation tower, offering a bird's-eye view of the surrounding Stag's Leap region.

Rick Steltzner is a third-generation Californian who grew up in Livermore working part time for Wente Brothers Winery. He earned an MFA degree at Sacramento State College. Soon his life as an artist on St. Helena's Lodi Lane forced a change of career in order to stay in the Napa Valley.

Rick bought some land in the Stag's Leap District in 1964 (smart move) and began to grow grapes, drawing on his childhood memories of his mentor, Ernest Wente. Since he turned out to be good at caring for vineyards, Rick established and

STELTZNER VINEYARDS TOWER AND
CAVE ENTRANCE

managed vineyards for other growers and wineries. He then started his own winemaking operation in a converted prune-dehydrating shed. He now enjoys high ratings from many reviewers.

Fine points: Tasting fee: $3.00. Featured wines: Sauvignon Blanc, Chardonnay, Claret, Merlot, Cabernet Sauvignon, Sangiovese, Merlot Grappa. Owners: Richard and Christine Steltzner. Winemaker: Charles W. Hendricks. Cases: 15,000. Acres: 100.

❧ *Steltzner Vineyards, 5998 Silverado Trail, Napa 94558; phone (707) 252–*

7272, fax (707) 252–2079, Web site www.steltzner.com. Open from 10:00 A.M. to 5:00 P.M. Monday–Saturday, noon to 4:30 P.M. Sunday. Visa and MasterCard. Wheelchair-accessible.

As you leave Steltzner, turn left (south) and head south on the Silverado Trail for 0.5 mile to STAG'S LEAP WINE CELLARS, whose sign comes up quickly down a hill on the left (east). Stag's Leap's world-class Cabernet Sauvignon won the Paris Bicentennial Tasting in 1976, causing French judges at the blind tasting to proclaim, "At last a good French wine!"

Stag's Leap is actually an old Indian name given to a rock formation on the hillside and later applied to the local wine appellation. Be sure to notice co-owner Barbara Winiarski's artistic sandstone floors in the reception hall, as well as her gardens and comfortable design concepts. Employees and visitors enjoy picnic lunches at tables, and children are offered juices.

Founder Warren Winiarski was born in Chicago of Polish parents. His last name means "from the vine" or "winemaker's son." Warren should have known that, since his father made dandelion wine and fruit cordials in their home basement, he was fated to make elegant wines someday instead of following his liberal arts degree or the political history and theory he studied in Italy. While a liberal arts lecturer at the University of Chicago, he and his wife, Barbara, began to think of farming as an alternative to big-city life.

The Winiarskis moved to California in 1964. Warren first worked as an apprentice for Lee Stewart at Souverain Winery, then as assistant winemaker for Robert Mondavi in 1966, while looking for land similar to Nathan Fay's, whose wines he admired greatly. He found forty-four acres next to Fay Vineyard. Partly planted by Barbara and their children, it is now Stag's Leap Wine Cellars.

 Fine points: The Smithsonian Institution recently completed a yearlong project of recording life at Stag's Leap. Tasting fee: $5.00 including glass. Featured wines: Chardonnay, Sauvignon Blanc, White Riesling, Cabernet Sauvignon, Merlot, Hawk Crest Merlot, Petite Sirah. Owners: Warren and Barbara Winiarski. Winemaker: Michael Silacci. Cases: 60,000. Acres: 205.

❧ *Stag's Leap Wine Cellars, 5766 Silverado Trail, Napa 94558; phone (707) 944–2020, Web site www.cask23.com. Open from 10:00 A.M. to 4:30 P.M. daily. Visa, MasterCard, and American Express. Wheelchair-accessible.*

Be sure to go up the driveway to one of Napa's "ghost wineries," **REGUSCI WINERY,** to experience truly old Napa family vinting. Regusci's building is known as the Grigsby Building Occidental Winery, because Terrill and Charles Grigsby had it constructed here in 1878 by Caucasians, partly in response to the

REGUSCI WINERY'S GRIGSBY BUILDING

St. Helena Star's anti-Chinese call to oust Chinese laborers.

The building features 2-foot-thick hand-cut lava stone walls, which provide natural cooling. The original winery operated on a gravity system, with crushing on the third floor; the juice was gravity fed to the second floor for settling and fermentation, then down to the bottom floor for barrel storage and aging. During Prohibition, the third floor became a distillery for bootleg wine, and the second floor became a dairy.

Gaetano Regusci bought the property in 1932 and made his own wines, while farming corn, hay, prunes, and walnuts, and raising cattle and hogs. Eventually, Gaetano's son Angelo took over, and after the family grew grapes for others for years. Angelo's son Jim and Jim's wife, Diana, reestablished the winery, with their first vintage crush in 1996.

Enjoy the cool, historical tasting room, with olive oil tastes and fun historic posters.

Fine points: Tasting fee: $5.00. Featured wines: Estate grown Chardonnay, Riesling, Zinfandel, Merlot, Cabernet Sauvignon. Owners: Jim and Diana Regusci. Winemakers: Angelo Regusci and Charles Hendricks. Cases: 3,500. Acres: 200.

❧ *Regusci Winery, 5584 Silverado Trail, Napa 94558; phone (707) 254–0403, fax (707) 254–0417. Open from 10:00 A.M. to 5:00 P.M. by appointment. Visa, MasterCard, and American Express. Wheelchair-accessible.*

Next in our progression southward on the Silverado Trail is CHIMNEY ROCK WINERY, located in a large, white, monastic-looking building, a replica of a South African winery with the Dutch Huguenot architectural influence of Capetown. Drive 0.8 mile south of Stag's Leap Wine Cellars and turn left when you see the signs.

Poplar trees line the buildings. You can sip in the beautiful courtyard, but no picnicking is allowed.

Co-owner Sheldon (Hack) Wilson developed the Pepsi market throughout Africa as the founding bottler on the African continent. He also served as president of Pepsi United Bottlers for Los Angeles, Mexico, and Puerto Rico. Hack explored vineyard property in Bordeaux but directed his attention to the Napa Valley with the encouragement of his friend, the late Alexis Lichine.

Hack purchased the Chimney Rock Golf Course and the adjacent mountain in 1980, bulldozed nine holes (seventy-five acres), and planted his vineyard estate. The Wilsons and their partners, the Terlato Wine Group, in 2000 decided to replace the remaining nine holes of the golf course with new vineyards.

Fine points: Behind the counter in the tasting room, you can get up close and personal with special-label Chimney Rock bottles made for the final cast party of *Cheers*; parties for television shows *Wings* and *Empty Nest*; the movie *Victor-Victoria*; the Long Beach Grand Prix; and NBC's *Today* show. Tasting fee: $7.00 per glass, including glass. Featured wines: Chardonnay, Fumé Blanc, Arneis, Rosé of Franc, Cabernet Sauvignon, Cuvée, Elevage. Owners: Stella and Sheldon Wilson, the Paterno Group, and the Terlato Wine Group. Winemaker: Douglas Fletcher. Cases: 30,000. Acres: 65.

❧ *Chimney Rock Winery, 5350 Silverado Trail, Napa 94558; phone (707) 257–2641 or (800) 257–2641, fax (707) 257–2036, Web site www.chimney rock.com. Open from 10:00 A.M. to 5:00 P.M. daily. Visa, MasterCard, and American Express. Wheelchair-accessible.*

Right next door, to the south of Chimney Rock, is CLOS DU VAL, which means "a small vineyard estate in the valley"—appropriate for a family whose roots are in France. As you approach the winery, notice the American and French flags, loads of California poppies, magnolia trees, a little lake, roses along the paths, and an herb garden of lavender, rosemary, and thyme.

Owner John Goelet descends from a distinguished French wine family. His mother, Anne Marie Guestier, was a descendant of François Guestier, who

CLOS DU VAL

worked for the Marquis de Segur, owner of Chateaux Lafite and Latour. His son, Pierre François Guestier, owned Chateau Beychevelle and was a partner in the Barton & Guestier wine firm.

Goelet was introduced to Bernard Portet, a native of the Médoc region of Bordeaux and then a recent graduate in agronomy, viticulture, and enology from the renowned University of Montpellier in France. Portet came from a family involved in winemaking in Cognac and Bordeaux for generations. The two men searched the world and decided that this was the perfect site for their winery.

The interesting Clos du Val wine labels introduce you to the Three Graces—Aglaia (Splendor), Euphrosyne (Mirth), and Thalia (Good Cheer)—daughters of Zeus and Eurynome, and thought to be the loveliest figures of Greek mythology. When the Greek gods planned a banquet, the Three Graces were the first to be invited. They subsequently enchanted the gods, and no banquet was complete without them. Clos du Val hopes you will feel the same way about their wines.

Don't miss the Ronald Searle whimsical wine illustrations commissioned by John Goelet in 1977, which you can purchase for a bargain $9.00 in the fun and elegant tasting room. Check out the specially etched wine bottles.

Fine points: Clos du Val also sponsors the Napa Chamber Music Series in S. Anderson's champagne caves. Tasting fee: $5.00. Featured wines: Sémillon, Ariadne, Vin Gris, Chardonnay, Zinfandel, Sangiovese, Pinot Noir, Merlot, Cabernet Sauvignon. Owner: John Goelet. Winemaker and President: Bernard Portet. Cases: 70,000. Acres: 300.

Clos du Val, 5330 Silverado Trail, Napa 94558; phone (707) 259–2225, fax (707) 252–6125, Web site www.closduval.com. Open from 10:00 A.M. to 5:00 P.M. daily. Visa, MasterCard, American Express, and Discover. Wheelchair-accessible.

A mile and a half south of Clos du Val, also on the east side of Silverado Trail, you will find the elegant SIGNORELLO VINEYARDS. Its driveway is lined with plum trees and Italian junipers as you climb through vineyards. The modest, tasteful Italian decor includes painted arches and a glass desk in the cozy vestibule.

The tasting bar is right in the tank and aging room. Tasting is hosted by Kathy Wood. You will enjoy the scale of everything here. Be sure to notice the barrel wall mural.

Fine points: You can't miss the Dan Marino football jersey personally signed to owner Ray Signorello. Signorello's wines receive high ratings from *Wine Spectator*. Tasting fee: $5.00. Featured wines: Chardonnay, Sémillon, Vin Gris de Pinot Noir, Merlot, Cabernet Sauvignon, Pinot Noir. Owners: Ray Signorello, Sr. and Jr. Winemakers: Pierre Birebent and Ray Signorello, Jr. Cases: 8,000. Acres: 100.

Signorello Vineyards, 4500 Silverado Trail, Napa 94558; phone (707) 255–5990. Open from 10:00 A.M. to 5:00 P.M. daily, by appointment. Visa, MasterCard, and American Express. Wheelchair-accessible.

One of the most intriguing wineries growing on the east side of Silverado Trail promises to be DARIOUSH WINERY, the passion of Darioush Khaledi, owner of Value Plus Marts in Los Angeles and a 1970s immigrant from Iran. Currently you can taste the excellent wines in the most elegant mobile home tasting room around.

When all the building is completed, Darioush Winery will feature formal Mediterranean gardens with plants native to the Middle East, stone from the same source as that used for Persepolis, and an elegant architectural and cultural experience unparalleled in the Napa Valley. You can peruse Persian cookbooks, history books, and substantial cultural brochures. Complimentary fruit juices and water are available on request—what a gracious idea!

Darioush smartly hired Bernard La Borie as president, Steve Devitt, formerly winemaker at neighbor Signorello Vineyards, and Aleta La Borie, former international marketing director at Beringer, to make his dream a reality.

 Fine points: Tasting fee: $4.00. Featured wines: Chardonnay, Cabernet Sauvignon, Merlot, Viognier, Vin Gris, Shiraz. Owner: Darioush Khaledi. Winemaker: Steve Devitt. Cases: 1,000. Acres: 28.

❧ *Darioush Winery, 4240 Silverado Trail, Napa 94558; phone (707) 257–2345, fax (707) 257–3132, Web site www.darioushwinery.com. Open from 11:00 A.M. to 5:00 P.M. daily. Visa, MasterCard, American Express, and Discover. Wheelchair-accessible.*

To get to **MONTICELLO CORLEY FAMILY VINEYARDS,** take Oak Knoll Lane west from the Silverado Trail or east from Highway 29. It is closer to Silverado Trail. Turn south on Big Ranch Road, then east into Monticello's driveway.

You will be amazed at the resemblance of Jay Corley's "Jefferson House" to Thomas Jefferson's estate in Virginia. One-third the size of the original, Corley's is decorated in colonial furnishings and incorporates Jefferson's own designs throughout, since local architect Lou Gerhardt used actual plans from Jefferson's Monticello. Even the vast gardens are planted on Jefferson's principle of having something in bloom at all times. The Corleys honor Jefferson as

MONTICELLO CORLEY FAMILY VINEYARDS

"the first American Viticulturist," among his many other accomplishments.

Monticello wines have been served at White House dinners honoring Thomas Jefferson. Enjoy the relaxing historic atmosphere. The tasting room staff is lively and lots of fun.

 Fine points: Tasting fee: $5.00. Featured wines: Chardonnay, Chenin Blanc, Cuvée Cabernet Sauvignon, Pinot Noir, Merlot, Zinfandel, Merlot Chateau M (Sauvignon Blanc/Sémillon blend), Domaine Montreaux Vintage Brut. Owner: Jay Corley. Winemaker: Geoff Murray. Cases: 18,000. Acres: 80.

Monticello Corley Family Vineyards, 4242 Big Ranch Road, Napa 94558; phone (707) 253–2802 or (800) 743–6668, fax (707) 253–1019, Web site www.monticellovineyards.com. Open from 10:00 A.M. to 4:30 P.M. daily. Visa, MasterCard, American Express, and Discover. Wheelchair-accessible.

Just south of Monticello Corley Family Vineyards, don't miss **ANDRETTI WINERY,** of, yes, that Mario Andretti. Andretti has built a lovely Tuscan villa with all the feeling of his native Italy, complete with piazza, bubbling fountain, handworked iron balustrades on the residence, display kitchen for parties and cooking demonstrations, bocce-ball court, and demonstration vineyard. You can buy exquisite rare Andretti race car driving books, shirts, and hats, to say nothing of the great wine.

Bob Pepi, who began Pepi Winery with his father, Robert Pepi, has been

ANDRETTI WINERY'S TUSCAN VILLA COURTYARD

with Andretti from its founding in 1995. Indianapolis 500 and Daytona 500 winner Andretti partnered with long time pal and former K-Mart president and CEO Joe Antonini to start the winery.

 Fine points: Tasting fee: $3.00. Featured wines: Chardonnay, Sauvignon Blanc, Cabernet Sauvignon, Pinot Noir, Merlot, Sangiovese, Sauvignon/Sémillon, Claret, Lugana Bianco, Rosso. Owners: Andretti Wine Group. Winemaker: Bob Pepi. Cases: 15,000. Acres: 43.

❧ *Andretti Winery, 4162 Big Ranch Road, Napa 94558; phone (707) 255–3524 or (888) 460–8463, fax (707) 259–6776. Open from 10:00 A.M. to 4:30 P.M. daily. Visa, MasterCard, and American Express. Wheelchair-accessible.*

LUNA VINEYARDS, one of Napa Valley's newest wineries, was started in 1995 by George Vare and Mike Moone, neither of whom was new to the wine business. Vare had organized Geyser Peak, and Mike Moone had been in sales with Beringer for years. Combine those talents with those of winemaker John Kongsgaard, a thirteen-year veteran of Newton Vineyards, and you have a full set of "Lunatics."

Vare and Moone bought St. Andrews winery at this location and replanted the old Chardonnay vineyard to Pinot Grigio, now the largest planting of Pinot Grigio in Napa Valley. The "Lunatic" partners even play classical music for their vines, and the vines respond in kind.

The newly remodeled tasting room offers a quiet respite from downtown Napa or the bustle of the rest of the Valley, with a large tasting bar, cool tile, and enough space to breathe. For now, the Lunatics are making only a few Italian varietals, and making them very well.

 Fine points: Tasting fee: $3.00. Featured wines: Estate Pinot Grigio, Sangiovese, Merlot. Owners: Silverado Partners (George Vare, Mike Moone, and John Kongsgaard). Winemaster: John Kongsgaard. Cases: 20,000. Acres: 50.

❧ *Luna Vineyards, 2921 Silverado Trail, Napa 94558; phone (707) 255–5862, fax (707) 255–6385, Web site www.lunavineyards.com. Open from 10:00 A.M. to 5:00 P.M. daily; tours by appointment. Visa, MasterCard, American Express, and Diners Club. Wheelchair-accessible.*

The most southern winery on the Silverado Trail is homey VAN DER HEYDEN, the pride and joy of Andre and Sande Van der Heyden and their family. Van der Heyden claims to be the only winery in the world that produces a Late Harvest Cabernet Sauvignon. It, like all their wines, is sold only here in the tasting room.

NONNA RINA'S LAMB ROAST
from Mario Andretti's mother, Rina Andretti

INGREDIENTS:

> 7 lb leg of lamb
> fresh lemon
> 2 Tbs fresh or dried rosemary
> 1 cup Andretti Winery Pinot Noir
> 3 cups water
> 2 stalks celery, diced
> 1 carrot, diced
> 1 onion, diced
> Accent
> salt
> pepper

PREPARATION:

Remove all fat from the leg of lamb. Wash the lamb in water and pat dry. Cut a fresh lemon in half and rub vigorously over the lamb. Then rub 2 Tbs of rosemary over the skin. Sprinkle Accent, salt, and pepper over the leg, to taste.

Preheat oven to 350°F. Next, mix 3 cups of water and 1 cup of Andretti Winery Pinot Noir. Add the diced celery, carrots, and onion to the broth mixture.

Put broth in pan, then lay in leg of lamb. Bake at 350°F for 3 hours or until done. (Meat should fall away from the bone.) When done, remove lamb and slice into pieces.

For gravy for lamb roast: Put all the juice through a strainer into another pot and bring to a boil. Take 1 or 2 Tbs of cornstarch and dilute in ½ cup water. Pour slowly into boiling juice, mixing constantly for 1 minute. Once mixed, pour gravy over meat. Serve warm.

To get here, turn right (west) at the multicolored flags to the Van der Heyden home. There are lots of RVs near the vineyard. The small, homemade, slightly funky tasting room is in the rear. Cut wooden Dutch people hold signs

SCALLOPS AND MUSHROOMS IN CREAM SAUCE
from Jim Elder, Vice President of Sales, Luna Vineyards

INGREDIENTS:

2 Tbs butter	1 cup heavy cream
2 Tbs finely chopped shallots	1 lb scallops
¼ lb fresh mushrooms, thinly sliced	¼ cup orange juice
1 tomato, peeled, seeded, and diced	¼ tsp orange zest
2 Tbs cognac	salt and pepper to taste

PREPARATION:

In a sauté pan melt butter over medium heat; add shallots, stirring for about 30 seconds. Add mushrooms and cook, stirring for about 2 minutes. Add scallops, salt, and pepper, and cook, stirring about 1½ minutes. Add cognac and cook briefly.

Transfer scallops and mushrooms to a sieve placed in a bowl to collect the juice. Add diced tomato, orange juice, and orange zest, and cook, stirring about 1 minute. Add cream and any liquid that has accumulated from the scallops. Bring to a boil and cook over high heat for 2 minutes. Add scallops and mushrooms to sauce and heat briefly.

Serve with steamed rice. Serves 4.

directing you to the tasting room. If the American flag is out, the winery is open.

House cats sit on needlepoint chairs and Oriental rugs, and the ceiling is taped together here and there, but who's looking? A football signed by the whole San Francisco '49ers football team sits in a glass case, alongside Dutch porcelain figurines.

A former furniture-business owner, Van der Heyden first made wine in his basement and gave winemaking classes in a Piedmont, California, lawyer's basement. He used to sell lots of his wine in the Netherlands, a result of the Dutch ambassador to the United States taking some of these wines home, but his wines have become so popular that he now sells it all right here at the winery. He also does wine-tasting cruises and tastings in conjunction with Holland America Line.

Fine points: This place is a don't-miss, once-in-a-lifetime experience. Andre sells chocolate truffles for $2.50 to accompany sips of his rare Late Harvest Cabernet Sauvignon. Tasting fee: $5.00. Featured wines: Chardonnay, Cabernet Sauvignon, Late Harvest Cabernet Sauvignon. Owner, winemaker, "and janitor and everything in between": Andre Van der Heyden. Cases: 2,500. Acres: 13.

❧ *Van der Heyden, 4057 Silverado Trail, Napa 94558; phone (707) 259–9473. Open from 10:00 A.M. to 6:00 P.M. daily. Visa, MasterCard, American Express, Discover, and JCB. Wheelchair-accessible.*

Barely south and across the Silverado Trail from Van der Heyden, you might want to stop into the SODA CANYON STORE for excellent sandwiches and salads, Seattle's Best Coffee espresso drinks, last-minute supplies, and lots of local color.

❧ *Soda Canyon Store, 4006 Silverado Trail, Napa 94558; phone (707) 252–0285. Open from 6:00 A.M. to 7:00 P.M. Monday–Friday, 6:30 A.M. to 7:00 P.M. Saturday, 7:00 A.M.–7:00 P.M. Sunday. Visa and MasterCard. Wheelchair-accessible.*

Hardman Avenue, which leads to Silverado Golf Course and Resort and William Hill Winery, is off to the left (east) from Silverado Trail, 1 mile south of the Soda Canyon Store. Hardman follows the ups and downs of the local landscape and runs right into the SILVERADO COUNTRY CLUB, a vast resort focused on golf at two courses. If you're a golf devotee, this is it in Northern California.

Individuals own the cottages here and rent them to guests through the club. The restaurant is elegant, and locals like the Sunday brunch.

❧ *Silverado Country Club, 1600 Atlas Peak Road, Napa 94558; phone (707) 257–0200. Visa, MasterCard, American Express, Discover, Diners Club, and Carte Blanche. Wheelchair-accessible.*

Turn left onto Atlas Peak Road when you reach Silverado Country Club and follow WILLIAM HILL WINERY's signs up the hill. Here you can inhale the most spectacular view in the southern Napa Valley.

William Hill began his winery in 1976, developing prize vineyards on the Silverado bench, and produced excellent Chardonnay and Cabernet Sauvignon. He built this new winery in 1990. It was so impressive that the Wine Alliance of William Hill, Atlas Peak, Clos du Bois, and Callaway near Temecula in Southern California were bought by Hiram Walker and Allied Domecq in 1991.

Try to visit Friday through Sunday, when the staff offer food and wine pairings, which might include tapenades and fresh local strawberries. Enjoy relax-

NAPA VALLEY VIEW FROM WILLIAM HILL WINERY

ing, tasting the wines, and soaking in the view from wrought-iron tables and chairs on the patio.

Fine points: William Hill's wine labels all feature biologically accurate representations of the Chardonnay, Cabernet Sauvignon, and Merlot vine leaf appropriate to the wine in the bottle, with interesting explanations of the leaf's qualities. Tasting fee: $3.00, reserves $5.00. Featured wines: Chardonnay, Merlot, Cabernet Sauvignon. Owner: Wine Alliance (Hiram Walker). Winemaker: Jill Davis. Cases: 90,000. Acres: 130.

❧ *William Hill Winery, 1761 Atlas Peak Road, Napa 94558; phone (707) 224-4477, fax (707) 224-4484, Web site www.williamhillwinery.com. Open from 10:00 A.M. to 4:30 P.M. daily. Visa, MasterCard, and American Express. Wheelchair-accessible.*

As you leave William Hill Winery or Silverado Country Club, continue south on Atlas Peak Road to the historic **HEDGESIDE VINTNERS, HEDGESIDE WINE GALLERY,** and **DEL DOTTO CAVES** in the old Hedgeside Distillery, one of Napa Valley's "ghost wineries." Further down Atlas Peak is the Jessel Gallery at the corner of Trancas Boulevard.

WILD MUSHROOM PÂTÉ
from William Hill Winery

INGREDIENTS:

2 cups chicken broth
2 oz dried porcini mushrooms
8 Tbs unsalted butter
3 lbs mixed wild and white mushrooms
1–2 tsp fresh thyme, chopped
4 oz softened cream cheese
2 Tbs fresh chives, chopped
1½ cups chopped shallots
salt and pepper to taste

PREPARATION:

Heat chicken broth to simmer, and add porcini mushrooms. Let soak 20–30 minutes. Strain mushrooms through cheesecloth or paper towels and reserve liquid. Wash porcinis to remove any extra sand.

In a large skillet, heat butter and shallots for 5+ minutes, until golden. Add wild and white mushrooms and thyme and continue to simmer until mushrooms are golden. Add porcinis and strained soaking liquid and simmer until most of the liquid has evaporated. Stir in cream cheese, chives, salt, and pepper. Cook until cheese has melted.

Transfer mixture into food processor and blend until smooth. Serve with sourdough bread or melba toast.

Note: Use only those wild mushrooms you can identify..

The ivy-covered Hedgeside winery building was built in 1885 by Morris M. Estee from Pennsylvania, who became a lawyer, a member of the California legislature, a law book author, and an organizer of the Napa Vinicultural Society. Closed by Prohibition, Hedgeside reopened right after repeal as a new distillery and produced alcohol for the government during World War II. Notice the old local stone exterior, marble floors, and mahogany cabinets.

David and Yolanda Del Dotto have lovingly restored the Hedgeside building and offer their own superb wines in their 200-foot natural limestone caves, as well as tasting opportunities of rare boutique wines from Del Dotto, Conn Valley, Chateau LoVecchio, Big Horn, Viviani, Caldwell, and Saddleback. Richard Albert operates the lush Hedgeside Wine Gallery, where you can purchase rare old French and Italian vintage imports. A collector's heaven!

 Fine points: Tasting fee: $10, or $20 for one-hour tour and barrel tasting. Featured wineries and wines: Del Dotto's estate-grown Cabernet Sauvignon, Cabernet-Sangiovese blend, Merlot, Cabernet Franc; Conn Valley, Chateau LoVecchio, Big Horn, Viviani, Caldwell, and Saddleback labels.

❧ *Del Dotto Caves/Hedgeside Vintners, Hedgeside Wine Gallery, 1055 Atlas Peak Road, Napa 94558; phone (707) 256–3332 (Hedgeside), (707) 255–5087 (Del Dotto), Web site www.deldottovineyards.com. Open from 11:00 A.M. to 5:00 P.M. daily. Visa, MasterCard, and American Express. Wheelchair-accessible.*

Now head south to Trancas Boulevard, turn right (west), and you're on your way back to Highway 29.

Salud!

CHAPTER 5

WHERE TO STAY IN THE NAPA VALLEY

*H*ere *we list each establishment's price range, valid from late spring into fall; prices are typically lower the rest of the year. The prices also vary between weekdays and weekends and are subject to change without notice. Many places require a two-day minimum. Under California law no indoor smoking is allowed.*

NAPA

Hotels, Motels, and Inns

The hostelries in the city of Napa are all of good quality and are listed here in order, based on the distance from Highway 29.

EMBASSY SUITES—NAPA VALLEY, 1075 California Boulevard, Napa 94558; phone (707) 253–9540, fax (707) 253–9202; 205 suites in three Mediterranean style stories; $234 Sunday–Thursday, $284 Friday–Saturday. Restaurant in atrium, giant fireplace in lobby, indoor and outdoor pools.

BEST WESTERN ELM HOUSE INN, 800 California Boulevard, Napa 94558; phone (707) 255–1831, fax (707) 255–8609; 17 large units in three stories; $119–$219. Some fireplaces, whirlpool, and spa.

NAPA VALLEY TRAVELODGE, 853 Coombs Street, Napa 94558; phone (707) 226–1871, fax (707) 226–1707; 44 units; $59–$119 Sunday–Thursday, $139–$169 Friday–Saturday. Small pool.

NAPA RIVER INN, 500 Main Street, Napa 94558; phone (707) 251–8500, Web site www.napariverinn.com; 66 rooms, including 8 deluxe historic suites; newest hotel in town (opened June 2000), part of Hatt Building restoration; all rooms have river boat theme; $149–$169, suites $229–$309.

THE CHABLIS INN, 3360 Solano Avenue, Napa 94558; phone (707) 257–1944, fax (707) 226–6862, Web site www.chablisinn. com; 34 units, some efficiencies; May–November 15: $90–$115 Sunday–Thursday, $130–$150 Friday–Saturday; remainder of year: $75–$95 Sunday–Thursday, $95–$125 Friday–Saturday. Pool, spa, and whirlpool.

NAPA VALLEY MARRIOTT, 3425 Solano Avenue, Napa 94558; phone (707) 253–7433, fax (707) 258–1320, Web site www.mariott.com; 191 units; $239–$274 (some include breakfast). Recently renovated. Harvest Cafe Restaurant, heated pool, two lighted tennis courts, and spa.

NAPA VALLEY BUDGET INN, 3380 Solano Avenue, Napa 94558; phone (707) 257–6111, Web site www.napavalleybudgetinn.com; 58 rooms; $66–$120. Pool. Pets OK.

THE CHATEAU, 4195 Solano Avenue, Napa 94558; phone (707) 253–9300, fax (707) 253–0906, Web site www.napavalleychateauhotel.com; 115 units; April–November: $110 Sunday–Thursday; $140 Friday–Saturday; remainder of year: $100. Pool, spa, meeting facilities, free movies.

JOHN MUIR INN, 1998 Trower Avenue, Napa 94558; phone (707) 257–7220; fax (707) 258–0943, Web site www.johnmuirnapa.com; 59 units in three stories, some efficiencies; $105–$190. Pool, continental breakfast.

BEST WESTERN INN AT THE VINES, 100 Soscol Avenue, Napa 94558; phone (707) 257–1930, fax (707) 255–0709, Web site www.innatthevines.com; 68 units, including deluxe; $100–$175. Pool, whirlpool. No pets.

Bed-and-Breakfasts

These entries are listed from downtown Napa to farther out in the countryside. They are an architectural historian's delight. Almost all require a two-night minimum stay on weekends.

THE BEAZLEY HOUSE, 1910 First Street, Napa 94558; phone (707) 257–1649, Web site www.beazleyhouse.com; 11 darkly romantic rooms; $125–$255. This 1902 Colonial Revival was Napa's first B&B (in 1981).

THE 1801 INN, 1801 1st Street, Napa 94558; phone (707) 224–3739, Web site www.the1801inn.com; 5 rooms; $150–$249. A 1903 Queen Anne Victorian.

THE OLD WORLD INN, 1301 Jefferson Street, Napa 94558; phone (707) 257–0112, Web site www.oldworldinn.com; 8 rooms; $135–$235. A Victorian house. One room with whirlpool, some canopied beds.

CEDAR GABLES INN, 486 Coombs Street, Napa 94558; phone (707) 224–7969, fax (707) 224–4838, Web site www.cedargablesinn.com; 6 rooms; $169–$239. Sixteenth-century–style shingled English 1892 manor house.

HENNESSEY HOUSE B&B INN, 1727 Main Street, phone (707) 226–3774, fax (707) 226–2975, Web site www.hennesseyhouse.com; 10 rooms; $105–$250. An 1889 Queen Anne Victorian and carriage house. National Register of Historic Places.

THE BLUE VELVET MANSION, 443 Brown Street, Napa 94558; phone (707) 253–2583, fax (707) 257–8205, Web site www.bluevelvetinn.com; 14 rooms, 1 2-room suite; $189–$359. An 1886 Queen Anne Victorian.

CHURCHILL MANOR, 485 Brown Street, Napa 94558; phone (707) 253–7733, fax (707) 253–8836, Web site www.churchillmanor.com; 10 rooms; July–November: $145–$215, remainder of year: $125–$195. This 1889 Second Empire mansion is in the National Register of Historic Places.

McCLELLAND-PRIEST B&B, 569 Randolph Street, Napa 94559; phone (707) 224–6875 or (800) 290–6881, Web site www.historicinnstravel.com; 5 rooms; $159–$259. An 1879 house, elegantly decorated. Large suites, Jacuzzis.

LA BELLE EPOQUE, 1386 Calistoga Avenue, Napa 94558; phone (707) 257–2161, Web site www.labelleepoque.com; 6 rooms; $170–$250. An 1893 Queen Anne Victorian.

ARBOR GUEST HOUSE, 1436 G Street, Napa 94558; phone (707) 252–8144, Web site www.arborguesthouse.com; 5 rooms; $145–$200. A 1906 Colonial style home, with choice of fireplace or spa in carriage house or garden.

THE NAPA INN, 1137 Warren Street, Napa 94558; phone (707) 257–1444, Web site www.napainn.com; 6 rooms; $140–$195 Sunday–Thursday, $155–$210 Friday–Saturday (scheduled to increase by January 2001). An 1899 Victorian on residential street, stained-glass windows.

CHARDONNAY LODGE, 2640 Jefferson Street, Napa 94558; phone (707) 224–0789; 20 rooms; $55–$110. Recently renovated.

STAHLECKER HOUSE, 1042 Easum Drive, Napa 94558; phone (707) 257–1588, Web site www.stahleckerhouse.com; 4 rooms; $135–$295 with possible discounts. Country inn beside running creek.

CANDLELIGHT INN, 1045 Easum Drive, Napa 94558; phone (707) 257–3717, Web site www.candlelight.com; 9 rooms; $135–$255. A 1929 English Tudor with modern amenities, in park on the bank of Napa Creek.

OAK KNOLL INN, 2200 East Oak Knoll Avenue, Napa 94558; phone (707) 255–2200; 3 large rooms; April–Thanksgiving: $395–$450, remainder of year: $285–$395. French-style country inn built in 1984. Given 4 kisses by "Best Places to Kiss in Northern California."

INN ON RANDOLPH, 411 Randolph Street, Napa 94558; phone (707) 257–2886, Web site www.innonrandolph.com; 5 rooms; $129–$259. Lovingly restored 1860 landmark Gothic Revival Victorian.

LA RESIDENCE COUNTRY INN, 4066 Highway 29, Napa 94558; phone (707) 253–0337, Web site www.laresidence.com; 20 rooms (including 4 suites); $185–$315. An 1870 Gothic Revival mansion and "French Barn".

BROOKSIDE VINEYARDS B&B, 3194 Redwood Road, Napa 94558; (707) 944–1661, fax (707) 252–6690; 3 rooms; $135–$175. A 1955 California Mission–style set in vineyard, patio, gazebo.

COUNTRY GARDEN INN, 1815 Silverado Trail, Napa 94558; phone (707) 255–1197, fax (707) 255–3112, Web site www.countrygardeninn.com; 8 rooms; $135–$155. English style inn in an 1860 carriage house beside river.

Resorts

SILVERADO COUNTRY CLUB RESORT, 1600 Atlas Peak Road, Napa 94558; phone (707) 257–0200, fax (707) 257–5400, Web site www.silveradoresort.com; 260 units; $165–$535, with condos up to $1,300.

YOUNTVILLE

Hotels, Motels, and Inns

VINTAGE INN, 6541 Washington Street, Yountville 94599; phone (707) 944–1112, fax (707) 944–1617, Web site www.vintageinn.com; 80 rooms; November–March: $175–$275, April–July: $200–$300, August–October: $250–$325. Built in 1970s, several buildings designed by Kipp Stewart. All units have fireplace, balcony or patio, whirlpool tub, handcrafted furniture.

NAPA VALLEY LODGE, 2230 Madison Street, Yountville 94599; phone (707) 944–2468, fax (707) 944–9362, Web site www.woodsidehotels.com; 55 rooms; $220–$535 (5 high-end suites). Spanish-style buildings, elegant lobby with large fireplace, conference facilities.

NAPA VALLEY RAILWAY INN, 6503 Washington Street, Yountville 94599; phone (707) 944–2000, Web site www.10Kvacationrentals.com; November–April: $75 Sunday–Thursday, $95 Friday–Saturday, May–October: $95 Sunday–Thursday, $125 Friday–Saturday. An unusual inn constructed of 9 old railroad cars (including 3 cabooses).

VILLAGIO INN & SPA, on Washington Street, Yountville 94599; phone (707) 944–4444, Web site www.villagio.com; 112 rooms; November–March: $250–$635, April–July: $225–$635, August–October: $250–$710.

Bed-and-Breakfasts

OLEANDER HOUSE, 7433 St. Helena Highway (Highway 29), Yountville 94599; phone (707) 944–8315, Web site www.oleander.com; 5 rooms; $145–$180. Two-story French Country home built in 1982.

MAISON FLEURIE, 6529 Yount Street, Yountville 94599; phone (707) 944–2056, fax (707) 944–9362 or 944–9342, Web site www.foursisters.com; 13 rooms; $115–$260. If you're looking for a colorful past, this is the place. Built of fieldstone and brick in 1873 as an inn, it became a bordello, then a speakeasy.

PETIT LOGIS INN AND B&B, 6527 Yount Street, Yountville 94599; phone (707) 944–2332, Web site www.petitlogis.com; 5 rooms; $160 Sunday–Thursday, $195 Friday–Saturday. Full breakfast.

BORDEAUX HOUSE, 6600 Washington Street, Yountville 94599; phone (707) 944–2855, Web site www.bordeauxhouse.com; 7 rooms; $115–$145. Air conditioning, some fireplaces and balconies, buffet breakfast. No pets.

BURGUNDY HOUSE, 6711 Washington Street, Yountville 94599; phone (707) 944–0889, Web site www.burgundyhouse.com; 5 rooms; $125–$160. An 1893 French-style stone inn originally built as a brandy distillery.

TRUBODY RANCH, Yountville 94599; phone (707) 255–5907, Web site www.napanet.net/~trubody/, 3 rooms; $205 Sunday–Thursday, $265 Friday–Saturday. A restored 40-foot water tower and a cottage set in a 140-acre vineyard; original antiques, fireplaces, clawfoot tubs.

HILLVIEW COUNTRY INN, Yountville 94599; phone (707) 224–5004, Web site www.hillviewinnnapa.com; 3 rooms; $175–$200. A century-old farmhouse in the middle of vineyards, with farm furniture.

RUTHERFORD

Hotels, Motels, and Inns

RANCHO CAYMUS INN, 1140 Rutherford Cross Road, Rutherford 94573; phone (707) 963–1777, fax (707) 963–5387; 26 rooms; $175–$345. Beautifully designed Spanish-style, with tiled roof, open-beamed ceilings, courtyard, gardens, handcrafted furniture from Mexico and Ecuador.

Resorts

AUBERGE DU SOLEIL, 180 Rutherford Hill Road, Rutherford 94573; phone (707) 963–1211, Web site www.aubergedusoleil.com; 50 rooms (19 are suites); $350–$2,500. Southern France country style with wooden shutters. Private entries, terraces, refrigerators, wet bars, elegance throughout. This resort is set on 33 hillside acres among olive trees, and grew from the world-famous Auberge du Soleil restaurant. If price is no object, then this is the tops in Napa Valley luxury. Three tennis courts, pool, spa, exercise room, whirlpool. Not recommended for children. No pets.

ST. HELENA

Hotels, Motels, and Inns

HARVEST INN, One Main Street (Highway 29), St. Helena 94574; phone (707) 963–9463, fax (707) 963–4402, Web site www.harvestinn.com; 54 rooms; $149–$649 (executive suite). Tudor-style stone building situated in vineyard. Two pools, Jacuzzis, many fireplaces, wet bars, balconies.

EL BONITA MOTEL, 195 Main Street (Highway 29), St. Helena 94574; phone (707) 963–3216, fax (707) 963–8838, Web site www.elbonita.com; 42 rooms, some efficiencies; $119–$159 Sunday–Thursday, $159–$199 Friday–Saturday.

VINEYARD COUNTRY INN, 201 Main Street (Highway 29), St. Helena 94574; phone (707) 963–1000, fax (707) 963–1794; 21 two-room suites, $220. All rooms in this beautifully appointed French country inn have wood-burning fireplaces, wet bar, and fridge; most have balconies.

THE INN AT SOUTHBRIDGE, 1020 Main Street (Highway 29), St. Helena 94574; phone (707) 967–9400; 21 large rooms; $275–$450 Sunday–Thursday, $395–$535 Friday–Saturday. Designed by architect William Turnbull, Jr., with a winery theme, and completed in 1995.

HOTEL ST. HELENA, 1309 Main Street (Highway 29), St. Helena 94574; phone (707) 963–4388, fax (707) 963–5402; 18 rooms; $125–$185 Sunday–Thursday, $165–$175 Friday–Saturday. This 1881 historic hotel had deteriorated into a fleabag before it was recently rebuilt and lovingly restored with its original nineteenth-century feeling.

WINE COUNTRY INN, 1152 Lodi Lane, St. Helena 94574; phone (707) 963–7077, Web site www.winecountryinn.com; 25 rooms; $176–$345. Most rooms in this New England–style inn have antiques, balconies or decks.

Resorts and Spas

St. Helena has two resorts, which are also spas providing mineral and mud baths and a variety of healthy "treatments" to bring pleasure and tone up your system.

MEADOWOOD NAPA VALLEY, 900 Meadowood Lane, St. Helena 94574; phone (707) 963–3646, fax (707) 963–3532, Web site www.meadowood.com; 99 rooms; $420–$535, lower in winter and early spring.

WHITE SULPHUR SPRINGS, 3100 Sulphur Springs Road, St. Helena 94574; phone (707) 963–8588, Web site www.whitesulphursprings.com; 14 rooms and 9 cottages; $110–$225. The oldest resort in Napa County, established in 1852. Set in a canyon, surrounded by redwood and fir trees on 330 acres.

Bed-and-Breakfasts

THE INK HOUSE, 1575 St. Helena Highway South (Highway 29), St. Helena 94574; phone (707) 963–3890, Web site www.inkhouse.com; 7 rooms; $100–$205. An 1884 Italianate Victorian, in Register of Historic Places.

ROSE GARDEN INN, 1277 St. Helena Highway South (Highway 29), St. Helena 94574; phone (707) 963–4417, Web site www.rosegardeninn.net; 4 rooms; $135–$180. Turn-of-the-century farmhouse set among vineyards.

SHADY OAKS COUNTRY INN, 399 Zinfandel Lane, St. Helena 94574; phone (707) 963–1190, fax (707) 963–9367, Web site www.shadyoaksinn.com; 4 rooms, 2 in 1920s Craftsman house and 2 in 1880s-era stone winery; $179–$239. Antiques, patio with pillars entwined by century-old wisteria.

ZINFANDEL INN, 800 Zinfandel Lane, St. Helena 94574; phone (707) 963–3512, Web site zinfandelinn.com; 3 rooms; $250–$330 (with lower off-season rates). English Tudor–style house.

LA FLEUR B&B, 1475 Inglewood Avenue, St. Helena 94574; phone (707) 963–0233; 3 rooms; $195. An 1882 Queen Anne Victorian in the midst of a working vineyard and winery.

SUNNY ACRES B&B, 397 Main Street (Highway 29), St. Helena 94574; phone (707) 963–2826; 2 rooms; $125–$150. Restored 1879 Victorian originally built for Dr. George Belden Crane, one of the valley's first grape growers, in midst of 20 acres of vineyard.

AMBROSE BIERCE HOUSE, 1515 Main Street (Highway 29), St. Helena 94574; phone (707) 963–3003, Web site www.ambrosepiercehouse.com; 2 rooms, 1 suite; $99–$159. An 1872 Victorian where once lived acerbic journalist Ambrose Bierce.

ADAGIO INN, 1417 Kearney Street, St. Helena 94574; phone (707) 963–2238, Web site www.adagioinn.com; 3 rooms; $159–$269. New owners Betsy and Scott Buckwald, in 1999 completely redecorated, added new furnishings, VCRs and complimentary video.

CINNAMON BEAR B&B, 1407 Kearney Street, St. Helena 94574; phone (707) 963–4653, Web site www.bedandbreakfast.com; 3 rooms; $125–$225. A 1904 Craftsman house. Veranda around house.

BYLUND HOUSE, 2000 Howell Mountain Road, St. Helena 94574; phone (707) 963–9073, Web site www.bylundhouse.com; 2 rooms; $95–$200. Modern Italian villa with sweeping valley views, balconies.

HILLTOP B&B, 9550 St. Helena Road, St. Helena 94574; phone (707) 944–0880, Web site www.traveldata.com (also www.cabbi.com/innaccess, then click on bamboo virtual tour); 4 rooms; $145–$225. Modern ranch house in the Mayacamas Mountains 6 miles west of town.

OLIVER HOUSE COUNTRY INN, 2970 Silverado Trail North, St. Helena 94574; phone (707) 963–4089 or (800) 682–7888, Web site www.oliverhouse. com; 4 rooms; $145–$295. Swiss Bavarian chalet.

GLASS MOUNTAIN INN, 3100 Silverado Trail North, St. Helena 94574; phone (707) 968–9400 or (877) 968–9400, fax (767) 968–9480, Web site www.glassmountaininn.net; 3 rooms; $165–$295. Shingled house with steeple roof. Old wine cave on premises.

SPANISH VILLA, 474 Glass Mountain Road, St. Helena 94574; phone (707) 963–7483; 3 rooms; $125–$175. Spanish-style country inn.

BARTELS RANCH AND B&B COUNTRY INN, 1200 Conn Valley Road, St. Helena 94574; phone (707) 963–4001, Web site www.bartelsranch.com; 4 rooms; $175–$425. Jami Bartels originally designed this large rock-and-red-wood ranch house for a household of children (including a succession of exchange students) in the middle of 60 acres. For honeymooners and lovers there is the "Heart of the Valley Suite," with heart-shaped whirlpool and steam shower for 2.

ELSIE'S CONN VALLEY INN, 726 Rossi Road, St. Helena 94574; phone (707) 963–4614; 3 rooms; $185–$275 (call for off-season rates). Rose garden, views.

ERIKA'S HILLSIDE, 285 Fawn Park Road, St. Helena 94574; phone (707) 963–2887; 3 suites; $95–295. Swiss chalet on 3-acre hillside garden, terraced rock walls, shaded by oak trees.

WINE COUNTRY VICTORIAN AND COTTAGES, 400 Meadowood Lane, St. Helena 94574; phone (707) 963–0852, Web site www.anotherplanet.to; Queen Anne Suite in classic Victorian and 2 cottages on woodland estate; $185–$245. Decorator furnishings.

RUSTRIDGE RANCH AND WINERY, 2910 Lower Chiles Valley Road, St. Helena 94574; phone (707) 965–2871, Web site www.rustridge.com; 3 rooms; $150–$200.

CALISTOGA

Spas, Resorts, and Baths

Nowadays the spas and baths are the centerpieces of the resorts in Calistoga.

In most cases you do not have to stay at the resort to enjoy spa privileges. Here we list only those places with lodging.

DR. WILKINSON'S HOT SPRINGS RESORT, 1507 Lincoln Avenue, Calistoga 94515; phone (707) 942–4102, Web site www.drwilkinson.com; 42 rooms, many with kitchenettes; $99–$159; $129–$169 for the Victorian suite.

INDIAN SPRINGS RESORT AND SPA , 1712 Lincoln Avenue, Calistoga 94515; phone (707) 942–4913, Web site www.indianspringscalistoga.com; 16 cottages; $175–$500 (3 bedrooms). Calistoga's oldest continuing resort. Site of centuries-old Indian sweat house.

CALISTOGA VILLAGE INN AND SPA, 1880 Lincoln Avenue, Calistoga 94515; phone (707) 942–0991, fax (707) 942–5306, Web site www.greatspa.com; 41 rooms; $79–$159. Mineral water spa and pool with views of hills.

CALISTOGA SPA HOT SPRINGS, 1006 Washington Avenue, Calistoga 94515; phone (707) 942–6269, Web site www.calistogaspa.com; 57 units, all with kitchenettes; $100–$150.

EUROSPA AND INN, 1202 Pine Street, Calistoga 94515; phone (707) 942–6829, Web site www.eurospa.com; 16 rooms; packages include room for 2, spa treatment, and meal. $149–$199; packages, $269–$289 individual, $369–$389 per couple. Pool, Jacuzzi, continental breakfast.

GOLDEN HAVEN HOT SPRINGS AND RESORT, 1713 Lake Street, Calistoga 94515; phone (707) 942–6793, Web site www.goldenhaven.com; 30 rooms, many with kitchenettes; $59–$165. Set in oaks with gardens.

SILVER ROSE INN AND SPA, 351 Rosedale Road, Calistoga 94515; phone (707) 942–9581, Web site www.silverroseinn.com; 20 rooms; $160–$250 Monday–Thursday, $190–$280 Friday–Sunday. Packages available. Rooms split between 2 lodges, on knoll and in vineyard. Individually decorated rooms.

Hotels, Motels, and Inns

CALISTOGA INN AND BREWERY, 1250 Lincoln Avenue, Calistoga 94515; phone (707) 942–4101, Web site www.napabeer.com; 17 rooms; $60 Sunday–Thursday, $90 Friday–Saturday. A turn-of-the-twentieth-century hotel in heart of town, above restaurant and brew pub. Shared bathrooms and showers.

ROMAN SPA, 1300 Washington Street, Calistoga 94515; phone (707) 942–4441, Web site www.tales.com; 60 rooms, 26 with kitchens, 1 with 2 bedrooms; June 15–Labor Day: $106–$200, remainder of year: $86–$168.

MOUNT VIEW HOTEL, 1457 Lincoln Avenue, Calistoga 94515; phone (707) 942–6877, Web site www.mountview.com; 34 rooms; $130–$250. Restored 1919 Mission Revival hotel with some cottages. Once Calistoga's prestigious European Hotel, it is listed in the National Register of Historic Places. It now has 9 elegant suites with period furniture, redecorated art deco lobby.

HIDEAWAY COTTAGES, 1412 Fairway, Calistoga 94515; phone (707) 942–4108, Web site www.hideawaycottages.com; 17 cottages, some with kitchenettes; $75–$200 (2 bedrooms). Next to Dr. Wilkinson's Hot Springs Resort.

COTTAGE GROVE INN, 1711 Lincoln Avenue, Calistoga 94515; phone (707) 942–8400, fax (707) 942–2653, Web site www.cottagegrove.com; 16 cottages; $215 Sunday–Thursday, $275 Friday–Saturday. Historically on promenade of Sam Brannan's resort of mid-1880s.

BEST WESTERN STEVENSON MANOR INN, 1830 Lincoln Avenue, Calistoga 94515; phone (707) 942–1112; 34 rooms; $80–$189. Renovated in fall 2000, after fire.

COMFORT INN NAPA VALLEY NORTH, 1865 Lincoln Avenue, Calistoga 94515; phone (707) 942–9400, fax (707) 942–5262, Web site www.callodging.com; 54 rooms, many with views; $65–$199. Sauna, small pool, whirlpool. Free breakfast. Preregistration urged to get scenic rooms. No pets.

CARLIN COUNTRY COTTAGES, 1623 Lake Street, Calistoga 94515; phone (707) 942–9102, fax (707) 942–2295, Web site www.carlincottages.com; 15 rooms, 8 with kitchens; $89–$150 Monday–Thursday, $125–$195 Friday–Sunday.

Bed-and-Breakfasts

LARKMEAD COUNTRY INN, 1103 Larkmead Lane, Calistoga 94515; phone (707) 942–5360, Web site www.larkmeadinn.com; 4 rooms; $150. Early 1900s Palladian-style house. One room with king-size brass bed.

THE ELMS, 1300 Cedar Street, Calistoga 94515; phone (707) 942–9476, fax (707) 942–9479, Web site www.theelms.com; 7 rooms; $135–$225. An 1873 French Second Empire–style house; National Register of Historic Places.

LA CHAUMIERE, 1301 Cedar Street, Calistoga 94515; phone (707) 942–5139 or (800) 474–6800, Web site www.lachaumiere.com; 2 rooms, plus a log cabin; $135–$185. A Cotswold cottage with lush garden, patio.

HOTEL D'AMICI, 1436 Lincoln, Calistoga 94515; phone (707) 942–1007; 4 suites; $150–$250. Formerly Brannan's Loft. In 1998 the Pestoni family—longtime owners of the hotel and Rutherford Grove Winery—completely remodeled this venerable inn and changed its name.

BRANNAN COTTAGE INN, 109 Wapoo Avenue, Calistoga 94515; (707) 942–4200, Web site www.brannancottageinn.com; 6 rooms, including 2 suites; $145–$160. An 1860 Greek Revival inn, the only survivor from Sam Brannan's Hot Springs Resort. The oldest building in Calistoga, fully renovated in 1990s, listed in National Register of Historic Places.

SLEEPY HOLLOW B&B, 911 Foothill Boulevard, Calistoga 94515; phone (707) 942–4760, fax (707) 963–0181; $100–$125. Country-style inn.

CHRISTOPHER'S INN, 1010 Foothill Boulevard, Calistoga 94515; phone (707) 942–5755, Web site www.christophersinn.com; 22 rooms, including 9 suites; $165–$395. Country Georgian–style inn.

CALISTOGA'S WINE WAY INN, 1019 Foothill Boulevard, Calistoga 94515; phone (707) 942–0680, Web site www.napavalley.com/wineway; 6 rooms; $90–$165. A 1915 Craftsman home.

THE PINK MANSION, 1415 Foothill Boulevard, Calistoga 94515; phone (707) 942–0558, fax (707) 942–0558, Web site www.pinkmansion.com; 6 rooms; $145–$275. An 1875 Victorian house.

CALISTOGA WAYSIDE INN, 1523 Foothill Boulevard, Calistoga 94515; phone (707) 942–0645, Web site calistogawaysideinn.com; 3 rooms; $140 Monday–Thursday, $165 Friday–Sunday. A 1920 Spanish-style home with waterfall into pond, gardens for meditation.

CULVER MANSION, 1805 Foothill Boulevard, Calistoga 94515; phone (707) 942–4535, Web site www.culvermansion.com; 6 rooms; $160–$190. An 1875 Victorian—Registered Historical Landmark.

CALISTOGA COUNTRY LODGE, 2883 Foothill Boulevard, Calistoga 94515; phone (707) 942–5555, fax (707) 942–5864, Web site www.countrylodge.com; 6 rooms; $120–$175. A 1910 Southwest-style lodge.

FOOTHILL HOUSE, 3037 Foothill Boulevard, Calistoga 94515; phone (707) 942–6933, fax (707) 942–5692, Web site www.foothillhouse.com; 4 suites; $165–$295. An 1897 renovated farmhouse and cottage.

SCARLETT'S COUNTRY INN, 3918 Silverado Trail, Calistoga 94515; phone (707) 942–6669, Web site www.members.aol.com/scarlett; 3 suites; $125–$185. Lawns, pines, vineyards, pool, fireplace, air conditioning.

TRAILSIDE INN, 4201 Silverado Trail North, Calistoga 94515; phone (707) 942–4106, Web site www.trailsideinn.com; 3 suites; $120–$150. A 1930s farmhouse with fireplaces, vineyard, air conditioned, pool.

QUAIL MOUNTAIN B&B, 4455 North St. Helena Highway, Calistoga 94515; phone (707) 942–0316; 3 rooms; Decemeber–March: $140–$170, April–November: $160–$190. Set about 300 feet above highway, on 26 acres.

Ranches

MOUNTAIN HOME RANCH, 3400 Mountain Home Ranch Road, Calistoga 94515; phone (707) 942–6616, Web site www.mtnhomeranch.com; 7 cabins, 7 hotel rooms, 8 cabanas; $65–$135 high season, $45–$155 rest of year.

TRIPLE-S RANCH, 4600 Mountain Ranch Road, Calistoga 94515; phone (707) 942–6730, Web site www.triplesranch.com; 7 cabins; $85 for 2, $10 for each additional person. Hiking, bocce ball.

ANGWIN

Bed-and-Breakfast

FOREST MANOR, 415 Cold Springs Road, Angwin 94508; phone (707) 965–3538, Web site www.forestmanor.com; 3 rooms; $210–$395. In English Tudor inn on 20 acres, vaulted ceilings.

CHAPTER 6

BEYOND WINE TASTING

*W*ining and dining and general gastro-touring are primary activities in the Napa Valley, but there are many other wonderful things to do in this heaven on Earth. Here we tell you about where to find some of the favorites, including ballooning, biking, horse-back riding, gliding, and golfing. We also describe less active pursuits, such as getting spa treatments, meandering through farmers' markets, and taking river cruises. So here we go—up, up, and away.

BALLOONING

Ballooning is best and most peaceful in the early morning, when winds are calm and the air is cool. Most balloon flights in the Napa Valley end with brunch in a restaurant, and some include champagne. Most flights cost $115–$185 for adults and $150 for children ages one to sixteen. Here's an alphabetical list of balloon-flying companies. All of them encourage you to bring cameras and personal video equipment.

ADVENTURES ALOFT OF THE NAPA VALLEY, P.O. Box 2500 at Vintage 1870, Yountville 94599; phone (707) 944–4408 or (800) 944–4408, e-mail ballooning @nvaloft.com, Web site www.nvloft.com. Claims "the world's most experienced pilot team" and offers a seated champagne breakfast hosted by your pilot.

BALLOON AVIATION OF NAPA VALLEY, 6525 Washington, Yountville 94559; phone (707) 944–4400 or (800) FOR–NAPA. Sunrise launches in vintage 1870 balloon; champagne lunch.

BALLOONS ABOVE THE VALLEY, 5091 Solano Avenue, Napa 94558; phone (800) GO–HOT AIR.

BONAVENTURA BALLOON COMPANY, 133 Wall Road, Napa 94558; phone (707) 944–2822 or (800) FLY–NAPA; Web site www.bonaventuraballoons. com. Has been used and recommended by *Forbes* magazine, Universal Studios/ABC-TV, and *Gourmet* magazine. Includes champagne.

CALISTOGA BALLOON ADVENTURES, P.O. Box 932, Calistoga 94515; phone (707) 942–2282 or (800) 400–0162. Hour-long flights from Calistoga meadow; you are allowed to pitch in for the balloon setup if you wish; the price includes brunch at Cafe Sarafornia in Calistoga.

NAPA VALLEY BALLOONS, P.O. Box 2860, Yountville 94599; phone (707) 944–0228 or (800) 253–2224. The hour-long flight with Napa's oldest ballooning company culminates with a catered sparkling-wine brunch.

BICYCLE RIDING AND BIKE RENTALS

Napa Valley is an ideal locale for biking as, except for a few slight climbs, it's pretty flat. The heavy traffic makes cycling on Highway 29 hazardous, but bike lanes run the full length of the Silverado Trail. The Trail also has fewer cars and a generally quieter ride and ambience than Highway 29.

Here's an alphabetical list of bike rental (and repair) shops. Most charge about $25.00 a day, or $7.00 an hour for rentals.

BICYCLE TRAX, 796 Soscol Avenue at the corner of Third Street, Napa 94559; phone (707) 258–8729. Voted "Best Bike Shop in the Napa Valley."

BIKE TOURS OF THE NAPA VALLEY, 4080 Byway East (at Trower), Napa 94559; phone (707) 255–3377 or (800) 707–2453. Bike rentals and tours.

PALISADES MOUNTAIN SPORT, 1330 Gerard, Calistoga 94515; phone (707) 942–9687. Mountain and hybrid bike rentals and expert mechanics available.

ST. HELENA CYCLERY, 1156 Main Street, St. Helena 94574; phone (707) 963–7736, fax (707) 963–5099. Rentals of hybrid bicycles for touring; the rental fee includes helmet, lock, water-bottle cage, and rear rack.

YOUNTVILLE BIKE RENTALS, Vintage 1870 on Washington Street, Yountville 94599; phone (707) 944–9080. Includes helmet and a map of Napa Valley.

BOCCE BALL

When was the last time you played bocce ball? Give it a try. Public bocce courts are located right in downtown Yountville, south of new hotels and The Diner on the west side of Washington Street. Take the Yountville exit off Highway 29, turn right (east) to Washington Street, and turn right (south) again. The bocce ball courts will be on your right. Bocce balls are available at a small rental fee. Call Brent Randol (707) 483–3630 to schedule free games.

HANG GLIDING

CALISTOGA GLIDERS, 1546 Lincoln Avenue, Calistoga 94515; phone (707) 942–5000, fax (707) 942–4520. Your affable glider pilots recommend that you "surf the invisible waves of air breaking over the mountains as your glider swoops and soars on silent wings." Go ahead! Open every day, weather permitting, Calistoga Gliders will have you take off heading down the Napa Valley from its northern tip. Maximum combined weight is 340 pounds. The cost ranges from $79 for one person for twenty minutes to $179 for two people for thirty minutes.

GOLFING

Not surprisingly, Napa Valley has lovely golf courses. Most of the courses are open to the public; two are not.

Courses Open to the Public

AETNA SPRINGS GOLF COURSE, 1600 Aetna Springs Road, Pope Valley 94567; phone (800) 675–2115. Nine holes, driving range, picnic and BBQ facilities, forty-five minutes north of Napa. Greens fees: $13 weekdays, $18 weekends.

CHARDONNAY GOLF CLUB, 2555 Jamieson Canyon Road (Highway 12 between American Canyon and Highway 80), Napa 94558; phone (707) 257–8950. Two eighteen-hole courses, lovely setting, restaurant. Greens fees: $60 weekdays, $80 weekends.

MOUNT ST. HELENA GOLF, Napa Valley Fairgrounds, Calistoga 94515; phone (707) 942–9966. Flat nine holes, BBQ area, RV park, seniors' programs, snack bar. Greens fees: $12 weekdays, $18 weekends; seniors $9 weekdays, $12 weekends.

NAPA MUNICIPAL GOLF COURSE at John F. Kennedy Park, 2295 Streblow Drive, Napa 94558; phone (707) 255–4333. Eighteen holes, cocktail lounge, restaurant, outside deck. Greens fees: $15 residents, $21 nonresidents weekdays; $20 residents, $25 nonresidents weekends.

YOUNTVILLE GOLF COURSE, 7801 Solano Avenue, Yountville 94599; phone (707) 944–1992. Nine holes, restaurant, beer and wine bar, new management, increased length to 3,000 yards, par 34. Greens fees: $14, $10 early bird before 8:00 A.M.

Private Courses

MEADOWOOD RESORT, 900 Meadowood Lane, St. Helena 94574; phone (800) 458–8080. Open to members and resort guests only. Members of other clubs may play. Nine holes. Greens fees: $35.

SILVERADO COUNTRY CLUB, 1600 Atlas Peak Road, Napa 94558; phone (707) 257–0200. Open to members and resort guests only. Greens fees: resort guests $115, members of reciprocal clubs $135, including cart.

TENNIS

The climate in Napa Valley makes for some fantastic tennis. Try out these courts on your visit. They are open to the public and are available on a first-come, first-serve basis.

Public Courts

CALISTOGA PUBLIC TENNIS COURTS, Stevenson and Grant Streets; phone (707) 942–2838. Four courts, lighted at night.

NAPA PUBLIC COURTS, Napa Valley College (Highway 12 south of Napa); phone (707) 257–9529 and at Vintage High School, 1275 Trower Avenue, Napa High School, 2475 Jefferson Street, and Silverado Middle School, 1133 Coombsville Road, all in Napa.

ST. HELENA PUBLIC TENNIS COURTS, Robert Louis Stevenson School, 1316 Hill View Place; St. Helena High School, 1401 Grayson Avenue; Crane

Park off Crane Avenue; phone (707) 963–5706.

Private Courts

MEADOWOOD RESORT, 900 Meadowood Lane, St. Helena 94574; phone (707) 963–3646. Courts open to members and guests only.

SILVERADO COUNTRY CLUB AND RESORT, 1600 Atlas Peak Road, Napa 94558; phone (707) 257–0200. Courts open to members and guests only.

TOURS

Every entrepreneur in the Napa Valley is some sort of tour guide, some more reputable than others. Here we identify a few—but perhaps our book will help you be your own best guide.

NAPA VALLEY WINE TRAIN, 1275 McKinstry at Soscol Avenue, Napa 94559; phone (707) 253–2111 or (800) 522–4142. The Wine Train is a more than three-hour, 36-mile ride up the spine of the Napa Valley along the tracks built by Samuel Brannan for the Napa Valley Railroad Company in 1864 and last owned by the Southern Pacific. It is also an elegant gourmand trip into the past, with plush railroad cars and the best Napa Valley wines and excellent food served in a 1917 Pullman Dining Car.

Golden Grain (Rice-a-Roni) Macaroni Company and Ghirardelli Chocolate president Vincent de Domenico perseveres with his Wine Train. (Mrs. de Domenico told Kathleen, "He never had a model train as a child.") It runs at 11:30 A.M. and 6:30 P.M. weekdays, 8:55 A.M. and 12:30 and 6:00 P.M. weekends. The food is excellent and reasonably priced. Reservations are necessary—and mandatory for the winemakers' lunches on Fridays. Jackets suggested on dinner train. Prices range from $25 to $60; a children's menu is available.

GRAND ROMANCE NAPA RIVER CRUISES, Main and Third Street Dock, Napa 94558; phone (707) 554–2100 or (800) 750–7501. An enterprising group captured one of the old Petaluma riverboats and restored it to recapture the glamour and romance of the golden days of paddlewheeler travel. Two-and-a-half-hour cruises on the Napa River include lunch or dinner at $34.95 or $39.95 per person, leaving from Napa; or you might enjoy the Sunset Dinner Dance ($49.95), Sunday Champagne Brunch Cruise ($29.95), or the Music Cruise on Sunday afternoons ($15.95), all departing from the Vallejo Waterfront.

BRIDGEFORD FLYING SERVICE (Napa Valley Airport; 707–224–0887 or 707–644–1658) offers sensational tours by air in its Cessna Skyhawk or Cessna Centurion, for groups of any size. Fly over the Napa Valley, Lake Berryessa,

Golden Gate Bridge and San Francisco Bay, and along the Pacific Coast and the Russian River in Sonoma County. Make up your own tour—they'll fly you. ANTIQUE TOURS LIMOUSINE SERVICE, phone (707) 226–9227. Tour in elegantly restored, 1947 convertible Packard limousines for an unforgettable Gatsby-esque experience. The cars are equipped with stereo, electronic bar, champagne bucket, gourmet picnic lunch, and privacy window. These limos accommodate up to six passengers in the rear, and two more up front. Rates: $60 per hour weekdays, $80 per hour weekends, both with three hour minimums. Let your guides select the wineries to visit, or go to those of your choice.

ROYAL COACH LIMOUSINE SERVICE, INC., phone (800) 995–7692, has basically the same features as Antique Tours, but without lunch. Royal coach features more traditional cars. Executive Limousine, (707) 257–2949, offers sedans, stretches, and super-stretches for transportation and wine tours, as do Napa Valley Crown Limousine, (707) 257–0879, (707) 226–9500, and (800) 286–8228; Classic Limousine, (707) 253–0999; Odyssey Limousine, (800) 544–1929; Premier Limousine, (707) 226–2106; and Napa Valley Limousine Services, (707) 258–0689, which also has "licensed bodyguards."

BEAU LIMOUSINE NAPA WINE TOURS; phone (800) 387–2328, Web site www.beaulimousine.com. Choose from a variety of packages, from a $49 five-hour wine tour to a $168 dinner on the Wine Train and a five-hour wine tour. Prices are based per person ($168 per person, with a minimum of six people) and include champagne. Stretch limousine or "limousine party bus."

DESTINATION: NAPA VALLEY HISTORICAL TOURS, phone or fax (707) 965–1808. Covers history and historical wineries, native cultures and pioneer settlers, St. Helena's nineteenth-century architecture, Calistoga spas and silver mines, enology, stone bridges, water towers, Victorian homes, landmarks, and ranchos; $39 for a half-day tour.

NAPA VALLEY HOLIDAYS, phone (707) 255–1050, uses "mini-coaches" to wineries, hiking trails, restaurants; $30 per person.

VILLA CA 'TOGA HOUSE TOUR, from Sharpsteen Museum, 1311 Washington Street, Calistoga 94515; phone (707) 963–4171. Artist Carlo Marchiori conducts a tour once each May. Shuttle buses from the Sharpsteen Museum; $20 donation to the museum. The museum also sells detailed books for self-guided auto or foot tours.

SPAS

Calistoga majors in spas, mud baths, massages, and mineral baths from the natural wells located in the area. Spas abound in Napa Valley; some provide lodging, while others are day spas. Here we tell you about a few of the best. They all take major credit cards and reservations.

CALISTOGA SPA HOT SPRINGS, 1006 Washington Street, Calistoga 94515; phone (707) 942–6269.

DR. WILKINSON'S HOT SPRINGS, 1507 Lincoln Avenue, Calistoga 94515; phone (707) 942–4102.

INDIAN SPRINGS, 1712 Lincoln Avenue, Calistoga 94515; phone (707) 942–4913, fax (707) 942–4919.

LAVENDER HILL SPA, 1015 Foothill Boulevard, Calistoga 94515; phone (707) 942–4495 or (800) 528–4772. No lodging.

MOUNT VIEW SPA AT THE MOUNT VIEW HOTEL, 1457 Lincoln Avenue, Calistoga 94515; phone (707) 942–5789 or (800) 772–8838.

NANCE'S HOT SPRINGS, 1614 Lincoln Avenue, Calistoga 94515; phone (707) 942–6211.

FARMERS' MARKETS

Every week three farmers' markets attract locals and visitors alike to the freshest of fresh vegetables and flowers from the Napa Valley and other prime California agricultural sources.

NAPA CHEF'S MARKET, at the Napa Town Center, on and off First Street, Napa 94558; phone (707) 255–8073; Friday 4:00–9:00 P.M., May–September. Good family fun in this downtown mall atmosphere. Many different vendors set up on First Street, in the walkways within the open-air mall. Napa Valley chefs give cooking demonstrations at 6:00 P.M., and local bands play live music.

NAPA DOWNTOWN FARMERS' MARKET, in the parking lot on West Street between First and Pearl Streets, Napa 94558; phone (707) 252–7142; Tuesday 7:30 A.M.–noon, May–October. This market features some local produce in a neighborhood atmosphere. If you time it right, you can stay on for lunch at nearby restaurants.

To get to the ST. HELENA FARMERS' MARKET, in Crane Park, turn west off Highway 29 onto Grayson Avenue between the A&W root-beer restaurant and St. Helena High School, St. Helena, 94574; phone (707) 252–2105, Fridays 7:30–11:30 A.M. May–October. This market has the most gourmet atmosphere and delicacies; a must for food lovers visiting the Napa Valley.

CHAPTER 7

HISTORY OF THE NAPA VALLEY

*O*nce upon a time there were no grapevines, no wineries, and
no wine in Napa Valley. There was just a long, narrow valley—no more
than 5 miles wide at any point—with a river meandering southward
down to a gigantic bay sheltered from the ocean. At the head of the valley was a dark mountain, which, at 4,343 feet, was the highest for a
hundred miles in any direction.

Within the shadow of that mountain, along the shores of the river, beneath
the canopy of thousands of oak, fir, and redwood trees, and in the hills that bor-
dered the valley, lived more than 5,000 Native Americans. Their ancestors had
first migrated to the valley more than 7,000 years earlier.

By the time Europeans discovered the valley, it was home to several peoples,
including a Coast Miwok tribe (which the Mexicans named Wappos, a corruption of the Spanish *guapos*, meaning "brave ones"). These people called themselves Mayacamas. They lived northwest of the Pomo and Wintun groups, who
had come across the hills from the Sacramento Valley. Tribelets included the
Callajomans, near St. Helena and Oakville; the Caymus, around Yountville; the
Napa (spelled *Nappa* by the first white settlers), between the river and present-
day Napa city; the Ulcas, east of the Napa River; and the Suscol, south toward
the bay. A Miwok band, the Huichica, spilled over from Sonoma Valley in the
southwest, in what is now called the Carneros District. To the southeast, at the
present-day city of Vallejo and beyond, lived the brave and combative Suisun.

Hunters and gatherers, these peoples lived on game, fish, roots, berries, and
a rough bread made from acorns ground with a mortar and pestle. There was
no agriculture. Simple thatched huts provided shelter from late autumn to early
spring; then they set up outdoor camps for hunting and fishing closer to the
shores of rivers, streams, and the bay.

Like most Natives of northern California, these first denizens of the Napa
Valley were far more hygienic than the white invaders, bathing every day. The

men and boys regularly and purposely perspired in a sweathouse, waiting until
the heat was nearly unbearable before rinsing off in a cold stream. These buildings doubled as a meeting place for the elders. It was an existence lived in har-
mony with nature.

FATHER ALTIMIRA "DISCOVERS" THE VALLEY

San Francisco Bay was "discovered" in 1769 by a company of Spanish soldiers led by Gaspar de Portola, who sent Sergeant Jose Ortega circling the bay
to find a route to Drake's Bay to the north. Ortega stopped at Carquinez Strait,
across the bay from the delta of the Napa River, and turned back. Thus Napa
Valley remained little more than a rumor to the outside world for another fifty
years. In 1817 a small mission was built in San Rafael as a sanitarium for sick
Indians.

When the Mexicans gained independence from Spain in 1822, their government was anxious to counter possible Russian movement from Fort Ross at
Bodega Bay, and the Franciscan friars wanted to found a northern mission
where food could be produced. A young Spanish priest, Father Jose Altimira,
was sent from Mission San Francisco de Assisi (Mission Dolores) in Yerba
Buena with a troop of mounted soldiers to locate a likely site. Altimira passed
through San Rafael on June 16, 1823, and headed over the first range of hills to
the Petaluma plain. He then led his party over the next range of hills eastward
and for two days explored Sonoma Valley.

Altimira and his military escort turned east again and rode over the hills
more or less along the route of current Highway 121—they were the first non-
natives to see the Napa Valley. It was July 1, 1823. After crossing the Napa
River, they climbed a hill east of the present-day site of Napa State Hospital,
from which they could see the sweep of the southern valley. After another day
of exploration, they returned to the Sonoma Valley. There he started construction of Mission San Francisco Solano. It was dedicated on April 4, 1824.

The Napa Valley was just too distant from the mission in San Rafael to be
considered for a new mission location. However, this verdant valley and its
"pagan natives" easily came within the expanding control of the Sonoma
mission.

Some 1,300 Natives were baptized between 1823 and 1834, and as many as
700 lived under serf-like conditions in or around the Sonoma mission. The
whip was used to enforce rules and punish runaways. Most of the Indians in the
Napa Valley avoided living at the mission.

VALLEJO AND THE MEXICAN LAND GRANTS

In 1834 the Mexican government decreed that the missions be "secularized" and their lands and buildings taken over by the government. Sent north from Monterey was twenty-nine-year-old Lieutenant Mariano G. Vallejo, who assumed control of the mission lands covering the region from present-day Petaluma, through Sonoma Valley, and all of Napa Valley.

The first American to settle in the Napa Valley was George C. Yount, guided there in 1831 by twenty-four-year-old frontiersman Guy Freeman Fling, who had "gone native," living with Indians around Monterey and adopting their ways. As he stood on the cusp of Mount St. Helena (not yet so named), Yount reputedly announced to the wind that "in such a place I would like to live…." A North Carolinian with a wandering foot, he had left his wife Eliza and their three children in Missouri one day in 1826 to lead a pack train to New Mexico—and never returned. He hunted everything from elk to otters, for a time made shingles, and in 1833 became sort of a jack-of-all trades for both the San Rafael and Sonoma missions.

When Mariano Vallejo took command of Sonoma, he contracted with Yount to make shingles for the roofs of the mission building he was having restored, and for his own palatial adobe facing the Sonoma eight-acre plaza. Yount told Vallejo that his one desire was to have land of his own, and he knew just the place. With Vallejo's endorsement, on March 23, 1836, Yount received a grant of 11,814 acres in the heart of the Valley, called Rancho Caymus after the Caymus tribe. With the labor of Natives from the Sonoma mission, he built a two-story blockhouse that served as both a home and a bastion from which Indian attacks could be repelled.

In May 1836 Vallejo gave two grants to Nicolas Higuerra: one where Napa City now stands, and another in the Carneros—a total of 2,638 acres. Higuerra built an adobe house and planted beans.

A native Californio, born in Monterey like General Vallejo, was Cayetano Juarez, who had come to Sonoma as a seventeen-year-old soldier in 1827. He received a two-square league (8,865 acre) grant called Tulucay, on the east shore of the Napa River, southeast of present-day Napa city. Juarez built an adobe house. Today it is the oldest building still standing and houses the Old Adobe Restaurant.

The next beneficiary of the largesse of General Vallejo was brother Salvador Vallejo. Salvador was granted the traditional two square leagues, which comprised two tracts, called the Trancas and the Jolopa. He built a good-sized adobe home for himself off what is now called the Silverado Trail, and two more for ranch workers. Later he received an additional 6,652 acres.

The Berryessa family was given two large grants in 1836 totaling over 17,000 acres. This land was called the Mallocomas (or Mayacamas), which covered the northern end of the Valley, including today's Calistoga. In 1843 they acquired an even bigger grant, more than 35,000 acres, much of which was then Berryessa Valley and is now under man-made Lake Berryessa. This grant was, oddly, named Las Putas Rancho (*puta* is Spanish for "whore"). The name survives as Putah Creek.

Edward Bale was an eccentric, twenty-nine-year-old English physician when he landed in Monterey from a ship out of Boston. For a couple of years, he practiced medicine in Monterey. He wooed and wed the young niece of General Vallejo, Maria Soberanes, converted to Catholicism, and became a naturalized Mexican citizen. While in Monterey he obtained a permit to open a drug store but began selling liquor, which was against the law. For this he was arrested and fined. Despite Bale's indiscretion, Vallejo appointed him "Surgeon of the California Forces," since he was the only doctor around. Bale and his wife moved to Vallejo's headquarters in Sonoma.

But Bale soon ran afoul of brother-in-law Salvador, accusing him of making a pass at Bale's wife, who was also Salvador's niece. Salvador administered a whipping to Bale. A battered and humiliated Bale responded with two shots at Salvador, missed, and was thrown into what passed for a jail in Sonoma. Through the intervention of the British consul in Monterey, no punishment was meted out.

Despite all this discord, in 1841 General Vallejo arranged a two-square league grant for Bale in Napa Valley—perhaps to get him out of town—between the grants to Yount and the Berryessas, and including the future site of St. Helena. It was officially given the unusual name of Carne Humana—literally "human flesh" (and you thought Whore's Ranch was bad)—which was apparently a corruption of an Indian name for the area. The Spanish and English ears for native tongues were notoriously weak, and the newcomers seemed to care little for the names the Natives gave to land that was being stolen from them.

In the area where Highway 121 links Napa and Sonoma Counties today, another expatriate American, Jacob Leese, who happened to be married to Vallejo's sister Rosalie, received the Huichica grant in exchange for property in Yerba Buena (San Francisco), where he was a trader, and moved to Sonoma.

Two Americans settled and received grants beyond the eastern hills. William Pope, a former trapper and hunter in the southwest who had been living in the Los Angeles pueblo with his Mexican wife and children, was given Pope Valley. Pope had only six months to enjoy his land, for he suffered a near-amputation of his leg when an ax slipped, and he bled to death. The other to receive a land grant was Colonel John Chiles, an old Indian fighter and guide across the plains as early as 1841, who brought Yount's children from Missouri in 1843. The following year he received the Chiles Valley grant. He continued his guiding work, settled permanently with his family in 1852, and built a flour mill.

THE DEHUMANIZATION OF THE INDIANS

But what of the original residents: the Wappo, Pomo, Coast Miwok and all their subnations, the Mayacamas, Caymus, Suscol, Huichica, and Nappa?

Many of the Indians had become restless under mission life. They often ran away, only to be hunted down by the Mexican soldiers assigned to the Sonoma mission. Between 1837 and 1839 a smallpox epidemic killed hundreds of Natives, who lacked immunity to the European malady. Other diseases, such as cholera, and the consumption of hard liquor (unknown to the Indians before the Europeans came) reduced the population.

Fearful of Indian attacks, Mariano Vallejo put the problem in the hands of his brother Salvador, who used his small troop of soldiers to show force. In the one outright battle fought in the Soscoal (a Spanish spelling of Suscal) area between Mexican soldiers and a large band of rebelling Indians who had invaded from the southeast, the Natives lost more than 200, against the deaths of only two Mexicans.

However, General Vallejo soon entered into peace treaties or alliances with several of the chiefs of neighboring tribes. The most valuable of these arrangements was a long-term pact with Chief Solano (a name given when he was baptized at the mission) of the Suisun. The imposing Solano stood 6 feet 7 inches and was probably the biggest Native in Northern California. He was smart and loyal to Vallejo. The Suisun were willing to fight off any tribes that had any ideas of threatening the Mexican settlement. It was Solano who arrested Dr. Bale when he ran off after shooting at Salvador Vallejo.

Nevertheless, the Natives had become dehumanized in the eyes of Salvador and his squad, as well as some of the early settlers. In 1841, responding to reports of cattle being stolen by Natives in the upper Napa Valley, a group of soldiers and settlers under the direction of Salvador Vallejo surrounded a sweat house near Mount St. Helena. As the Indian men and boys stepped out, one by one they were shot and killed—more than a hundred in all. An entire village lost its menfolk.

George Yount, on the other hand, was friendly with the Indians. He hired them to build his blockhouse and an adobe home. Only once were shots fired

GEORGE YOUNT

at Yount's blockhouse. Most settlers found that the Indians were good workers and trustworthy if treated fairly and given respect.

Eventually, some of the Native survivors were induced to move to a reservation in Mendocino County, established in 1856.

In 1841 the Russians at Bodega Bay sent an exploring party eastward to Mount St. Helena, where they planted a copper tablet memorializing the visit on the mountain's western peak and raised a Russian flag. That symbolic effort was the last Russian move to enlarge their influence in California, and they soon sold Fort Ross to John Sutter.

The origin of the name St. Helena has several versions. In 1823 Father Altimira declared that it looked like "Saint Helena on her bier," referring to the sculptured tomb of the saint at the abbey in Rheims. Some suggest that it was named for Saint Helena, patron saint of Russian royalty. Others theorize that the name honored the wife of the governor-general of Siberia and Fort Ross or for a ship of that name that brought supplies to Fort Ross. Take your pick, but Altimira was there first.

THE BEAR FLAG REVOLT

Meanwhile, by 1840 wagon trains were beginning to wend their way west, mostly to Oregon. The Kelsey family train (including Ben Kelsey's wife, Nancy, the first white woman to cross the plains) came down from the Columbia River in 1844 to the Napa Valley. Those who trekked over the Sierra Nevadas stopped at Sutter's Fort and then dispersed from there.

By 1846 about 10 percent of the population of Alta California were transplanted Americans. In Napa Valley there were maybe a dozen houses and a non-Native population of less than fifty.

U.S. President James K. Polk had an acquisitive eye on California and the Southwest. Captain John C. Fremont ("The Pathfinder") was sent roaming about southern Oregon beyond the reach of Mexican authorities, with a crew of "topographical engineers," including scout Kit Carson, with secret orders. In early June 1846 Fremont rode south to Sutter's Fort, where he encountered an irregular company of twenty-two American settlers desirous of throwing off Mexican rule. Fremont urged them to intercept a herd of horses being sent by General Vallejo to General Jose Castro in Santa Clara, and they did so.

Now with first-class mounts, the Americans decided they would capture Sonoma, the frontier capital of Mexican authority. Led by Ezekiel Merritt, a Fremont man, they set out for Sonoma and on June 13 stopped at the Bale rancho in Napa Valley, where they met a group of Napa Valley settlers, whose spokesman was John Grigsby. Eleven of the Napa Valley men, including Grigsby, three Kelsey brothers (Ben, Sam, and Andy), and teenager Nathan Coombs, agreed to become part of the force. Late at night the thirty-three riders headed westward over the hills.

They galloped into the Sonoma plaza shortly after dawn on June 14. General Vallejo was asleep. Awakened by the whoops and hollers of a rowdy-looking band of armed riders, Vallejo invited in the leaders. He offered them brandy and wine and spoke of having a discussion on a "friendly" basis until interrupted by Merritt, who announced that they "meant business" and intended to set up an independent California government. Merritt also placed under arrest General Vallejo, his brother Salvador, brother-in-law Jacob Leese, and his secretary Victor Prudon.

Nevertheless, General Vallejo ordered wine for all the men under Merritt's command. Some of the men drank too much and began talking about looting, until William Ide, the co-leader of the Grigsby-Ide wagon train, made a stirring speech reminding the invaders that their goal was to form a republic free of Mexico. His oratory caused them to elect Ide the first and only president of the Republic of California.

President Ide prepared a proclamation printed in English and Spanish, while William Todd (nephew of Mary Todd Lincoln) made a flag out of a petticoat and a chemise, drew a red star in the corner, ran a strip of red flannel along the bottom, and drew a bear, which looked for all the world like a misshapen pig. With "poke juice" he printed in the words CALIFORNIA REPUBLC, but then had to blot out the last syllable to insert the missing *I*. The concept of a bear flag was apparently the idea of Napa Valley's Peter Storm, who in later years would display his version with a bear standing on its hind legs. Vallejo and his aides were taken to Sutter's Fort and put in jail, where they languished for two months.

The California Republic lasted just twenty-five days. Before June was over Fremont showed up in Sonoma and incorporated the Bear Flaggers into what he called the California Battalion, making Grigsby commander of one of three companies. On May 13, 1846, the United States had declared war on Mexico, supposedly over a border dispute along the Rio Grande. However, official news of the war did not reach Monterey until the second week in August.

When the Mexican War ended with the Treaty of Guadalupe Hidalgo in 1848, California became American land. All Californios were granted full benefits of American citizenship; and the vast majority of former Mexican citizens, including the Vallejos and the Napa Valley Californios, swore loyalty to the United States.

NATHAN COOMBS LAYS OUT NAPA

George Yount, in 1837, and Dr. Bale, in 1846, built grist mills for grinding grain into flour, as well as lumber mills. The Bale grist mill still exists in Bale Grist Mill Historical Park on Highway 29. Yount's blockhouse, adobe house, and mills are no more, but they are commemorated by a stone monument just north of Yountville on Yount Mill Road.

The principal commercial activities in the Valley before 1850 consisted of cattle raising (hides for leather always made for good business), grain (wheat, barley, beans, and corn), a few orchards, the beginning of a lumber industry, and some quarrying. A primitive embarcadero was built on the Napa River from which Nicolas Higuerra shipped lime on a small sail-powered freight boat as early as 1844.

Nathan Coombs was a young man from Massachusetts who came to the Sacramento Valley in 1843, worked on a ranch, married the boss's daughter, and in 1845 moved to the Napa Valley. Coombs and John Grigsby were hired by pioneer Higuerra in 1847 to build his adobe residence to replace the thatch-and-mud cabin he had built himself. In payment, Higuerra gave them a large plot of land on the Napa River. Coombs soon bought out Grigsby's interest.

Just twenty-one, Coombs laid out the proposed town of Napa on his newly acquired property, using James Hudspeth as surveyor. Then Coombs began to sell lots. The first building erected was Harrison Pierce's Empire Saloon (first things first!), on Third Street near the Napa River. The streets were not marked clearly, and the saloon was framed out in the middle of Main Street and had to be rolled to its proper location. In 1848 J. T. Thompson opened the first store at the foot of Main Street, followed by a store built for Vallejo and Frisbie (the general and his son in law), and a spate of others in 1849. The spelling of *Napa* with a single *p* was settled, and the use of *Nappa* was abandoned by 1851.

After the discovery of easy gold in 1848 at Sutter's Mill near Coloma, Napa was virtually deserted by those who rushed to locate a claim and a fortune. Most would be disappointed, but Napa eventually benefited by the influx of immigrants pouring into northern California through San Francisco.

The Napa Valley's first school was established in 1847 by a survivor of the snow-trapped Donner Party, Sarah Graves Fosdick, the first American schoolteacher in California, who taught outdoors under the trees on the Bale property until a school was built for her in 1849. The first public elementary school opened in Napa in 1855.

In 1848 a ferry service across the Napa River was instituted. The first steamboat from San Francisco arrived at the Napa embarcadero at Soscol in 1850, and two years later it blossomed into regular commercial

NATHAN COOMBS

runs three times a week. From there stages and wagons transported passengers and goods northward. Soscol was a natural port, since the Napa River was still navigable there at low tide. Roads from Napa to Sonoma and Vallejo were improved in the early 1850s.

Napa County was one of the original twenty-seven California counties created in September 1850. It originally included present-day Lake County, which was split off in 1861. The first official census in 1850 numbered Napa County's population at 405, with 159 in the town of Napa. In two years it would multiply five times.

With increased population came crime. The most spectacular case stemmed from a minor lawsuit in 1850 between pioneers George Yount and Isaac Howell, which Justice of the Peace S. H. Sellers had decided in Howell's favor. A few days later a relative of Yount's, Hugh McCaully, encountered Judge Sellers at a store and began giving him an earful about the decision. The judge, who was sitting on a barrel, in effect told McCaully to "get lost." In response, McCaully pulled a large knife and stabbed Sellers in the back. The judge died instantly, and McCaully was tried, convicted, and sentenced to hang.

The killer's friends went to the state capital, which was in nearby Benicia (named for General Vallejo's wife) for that year, and convinced the governor to issue a reprieve. Friends of the slain judge were in Benicia and heard about the reprieve, so they chartered a little steamer to race to Napa, while the officer coming with the governor's order headed overland. To delay the officer, they stopped long enough to disable the ferry so that it could not cross the Napa

River, thus forcing the officer to ride upstream to the Trancas area before crossing. In the meantime, the judge's friends invaded the temporary jail, located above a general store at Main and Second, threw a rope over a rafter, and lynched McCaully. No witnesses could be found.

Coombs built the American Hotel in 1850, the first hostelry in the Valley, which was followed by the Napa Hotel and inns connected with new saloons. Some of the enterprises were run in structures that were half wood and half tent, but were soon replaced by something more substantial. Restaurants, a blacksmith shop, a butcher shop, and houses—a couple built of brick—made their appearance in the early 1850s.

Unfortunately, the quality of so-called streets did not match the development of businesses and homes, for they were unimproved mudholes part of the year, and rough trails in summer. Vehicles were constantly getting stuck or tipping over. Inadequate bridges were built across neighboring creeks and the Napa River. Most of them collapsed or were swept away in heavy rains.

Coombs started a freight shipping line and from his ranch, The Willows, became the state's leading breeder of thoroughbred racehorses. He served two terms in the State Assembly. When he died at age fifty-one in 1877, his funeral cortege included 150 carriages and a procession of fifty Napa County pioneers.

The Birth of St. Helena

In 1849 Dr. Bale died, at just forty-one years of age, leading to the sell-off of portions of his property in the 1850s. One of the early buyers was Henry Still. In 1853 Still built a home and a general store in the middle of the upper portion of the Napa Valley. Trouble was, the population was so sparse that he could look miles in each direction and seldom spot a customer. So Still devised a remarkable strategy: He would give away—free, gratis—a lot of land to anyone willing to start a business on the property. Shortly there were takers—a shoe shop, a blacksmith, a wagon-building and -repair business, a hotel, and then two saloons. Houses soon followed, and the Baptists and the Cumberland Presbyterians built churches. The town of St. Helena had been born.

The county rejoiced when the rough trail up the center of the Valley was designated a county road, and development work began in 1852. Five years later a stagecoach service operating throughout the county and over the hills to Clear Lake was founded by William F. Fisher, who had been a station agent for Coombs. However, the main county road was not fully improved with gravel and oil until 1860. A telegraph line was strung between Vallejo and Napa in 1858, seven years before the telegraph reached the west coast from the east in 1865.

THE FIRST TRICKLE OF WINE

Still no wine? Well, barely. George Yount brought a few cuttings from the Sonoma mission vineyard when he first received his land grant in 1836, and he planted and nurtured these vines into a small vineyard, primarily for table grapes. He made a little bit of wine for serving to guests, with the grapes in leather bags stomped by foot.

John M. Patchett was fifty-three years old when he arrived at Napa in 1850, after gradually making his way west. He purchased a hundred-acre tract in 1852. It became known as "Patchett's Addition" to Napa between First Street and Laurel west of Jefferson. On it he planted a vineyard of Mission grapes and an orchard. In 1857 he crushed enough Mission grapes to produce six barrels and 600 bottles of wine, charging $2.00 a gallon. He built the Valley's first winery in 1859, a 50-by-33-foot stone structure in the city of Napa

Napa Valley's first nurseryman was Simpson Thompson, a Pennsylvanian who arrived in 1852 and, with his brother, William, purchased a hundred acres of the Soscol Rancho south of the town. With a system of ditches and dikes, he established orchards and a great variety of fruit-bearing trees and plants, including forty-five varieties of grapevines by 1856. Just north of Napa at Oak Knoll, another orchardist, Joseph Warren Osborne, was also experimenting, in his case with 3,000 vines of European varietals, including Zinfandel, by the late 1850s.

Hungarian Augoston Haraszthy had fled his home country after an abortive attempt by army officers to liberalize the autocratic rule of the Hapsburgs. In Wisconsin, Illinois, and California, he had unsuccessfully searched for the ideal location for growing wine grapes equal to those of Europe. He wangled a job as the director of the U.S. mint in San Francisco, but was sacked when accused of keeping the gold-dust sweepings.

Haraszthy visited the old Mission vineyard and Vallejo's little home vineyard at Sonoma in 1856. He believed that he had found the soil and climate he had been seeking. He purchased land and planted a vineyard, which he named Buena Vista, and crushed some purchased grapes in 1858. Ironically, he had to look to Napa Valley for cuttings of European varietals (vinefera) to plant his vineyard in Sonoma. He purchased cuttings of a relatively unknown varietal, Zinfandel—from either or both Simpson Thompson and Joseph Osborne— and planted them at Buena Vista.

In 1863 Osborne was shot and killed in his orchard by a disgruntled laborer in a dispute over a bounced paycheck. The murderer was convicted in a jury trial and became the first person legally hanged in Napa County.

Haraszthy inveigled the governor of California to appoint him official emissary to vineyardists in Europe so that he could explore the potential of bringing varietals to supplant the second-rate-tasting Mission grapes. He returned in 1861 with 100,000 seedlings for Sonoma and for distribution throughout California. Haraszthy's pioneering efforts launched California's commercial wine business big time and gave Sonoma Valley a running head start.

However, Napa Valley was already getting on the wine-grape bandwagon, without Haraszthy's help. Patchett, Thompson, and Osborne may have been first, but others were soon also busy. The number of vines climbed from 22,000 in 1856 to 90,000 in 1858, when there were thirteen grape growers in the Valley, including the Valley's first woman vintner, Lolita Bruck, in the St. Helena area.

Charles Krug had emigrated from Germany, winding up in California in 1852. He planted a small vineyard in San Mateo County, south of San Francisco, as had Haraszthy, and then became an assistant to the Hungarian at the U.S. Mint. Krug followed Haraszthy to Sonoma and planted 16,000 vines on land he had purchased next to Haraszthy's Buena Vista.

Using an apple press at Patchett's place, Krug crushed some grapes for wine in 1858. The next year he made a little wine for Dr. Bale's widow, and in 1860 he became winemaker for George Yount's small vineyard. Then, in rapid succession, Krug put his Sonoma vineyard up for sale in August 1860, became engaged to Caroline Bale—heiress to a substantial portion of the unsold lands of the late doctor—and married her the day after Christmas.

The newly wed Krug found himself master of a tract of 800 acres, and he planted 15,000 vines there in 1861. Within a few years he extended the planting to 60,000 vines, two-thirds in European varietals. Starting with a crude 14-by-20-foot wine cellar, each year Krug expanded, until he eventually built a new, concrete two-story winery.

Parallel to Krug's vineyard development was the operation of Dr. George Belden Crane, a physician '49er from New York, who had been director of the City and County Hospital in San Jose before moving to Napa Valley in 1858. Crane planted vines in St. Helena—the first in that township—and produced 300 gallons of varietal wines in 1864, a year before Krug's first vintage. Crane hired Swiss-born Henri Alphonse Pellet away from Patchett to manage his vineyard, where he planted sixty varieties.

Highly respected for his viticulture knowledge, Pellet eventually created Pellet & Carver Winery, with financing from partner D. B. Carver. Pellet also built the first steam-powered mill in the Valley. He later was elected city trustee of St. Helena and to two terms as a county supervisor.

Various pioneers had begun planting small vineyards along with orchards

CHARLES KRUG WINERY – 1870S

and grain, including John York, David Hudson, and George Tucker. Cattle raising suffered a blow in the late 1860s from legislation that permitted fencing of open spaces. The number of cattle in Napa County dropped from more than 10,000 to 5,000 by the end of the decade. However, well into the 1870s dairies were still the leading agricultural occupation in the Napa Valley.

George Yount died in 1865, leaving a will that provided that several thousand of his acres be divided into fifty-acre parcels and sold at public auction. The sun had set on the day of the giant land-grant ranchos. Two years after his death, the community that had grown up around his home, which he had named Sebastopol, officially changed its name to Yountville.

SAM BRANNAN'S CALISTOGA, SARAFORNIA

In 1848 John York had discovered natural hot springs on the Bale property. This was later named White Sulphur Springs, and a hotel catering to the wealthy of San Francisco was erected in 1855. When it burned down in 1859, it was rebuilt, and the grounds were developed by one Swen Alstrom, who built cottages and other amenities, including a private telegraph line to the financial district of San Francisco.

Sam Brannan was something of a rogue. He arrived in 1846 at the village of Yerba Buena, in charge of a shipload of Mormons and money to purchase land for Mormon colonies in California. He used some of those funds to acquire property for his own account. He opened a general store in the future San Francisco but needed more population to make it the success he envisioned.

While visiting Sutter's Fort, Brannan heard the details of James Marshall's gold discovery at Sutter's Mill. John Sutter was desperate to keep it quiet, fearing that an influx of settlers would overrun his inland empire. Brannan, with his eye on the gold ring, did not care what Sutter wanted to hide, for the Mormon colonist wanted California—just acquired by the United States—to be flooded with immigrants, who would be his customers. So he took a small bag of gold dust back to San Francisco and dramatically rode through the center of the little village shouting, "Gold. Gold at the American River." The secret was out, the gold rush began, and Brannan emerged a rich man.

Learning of the hot waters that bubbled to the surface in the northern part of the Napa Valley (actually then called The Springs Township), in 1859 Brannan paid top dollar for a large parcel of property. He immediately began development of a resort for the recreation of the people of the San Francisco Bay Area—particularly the wealthy. He spent money on bathhouses, into which was pumped sulfurous hot water from the ground, twenty-five cabins, and a lavish community plan. After several drinks one night, he described his scheme to create a west coast resort in the mode of the upscale Saratoga in New York: "It'll be the Calistoga of Sarafornia," he slurred. And the name stuck.

Brannan's Calistoga resort opened with a huge splash in 1862, when a chartered ship full of guests from San Francisco was met by coaches and carriages that carried them from the dock in Vallejo to a huge feast. There was champagne for the rich and influential—and free kegs of beer and barbecue for the multitudes. They found a racetrack, swimming pool, skating rink, exotic landscaping tended by Japanese gardeners, and an observatory from which to view the entire utopia. There was a private water reservoir, a distillery for making brandy, a winery, and 100,000 newly planted vines.

Almost immediately businesses to support this operation were attracted to Calistoga. But the road north of St. Helena was still too bumpy for the tender backsides of the ladies whom Brannan hoped to attract. What he and the Valley needed was a railroad. The legal means were in place.

THE NAPA VALLEY RAILROAD

Ex-judge Chancellor Hartson from Napa was elected to the State Assembly for the 1864 session. Shortly before taking office Hartson organized the Napa Valley Railroad Company. Assemblyman Hartson's number-one priority was to shepherd a bill chartering the company with the right to receive subsidies of between $5,000 and $10,000 per·mile, to be guaranteed by a bond issue submitted to the voters of Napa County. What the proposed railroad needed was a promoter, and Brannan was that man.

The bond issue was adopted easily, $60,000 was subscribed to meet additional costs (including $30,000 advanced for railroad cars by the corporation's directors), and farmers along the proposed route gladly donated the right-of-way.

The inaugural train ran from Soscol to Napa in June 1865—the first railroad in California. With the help of another Hartson bill, the Napa Valley Railroad was extended to Calistoga by August 1868. Winery owners were ecstatic, since they and other agriculturists could ship cheaply and travel from doorstep to San Francisco via rail and ferry in just six hours. In 1869 the Napa Valley line was connected to a railway running from Vallejo to Sacramento, and shortly thereafter with the transcontinental railroad.

But life was going downhill for the enthusiastic Brannan. In April 1868, when he personally tried to foreclose on a neighboring mill, the owner shot Brannan, hitting him eight times from neck to hip. Brannan almost died. Still, as the first train arrived in Calistoga in August, Brannan had recovered sufficiently to throw a party at his resort for 3,000 celebrants. It was to be his last hurrah.

To finance the elegance of his Calistoga Hot Springs resort and extravagant living, Brannan had borrowed heavily, with the resort put up as security. The Sacramento Savings Bank finally foreclosed in the early 1870s. In 1879 the bank began selling off twenty-five- to 200-acre parcels. His wife divorced him, he drank more heavily, and died impoverished in Southern California.

Calistoga (population 1,259 in 1880) and the railroad were his heritage to the Napa Valley.

The Napa Valley Railroad also went into foreclosure and was purchased by the California Pacific, and through a series of mergers eventually became part of the Southern Pacific.

PIONEER DAYS IN THE '60S AND '70S

Crimes in Napa Valley during the 1860s and 1870s were often exotic. There was the case of the adventurer Gilbert Jenkins, for instance, who killed the father of a seventeen-year-old woman of both beauty and wealth whom he hoped to seduce with her dad out of the way. Not only was he caught, but he owned up to eight murders across the country before he was hanged.

Winery owner John Patchett was slipped knock-out drops in his drink so that he would be unconscious; then two masked men terrified his housekeeper, ransacked his home, and burglarized the houses of the public administrator and a former judge. Hunters spotted two suspicious men by a cave in the hills. A notorious ex-con named "Black Jack" Bowen and his partner were soon surprised by a posse and packed off to San Quentin Prison.

When the manager of a bar with a bordello upstairs fired at some unruly customers outside and killed one, he was soon taken from jail by a small mob. They hanged him from a tree, apparently to prevent a trial in which testimony of witnesses would have revealed the names of the customers of the bawdy house. A conspiracy of silence protected the lynchers.

With a population in which men outnumbered women ten to one, in the 1860s Napa County held the distinction of having the most prostitutes per capita of any county in California.

To illuminate Napa city, a gas company was founded in 1867, with sixty-five customers. Lamps on principal streets were lit by a lamplighter who rode around town at dusk. The first public library opened in 1870. An imposing stone library (The Goodman Library) erected in 1902 is now the home of the Napa County Historical Society.

Adding to the tourist attraction of the Valley was the discovery in 1870 of the petrified forest—ancient trees turned to stone—by "Petrified Charlie" Evans, northwest of Calistoga.

NAPA WINES GROW AND GO NATIONAL

On the heels of Krug and Crane came Jacob Schram, an unlikely vintner in an unlikely place, who purchased his first land in Napa Valley in 1862. A barber by trade, Schram landed in New York from Germany in the mid-1850s and headed to San Francisco. Upon visiting Napa Valley Schram became convinced that he could succeed at making wine. The only land he could afford was a chaparral- and tree-studded slope of the Mayacamas north of St. Helena. He cleared a patch of land himself, cut hair at White Sulphur Springs resort on weekends to put food on the table, and in 1863 planted his first vineyard. By 1867 he had 14,000 vines.

Schram's first vintage encouraged another German, San Francisco wine merchant Gottlieb Groezinger, to buy vineyard land, plant vines, and produce wines. Groezinger was particularly interested in improving the quality of California wine to provide real competition for European wines being sold on the east coast market. A San Francisco outfit, Kohler & Frohling, had begun shipping some California wines and brandy around the Horn to New York as early as 1857, but the price received (75 cents a gallon on average) was well below that of French and German products, and the reputation for quality was shaky at best.

Schram and Groezinger were the harbingers of a new wave of winemakers in the Napa Valley, including brothers John and Theodore Sigrist in Brown's Valley, west of Napa, who built a winery with a capacity of 100,000 gallons. John Lewelling was a noted nurseryman, whose brothers had brought west the seedlings that launched Oregon's agriculture. He had planted orchards in what he called Fruitvale (now a neighborhood in Oakland) and gave up his post as a county supervisor in Alameda County to move to Napa Valley, where he planted orchards and 35,000 vinifera grape vines in St. Helena.

By 1866 there were 700,000 grape vines in Napa County. However, wheat, particularly in Berryessa Valley, was still the leading farm product, ground into flour by local mills.

Alexander J. Cox, a printer who came west as a soldier with the regiment that took over Sonoma during the Mexican War, had started a newspaper there called *The Sonoma Bulletin*, which he shut down in 1855. He carted his old press to Napa and, on July 4, 1856, began publishing the four-page *Napa County Reporter*, which was erratically issued until 1858, when Cox moved on to Healdsburg. New ownership, led by the hard-drinking but popular writer R. T. Montgomery, took over and acquired a new press. For several years it was an influential newspaper. It went out of business in 1888.

The Napa Register came out as a weekly in August 1863 and went through a series of ownership changes. Popular from the outset, in December 1872, under new publisher G. W. Henning, the *Register* became a daily. It is still Napa's principal newspaper. Other journalistic attempts failed after short runs, including *The Pacific Echo*, a rabidly anti–President Lincoln paper—which died the day of Lincoln's death.

The *St. Helena Star* was founded in 1874 as a weekly newspaper. It has been in continuous publication ever since—one of the oldest weeklies in the state. Another survivor of the numerous pioneering publication efforts in the county is *The Weekly Calistogan*, which first came off the press in 1877.

Cinnabar, the ore that contains quicksilver, was discovered in Pope Valley in 1861, and later near Oakville. Various attempts were made to mine and process the ore, but the work stumbled along for a decade under various companies until the major mining efforts were consolidated under the Napa Mining Company in 1873. For more than sixty years thereafter, quicksilver was profitably mined in substantial amounts.

Silver mining in Napa County was a flash in the pan. In 1872 a vein of silver was discovered north of Calistoga, on the southeast slope of Mount St. Helena, near the toll road to Lake County. Alexander Badlam, a nephew of Sam Brannan, staked a claim, laid out a small town called Silverado City, dug a mine, and built a mill to process the ore. This activity triggered a silver rush, which drew 1,500 people, a host of mining claims in the hills, the Silverado Hotel, a stage station, several businesses, and the inevitable saloons. The silver was played out by the autumn of 1875 (the total was a puny $92,000 worth), and the population disappeared.

Chinese laborers had first arrived in the Valley after they had been drawn to the gold diggings in the mountains as early as 1849. By the time they had helped substantially to build the transcontinental railroad, completed in 1869, at least 400 had settled in the Valley. Grouped in "Chinatowns" on the outskirts of Napa, St. Helena, and Calistoga, they provided the brawn for building stone fences (which still exist), planting vineyards, digging mines, and harvesting crops. Some worked as cooks, gardeners, and household servants, while a few operated their own laundries. When the Chinese Exclusion Act was enacted in 1882, barring further immigration, Terrell Grigsby, owner of the Occidental Winery, personally fought off a mob intent on chasing out his Chinese workers. The wine industry needed their loyal, inexpensive labor. Eventually, most Chinese migrated to the cities.

THE BUILDING BOOM

The Uncle Sam Wine Cellar was founded in 1870, in a large building at the corner of Main and Fourth Streets in Napa, with a storage capacity of 500,000 gallons for the bulk wine it made from the grapes of several growers. The structure still stands, albeit substantially altered.

Napa was chosen by a state commission as the site of the State Hospital for the Insane (now called Napa State Hospital). A five-story Gothic institution with seven towers was subsequently erected on spacious grounds southeast of Napa city, where Father Altimira had first camped. Despite its rococo façade, it was extremely modern in amenities for the time (fire hydrants on every floor, lots of toilets, central steam heating, and gas lighting). In 1875 it opened to handle more than 600 patients.

A courthouse of classic design was dedicated in February 1879, built for a cost of $51,000 in downtown Napa. Amazingly, it still functions as Napa County's courthouse, almost without change from the day it opened, except that a nonfunctional tower was added and then later removed.

PALACE HOTEL IN THE 1870S

In Napa city the luxurious Palace Hotel, with seventy rooms, all with baths and fireplaces, opened in 1875 at the corner of Third and Soscol. When the old Napa Hotel, dating from 1851, burned down in 1884, it was immediately replaced by a brick structure just south of the Opera House. There was also the wooden Revere House, which was the largest building in Napa to collapse during the 1906 San Francisco earthquake.

Napa Valley was fortunate that Mark Strong, a photographer with an artistic eye and feel for history, came to town in 1886. From then on, almost to the day of his death in 1946, Strong recorded on film the changes in the city and Valley.

With the transcontinental railroad's completion in 1869, it became easy to ship goods to the east, and practical to travel to New York and other business centers. Dr. Crane visited his native New York to promote Napa Valley wines, met with skepticism, and was discouraged. Charles Krug followed, and his enthusiasm carried the day. Krug's greatest contribution was to convince the eastern wine distributors that the best wines in the Western Hemisphere came from the Napa Valley.

Krug, Jacob Beringer (Krug's former winemaker who launched his own winery, Beringer Brothers, in 1875), and M. G. Ritchie established the Napa Valley Wine Company to combine forces to distribute wines. John Lewelling and H. W. Crabb, who had followed Lewelling from Alameda County to found his Hermosa Vineyards in Oakville, emulated the Krug/Beringer/Ritchie example by contracting with eastern distributors. Lewelling and Crabb pioneered the shipment of grapes packed in freight cars filled with ice.

The results are in the statistics. By 1873 Napa Valley wines were being shipped to the east coast by the carload. The gallonage of wines vinted reached almost 500,000 that year, a far cry from the piddling 8,745 in 1860. Still, Napa County continued to trail Sonoma County production. In 1877 Napa produced 640,000 gallons and Sonoma, 2,500,000. But that was soon to change. Total shipments of California wine to the midwest and east coast climbed to 1,243,000 gallons in 1878. In 1880 Crabb produced 300,000 gallons and Krug, 280,000. While Krug was the chief publicist for Napa's wines, Crabb became the Valley's most innovative experimenter. He later gave twenty acres to the University of California for enological testing.

STEVENSON AND OTHER CHARACTERS

An itinerant Scottish travel writer, Robert Louis Stevenson, showed up in Calistoga in the summer of 1880, on a honeymoon with his wife, Fanny, a divorcee he had just married. The Stevensons lived for most of the time at the old hotel in the ghost town of Silverado. The writer and winemaker Schram became friends who talked for hours. Three years later Stevenson burst on the literary world with his novel *Treasure Island*, in which the physical description of the island's interior was based on Mount St. Helena. In November and December 1883, Stevenson had two articles published in the magazine *Century Illustrated* about the Stevensons' stay, which were later issued in a small volume entitled *Silverado Squatters*.

The tubercular Stevenson died in 1894, before anyone in the Valley paid any attention to this book. His death was reported in just half a dozen lines in the *St. Helena Star*, with no mention at all in the *Register* or *Calistogan*.

Several prominent characters moved to the Valley during this period, including S. Clinton Hastings, chief justice of the California Supreme Court and founder of the state's first law school, Hastings College of the Law in San Francisco (now part of the University of California system); and Lilburn W. Boggs, former governor of Missouri, who had come west expecting to be appointed first governor of California. The highest West Coast office that Boggs achieved was alcalde (mayor/judge) of Sonoma. Former speaker of the Assembly, and losing candidate for governor and U.S. Senate, Morris M. Estee built a winery on Atlas Peak in 1885 (it is still used for wine storage).

Former Union general and U.S. Senator John F. Miller purchased a large parcel east of Napa, upon which he built a fourteen-room mansion, which today is the Silverado Country Club.

Concerned with the condition of disabled veterans of the Civil War, the San Francisco chapter of the Grand Army of the Republic (GAR), with the assistance of a Mexican War veterans group, bought 910 acres just west of Yountville for $17,500 in 1881. With donated funds, the Veterans' Home Association opened its first building in 1884, to house forty-two veterans. Soon the legislature approved expense payments of $150 a year for each resident. The Veterans' Home expanded rapidly but was always short of funds. Finally, in 1897 the state took over the Home's operation, when it was the residence for 800 veterans.

OF BERINGER, NIEBAUM, AND BANDITS

Over the hills to the west, disaster struck the vineyards of Sonoma Valley, where phylloxera, plant lice that attacks vine roots, caused most vineyards to wither and die between 1876 and 1879. For the first time Napa County surpassed Sonoma County in wine production. Napa vineyardists breathed a collective sigh of relief that they had been spared. Their elation would prove to be premature.

New and larger wineries were constructed in the late 1870s and early 1880s. Jacob Beringer, with financing from brother Frederick in New York, built a three-story winery with a deep, cool cave in St. Helena. Nearby, John C. Weinberger erected a winery in 1876, which he soon enlarged to hold 180,000 gallons—it is now the location of the Markham Winery. In 1874 Napa grocer Giuseppe Migliavacca became the first Napa resident of Italian heritage to develop a major winery, and he was followed by Vittorio Sattui in 1885 and Anton Nichelini shortly thereafter. As early as 1882 some Valley growers began using smudge pots to ward off extreme frosts—now often replaced by more environmentally acceptable wind machines. In 1888 Greystone Winery in St. Helena became the first run by electricity from a gasoline-powered generator.

Gustave Niebaum, a Finnish sea captain, had made a fortune in the northern Pacific fur trade. When he became interested in winemaking, he had the time, money, and inclination to be a perfectionist. West of the hamlet of Rutherford, Niebaum found a poorly maintained attempt at a winery, which he bought. Its name: Inglenook (Scottish for "a seat by the fire.")

During the early 1880s Niebaum expanded and cleared his acreage, went to Europe and brought back cuttings, read every book he could get in any language about winemaking, ordered the best equipment, and created cellars to maintain constant temperatures. And, to house it all, he had constructed an imposing stone mansion that overlooked the plain. Seven years after Inglenook's first wine release, Niebaum's winery was given the award for "excellence and purity" at the Paris Exposition in 1889. Other Napa Valley wineries brought home twenty medals—including a gold for Migliavacca—more than any American wine region. Napa Valley had secured its place on the international wine map.

Stagecoaches and delivery wagons that climbed the hills from Napa Valley to Lake County were occasionally robbed in the 1880s. In the '90s the highwaymen became a plague, time and again forcing drivers to "throw down the box" and passengers to empty their pocketbooks. In May 1895 one of a pair of robbers beat up a Chinese passenger, immediately casting suspicion on one Buck English, known to be a foul-mouthed Sinophobe. Sheriff George McKenzie put together a four-man posse, which included twenty-three-year-old District Attorney Ted Bell. They trailed English to the village of Monticello in Berryessa Valley. A Wild West–style chase followed, in which English was punctured by fifty-two shotgun pellets before being captured more dead than alive.

A couple of years later, David Dunlap, the leader of the local Democratic party, was elected sheriff. With prior experience as a sheriff in Nevada, Dunlap looked like a Central Casting version of the western lawman: tall, erect, with a drooping mustache and steel-blue eyes. A new gang of stage robbers went into business, and the frustrated sheriff kept losing their tracks in the hills. One newspaper began referring to Dunlap as "no catch-'em Dave." Finally, he and his deputies chased down and arrested the county's last highwayman. (The newspaper was unimpressed, calling the sheriff "no catch-'em Dave, except once.") At the turn of the twentieth century Napa was the scene of California's last public hanging, with tickets issued to spectators.

Frank Coombs, son of Nathan Coombs, was the county's most successful political figure. He was elected district attorney in 1880 at age twenty-seven as a Republican. His next successes were his election to the state assembly on seven occasions between 1887 and 1927. Coombs was twice chosen speaker of the assembly; was appointed U.S. minister to Japan in 1892; served a term in Congress; and for several years was U.S. attorney for Northern California.

His son, another Nathan Coombs, was elected state senator as a Republican in the 1950s. The sister of Senator Coombs married the son of Sheriff David Dunlap. Their union produced four sons; a farmer and three lawyers. One of them, Frank Dunlap, was Napa city attorney for many years. Another, Democrat John F. Dunlap, was elected to four terms as state assemblyman and served four years as state senator in the 1970s. He and his wife, Janet, still reside on a portion of founder Nathan Coombs' ranch.

KRUG'S DEATH AND THE BATTLE AGAINST PHYLLOXERA

A slump in wine prices drove Charles Krug into bankruptcy in 1885—he had gotten easy credit based on his reputation—and forced the sale of his winery to a San Francisco banker. His wife, Caroline, went from eccentricity—like her father Dr. Bale—into outright insanity before she died in December 1885. Krug, the man who loved to talk to reporters, lost the power of speech. The "Father of Napa Valley Wines" died on November 1, 1892.

The insidious phylloxera had made their migration gradually from Sonoma Valley into vineyards in the Carneros region, shared by Sonoma and Napa Valleys by 1890. In 1893 a report commissioned by the state Board of Viticultural Commissioners revealed that 244 out of 577 Napa County vineyards showed signs of the voracious louse.

Napa's winegrowers benefited from Sonoma's experience with the bug, since Sonoma growers had found some root stock resistant to phylloxera. There was also the expertise available from the University of California's new enological study department. The state board pointed out that Judge John Stanly's vineyards in Carneros had not been harmed by the louse since they were planted in *Riparia* roots, proving they were resistant.

University of California professor Arthur Hayne argued that the root stock *Rupestris* was superior to *Riparia* in California soil. Although most growers were slow to accept Hayne's view, George Schonewald met with remarkable success with grafting to *Rupestris*. A new face on the scene, French immigrant Georges de Latour, in 1900—the depth of the phylloxera calamity—ordered millions of *Rupestris* root stock from France, which he sold throughout Northern California.

While Napa wines continued to win medals through the 1890s at various state and national expositions, by the turn of the century, there remained fewer than 5,000 acres in vines. Although some growers switched to fruit growing— French prunes were a new favorite—others began pulling vines in favor of replanting first with *Riparia* and then *Rupestris* root stock.

There were other industries in the Valley besides winemaking, however. There were fruit orchards, olive groves, dairying, the resort business, the bottling of mineral waters, and the processing of leather, which dated back to the 1860s. In fact, "Napa Leather" became a dictionary definition for soft leather.

Newcomer de Latour, barely speaking English and previously perpetually near-broke, became the leader of Napa Valley's winery resurgence. With the profits from his chancy purchase of root stock—primarily on credit—he finally had some funds to purchase property and build a winery, which he opened in Rutherford in 1907, named Beaulieu Vineyards, meaning "beautiful place."

De Latour planted extensively, obtained the endorsement of the San Francisco Catholic Archdiocese for use of his wine by churches, bottled bulk wine under his label while waiting for vines to mature, and soon was vinting large amounts of Bordeaux-type wines. By 1910 Beaulieu was Napa Valley's most famous winery—a far cry from the days when de Latour, a chemist trained in France, scraped out a living by making cream of tartar from wine-barrel leavings.

Victory over phylloxera encouraged new investors who built large wineries. The Salmina family built Larkmead, and Antonio Forni leased and rejuvenated Josephine Tychson's winery and vineyards.

The 1903 invention of a machine that would mass-produce glass bottles made bottles cheap and plentiful. This allowed each winery to identify its product with labels on the bottles and increased the Napa Valley wine exposure. Annual wine production in Napa County was reaching 4 million gallons.

It appeared that there were clear skies ahead for the Napa Valley wine industry. But there was one cloud on the horizon. It was called Prohibition.

PROHIBITION SHUTS DOWN THE WINERIES

What started as a movement to close down saloons, by the second decade of the century had become a crusade, with accelerating political momentum, to put an end to all alcohol manufacture and sale, but the margin was increasingly close. Many winemakers, as producers of the drink of moderation, hoped that, if alcohol were prohibited, wine would be exempt as "food."

Congress passed the Eighteenth Amendment on December 18, 1917, and submitted it to the state legislatures. The California Assembly and Senate approved it on January 11, 1919, and five days later the last necessary state legislature ratified Prohibition, to take effect in 1920. There were exceptions: Wine for sacramental and medicinal purposes could be made and sold (on the technicality that it was not used for "beverage purposes"), and limited production of wine—200 gallons a year—for personal use was permitted.

The sacramental-wine exemption became a saving grace for de Latour and his Beaulieu, since he had one of ten permits to provide wine for church altars.

More than 120 wineries in Napa County officially shut down. Grape growers could still ship grape juice or grapes—sometimes with the warning not to add yeast, which might cause "illegal fermentation." Many tore out their vines and substituted prunes, cherries, or walnuts.

Of course, like many Americans, there were winemakers who sneered at Prohibition as a joke, and they continued to make wine far in excess of personal needs. Although local law enforcement and federal officials were primarily concerned about halting the bootlegging of hard liquor, wine occasionally became the target. One day the revenuers raided large storage tanks on Dunaweal Lane and delighted in smashing them with axes. The resulting wine flood turned the road into what old-timers still call "the river of red."

The Sawyer Tanning Company, which had been in business since 1872, expanded with new products such as patent-leather shoes and softball covers. In 1915 Napans Peter Jensen and Edwin Pridham invented the loudspeaker, which they named Magnavox. As the company grew it moved to Indiana.

Napa County was essentially on hold: Between 1910 and 1930 the population increased slightly, from 19,800 to 22,879. In the 1920s the number of residents of the city of Napa actually dropped, from 6,757 in 1920 to 6,437 in 1930.

The Napa Valley Railroad eliminated passenger service in 1929, and the electric line from Vallejo to Calistoga shut down in 1939, giving way to the bus and automobile.

REPEAL AND RECOVERY

Like the rest of the nation, the Napa Valley was stagnant after the onset of the Great Depression in 1929. The resort business was hurt by the lack of personal income available for entertainment, and agriculture suffered from low prices. One hope would be the repeal of Prohibition, which finally occurred on December 7, 1933.

Beaulieu Vineyards was first out of the gate, since it had been making sacramental wine during the twelve years of Prohibition and because shrewd de Latour built up a large pre-repeal inventory of wine, which he could ship immediately. Close on his heels was forty-three-year-old Louis M. Martini, a tall, blond native of Italy, who since 1922 had run a company at Kingsburg in the San Joaquin Valley that made grape concentrate for sale to amateur winemakers. Martini built a winery in St. Helena, planted vineyards of Cabernet Sauvignon and Zinfandel in both Napa and Sonoma Counties, and began producing full-bodied wines at modest prices. They were an instant success. He was a founder of the California Wine Institute and the prime mover in creating a gathering of winery owners, the Napa Valley Vintners Association.

The leadership of Inglenook devolved on the grand-nephew of founder Captain Niebaum, young John Daniel. The handsome 1933 Stanford engineering graduate felt obligated to restore the old winery's preeminence and honor the legacy of Captain Niebaum. He studied viticulture with Sonoma wine sage Carl Bundschu. When John's aunt died in 1937, he took full command of the winery (owned jointly with his sister, who was not interested in its operation). Daniel hired an expert winemaster, George Deuer, diversified wine vintages, joined the Wine Institute Board in 1941, and put "Napa Valley" on Inglenook labels, which were vintage-dated.

Charles de Latour got another step on the competition in 1938, when he induced Andre Tchelistcheff to leave Paris and work for Beaulieu as a winemaster. Tchelistcheff was a dapper Russian refugee from the Communist regime who had studied agronomy in France and was an expert on grapes. Despite doubts about coming to America, Andre and his wife and child came to Napa.

He cleaned up Beaulieu Winery, had tanks scrubbed, set up a laboratory, and insisted on new equipment, including a corking device. The sensitivity of his taste buds for wines was remarkable, and Beaulieu's quality rose. For the next forty years he would be the United States' ruling authority on wines and winemaking. His influence on disciples like Joe Heitz, Mike Grgich, and Warren Winiarski raised the standard that winemasters expected. Tchelistcheff ushered in the era of the professional winemakers, who were often graduates of the University of California at Davis.

Beringer was back in business with absentee ownership. On land owned by the Catholic order for three-quarters of a century, the Christian Brothers were making wine and brandy. They would gain fame under the legendary winemaker Brother Timothy. But it was still the Depression, and the wine industry was only a shadow of what it would become.

Cesare Mondavi was an Italian immigrant who had settled in Lodi, California, where he shipped grapes to home winemakers around the country during Prohibition. Shortly after repeal he bought a small, vacant stone winery in St. Helena. Cesare sent his older son, Robert, fresh out of Stanford, to build up a bulk wine business there. Robert soon was crushing enough grapes to yield a million gallons a year. At the urging of his sons, Robert and Peter, Cesare bought the dilapidated Krug winery and property for $87,000 (mostly borrowed) in 1943, on the condition that Robert, as general manager, and Peter, as winemaker, would run the winery.

THE 1940S AND BEYOND

A military airport south of Napa city was built during the war and became Napa County Airport in 1946.

Famous people living in the valley included Jessamyn West, wife of Superintendent of Schools Harry McPherson, who wrote *Friendly Persuasion* in 1940. Her book became a best-seller and a popular movie. West (the outspoken Democratic cousin of Republican Richard Nixon) also authored another best-seller, *The Witch Diggers*. M. F. K. (Mary Frances Kennedy) Fisher, was already famous for her classics on food appreciation and travel like *How To Cook a Wolf*, when she moved to St. Helena in the early 1960s. During the time she lived there, she wrote regularly for *The New Yorker* magazine. Canadian writer Arthur Hailey lived in a large house overlooking St. Helena while writing several of his very popular novels like *Airport*, *Hotel*, and *The Bankers* in the 1970s and 1980s, before leaving for a home in the Bahamas.

Scarcely noticed in 1947 was the purchase of the old Sutter Home Winery by Mario Trinchero and his family from New York. Mario and his brother were so strapped for cash that they could not pay the $12,000 for the century-old Victorian next to the vineyards on Highway 29 in St. Helena.

In the meantime, John Daniel came to love Inglenook, but his beautiful wife, Betty, came to hate it. Isolated from the city society she enjoyed, she suffered depression, began drinking too much, and became involved in notorious affairs, which eventually led to their divorce. In 1964 John finally sold Inglenook to United Vintners, whose management promised to maintain Inglenook's integrity. With the winery out of his system, John and Betty reconciled and remarried. But United Vintners turned the main building into a storage house and began producing jug wine under the venerable Inglenook name. Soon thereafter John Daniel died of a heart attack, induced by an overdose of barbiturates. The cause was considered suicide, but some said that it was really a broken heart.

BIG BUSINESS AND BIG WINNERS

The sale of Inglenook was an omen. Big corporations were attracted to the existing wineries and had the bucks to make tempting offers. Soon Heublein, Coca-Cola, Seagram's, Nestlé, R. J. Reynolds, and Grand Metropolitan of London (which had bought Reynolds, which had bought Heublein) became owners. There would be others. Some cared about excellent wines; others were primarily interested in profits.

Tensions existed between brothers Robert and Peter Mondavi at Charles Krug Winery even before their father, Cesare, died. It was almost inevitable that Robert, as "Mr. Outside," and Peter, as "Mr. Inside," would not agree. Robert was outgoing and willing to spend money for promotion, while Peter was cautious and introverted.

The brothers argued over the future participation of their sons in the business. In 1965, when Robert set up a corporation to establish a small winery for his sons, which he called Robert Mondavi, Peter and mother Rosa—who owned the majority of the stock in Krug—pulled the plug. Robert was put on involuntary "leave," which really meant that he was out.

Robert Mondavi lined up financing, bought property in Oakville on Highway 29, and built a winery. The family split had a much greater impact on Napa Valley than the addition of another winery. It meant that Robert Mondavi was turned loose to promote himself, his winery, his wines, and Napa Valley.

The elegant mansion and grounds created by General Miller in the last century was purchased in 1967 by Amfak Corporation. Amfak spent $100 million to turn the estate into the private Silverado Country Club, with two golf courses designed by Robert Trent Jones, 400 condos, a spacious clubhouse, tennis courts, and a renovated mansion.

May 24, 1976, was a landmark date for Napa Valley wines. At a prestigious blind tasting in Paris that day, the Cabernet Sauvignon of Stag's Leap Cellars (Warren Winiarski, owner and winemaker) was rated the "Best Red," and the Chardonnay of Chateau Montelena (James Barrett, owner and winemaker) was named best of the white Burgundies. Their competition were the elite wineries from Bordeaux and Burgundy. These tasting triumphs proved that Napa Valley wines belonged among the best international wines and signaled that Napa Valley wineries should shift toward varietals rather than "jug" wines. Within the next twenty years, sales from Napa varietals leapt from $150 million to $2.5 billion.

THE POLITICS OF PRESERVATION

Political controversies over the future of Napa County broke out in the late 1960s and continued for the next thirty years. The first scrimmage came in 1968, when the Board of Supervisors had to decide whether to authorize "agricultural preserves" pursuant to the recently adopted state Williamson Act. Under that act, an owner of agricultural land could contract with the county to keep the property in agriculture (and not a subdivision) perpetually until ten years after the owner filed a notice of intent to cancel the contract. In return, the county would give the owner a property-tax reduction.

The Board of supervisors had to pass an ordinance agreeing to county participation. "Ag preserves" are common today, but were novel in the 1960s. Those Napans concerned with overdevelopment were in favor of permitting such preserves in Napa County, as were some vintners, including Louis Peter Martini, of the new generation of Martinis, and Jack Davies, who had just purchased the old Schramsberg winery, which he and his wife, Jamie, were restoring. At the crucial meeting of the board, one winery owner was so abusive to the supervisor from St. Helena, fence-sitter Julius Caiocco, that Julius voted to make it unanimous to approve agricultural preserves, saying "Nobody's gonna shake a finger at me."

In 1972, supported by a coalition of environmentalists and neighborhood organizations, Virginia (Ginny) Simms, John Tuteur, and Henry Wigger were elected to the Board of Supervisors. They had pledged to enact zoning that would limit home sites on rural hillsides to forty acres per home. That limitation was adopted in 1973. For the next two decades, bitter supervisorial elections—unlimited development versus limited growth—were held every two years, with the Board split one way or the other each term. The hillside limitation bounced down to twenty acres and then back up to forty. In 1989 a pro-development board majority abruptly dismissed the entire Planning Commission and fired the county's long-time planning director.

Another area of conflict needed to be resolved. Volker Eisele, with a Ph.D. from UC Berkeley, and his landscape architect wife, Liesel, had bought an old vineyard and rusty winery. He soon organized the Napa Valley Grape Growers Association, to represent the position of independent growers not employed by major wineries. The local growers were concerned with the use of the Napa Valley address on bottles of wine made from so-called foreign grapes shipped in from outside the county. This was particularly true of wineries that had a second label with wine of lower quality. The growers' proposal: In order to use a Napa address or Napa appellation, or to become a new or expanded winery in Napa County, 75 percent of the wine had to be vinted from grapes grown in the county.

The 240 members of the growers' association were unanimous in favor, but the wineries were divided. It took almost three years of discussions, a moratorium on new winery permits, and two supervisorial elections before a compromise—first proposed by the growers—was adopted by the Board of Supervisors in the county's "definition" of wineries for permits. The ordinance allowed already existing wineries to continue any practices they were employing (including use of "foreign" grapes), but new wineries had to use 75 percent Napa grapes and could not have public tours and tastings. It did allow food to be served for promotional services. Any expansion of an existing winery had to meet the 75 percent requirement. In part, this explains the reason why many wineries today—even elegant facilities like Joseph Phelps—require visitors to call ahead for an appointment for tasting, to avoid the "open to the public" tasting-room prohibition.

As the 1990s opened there was an important shift of sentiment: More and more vineyardists and winemakers became convinced that subdivisions and vineyards did not mix. Since Napa Valley wineries were a crucial business as well as a great tourist draw, maintaining the beauty of the hills and restricting the areas available for malls, outlet centers, and subdivisions made economic as well as aesthetic sense.

THE NEW WAVE

Napa Valley saw many changes in the 1980s and 1990s. Robert Mondavi won a large judgment against his brother Peter and the Krug winery. A lawsuit that began over the use of the Mondavi name on a company Peter set up climaxed in a ruling that Robert was owed millions for being forced out of Charles Krug. In 1980 he married Margrit Biever, who worked closely with him in developing his Robert Mondavi Winery. With his financial and personal conflicts in the past, Robert Mondavi had more time to spend as spokesman of Napa Valley wines to the world. He was not the only one, but certainly was the most ubiquitous.

Robert Trinchero, the son of Mario, who had bought little Sutter Home, experimented with making a white wine from Zinfandel grapes, after trying dozens of different varieties. He came out with 350 cases of his "invented" White Zinfandel in 1974. He caught the popular trend toward whites and surpassed the 4-million-cases mark early in the 1990s, to become Napa Valley's largest producer. The headquarters is in the lovely Victorian house that his father and uncle could not afford to buy for $12,000.

Motion picture director Francis Ford Coppola (*The Godfather, Peggy Sue Got Married, Apocalypse Now*) purchased—some say "rescued"—Inglenook from Heublein, changed the name to Niebaum-Coppola Estate, and created a museum of cinematic history. Art and wine were linked with architectural innovation, exhibits and museums, including avant-garde Clos Pegase and the winery/art museum called The Hess Collection.

More and more people from other disciplines and professions—doctors, lawyers, Silicon Valley pioneers, businesspeople, a rocket scientist—planted grapes and opened wineries, all dedicated to a search for quality. There were several new owners and winemakers who had grown up with European wine traditions. The number of wineries rose at a dizzying pace, as did the ratings by such magazines as *Wine Spectator* and *Wine Enthusiast.*

Resort business was also making a comeback. In the 1980s Auberge du Soleil and Meadowood, both rated among the best resorts in the world, became instant tourist magnets. Old mansions were being converted to bed and breakfasts every year. Upscale restaurants were drawing crowds. The Culinary Institute of America, the nationally known school for high-caliber chefs, purchased the old Greystone Cellars, restored the facility exquisitely, and opened its western campus in 1995.

Finally, in 1998 the voters passed a bond issue to pay for rerouting the Napa River to prevent the periodic flooding that has swept the city of Napa regularly since the days of Nathan Coombs.

The population of Napa Valley now exceeds 150,000—compared to the 5,000 native Americans living there when Father Altimira surveyed the Valley from a hill in the Soscol, or when George Yount built his blockhouse. The glory is that the natural beauty remains.

CHAPTER 8

THE NAPA VALLEY LIST OF LISTS

*I*n this chapter we give you lots of handy information that we like to have ourselves when traveling, and we hope that it comes in handy for you, too. In each case, we list the best available.

WINERIES REQUIRING APPOINTMENTS FOR TASTING

Under Napa County regulations many wineries require that visitors make appointments to taste wines. Here are wineries that require appointments:

Anderson's Conn Valley Vineyards, 680 Rossi Road, St. Helena; (707) 963–8600.

Bouchaine Vineyards, 1075 Buchli Station Road, Napa; (707) 252–9065. Open 10:00 A.M.–4:00 P.M. Monday–Friday.

Calafia Cellars, 629 Fulton Lane, St. Helena; (707) 963–0114.

Caymus Vineyards, 8700 Conn Creek Road, Rutherford; (707) 967–3010. Open 10:00 A.M.–4:30 P.M. daily.

Chappellet Winery, 1581 Sage Canyon Road, St. Helena; (707) 963–7136.

Chateau Woltner, 3500 Silverado Trail, St. Helena; (707) 963–1744.

Chrichton Hall, 1150 Darms Lane, Napa; (707) 224–4200.

David Arthur Vineyards, 1521 Sage Canyon Road, St. Helena; (707) 963–5190.

Deer Park Winery, 1000 Deer Park Road, Deer Park; (707) 963–5411. Open 10:00 A.M.–4:00 P.M. daily.

Domaine Charbay Winery & Distillery, 4001 Spring Mountain Road, St. Helena; (707) 963–9327. Open 10:00 A.M.–4:00 P.M. daily.

Domaine Montreaux, 4242 Big Ranch Road, Napa; (707) 253–2802.

Duckhorn Vineyards, 1000 Lodi Lane, St. Helena; (707) 963–7108. Open 9:00 A.M.–4:30 P.M. Monday–Friday; no tasting.

Dunn Vineyards, 805 White Cottage Road North, Angwin; (707) 965–3642.

Frog's Leap Winery, 8815 Conn Creek Road, Rutherford; (707) 963–4704. Open 9:00 A.M.–4:00 P.M. Monday–Friday, 10:00 A.M.–4:00 P.M. Saturday.

Graeser Winery, 255 Petrified Forest Road, Calistoga; (707) 942–4437.

Guilliams Vineyards, 3851 Spring Mountain Road, St. Helena; (707) 963–9059. Open 10:00 A.M.–5:00 P.M. daily.

Gustavo Thrace Winery, 880 Vallejo Street, Napa; (707) 257–6796. Open 10:00 A.M.–2:00 P.M. Monday–Friday.

Hansfahden Wineries, 5300 Mountain Home Ranch Road, Calistoga; (707) 942–6760.

Havens Wine Cellars, 2055 Hoffman Lane, Yountville, (707) 945–0921

Helena View Johnson, 3500 Highway 128, Calistoga; (707) 942–4956. Open 10:00 A.M. to 5:00 P.M. Saturday–Sunday.

Joseph Phelps Vineyards, 200 Taplin Road (east off Silverado Trail), St. Helena; (707) 963–2745. Open 9:00 A.M.–5:00 P.M. Monday–Friday, 10:00 A.M.–5:00 P.M. Saturday.

Kent Rasmussen Winery, 1001 Silverado Trail, St. Helena; (707) 963–5667.

Mayacamas Vineyards, 1155 Lokoya Road, Yountville; (707) 224–4030. Open 8:00 A.M.–4:30 P.M. Monday–Friday.

Moss Creek Winery, 6015 Steele Canyon Road, Yountville; (707) 252–1295.

Newton Vineyard, 2555 Madrona Avenue, St. Helena; (707) 963–9000.

Nichelini Winery, 2590 Sage Canyon Road, St. Helena; (707) 963–0717. Open 10:00 A.M.–6:00 P.M. Sunday and holidays; by appointment rest of week.

Opus One Winery, 7900 St. Helena Highway, Oakville; (707) 944–9442.

Robert Pecota Winery, 3299 Bennett Lane, Calistoga; (707) 942–6625.

Plam Vineyards, 6200 Washington Street, Yountville; (707) 944–1102. Open 9:00 A.M.–5:00 P.M. daily, 9:00 A.M.–3:00 P.M. Sunday.

Robert Keenan Winery, 3660 Spring Mountain Road, St. Helena; (707) 963–9177.

Roundhill Vineyards, 1680 Silverado Trail, St. Helena; (707) 963–5251. Open 10:00 A.M.–4:30 P.M. daily; sales, no tasting.

Saintsbury, 1500 Los Carneros Avenue, Napa; (707) 252–0592. Open 9:00 A.M.–5:00 P.M. Monday–Friday

Schramsberg Vineyards, 1400 Schramsberg Road, Calistoga; (707) 942–4558. Open 10:00 A.M.–4:00 P.M. daily.

Schweiger Vineyards, 4015 Spring Mountain Road, St. Helena; (707) 963–4882.

Smith–Madrone Vineyards, 4022 Spring Mountain Road, St. Helena; (707) 963–2283. Open 10:00 A.M.–4:00 P.M. Monday–Saturday.

Spottswoode Vineyard and Winery, 1902 Madrona Avenue, St. Helena; (707) 963–0134.

Stony Hill Vineyard, 3331 St. Helena Highway North, St. Helena; (707) 963–2636.

Storybook Mountain Vineyards, 3835 Highway 128, Calistoga; (707) 942–5310.

Summit Lake Vineyards, 2000 Summit Lake Drive, Angwin; (707) 965–2488.

Swanson Vineyards, 1271 Manley Lane, Rutherford; (707) 944–0905.

Truchard Vineyards, 3234 Old Sonoma Road, Napa; (707) 253–7153.

Tudal Winery, 1015 Big Tree Road, St. Helena; (707) 963–3947. Open 10:00 A.M.–4:00 P.M. daily.

Van Asperen Vineyards, 1680 Silverado Trail, St. Helena; (707) 963–5251.

Viader Vineyards, 1120 Deer Park Road, Deer Park; (707) 963–3816.

Vine Cliff Winery, 7400 Silverado Trail, Oakville; (707) 944–1364. Open 10:00 A.M.–4:30 P.M. Monday–Friday.

W Winery, 1001 Silverado Trail, St. Helena; (707) 259–2800.

SOME FINE WINERIES GENERALLY NOT OPEN TO THE PUBLIC

Many Napa Valley winereies do not have tasting or sales facilities, but produce some of the best wines in the world. You can purchase their wines at fine wine shops, try them in restaurants, or get on winery mailing lists for newsletters and other special mailings.

Altamura Winery, 1700 Wooden Valley Road, Napa; (707) 253–2000.

Araujo Estate Wines/Eisele Vineyard, 2155 Pickett Road, St. Helena; (707) 942–6061.

Atlas Peak Vineyards, 3700 Soda Canyon Road, Napa; (707) 252–7971.

Azalea Springs Vineyards, 4301 Azalea Springs Way, Calistoga; (707) 942–4811.

Barnett Vineyards, 4070 Spring Mountain Road, St. Helena; (707) 963–7075.

Bacio Divino Cellars, 2610 Pinot Way, St. Helena; (707) 942–8101.

Benessere Vineyards, 1010 Big Tree Road, St. Helena; (707) 963–5853.

Buehler Vineyards, 820 Greenfield Road, St. Helena; (707) 963–2155.

Burgess Cellars, 1108 Deer Park Road, St. Helena; (707) 963–4766.

Cain Vineyard & Winery, 3800 Langtry Road, St. Helena; (707) 963–1616.

Colgin Cellars, 7830 St. Helena Highway, St. Helena; (707) 963–0999.

Conn Creek Winery, 8711 Silverado Trail, St. Helena; (707) 963–9100.

Corison Wines, P. O. Box 427, St. Helena; (707) 963–0826.

Dalla Valle Vineyards, 7776 Silverado Trail, Oakville; (707) 944–2676.

Diamond Creek Vineyards, 1500 Diamond Mountain Road, Calistoga; (707) 942–6926.

Diamond Mountain Vineyard, 2121 Diamond Mountain Road, Calistoga; (707) 942–0707.

Dominus Estate, 2570 Napanook Road, Yountville; (707) 944–8954.

Farella–Park Vineyards, 2222 North Third Avenue, Napa; (415) 954–4411.

Far Niente, 1 Acacia Drive, Oakville; (707) 944–2861.

Frazier, 40 Lupine Hill Road, Napa; (707) 255–3444.

Grace Family Vineyards, 1210 Rockland Road, St. Helena; (707) 963–0808.

Grandview Cellars, 1328 Main Street, St. Helena; (707) 967–9480.

Harlan Estate, 1551 Oakville Grade, Oakville; (707) 944–1441.

Harrison Vineyards, 1527 Sage Canyon Road, St. Helena; (707) 963–8271.

Honig Cellars, 850 Rutherford Road, Rutherford; (707) 963–5618.

Jaeger Family Wine Co., 4324 Big Ranch Road, Napa; (707) 255–4456.

Jarvis Vineyards, 2970 Monticello Road, Yountville; (707) 255–5280.

Lang & Reed Wine Company, 1961 Vineyard Avenue, St. Helena; (707) 963–3758.

Larkmead Vineyards, 1145 Larkmead Lane, St. Helena; (707) 942–6605.

Livingston Wines, 1895 Cabernet Lane, St. Helena; (707) 963–2120.

Lokoya Wines, 7585 St. Helena Highway, Oakville; (707) 944–2807.

Long Meadow Ranch Winery, 1775 Whitehall Lane, St. Helena; (707) 963–4555.

Louis Corthay Winery, 996 Galleron Road, Rutherford; (707) 963–2384.

Mount Veeder Winery, 1999 Mount Veeder Road, Yountville; (707) 963–7111.

Newton Vineyard, 2555 Madrona Avenue, St. Helena; (707) 963–9000.

Oakford Vineyards, 1575 Oakville Grade, Oakville; (707) 945–0445.
Oliver Caldwell Cellars, 3480 St. Helena Highway, St. Helena; (707) 963–2037.
Pahlmeyer Winery, 101 South Coombs Street, Napa; (707) 255–2321.
Paoletti, 4501 Silverado Trail, Calistoga; (707) 942–0689.
Paradigm, 683 Dwyer Road, Oakville; (707) 944–1683.
Quintessa, 1178 Galleron Road, Rutherford; (707) 963–7111.
Reverie on Diamond Mountain, 1520 Diamond Mountain Road, Calistoga; (707) 942–6800.
Screaming Eagle, P. O. Box 134, Oakville 94562; (707) 944–0749.
Seavey Vineyards, 1310 Conn Valley Road, St. Helena; (707) 963–8339 or 788–0800.
Silverado Hill Cellars, 3105 Silverado Trail, Napa; (707) 253–9306 or 253–9307.
Spring Mountain Vineyard, 2805 Spring Mountain Road, St. Helena; (707) 967–4188 or 967–4190.
Stag's Leap Winery, 6150 Silverado Trail, Napa; (707) 944–1303 or 944–4493.
Star Hill Winery, 1075 Shadybrook Lane, Napa; (707) 255–1957.
Tulocay Winery, 1426 Coombsville Road, Napa; (707) 255–4064.
Turley Wine Cellars, 3358 St. Helena Highway, Saint Helena; (707) 963–0940.
Villa Encinal Winery, 620 Oakville Crossroad, Oakville; (707) 944–1465.
Vineyard 29, 2929 Highwy 29 North, St. Helena,; (707) 963–9292.
Volker Eisele Family Estate, 3080 Lower Chiles Valley Road, St. Helena; (707) 965–2260.
Von Strasser Winery, 1510 Diamond Mountain Road, Calistoga; (707) 942–0930.

EVENTS AND FESTIVALS

The dates and times of regular events and festivals change from year to year. We encourage you to call the phone numbers listed for information.

February–March

Napa Valley Mustard Festival celebrates mustard in the vineyards at various locations, including the Culinary Institute of America, the Niebaum-Coppola Vineyards, and the Napa Fairgrounds in downtown Napa. The World Wide Mustard Competition is a big deal, with results announced with great fanfare at the opening party. It's all kicked off by the *Blessing of the Balloons* at Domaine Chandon Winery, 1 California Drive, Yountville 94599; phone (707) 259–9020, 944–8793, or 938–1133.

Taste of Yountville, along Washington Street in Yountville; phone (707) 944–0904. This event celebrates Yountville's claim that it has more world–class restaurants per square foot than any other town in the United States. And we are the beneficiaries, because they all cook and serve their delicacies at tables along the street. Lots of music and fun if it isn't raining.

April

Calistoga Maifest, Calistoga Fairgrounds; phone (707) 942–6524. This event takes place the first weekend in April (of course) and benefits the Rotary High School Scholarship Fund. Entertainment includes the Al Gruber band and mariachis. German and American food is available as well as German and local beers. Open from noon to 9:00 P.M.

April in Carneros, at all Carneros District wineries along the Sonoma–Napa border, promotes and celebrates the Carneros appellation with new wine releases, food, cigars, music, and general gustatory bliss; phone (800) 825–9475.

June

Beringer Celebrity Golf Classic, Chardonnay Golf Club, 2555 Jamieson Canyon Road east of Highway 12, Napa 94558; phone (707) 255–0950. This event benefits Justin–Siena Catholic High School in Napa, with big–name athletes mixing with lesser–known golfers. The fee is $375 to play with a celebrity of some sort.

Napa Valley Wine Auction, Meadowood Resort, 900 Meadowood Lane, St. Helena 94574; phone (707) 942–9783. This is the ultimate wine auction in the United States. The auction raises funds for local hospitals. The long weekend event includes barrel tastings, dinners with winemakers and owners, a Napa Valley collaborative chefs' dinner at Meadowood, and the auction itself. Most guests think the nearly $1,500 ticket price is well worth it.

Silverado Concours D'Elegance, Silverado Country Club, 1600 Atlas Peak Road, Napa 94558; phone (707) 428–3355; $10 in advance, $12 at the gate. This benefits the Children's Hospital of Oakland. Nearly 300 classic cars and their owners assemble to strut, wine, and dine. A fun event for all who enjoy a little elegance, old and new.

Yountville Italian Heritage Festival, at Vintage 1870 and other venues; phone (707) 968–2338. Friday evening–Sunday, third full weekend; golf, bocce ball, winemaker dinners at ten top restaurants.

Vintage 1870 Father's Day Invitational Auto Show, at Vintage 1870 in Yountville; phone (707) 944–2451; free. The name pretty much says it all.

July

Meadowood Croquet Classic, Meadowood Resort, 900 Meadowood Lane, St. Helena 94574; phone (707) 963–3646. Meadowood is the only winery with croquet courts and a full–time croquet pro. The U.S. Croquet Association holds this annual event of events, dressed all in white, of course. Inquire about new events and admission.

Napa Valley Shakespeare Festival, Rutherford Grove Winery, 1673 St. Helena Highway, St. Helena 94574; phone (707) 251–WILL, Web site www. napashakespeare.org. Each weekend during the month. The festival recently moved to this lovely site, with Shakespeare being performed on the lawn under huge shade trees.

August

Music in the Vineyards, phone (707) 578–5656, Web site www.napavalley music.org. Wednesday, Saturday, and Sunday, during first three weeks, classic music at several wineries. $25 per performance.

Napa Town and Country Fair, Napa Exposition Grounds, 575 Third Street, Napa 94558; phone (707) 253–4900. Second weekend. This is a truly local fair, more homey than a county fair for the southern end of the Napa Valley, featuring everything you would expect from 4–H projects living and cooked, carnivals, kids' games, wine tasting, cotton candy, and even a rodeo and—gads—a demolition derby.

September

Napa Symphony on the River, Third Street at the bridge, Napa; phone (707) 258–8762. Come here to celebrate life and music, with music from 7:00 to 9:00 P.M., food and fireworks in Veterans Park—it's a general down–home great time, held the Sunday of Labor Day weekend.

October

Calistoga Beer & Sausage Fest, Napa County Fairgrounds, 1435 North Oak Street, Calistoga 94515; phone (707) 942–0795. On the second weekend in October, twenty–four microbreweries from around Northern California show and pour, along with sausage– and mustard–making companies, local restaurants, and chili cook–off; $20 for everything, in toto. A wild–and–wooly time.

Harvest Festival, Hometown Style, Adams Street, St. Helena; phone (707) 963–5706. This is a resurrected and underpublicized local celebration of the grape harvest, held the last Saturday in October, with arts and crafts, run, carnival, and a pet parade (our favorite).

Old Mill Days, Bale Grist Mill State Historic Park, 3369 St. Helena Highway, St. Helena 94574; phone (707) 942–4575. Coopers, storytellers, millers, fiddlers, weavers, kids, and grownups all pretend it's 130 years ago. Why not. Great mill tours, grinding of flours of several kinds. A good healthy day.

November

Festival of Lights, Vintage 1870, Yountville; phone (707) 944–1171. This is held the Friday after Thanksgiving all over town, with Christmas carols, roasted chestnuts, Santa, street musicians and actors, and of course wine and food. Lots of fun for visitors and locals alike. The next day, Saturday, Santa moves on to Napa's Christmas Parade, beginning by the Cinedome multiplex theater at Pearl and Soscol. The parade and Santa, and a few throngs of locals, end up at the Napa Town Center to make the shopping season official and have a wee bit of sustenance.

Napa Valley Wine Festival, Napa Valley Country Club, 3385 Hagen Road, Napa 94558; phone (707) 253–3511. This event, held the first weekend in November, benefits the Napa Valley Unified School District. There are golf and tennis, fifty Napa Valley wineries, huge pasta dinner, and student music. A fun, charitable event. Tickets cost $30 in advance, $35 at the door.

Series

Jarvis Conservatory Opera, and other musical events, May–September, 1711 Main Street, Napa; phone (707) 255–5445.

ANTIQUES

Antique Fair, 6512 Washington Street, Yountville; phone (707) 844–8440

Elrod Antiques, 3000 St. Helena Highway; phone (707) 963–1901

European Country Antiques, 1148 Main Street, St. Helena; phone (707) 963–4666

Hacienda Hardware, 1989 St. Helena Highway, Rutherford; phone (707) 963–8850

The Irish Pedlar, 1988 Wise Drive, Napa 94558; phone (707) 253–9091
Jack Cole Antiques and Curios, 805 Washington Street, Calistoga; phone (707) 942–6712
Mandrake's Antiques, 6525 Washington Street in Vintage 1870, Yountville; phone (707) 944–9479
Neighborhood Antique Collective, 1400 First Street, Napa; phone (707) 259–1900
Red Hen Antiques, 5091 St. Helena Highway, Napa; phone (707) 257–0822
St. Helena Antiques, 1231 Main Street, St. Helena; phone (707) 963–5878
Tin Barn Collective, 1510 Lincoln Avenue, Calistoga; phone (707) 942–0618

BOOKSTORES

Bookends Book Store, 1014 Coombs Street, Napa; phone (707) 224–1077
Calistoga Book Store, 1343 Lincoln Avenue, Calistoga; phone (707) 942–4123
Copperfield's, 1303 First Street, Napa; phone (707) 252–8002
Main Street Books, 1315 Main Street, St. Helena; phone (707) 963–1338
Napa Children's Book Company, 1239 First Street, Napa; phone (707) 224–3893
Volume One Used Books, 1405 Second Street, Napa; phone (707) 252–1466
Waldenbooks, 1370 Napa Town Center, Napa, (707) 252–7326

CAMPGROUNDS

Bothe–Napa Valley State Park, Highway 29 south of Calistoga and adjoining Bale Mill State Park; phone (707) 942–4575 or (800) 444–PARK for state park reservations. Forty–nine tent and RV sites, nine tent only sites; picnic tables, fire pits and barbecues; rest rooms; showers; wheelchair–accessible; $1.00 fee for pets; $3.00 fee for swimming pool.

Calistoga Ranch Club Resort & Campground, 580 Lommel Road south of Calistoga; phone (707) 942–6565. Sixty tent only spaces, 84 RV sites, and some cabins. Enjoy 167 acres of trails, forest, fishing, swimming pool, and games. Facilities include barbecues, rest rooms, and showers.

Napa County Fairgrounds, 1435 North Oak Street, Calistoga; phone (707) 942–5111. Tents and RVs. Walk to downtown Calistoga. Pets OK on leash. *Napa Fairgrounds,* 575 Third Street, Napa; phone (707) 253–4905. Spaces for motor homes and 500 campers with cars. Facilities include rest rooms and showers; grocery store and laundromat nearby.

NIGHTCLUBS (SORT OF)

These are microbreweries, restaurants, and bars that occasionally have music.

Ana's Cantina, 1205 Main Street, St. Helena; phone (707) 963–4921. A local hangout featuring Mexican and El Salvadoran food and real drinks; rock, reggae, and country, 9:00 P.M. to 1:30 A.M. Thursday–Saturday; Sunday afternoon.

Calistoga Inn & Restaurant and *Napa Valley Brewing Company,* 1250 Lincoln Avenue, Calistoga; phone (707) 942–4101. Music in the bar Tuesday, Friday, and Saturday nights; on the patio occasionally in summer.

Club Bacchus, 1853 Trancas, Napa; phone (707) 258–1145. Disc jockey '50's funk Thursday–Saturday.

Cole's Chop House, 1122 Main Street, Napa; phone (707) 224–MEAT. Jazz, swing, Latin, 6:30 P.M. to 10:30 P.M. Saturday, 5:30 to 9:00 P.M. Sunday.

Downtown Joe's, 902 Main Street, Napa; phone (707) 258–2337. Microbrewery/restaurant with a lively rock, pop, and blues scene Thursday–Saturday. A $3.00 cover on weekends.

Hydro Bar & Grill, 1403 Lincoln Avenue, Calistoga; phone (707) 942–9777. Stays open late for great food, romantic bar–style jazz; Dixieland jam on Thursday.

Lord Derby Arms, Highway 29 (Lincoln Avenue) and Silverado Trail, Calistoga; phone (707) 942–9155. A distinctly British pub and hangout where local Irish singer John Kelley performs weekends.

Moore's Landing, 6 Cuttings Wharf Road, Napa; phone (707) 253–2439, Saturday evenings Cajun music on riverfront in summer.

Pacific Blues Cafe, 6525 Washington Street, Yountville; phone (707) 944–4455. Blues 6:00 to 9:00 P.M. Saturday, weather permitting.

Planet Rock, 3392 Solano Avenue, Napa; phone (707) 252–8200. Disc jockey, dancing with music style changing nightly. A $5.00 cover some nights. Call ahead for current details.

1351 Lounge, 1351 Main Street, St. Helena; phone (707) 963–1969. Jazz some evenings.

PICNIC SUPPLIES

Cantinetta Tra Vigne, 1050 Charter Oak Avenue, St. Helena; phone (707) 963–8888

Genova Delicatessen & Ravioli Factory, 1550 Trancas, Napa; phone (707) 253–8686, fax (707) 253–2487

Giugni Grocery Company, 1227 Main Street, St. Helena; phone (707) 963–3421

Oakville Grocery, 7856 St. Helena Highway, Oakville; phone (707) 944–8802

Pometta's, 7787 Highway 29, Oakville; phone (707) 944–2365

Sattui Winery, South St. Helena Highway, St. Helena; phone (707) 963–7774

Soda Canyon Store, 4006 Silverado Trail, Napa; phone (707) 252–0285

ABOUT THE
AUTHORS

*K*athleen and Gerald Hill are native Californians who divide their time between Sonoma in the Northern California wine country and Vancouver Island, British Columbia. As a team the Hills wrote *Sonoma Valley: The Secret Wine Country, Victoria and Vancouver Island: The Almost Perfect Eden, Northwest Wine Country: Wine's New Frontier, Montery and Carmel: Eden by the Sea, Santa Barbara and the Central Coast: California's Riviera, The Real Life Dictionary of the Law, The Real Life Dictionary of American Politics,* and an international exposé, *The Aquino Assassination.* Kathleen is the author of *Festivals USA* and *Festivals USA—Western States,* and she has written articles for *The Chicago Tribune, San Francisco Magazine, Cook's Magazine, San Francisco Examiner Magazine, James Beard Newsletter,* and other periodicals, while Gerald was editor and co-author of *Housing in California.* Gerald also practices law to support their writing habit. Together they have written for *National Geographic Traveler Magazine.*

Kathleen earned an A.B. at the University of California at Berkeley, a degree in French from the Sorbonne in Paris, and an M.A. at Sonoma State University. Gerald holds an A.B. from Stanford University and a J.D. from Hastings College of the Law, University of California.

INDEX

Acacia Winery, 6
Alan's Frames & Photography, 130
Alexis Baking Company and
    Cafe, 32
All Seasons Cafe and Wine
    Shop, 172
Amelia Claire, 121
Ana's Cantina, 136
Andretti Winery, 226
Angwin
    bed-and-breakfasts, 247
antiques, lists of, 296–97
Antique Fair, 48
appellations, x
Armadillo's, 123
Artesa Winery, 15
Artful Eye, The, 182
Atlas Peak Grill, 33
Auberge du Soleil, 194

Bale Grist Mill State Historic
    Park, 151
Bale Mill Pine Furniture, 152
Ballentine Vineyards, 146
ballooning, 249
Beaucanon Napa Valley, 92
Beaulieu Vineyards, 87
Bergman's, 121
Beringer's Vineyards, 139
bicycle riding and bike rentals, 250
Big Daddy's Drive-In, 175
Big Dipper, The, 128
Bird's Eye, The, 182
Bison, 132

Bistro Don Giovanni, 39
Bistro Jeanty, 47
bocce ball, 251
Bocconcini, 55
bookstores, lists of, 297
Boskos Ristorante, 171
Bothe Napa Valley State Park, 152
Bouchaine Vineyards, 8
Bouchon, 49
Brannan's Grill, 171
Brava Terrace, 148
Brix, 61
Buchanan's Stationery, 132

Cafe Sarafornia, 178
Cakebread Cellars, 75
California Veterans' Home, 60
Calistoga
    bed-and-breakfasts, 245
    hotels, motels, and inns, 244
    ranches, 247
    spas, resorts, and baths, 243
Calistoga Bookstore, 181
Calistoga Coffee Roastery, 175
Calistoga Inn and Restaurant, 168
Calla Lily, 121
campgrounds, lists of, 297–98
Cantinetta Tra Vigne, 119
Cardinale/Pepi Winery, 63
Carneros Creek Winery, 14
Casa Nuestra Winery, 190
Catahoula Restaurant &
    Saloon, 176
Ca'toga Gallery d'Arte, 182

Caymus Vineyards, 201
Celadon, 28
Chanterelle, 33
Charles Krug Winery, 143
Chateau Montelena, 164
Checkers Pizza & Pasta, 173
Chimney Rock Winery, 222
Cin Cin, 174
Claudia "K" Florist, 129
Clos du Val, 222
Clos Pegase, 157
Cole's Chop House, 30
Compadres Mexican Bar & Grill, 53
Cosentino Winery, 62
Culinary Institute of America
    at Greystone, 141
Creative Needle, 120
Cricket, 121
Cuvaison Winery, 186

D. Champaign, 121
Darioush Winery, 224
David's, 131
Dean & DeLuca, 102
Depot Hotel, 33
Di Rosa Preserve, 3
Diner, The, 46
Domaine Carneros, 4
Domaine Chandon, 56
Downtown Joe's, 27
Duckhorn Vineyards, 190
Dutch Henry Winery, 188

Edgewood Estate Winery, 111
Ehlers Grove and Cartlidge &
    Browne, 150
Erika Hills's "The Painted
    Illusion," 114
events and festivals, lists of, 293–96

farmers' markets, 255
Fideaux, 124
Flora Springs Wine Company, 101
Folie à Deux Winery, 149
Foothill Cafe, 34
Franciscan Vineyards, 93
Frank-Rombauer Cellars, 153
Frankie & Johnny & Luigi
    Too, 53
Free Time, 170
Freemark Abbey Winery, 146
French Laundry, The, 50
Frog's Leap Winery, 200

Gail's Cafe, 130
Gallery on Main Street, The, 130
Genoa Delicatessen & Ravioli
    Factory, 34
George C. Yount Pioneer cemetery
    & Ancient Indian Burial
    Grounds, 52
Georgie & Elsie Wood Public
    Library, 129
Gillwood's Cafe, 134
Giugni's Delicatessen, 135
golfing, 251
Good N Airy Angel, 172
Goodman's Since 1879, 132
Goosecross Cellars, 212
Gordon's Cafe and Wine Bar, 51
Grgich Hills Cellar, 90
Groezinger's Wine Shop, 49
Groth Vineyards & Winery, 206

Hacienda Hardware–Coleccion
    Mexicana, 89
Hakusan Sake Gardens, 20
hang gliding, 251
Heaven & Earth, 133

Hedgeside Vinters, Hedgeside Wine
    Gallery/Del Dotto Caves, 231
Heitz Wine Cellars, 107
Hess Collection, 37
House of Breads, 31
Hurd Bees Wax Candles and
    Gourmet, 148
Hydro Bar & Grill, 178

I. Wolk Gallery, 125
Imani Gallery, 31
Inti, 32

Jonesy's Famous Steak House, 36
Joseph Phelps Vineyards, 192

Keller's Market, 124
Kirkland Ranch Winery, 18

L. Funke & Son Department
    Store, 177
La Famiglia di Robert Mondavi
    Winery and Italian
    Marketplace, 67
La Toque, 89
Lakeside Grill, 45
Lee Youngman Galleries, 170
Livefire, 48
Lolo's Second to None Consignment
    Shop, 126
Louis M. Martini, 108
Luna Vineyards, 227

Madonna Estate/Mont St. John
    Winery, 11
Main Street Books, 134
maps
    Calistoga area, 169
    Carneros and Napa area, 2

downtown Napa, 26
Napa Valley, xi
Rutherford/Oakville area, 74
St. Helena area, 115
Yountville area, 45
Mario's for Men, 135
Markham Vineyards, 144
Meadowood Resort, 191
Merryvale Vineyards, 114
Milat Vineyards, 100
Miner Family Vineyards, 204
Miramonte, 137
Model Bakery, 130
Monticello Corley Family
    Vineyards, 225
Mosswood, 50
Mount View Spa and Mount View
    Hotel, 176
Mumm Napa Valley, 202
Mustards Grill, 61

Napa Ale Works, 22
Napa Cellars, 63
Napa Firefighters Museum, 31
Napa Valley, The
    bed-and-breakfasts, 236
    history of, 257–87
    hotels, motels, and inns, 235
    resorts, 238
Napa Valley Chocolates, 133
Napa Valley Coffee Roasting
    Company, 28, 128
Napa Valley Grapevine Wreath
    Company, 200
Napa Valley Grille, 53
Napa Valley Museum, 58
Napa Valley Olive Oil
    Manufactory, 119
Napa Valley Ovens, 181

Napa Valley Traditions and Futons
     & Furniture, 30
Napa Wine Company, 68
Nature Etc., 133
Newlan Vineyards & Winery, 43
Nichelini Winery, 198
Niebaum-Coppola Estate, 84
nightclubs, lists of, 298

Oakville Grocery, 69
Old Adobe Bar and Grille, 35
Old Faithful Geyser, 163
On the Vine, 122
Opus One Winery, 72
Overland Sheepskin Company, 56

Pacific Blues Cafe, 54
Pacifico Restaurante Mexicano, 183
Palladium, 132
Pat Quigle–Paper Tiger–Napa,
     127–28
Patina Fine Jewelry, 125
Peju Province, 82
Petrified Forest, 161
picnic supplies, lists of, 299
Pine Ridge Winery, 216
Pinot Blanc, 138
Plumpjack Winery, 204
Pometta's Delicatessen and
     Catering, 66
Prager Winery & Port Works, 113

Quail Ridge Cellars &
     Vineyards, 91

Ranch Market, 47
Raymond Vineyard & Cellar, 98
Red Hen Cantina, 35
Reed's, 122

recipes
     Asian crab cakes with lime-ginger
         sauce, 205
     black mussels steamed in
         Chandon brut, 59
     Caesar salad with garlic oil, 140
     caponata, 96
     Chevre and herb mousse, 6
     Colleen's flank steak, 212
     crispy & tangy lemon
         chicken, 80
     dungeness crab cioppino, 65
     fresh apple mirin cups, 21
     Grandma's pineapple upside
         down cake, 8
     grilled polenta with wilted greens
         and sausage, 77
     grilled portobello with braised
         greens and balsamic jus, 40
     grilled rack of lamb, 17
     lemon cream sauce, 47
     lemon tea bread, 211
     Louis M. Martini's Christmas
         Eve zabaglione, 110
     Maine crab cakes with sweet corn
         and peppers and grainy
         mustard sauce, 29
     Mitsuko's leg of lamb with
         vegetable medley and
         lentil-rice mix, 159
     Nonna Rina's lamb roast, 228
     Oakville polenta crostini with
         sun-dried tomato pesto, 71
     Old Bale Mill cheese spoon
         bread, 153
     peach walnut salad, 12
     Peju breaded turkey slices au
         Cabernet, 83
     pizza of the day, 162

polenta with wild mushrooms, 103
pork scaloppini with Pinot Grigio, caper sauce, 69
rabbit terrine with sliced apples and baguette, 59
roasted cornish game hens, 109
roasted garlic mashed potatoes, 214
roasted polenta and balsamic sauce, 118
saged Sangiovese veal chops, 216
scallops and mushrooms in cream sauce, 229
sesame sprout salad, 21
shrimp in dry riesling sauce, 42
smoked salmon and caper crostini, 73
spicy pork kebabs with Moorish flavors, 142
steamed clams with pancetta, Chardonnay, apple juice, and sage, 173
Toni's marinated olives, 86
truffle risotto, 13
Vietnamese five-spice chicken, 218
Whitehall Lane Napa Cabernet red risotto, 99
whole roasted pork loin wrapped with pancetta and stuffed with dried fruit, 97
wild mushroom pâté, 232
wildflower honey loaf, 19
Regusci Winery, 220
Restaurant at Meadowood, The, 191
Ristorante Piatti, 46
RMS Brandy Distillery, 9

Robert Mondavi Winery, 72
Robert Sinskey Vineyards, 209
Rombauer Vineyards, 189
Roundhill Family of Wines, 196
R.S. Basso Home Furnishings, 136
Rustridge Ranch & Winery, Bed & Breakfast, & Thoroughbred Home, 197
Rutherford
hotels, motels, and inns, 240
resorts, 240
Rutherford Gardens, 91
Rutherford Grill, 85
Rutherford Grove Winery and Napa Valley Grapeseed Oil Company, 95
Rutherford Hill Winery, 195

S. Anderson Winery, 210
Saintsbury, 10
Sawyer Cellars, 79
Schramsberg Vineyards, 154
Seguin-Moreau Napa, 22
Sequoia Grove Winery, 78
Shafer Vineyards, 213
Sharpsteen Museum, 180
Showplace North, 125
Signorello Vineyards, 224
Silver Oak Winery, 207
Silver Rose Cellars, 186
Silverado Country Club, 230
Silverado Museum, 128
Silverado Vineyards, 214
Soda Canyon Store, 230
Soo Yuan Chinese Food, 170
spas, 255
Sportago, 127
Spot, The, 104
St. Clement Vineyards, 145

St. Helena
  bed-and-breakfasts, 241
  hotels, motels, and inns, 240
  resorts and spas, 241
St. Helena Antiques & Other Fine
  Collectibles, 135
St. Helena Cyclery, 120
St. Helena Wine Center, 133
St. Supery Vineyards & Winery
  Discovery Center, 80
Stag's Leap Wine Cellars, 220
Steltzner Vineyards, 219
Sterling Vineyards, 157
Steve's Hardware and Homeware,
  Inc., 125
Stonegate Winery, 156
Sullivan Vineyards, 94
Summers Winery, 163
Susie's Bar, 181

Tantau, 127
Tapioca Tiger, 127
Taqueria Rosita, 31
Taqueria Santa Rosa, 170
Taylor's Refresher, 120
tennis, 252
Terra, 137
Tivoli, 126
Tomatina, 116
tours, 253
Tra Vigne, 117
Trattoria Green Valley, 123
Trefethen Estate Vineyards, 40
Trinchero Family Estates, 111
Trumbull Wine Cellars, 75
29 Joe's Coffee House, 102

Tuscany, 30

V. Sattui Winery, 104
Valley Exchange, 136
Van der Heyden, 227
Vanderbilt & Company–Napa
  Valley, 126
Vasconi's Drugs, 129
Vigil Vineyards, 161
Villa Mt. Eden Winery and Conn
  Creek Winery, 198
Vincent Arroyo Winery, 165
Vintage 1870, 54

Wappo Bar Bistro, 178
Wermuth Winery, 188
Wexford & Woods, 181
Whitehall Lane Winery, 98
Wilkes Sport, 135
William Harrison Vineyards/Mario
  Perelli-Minetti Winery, 193
William Hill Winery, 230
wineries, lists of, 289–93
  generally not open to public,
    291–93
  requiring appointments for
    tasting, 289–91

Yountville
  bed-and-breakfasts, 239
  hotels, motels, inns, 238
Yountville Park, 52

Zahtila Vineyards, 167
ZD Wines, 203